Penguin Books

Living Off Nature

Judy Urquhart went to ten different schools in England, Malaya, Austria and, finally, Scotland. It was here, living in the country, that she began to learn and read about natural history, an interest she pursued while married to the journalist and writer Brendan Lehane and continued while living in remote parts of Dorset, Somerset and County Cork in Ireland. In 1971 the *Daily Telegraph Magazine* commissioned them to write an article about an attempt to survive completely off the land. It was this experience, coupled with research over many years, that forms the basis of this book.

She is now based in London and is the author of two books: *Food From The Wild* and *Keeping Honeybees*.

LIVING OFF NATURE

Judy Urquhart

Illustrations by Vana Haggerty

Penguin Books

Penguin Books Ltd, Harmondsworth, Middlesex, England
Penguin Books, 625 Madison Avenue, New York, New York 10022, U.S.A.
Penguin Books Australia Ltd, Ringwood, Victoria, Australia
Penguin Books Canada Ltd, 2801 John Street, Markham, Ontario, Canada L3R 1B4
Penguin Books (N.Z.) Ltd, 182–190 Wairau Road, Auckland 10, New Zealand

First published by Allen Lane, 1980
Published in Penguin Books 1982

Made and printed in Great Britain by
Richard Clay (The Chaucer Press) Ltd,
Bungay, Suffolk
Set in Monophoto Plantin

Contents

INTRODUCTION 1

Part One

FOOD 11

Bees, Honey and Beeswax 14
Birds 18
Bread 32
Butter 36
Cheese 39
Cold Storage 42
Confectionery 44
Cooking 45
Eggs 50
Fats and Oils 52
Fire 55
Fish 62
Fungi 82
Herbs 88
Insects 92
Mammals 93
Milling 108
Molluscs, Crustacea, etc. 111
Nuts 119
Preserving 124
Puddings and Desserts 136
Rennet 141
Reptiles and Amphibians 141
Salad Plants 143
Salt 145
Sauces 147
Seaweed 150
Soup 155
Starving 158
Sugar and Other Sweeteners 161
Vegetables 163
Vinegar 168
Yeast 171

DRINKING 173

Beer 177
Brandy 179
Cider 181
Coffee 182
Gin 183
Liqueurs 183
Mead 185
Teas and Tisanes 187
Water 188
Whisky 192
Wine 194

SMOKING, SNUFF 203

Smoking Mixtures 204
Snuff 205

Part Two

SHELTER 209

Chimneys 212
Cleaning, Household 213
Drains and Damp Courses 213
Floor Coverings 215
Floors 221
Furniture 221
Houses 226
Lavatories 236
Light 237
Roofs 243
Stuffing 246
Wall Coverings 247
Windows 249

CONTAINERS 251

Baskets 252
Bowls 258
Containers 258
Nets 261
Plates 266
Pottery 266

TOOLS AND UTENSILS 273

Brushes 274
Forks 278
Knives 279
Nails 280
Pegs 280
Rakes 281
Sieves 282
Spoons 283

RAW MATERIALS 285

Charcoal 285
Glass 286
Glue 288
Lime 289
Metal 291
Paint 295
Potash 296
Rope and String 297
Tar 302
Turpentine 303
Wood 303

WRITING 312

Ink 312
Paper 313
Pen or Quill 316
Pencil 317

TIME AND MOTION 318

Boats 319
Direction and Pathfinding 323
Time 325
Weather Forecasting 327

CLOTHES AND CLOTHING 332

Cloth 334
Dyeing 337
Knitting 342
Leather 342
Sewing 347
Shoes 348
A Smock 350
Spinning 352
Weaving 355

GROOMING 361

Bathing 363
Combs 364
Cosmetics 365
Perfume 368
Soap 372
Teeth 375

HEALTH 377
Disinfectants 378
First Aid 379
Insecticides 383

SELECT BIBLIOGRAPHY 385

BOOKS RECOMMENDED
FOR IDENTIFICATION 391

NOTES 393

Acknowledgements

This book would never have been written or published without the help and encouragement of many people. I would like especially to thank my parents who gave much backing and had me to stay for long periods during its writing. Clare Glazebrook and Christopher Ollivant also gave me a roof at times when I needed it. My sisters Suky and Elspeth gave heart at many moments and my brother Adam and Patrick Scrivenor combined practical help with specialized information. Irene Cox typed the bulk of an extremely piecemeal manuscript and Liz Pitkethly finished off many ends. The staff of the Chard, Marylebone and London Libraries were most helpful over getting books and Anne Crane lent many from her collection. Dervla Murphy found the farmhouse at Monatrim which first gave me the idea and John Anstey commissioned the article which established it. Andrew Best gave invaluable advice and assistance and Michael Dover was a most understanding editor. And last, and most important, I would like to thank Brendan Lehane without whose knowledge I could not even have begun.

Introduction

For centuries people relied on their immediate surroundings for their daily needs. From Neolithic times until the end of the eighteenth century the greater part of the population lived exclusively off local produce, whatever they could make, hunt or grow. Blindfold, you could tell a region by its food and drink. Changes of stone and soil were reflected in the materials used for housing. With the coming of the Industrial Revolution this situation changed completely. Most people now live in towns; even country people depend almost entirely on standard produce, with perhaps a vegetable patch as a last vestige of self-sufficiency.

It was to see if it was possible to reverse this process, to return to dependence on nature, that Brendan and I set off for Exmoor. We settled near Dulverton, where we had been offered the run of a grassy valley which was soon to be flooded to make a reservoir. It had a small trout stream running through the middle, oak and beech woods on either side, Exmoor above and a wooden hut some Boy Scouts had built a few years before. Perfect, we thought, and certainly better than the alternative of a moor in Scotland covered with nothing but heather. Nonetheless it was not ideal.

Were I to start again, I would choose a site by a river and within easy reach of the sea. A southern site would be better than a northern one; the summer is longer, the winter less cold and the vegetation and wild life more varied and lush. The Isle of Purbeck in Dorset, the south of Wales where Carmarthen and Pembroke meet, the country round the Solway Firth, the part nearest the coast of the Lammermuir Hills in Scotland or parts of the south-west of England and the south of Ireland are all places where, within a ten-mile radius, there are enough of the right geographical features to make total survival in the wild possible. They all have streams and rivers which run into estuaries, a coast-line with sand and rocks, woods, arable land and upland. In such situations it should be possible to find everything necessary for living wild in a northerly climate: 'Food, Shelter, Clothing, and Fuel, for not until we have secured these are we prepared to entertain the true problems of life with freedom and a prospect of success.'[1]

From the springs and rivers you would get drinking water and freshwater fish: trout, perch, bream and carp. There would also be water-loving plants like watercress for salads and soup and willow trees for basket work.

To be near a large wood of deciduous trees is essential as wood is the basic raw material from which to build your house, make furniture, implements and utensils and, most important, to provide cooking fuel and heat. Most fungi grow in woods; deer, pigeon, pheasant and squirrels live there, and often swarms of wild bees too, in hollow trees.

Access to arable land would be useful, especially if you decided to continue with the way of life, as you would want to start some form of agriculture and keep some animals. The logic of agriculture is obvious: you can dictate what you eat rather than having to take a chance on what nature offers. Arable land is the natural home of many wild plants and of those cultivated ones which have escaped, often not very far, especially cereals and oil plants. Partridge, pigeons and small birds feed on arable land. In most parts of the country fields are surrounded by hedges. In these you will usually find the best brambles, sloes, crab apples, elderberries and haws. A hedgerow is the best place for laying traps, as rabbits and other small animals live in them. Ditches in between fields often have the best nettles for eating and cloth-making.

Upland is usually rough land; there you find bracken – edible and good for bedding and potash too – useful trees like rowan and birch and plants such as heather and bilberry. In the grassy bits you will find thyme, eyebright and speedwell for flavouring beer and, most certainly, rabbit warrens. In the wooded areas on the hillside badgers dig their sets; on the moorland live curlew, grouse and larks.

An estuary is the ideal place to evaporate salt and is the home of many molluscs, fish and water birds. A coast consisting of a mixture of rock and sand will have more seaweed and molluscs and as many fish as any other combination. If there are cliffs there will be gulls nesting in them; they and their eggs are well worth eating; the small feathers can be used for stuffing and the larger ones, if you have no geese, for quills. Clay is most easily dug from cliffs where a cross-section of geological deposits is exposed. From clay you can make pots and containers for cooking and storage. Ideally you would have a source of limestone too; this is the best building stone and also provides lime, used in so many articles. If there was metal as well your site would be complete.

The exact position of the house would be decided by the water supply. It would be near a spring for drinking water; preferably, one which develops into a stream so that once you became established a supply could be piped into the house. I would begin by building only a rudimentary shelter – a gipsy tent or a dugout and I would live in this to see how life was developing before building myself a more substantial structure. But both would be in places not too exposed to the west wind and on well-drained ground.

After establishing water and shelter the next consideration would be wood for fuel. The source of this should be close by as surprisingly large quantities are needed for even small amounts of cooking and heating. When we lived off the land we only had a fire in the evenings and even so we spent one or two days a week gathering fuel.

You will, for preference, begin your survival time in late spring or summer when wild food is at its most abundant and day-to-day eating is no problem. Your only worry should be to manage to preserve enough of the surplus to keep you through the lean winter months. Winter is the time when you will be most free to spin wool, weave, make baskets and carve wood into implements and utensils – a store of basic materials out of which these can be made should be put aside during the summer.

We planned to live off the land for two months only and we chose to go in August and September when, though many green leaves would be past their prime, berries, fungi and wild animals would be there in plenty. We also had the basics of a goat, four hens, a bag of crushed oats, a knife, an axe, snares, matches, a cooking pot, a change of clothing, a sleeping bag and books. I brought honey from my bees and candles, soap, salt and wine which I had made at home. We planned to make other things, like clothes, baskets, plates, pottery, paper and so on, while we were there.

The first night was bleak. The goat escaped; bracken on an ill-swept floor was very different from a bed; and it rained. The rain continued almost unabated for ten days, rations were scarce and uncooked owing to the lack of fire and I came to the conclusion that if this was what surviving meant I would rather not. But then I had no real driving force to keep me going.

It is notable that the most successful practitioners of self-sufficiency have been those sustained by religious conviction or Utopian desire. The first are personified by the early Cistercian monks, the Shakers and the Amish. St Bernard wrote that:

> Our life is a life of abjection, humility, voluntary poverty; of obedience, peace, joy in a rule, a discipline. Our life is a practice of silence, fasting, vigils, prayers, manual labour, and above all to follow the more excellent way which is charity, and to progress in all these things from day to day and persevere in them until the last day.[2]

Into the second category comes Thoreau, who lived for several years quite alone in the woods at Walden and wrote a classic book on the subject. W. B. Yeats expressed his longing for this way of life in 'The Lake Isle of Innisfree'. Thomas Traherne wrote:

> When I came into the country, and being seated among silent trees and meads and hills, had all my time in my own hands, I resolved to spend it all, whatever it cost me, in search of happiness, and to satiate that burning thirst which nature had enkindled in me from my youth. In which I was so resolute that I chose to live upon ten pounds and to go in leather clothes, and feed upon bread and water, so that I might have all my time to myself.[3]

Gipsies could be said to be successful long-term practitioners of self-sufficiency. Mr Jimmy Penfold expressed it thus:

> . . . to live. Nothing else matters. The simple reason is, we understand that during a period of seventy or eighty years, give or take a few years, you must learn to enjoy every minute of it.
>
> Don't become clots, we say, like the Gorjios,* get up at eight, work till five, watch television till ten, go to bed, get up at eight, back to work till

* Gorjios: non-gipsies.

five. Their clocks is what they serve, the Gorjios, they're automatons; well our people, we don't behave like that. We get up when we feel like it, we eat and drink when we're hungry and we're thirsty and we do what we want . . . We work to live rather than live to work.[4]

Living off nature requires a change of attitude as to which are the necessities of life – comfort must be the first to come under scrutiny. As Aldous Huxley wrote in 1927:

comfort is a thing of recent growth, younger than steam, a child when telegraphy was born, only a generation older than radio . . . Sixteenth-century popes lived in a discomfort that a modern bank manager would consider unbearable; but they had Raphael's frescoes, they had the Sistine chapel, and they had their galleries of ancient sculpture. Must we pity them for the absence from the Vatican of bathrooms, central heating, and smoking-room chairs? I am inclined to think that our present passion for comfort is a little exaggerated.[5]

Or, as Thoreau says, 'The life which men praise and regard as successful is but one kind. Why should we exaggerate any one kind at the expense of others?'[1] It is difficult, however, to readjust – we certainly found it so and I think anyone used to modern living would. But it is possible. As the weeks went on and I became more in tune with our new life I began to find a great satisfaction in providing for myself in this way, to enjoy the dependence on nature and the awareness of it.

When the weather cleared and stayed clear, the goat had been caught and become a friend and we had established a good routine, I came gradually to find pleasure in the daily routine of getting up, milking the goat, feeding the hens, eating a breakfast of oatcakes, honey and milk, fetching drinking water from the spring, getting wood and foraging for food. At first we would go for a long walk hoping to identify edible plants on the way, but as we became more familiar with the country we would make for certain known spots: places in the woods where there were good fungi, a part of the stream where watercress grew profusely, the edge of the moor thick with brambles, a clearing in the wood full of wild raspberries, a lane with an abundance of dandelion leaves and a meadow with more sorrel, yarrow and valerian than grass. After lunch we either lazed away in the sun with a book or spent the time weaving baskets, making pottery or other similar tasks.

Then in early evening Brendan would disappear to lay snares or to shoot a squirrel, rabbit or pigeon. This I would be given to cook, after the skin or feathers had been removed and put aside for treatment. Fishing was also an evening occupation; sometimes we would take a further walk for food. The goat was milked again and then we would light a fire, cook oatcakes and whatever else was for dinner, drink some wine and, as September advanced and the nights drew in, light a candle. But bedtime was always early and the candle was not alight for long.

In fact we slept a great deal. Partly because of all the fresh air and exercise but also because of a lack of food. Even when there was enough, the monotony of the diet drove away appetite. In spite of this we remained very healthy but both of us lost weight and the deficiency affected us in other ways too. I remember taking many rests during walks up hills, we had little energy and were uninventive. We failed to do many of the things we had intended to do, or could have done, if our minds had been full of their usual supply of ideas. The daily routine eventually became boring because it was always the same, devoted to the same pursuits – finding food and keeping dry and warm. I think perhaps this kind of life works best with a group of people. The work load could be spread and there would be a variety of company; it is extraordinarily difficult for anyone used to a modern urban environment with all its diverse entertainment to adapt suddenly to a completely different way of life – if you are used to outside stimulation you have withdrawal symptoms when it is removed.

As compensation there was the utter peace and beauty of the valley and the surrounding country. The feeling that if you wanted to sit and stare all day there was nothing – no telephone, no appointments, no radio with the news, no need to look smart – to prevent you doing it. We were able to think and read with a concentration and pleasure never before experienced. And as a couple we got on rather better than usual, the reason being, I think, that we relied totally on each other for survival.

So, when at last the time came to return to civilization, it was not the release that had been anticipated. Food tasted too rich and for a long time we lived on plain roast meat. The stimulation we thought we had craved came as an intrusion on an almost monk-like reserve that had built up over the weeks. I missed the closeness of the woods and the feeling that we were part of the chain of nature and dependent on each other for existence.

I first became interested in self-sufficiency from necessity during a summer spent in the south of Ireland. We were living in a stone farmhouse, four miles from the nearest village. There was no running water and I did all the cooking on a large open fire. Brendan was writing a book, there was very little money and very little for me to do. Always interested in wild plants, I would walk through the fields and along the river Bride. This part of Ireland, with its fairly chaotic approach to farming – fields seldom sprayed, replanted or drained – is rich in its variety of wild flowers. I therefore decided to supplement our poverty-stricken diet with any wild plants which were edible. I had with me André Simon's *Guide to Good Food and Wine* (the one cookery book I take with me as it covers everything from rhinoceros to dandelions) and, starting with this, began experimenting. I found that not only were there an enormous number of edible plants – over two hundred – but that many of them compared very well with ordinary garden vegetables. For instance, when we were invited to lunch by a rich American woman who had a country castle near by we were told that our first course was to be something really special. It turned out to be sorrel soup, which we were rather tired of, as we had been making it from the sorrel in the field outside the farmhouse. Hers had been grown from seed imported from France, but there was no difference in the taste.

We spent the following year in London where I pursued my researches into edible wild foods. That winter several strikes made me expand my researches into other related fields; I thought that it might be useful to know how to make things for myself as machines and the men who manned them were obviously unreliable. This led me to learn something of the crafts of a pre-industrial society and how they fitted in with an interdependent village system.

When the editor of the then *Daily Telegraph Magazine* suggested that we should live in the wild for two months and write an article about it, we agreed. This book is the accumulation of all the information I would have liked to have had with me in one volume during that time.

Part One

Food

Bodies need food in order to function. An obvious remark, but the truth of this statement never had any meaning for me until I was in a position of not having enough food. It is estimated that for hard physical labour the average person requires 4,000 calories a day, for light office work 2,500 and for a day in bed 1,800. These calories should be made up of a mixture of protein of which the richest sources are meat, fish and nuts; carbohydrates which come mostly from grain, roots, sugar; fats of various forms; and vitamins which occur in varying amounts in all foods but especially in vegetables, fats, eggs, grains and liver. While we were living off the land our intake of calories was usually sufficient for a day in bed but not for the physical labour which the life entailed. There were days which were spent almost entirely on foot searching for food and on which nothing more than leaves or berries were found. Though food, they were not enough, nor of the right kind, to compensate for the energy expended in getting them. This kind of day happened especially at the beginning when we were most inefficient at catching animals; it was soon apparent that the expertise with which a gipsy, poacher or gamekeeper lays traps and snares is acquired by a life-time's experience and judgement and cannot be gained in a matter of weeks from books. So our protein intake was low throughout our stay. This made us lethargic and I gave up much attempt at being original about food. Our daily diet, almost without exception, was made up of the following: *breakfast* of oatcakes, spread with honey and a cup of goat's milk; *lunch* of more oatcakes but eaten this time with goat's cream cheese and accompanied by a salad usually consisting of the more common leaves, sorrel, yarrow, dandelion, valerian and watercress, followed by fruit – raspberries or blackberries, whichever was in season; *supper*, except on the few occasions when we experimented with various types of cooking (like wrapping meat in clay and baking it in a pit in the ground) was invariably stew. The stew was of the type added to as the days went by; the typical gipsy cauldron full of whatever meat, fungi and vegetables were available, cooked in the juice of rowanberries. As the ingredients varied so did the taste, sometimes it was excellent and sometimes a bit peculiar. There was more salad to eat if required and berries. Occasionally we had fish but since the trout in the stream were very small, these could only be regarded as a starter to the meal. The same applied to snails, tiny nuggets of meat, which never amounted to much. The ones we ate were the little wood snails which after rain clustered thickly in a patch of nettles near the hut. They were easily gathered and I treated them as described on p. 117.

The largest source of meat we saw was pheasant and deer but, because we were living in our valley by courtesy of the late Auberon Herbert, who then owned the estate, we felt constrained, and confined ourselves to animals classed as vermin: squirrels, rabbits and pigeons. Rabbits were scarce as there had been myxomatosis the year before and the population had not yet recovered its former strength. We caught a rabbit perhaps every two or three days yet we could have eaten one each at a sitting. Squirrels were easy to get once we had acquired a gun. This we borrowed from the keeper who used to pass our hut sometimes; one item which I recommend you preserve from the twentieth century is a twelve-bore shot gun and a kit for reloading your own shells.* I do not know what the squirrels we shot had been feeding on but they tasted rank and needed a lot of dressing up to make them palatable. Though what we ate was on the whole tasty and good for us – we were never ill – the diet became monotonous, with the result that, even though hungry, we did not really feel like eating. I know more now about what you can eat and we could have been a great deal more adventurous, but even so part of the fault was our location. I recommend that if you are required to live off nature, select a coastal site if this is possible. Seaweed and molluscs are a large and easily accessible form of food. As it was, had we not had the goat, the hens and the bag of oatmeal we might on occasions have had to resort to some of the food in the section on starving (p. 158 ff.).

But given the right site, with a selection of all types of habitat and with some planning and preservation, it should be possible to feed yourself adequately all the year round. Nowadays we eat much the same food all year, but a diet tied to what nature has to offer would have to vary according to the season. In spring there would be more

* Both can be bought from Thomas Bland & Sons, 21–22 New Row, London W2.

green leaves for salad and vegetable, fish which would be returning to the shore after their winter migrations, and gulls' eggs. It would be the time to tap maple and birch for their sugary sap. In late spring and early summer there would be seaweed and molluscs and many flowers to be made into wine. This is also the time when grass is at its richest and, if you have livestock, when their milk makes the most succulent cheese. The moment the weather gets warmer too it is worth starting to evaporate sea water for salt. In summer as plant seeds ripen those for flour and oil can be collected, animals and birds will have finished breeding and be coming into prime condition and there will still be enough green leaves and seaweed for vegetable. Thistles and samphire are also ready at this time and ash keys for pickling. Fungi and nuts and animals are at their best in autumn and there will be berries in profusion; in late August honey from bees and roots to be dug. As winter comes on there should still be fish and seaweed laver until January. After this, if the store cupboard has not been stocked there could be a very lean two months until March, when the new growth starts again.

A wood fire improves the taste of food though cooking is certainly easier on a more modern stove. We had an old kitchen range which had been dug into the bank outside the hut and this was good enough for the amount of cooking we did. If I had to start from scratch I would begin with a camp fire and then, if I was going to remain in one place, I would try to build some kind of range along the lines of that described on p. 49.

We were allowed matches but this invaluable invention is comparatively recent. In the past sticks were rubbed together or a steel and flint was used to light fires or the problem was solved in other ways. One such was never to let the fire go out or get any lower than smouldering embers which could be fanned alight when needed.

A factor that has to be considered by anyone thinking of living off nature under today's conditions are the laws of trespass and the various preservation laws under which practically all flora and fauna are protected. These are very necessary in present circumstances, but since this book has been compiled with survival in mind I have assumed that they do not apply and have included several species of animal and bird which should not be taken except on exceptional occasions. Whenever a species is rare, or in danger of becoming rare, I have said so and hope it will be respected. At the moment seaweeds, fungi and molluscs are unprotected but there are comprehensive laws protecting birds and some animals, fish and flowers. However, whichever the species, you should never denude an area of a plant no matter how common, ring-bark a tree or irresponsibly kill any animal, bird or fish.

In this section I have tried to cater for those who feel they may some day need to survive off nature, for those in the same situation as ourselves and for those with some degree of civilization who have the time and opportunity for more elaborate cooking. But whichever state you are in a prerequisite is always to identify what you are eating, otherwise you may end up dying off the land, rather than living off the land, as happened to eight people who ate hemlock in the summer of 1976.

However, with reasonable care danger should be avoided. There is a vast supply of food going to waste because most of us are conditioned to buy, rather than collect, what we eat. I hope the following sections will show what is possible.

Bees, Honey and Beeswax

Keeping Bees

Modern science has brought about improvements in bee-keeping which have benefited not only the bees but their keepers as well. Hives with carefully calculated tiers and spacings and new equipment are all invaluable and anyone about to take up bee-keeping should get a National, WBC, Smith or Langstroth hive and a book on the subject. A practical demonstration by an experienced bee-keeper is invaluable.

For those without these resources, bee-keeping in the old way may be the only alternative. Africans keep bees in holes in trees and Levin in *Anna Karenina* kept them in hollowed-out stumps placed upside down.

He went into the shady lobby and from a peg in the wall took down his veil, put it on, and with his hands deep in his pockets entered the fenced-in apiary where – standing in regular rows and tied with bast to stakes – in the middle of a space where the grass had been mown, stood the old beehives, every one familiar to him, and each with a history of its own, while along the wattle fence stood the new hives with swarms hived that year.[21]

But the traditional way in this country was in a skep.

To make a skep

Take some supple willow or hazel branches and split them in four or more even strands with a sharp knife. Then take straw and damp it slightly twenty-four hours before use. To begin, bind straw round a small circular block of wood, and nail it in place. This is the centre of the top of the skep. Then wind round bunches of straw one coil after another and bind them in place with the split wood, threading it through the previous row. Form the skep into a dome shape at the top, with the sides almost straight. The straw should be bound so tightly that, when held up to the light, no daylight is visible. When the last circle is complete nail the skep to a wooden hoop with a slot cut in it – this is the doorway for the bees.

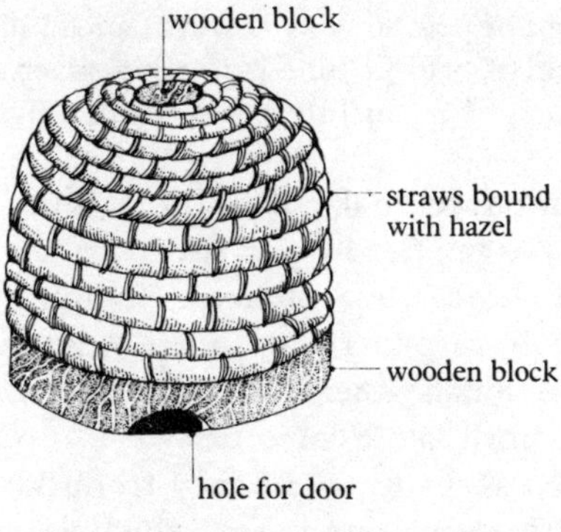

Acquiring Bees

When bees were widely kept, wild swarms or swarms which no one claimed were easy to come by. Today you will probably have to beg a nucleus from a neighbour or buy one from a commercial organization. Francis Galton gives the following ingenious way of finding wild bees.

Catch a bee, tie a feather or straw to his leg, which can easily be done (natives thrust it up into his body), throw him into the air, and follow him as he flies slowly to his hive; or catch two bees, and turning them loose at places some distance apart, search the place towards which their flights converge. But if bees are too scarce for either of these methods choose an open place, and lay in it a plate of syrup as a bait for the bees; after one has fed and flown away again, remove the plate 200 yards in the direction in which he flew, and proceed in the same sort of way until the nest is found.[19]

Swarms, incidentally, are very docile. The bees are full of honey and usually not aggressive. The vital part of capturing a swarm is to obtain the queen which is generally in the middle. If a skep is held under the swarm and the bees swept gently off whatever they are clinging to with a large feather, you should get her too. Cover the base of the skep and remove it to wherever you want to situate the hive. Turn it the right way up, stand it on something solid and firm with the doorway facing south or south-west and unimpeded so the bees have a clear flight path. If you failed to get the queen, the bees will return to her and you will have to start all over again.

A swarm of bees in May is worth a load of hay
A swarm of bees in June is worth a silver spoon
A swarm of bees in July is not worth a fly.

In early May swarms are small and in July it is too late in the season for the bees to make any headway; a late May or June swarm, however, given good weather and plenty of foraging material, should provide about 20 lb. surplus honey in late August. This is the time to collect honey – but heather honey, because the flowers bloom late, is not taken until late September.

To select which skeps to take honey from the bee-keeper goes along the row lifting each one to test which are the heaviest. The lighter ones he leaves to winter and to provide next year's crop of bees and honey. Using a smoker tin with a nozzle and bellows attached in which he lights some sulphur or a piece of saturated rag, he puffs smoke into the doorways of the heavy ones to kill the bees. Alternatively, he holds the whole skep over a pit filled with burning sulphur. The skep is then taken up, the comb cut from the inside, crushed and placed on a sieve for the honey to drain out. All this should be done wearing some form of protective clothing; trousers tucked into boots, a hat with a veil, gloves for the novice, and no gaps anywhere because if there is one the bees will find it.

Honey

The Honey in dry open Countries, where there is much Wild-thyme, Rosemary, and Flowers, is best. It is of three sorts, Virgin-honey, Life-Honey, and Stock-Honey. The first is the best. The Life-honey next. The Virgin-honey is of Bees, that swarmed the Spring before, and are taken up in Autumn; and is made best by chusing the Whitest combs of the Hive, and then letting the Honey run out of them lying upon a Sieve without pressing it, or breaking of the Combs. The Life-honey is of the same Combs broken after the Virgin-honey is run from it; the Merchants of Honey do use to mingle all the sorts together. The first of a swarm is called Virgin-honey. That of the next year, after the Swarm was hatched, is Life-honey. And ever after, it is Honey of Old-Stocks. Honey that is forced out of the Combs, will always taste of Wax. Hampshire Honey is most esteemed at London. About Bisleter there is excellent good. Some account Norfolk honey the best.[6]

Before the large-scale introduction of sugar in the eighteenth century honey was the only sweetener available. (If you use it instead of sugar in a modern recipe reduce the amount of water added by a fifth, as honey is more liquid). Honey was also used as a preservative and a cosmetic, and for making mead.

Beeswax

Beeswax was an essential part of the household economy, used to make candles, furniture polish, moulds and death masks, to waterproof leather, stopper bottles, and coat linen bandages for binding wounds. After the honey has drained out, the combs should be put, preferably in a muslin bag, in hot water (direct heat must never be applied as it ruins the wax) and left to melt down. As the water cools the impurities in the wax should sink to the bottom or be caught in the muslin and the solid wax will float on top. To store, squeeze into a ball and keep in a cool place.

Birds

A complete list of edible birds would include every known species. As far as I know no bird is poisonous, though many, especially sea birds, are too foul and too tough to eat. Others are too rare or live in inaccessible places. I have therefore included here only birds of which I have either personal experience, or good written evidence, of their having some gastronomic merit. Birds are given more protection by the law than any other wild species.

In Britain all birds, their nests and eggs, with a few exceptions, are protected by law. The main exceptions are certain game birds and species classed as pests. The current situation is that, of the birds included in the notes on pp. 20–28, cormorants, crows (carrion and hooded), doves (stock, collared and rock doves), gulls (great black-backed, lesser black-backed and herring), pigeons, rooks, starlings and house sparrows may be taken at any time *by authorized persons*; the game birds – grouse, pheasant and partridge – and coots, curlews (but not stone curlews), bar-tailed godwits, moorhens, plovers (golden and grey only), snipe (common and jack) and the species of geese and duck given in the notes may be killed outside their breeding season (1 February to 31 August unless stated otherwise). The rest are fully protected by the law at all times and are included here for historical interest. **Anyone intending to kill birds – or take their eggs – in Britain today must have a thorough knowledge of the Protection of Birds Acts 1954 and 1967 and the amendment of 1976 and must also have the authorization of the owner of the shooting rights.**

Unless otherwise stated all birds should be plucked and drawn before cooking. In general young birds are best roasted or halved and grilled, older birds casseroled. Since birds, with the exception of seabirds, carry little fat they should be basted with fat or butter while cooking; some bacon tied across the breast before roasting helps to prevent them drying up.

Other uses

The feathers of all birds should be kept, cleaned and dried out in a cool oven. They can be used for stuffing and the large wing feathers for pens. Oily seabirds can be rendered down and the oil used for light. Beaks and feet can be used as pegs and candle-holders.

Domesticated Birds

Until the eighteenth century the keeping and breeding of many species of birds was common practice. They provided a supply of fresh meat and eggs through the winter. However the development of root crops made it possible to feed animals through the winter and birds – especially pigeons, which consumed vast quantities of grain – became uneconomic.

Blackbirds, thrushes, fieldfares and other small birds

To feed these Birds, being taken old and wild, it is good to have some of their kinds tame to mix among them, and then putting them into great cages of three or four yards square, to have divers troughs placed therein, some filled with Haws: some with Hempseed and some with water; that the tame teaching the wild to eat, and the wild finding such change and alteration of food, they will in twelve or fourteen days grow exceeding fat, and fit for the use of the Kitchen.[6]

Duck: Wild duck were reared in small ponds set with willows and with small creeks to provide nesting places, and netted over. The duck were fed with bran or oats twice a day. (Mallard quickly become tame and the net would be superfluous in time.)

Partridge and pheasant: These might be kept in one room, with boxes for them to hide in. In the middle 'three wheat-sheaves, two with their ears upward, and one with the ears downward, and near unto them shallow tubs with water, that the fowl may pick wheat out of the ears, and drink at their pleasure; and by this manner of feeding, you shall have them as fat as is possible'.[6]

Pigeons: In the mid seventeenth century it was calculated that there were 26,000 dovecots in England, each holding from 500 to 1,000 birds. Pigeon holes were also built into the gables of houses, farm buildings and sometimes churches though most were kept in dovecots. Pigeon keeping was introduced into Britain by the Normans; their dovecots were massive, circular, low-domed, vaulted roofed buildings with a single hole to admit not only the pigeons but light and air as well. Nest holes covered the walls. Later other shapes, square, octagonal and oblong came into fashion, and the building was constructed of stone or brick or was half-timbered. Some had windows in the walls and a central post supporting a ladder so that high nests could be reached. The pigeons were supplied with fresh water, grit and corn but otherwise left to their own devices. The stock was begun by either taking young pigeons from their nests, or eggs, which were hatched out under broody hens.

Swans: Left to themselves to breed, the cygnets were caught and cooped in houses or courtyards or small ponds with some dry ground where they could sit and preen themselves. They would be fattened on barley, malt and water for four weeks before eating.

Wild Birds

Blackbird: 'Four and twenty blackbirds baked in a pie; when the pie was opened the birds began to sing, wasn't that a dainty dish to set before a king.' In 1590 the Lords of the Star Chamber paid 2s. a dozen for blackbirds. Mrs Beeton gives this recipe for blackbird pie.

Have ready some blackbirds, rump steak, veal forcemeat, hard-boiled eggs, good stock, paste, salt and pepper. Pick and draw the birds, and stuff them with veal forcemeat. Line the bottom and sides of a pie dish with rather thin slices of steak; put in the birds, cut in halves; season them with salt and pepper and intersperse sections or slices with hard-boiled eggs; half fill the dish with good stock, cover with paste and bake in a moderately hot oven from one and a quarter to one and three quarter hours, according to size. Add more stock before serving. Allow one blackbird to every two persons. A fat December blackbird was much esteemed in Paris where *Pâté de la foie de merle* was thought a great delicacy. The female blackbird is brown and you occasionally get albino ones, found everywhere in gardens, woodlands, hedges, etcetera, nesting in hedges and wood-piles.[7]

Bullfinch: One of the song birds still caught and eaten on the Continent.

Bunting: Formerly passed off as larks in Paris markets.

Coot: If skinned immediately after killing they are just edible and are said to appear disguised under classier names in some Soho restaurants. More appreciated in the past, in 1807 they were for sale at 1s. 6d. each, in 1922 for 8d. and in 1941 for only 6d. They like large expanses of open water and nest in reeds and other water vegetation.

Cormorant: Old birds have rank, dark flesh but young squabs were used in the north instead of pigeons in pies and are said to taste a bit like hares. All should be skinned before eating. They are found all round the British coast, especially in the west and north.

Crow – carrion and hooded: Eaten in earlier times by the French and Italians. They are tough birds, best skinned and stewed. They inhabit moors, cultivated country and sea-shores, nesting in trees and sometimes cliffs.

Cuckoo: Italians think that the flesh of the young cuckoo 'is a most delicious morsel'.[8] The cuckoo is more often heard than seen.

Curlew (except the stone curlew)*:* There is an old saying that 'A curlew lean or a curlew fat, Carries twelvepence on her back'. Good eating as long as they are inland birds fresh from feeding on moorland. Ian Niall writing in *Country Life* in 1965 says that he always tries to get a couple for the table in season if he is sure they are pasture fed. Roast. Curlew inhabit mud flats and estuaries but nest inland in moors, marshes and meadows.

Dove – stock, rock and collared: Similar to pigeons, but considered superior in taste, found in most of the same places, except for the rock dove which only inhabits coastal areas in Scotland and Ireland.

Duck: The close season for duck is from 1 February to 31 August (21 February to 31 August when below high water mark) and the following are all edible.

Mallard: Found throughout the country on almost any type of water.
Pintail: As long as its diet is not too fishy it is excellent eating. Found in the east of the country, it spends the winter on coastal waters, coming to inland water and marshes to breed during spring.
Pochard: Vegetarian by choice and consequently excellent eating. Widespread over most of the country, on lakes and backwaters. A diving duck.
Shoveller: Dr Muffet says that 'Shovelars feed most commonly upon the sea-coast upon cockles and shell-fish; being taken home,

and dieted with new garbage and good meat, they are nothing inferior to fatted gulls.'[10]
Teal: According to a mid-seventeenth-century authority: 'This bird for the delicate taste of its flesh and the wholesome nourishment it affords the body, doth deservedly challenge the first place among those of its kind.'[11] It is found everywhere except in the middle of England, on reedy pools and streams, marshes and moors.
Tufted duck: Good eating, though best when living on fresh water. A sociable bird, it inhabits lakes and pools throughout the country.
Wigeon: Good eating, similar to mallard and teal. It is found on salt and fresh water in Scotland, breeding on marshes and moors.

Fieldfare

Fieldfare: Juniper-fed fieldfares were held in high esteem on the Continent in the sixteenth and seventeenth centuries.

Gannet: Still eaten by some fishermen in the outer Hebrides (they are protected by law elsewhere in Britain). With the fulmar it was the principal food of the former inhabitants of St Kilda, who ate it fresh in summer and salted it down for winter use. The water poet Taylor described 'the Soleand Goose' in 1618 as 'a most delicate fowle, which has very good flesh, but it is eaten standing at a sideboard, little before dinner, unsanctified without garlic and after it is eaten it must be well liquered with two or three rowsers of sherrie or canarie sacks'.[13] Until the late nineteenth century gannets were still being shipped to London and the Midlands where they appeared on the menu in many of the cheaper restaurants.

Geese: All species of wild geese are edible though not thought as good as the domestic goose, being gamier and, on the whole, tougher. All but the greylag, which occasionally breeds in parts of northern Scotland, and the Canada goose, which is resident, are migrants in coastal areas, marshes and moors mainly in Scotland but also in parts of England, particularly East Anglia and estuaries elsewhere. Those most frequently eaten are the Canada goose, bean goose, greylag, pinkfoot and whitefront.

Godwit

Godwit, bar-tailed: Sir Thomas Browne called the Godwit 'the daintiest dish in England'.[9] They should be cooked without being drawn, like snipe, and are also good potted.

Grouse: André Simon says that 'there is between the birds shot in Derbyshire and those shot in Perthshire, as well as between the birds shot in one season and those of the previous year, the same degree of variation that exists between the different growths of the Côte d'Or of different vintages,'[9] and that they are best in their first year. They should be eaten the day that they are shot, or hung for not longer than a week. Wrapped in bacon and placed on toast, they should be roasted for twenty minutes until they are just cooked, pink but not raw. A variation is to stuff the bird with butter and rowanberries or even wild mountain raspberries. In season from 12 August to 10 December.

Gulls – great black-backed, lesser black-backed, herring and common: Domesticated in former times. Considered a delicacy and in 1590 cost 5s each (beef which was 20d. a stone). In Chard, Dorchester and Exeter, gull served with mustard and vinegar sauce was a regular dish in hotels. They inhabit coastal areas breeding on cliffs, islands and moors.

Heron: There was a time when herons were hunted with trained falcons. It is said that Henry II induced the Irish kings and chiefs he was entertaining in Dublin at Christmas 1171 to eat heron. Apparently they did not like it and did not touch it again. Certainly, herons were well liked in England. Some assert that they have a fishy flavour but it is thought that this is in the bones and if the heron is killed without any bones being broken, the flesh will be fine, dark red and slightly sweet. They should be skinned, not plucked. The Elizabethans stuffed heron with apples and served it in a pie – the pulp of the apple was said to draw out any fishy or oily flavour from the flesh.

An authority claims that

> it is acknowledged that the young heron is a great delicacy on the table, if killed at a proper time, and cooked by a *connoisseur* in the art. They should never be killed for the table until they have had, for the longest possible time, the benefit of the moonlight nights to gather flesh by fishing, and when killed, the bird should be enclosed in an earthenware jar, and buried underground for several days, by which means their brown colour becomes white, and the fishy flavour vanishes.[10]

House sparrow: These were commonly eaten in rural areas; Chard church wardens in 1657 debited the parish ninepence for one dozen sparrows.[15] According to a correspondent to *Country Life,*

> Some years ago we were staying at a farm-house in France and one of the favourite delicacies they gave us was grilled sparrows. They were skinned, then about six put on a skewer and grilled and we ate the breasts, which were tender and tasty. One sees thousands of these birds feeding on the farmer's corn, but no one seems to realize how good they are to eat.[16]

Another correspondent wrote:

> As a boy on a big mixed farm in Bedfordshire I ate sparrow pies, and very good they were. They were made in the same way as a game pie, that is to say the birds were plucked, drawn, with heads and feet removed, and put in the pie dish with beef steak or stewing beef and hard-boiled eggs, and covered with a pastry lid. They are, I think, best eaten cold . . .[17]

Lark: All species. Steak, oyster, kidney and lark pie was a traditional English dish and larks were cooked in great quantities. A seventeenth-century appreciation: 'Larks are of delicate taste in eating, light of digestion and of good nourishment.'[12] It should be plucked and the gizzard removed; then it should be wrapped in bacon, put in lark spits, run through from side to side, roasted for about ten minutes and served on toast.

Moorhen: 'Water-hen skinned and then fried in hot fat makes an excellent salmi or braise.' They inhabit ponds, slow streams and marshes, nesting in reeds and bushes near the water.

Partridge: Some consider this the best game bird but others prefer grouse, which, they say, has slightly more character. Egon Ronay, when asked on the radio programme Desert Island Discs what he would choose first to eat said a 'plain roast partridge'. Hang for no more than four days. They are best in October and when young. (The age can be told by looking at the first flight feather, which, in a young bird, is pointed at the tip and not rounded.) Roast with the breast covered with a strip of bacon for twenty-five minutes in a moderate oven or on a spit before the fire, basting with butter. Partridge over fifteen months can be tough and are best casseroled. Gipsies stuff them with mushrooms.

In season from 1 September to 1 February. They are resident all over Britain on farmland, pastures, moorland and waste land, nesting in well-hidden hedge bottoms and fields of corn.

Pheasant: Introduced into Europe from the Far East at an early date and fostered as a game bird. They live for up to fifteen years but any bird approaching that age should be stewed. Young ones may be roasted for forty-five minutes. The age can be told by the spurs: at one year they are rounded and pointless; at two, short and pointed; older than that, sharp and long. Hens have soft feet and a light plumage when young and rough feet and a darker plumage when old. Best from November to January. Hang by the head for about two weeks – when the tail feathers give they are ready to eat. Season 1 October to 1 February. They live on park and farm land and in shrubberies and woodland borders, nesting on the ground in low vegetation and bracken.

Plover – golden and grey: Used to be shot and netted in large quantities, and roasted like woodcock. Golden plovers are considered the best to eat but the grey plover is larger. Highly esteemed as a food, it used to be said of a discontented person that 'even a grey plover cannot please him'. Crab-apple juice and melted butter are often used as sauce. In Norfolk, where they are plentiful, plovers were made into pies. The grey plover is a winter visitor found chiefly on coastal flats near the shore line. The golden plover is a partial migrant found on hilly moors and, in winter, in fields and estuaries.

Puffin:

> Their flesh is excessively rank, as they feed on sea-weed and fish, especially sprats; but when pickled and preserved with spices, they are admired by those who love high eating. Dr Caius says that in his day the Church allowed them in Lent, instead of fish; he also acquaints us that they were taken by means of ferrets, as we do rabbits.[9]

They were also eaten on St Kilda, in the Faroe Islands and on all the Scilly Islands, which (except Tresco, which was owned by the Abbey of Tavistock) were for a long period held by the king for an annual rent of 300 puffins. In Henry VI's reign this was reduced to fifty puffins, a number then considered as equivalent to 6s. 8d. Much later in the seventeenth century the Earls of Derby used to have some 2,000 puffins a year sent from the Calf of Man. Certainly these Manx puffins (and probably those from the Scillies, too) were salted for human consumption.[14] The puffin is a summer visitor to the west and north-east coasts of Britain, breeding in holes excavated in the turf or in old rabbit burrows.

Quail: It should be eaten as soon as possible and cooked like snipe. It is very shy; it lives and breeds in rough pastures in southern England and south-west Ireland. Rare and heavily protected.

Ring ouzel: Gilbert White says that

> on the thirteenth of April I went to the sheep-down, where the ring-ousels have been observed to make their appearance at spring and fall, in their way perhaps to north or south . . . We shot a cock and a hen: they were plump and in high condition . . . I dressed one of these birds, and found it juicy and well-flavoured.[12]

Rook: Adult rooks are rank and not fit to eat but the breast and thigh tops of young squabs were once consumed in many parts of rural England. Skin and section as soon as possible after killing, soak overnight in milk, then casserole or wrap in strips of bacon and cook in a pie. Rooks inhabit agricultural areas, nesting in colonies in tree tops.

Snipe – common and jack: Among the finest game birds to eat. They should be plucked and roasted without being drawn; traditionally the head is left on and brought round so that the beak can be passed through the legs and body instead of a skewer. Brush with butter, cover with bacon, stand on a piece of toast to catch the juices and roast for about twenty minutes. The snipe is a small brown marsh bird preferring land where cattle have been kept. They are partial migrants and are found all over Britain. The close season is from 1 February to 11 August.

Starling: Boswell commented that while staying on Coll with Dr Johnson there were 'no black-cock, muir-fowl, nor partridges; but there are snipe, wild-duck, wild-geese, and swans, in winter; wild pidgeons, plover, and great numbers of starlings; of which I shot some, and found them pretty good eating'.[18] They are gregarious and are found in colonies in towns, and in the country nesting in holes in trees, buildings and cliffs.

Ring ouzel   Stonechat

Stonechat: 'The flesh of the stonechat is rather savoury.'

Swallow: Another songbird caught and eaten mostly by the Italians as it migrates across the continent.

Swan: Royal ownership of swans lapsed in the nineteenth century though on the Thames swan-rights are still exercised by the vintners and dyers livery companies. The former have the right to a feast of cygnets once a year. Until the end of the last century swans were fattened for Christmas in swan-pits taking their food from floating troughs. There are about 1,800 mute swans in Britain today all descended, even though the swan is a native bird, from semi-domestic stocks. Stuffed and roasted and served with a port wine sauce, the meat is rich and dark, but inclined to dry up during cooking unless kept well basted.

Thrush: Held in highest esteem by the Romans and similar in taste to a lark. They were fattened in large rooms for the table, two being allowed for each person. In many parts of France thrush dishes and thrush pâtés are great specialities, but the thrush is fully protected in Britain.

Waxwing: Eaten on the Continent, but uncommon in Britain.

Wheatear: Gilbert White noted that vast quantities are caught 'on the South Downs near Lewes, where they are esteemed a delicacy. There have been shepherds, I have been credibly informed, that have made many pounds in a season by catching them in traps.'[12]

The Compleat City and Country Cook (1732) says that 'They are a Tunbridge Bird; pick them very clean; season them with pepper and salt, put them in a pot, cover them with butter and bake them an hour; take them and put them in a cullender to drain the liquor away; then cover over with clarified butter and they will keep.'[9]

Wood-pigeon: Squabs or young pigeons under four weeks old are considered the most delicious. Young pigeons used to be fattened by tying them by the leg to the tree by the nest; as it was prevented from flying, its parents would continue feeding it for longer than usual. Pigeons feed on all kinds of crops and are easily decoyed by rubber pigeons. Roasted, potted or casseroled, 'Pygeons be easily dygested and are very holsome to them which are flammatike or pure melancholy.'[13] The wood-pigeon lives almost anywhere where there are trees, nesting in trees, hedges and old nests.

Capture

Game birds

Shooting: A twelve-bore shotgun or a .22 rifle is correct. Game birds are shot by walking them up – walking across their terrain, preferably helped by a well-trained dog, and shooting as the birds rise up in front. Or you can have them driven towards you – place yourself in a strategic position, down wind, by the side of a wood and get one or several people to beat through the wood towards you; shoot as the birds fly out. Game birds can be shot at any time during the day but ducks and geese fly in to water to feed at morning and evening and it is at these times that they are most easily shot. It is not considered sportsmanlike to shoot sitting game or to use any of the methods described below, **most of which are illegal.**

Kite: A paper kite in the shape of a bird flown above a field in which there are partridges will make them think that a hawk is aloft and will keep them on the ground from where they may be taken, by hand or by shooting.

Hooking: Corn and raisins, peas or acorns are scattered in a place where pheasants or pigeons feed. After the second or third day, when they have got accustomed to feeding, more peas or raisins are put down and less corn. In every raisin there is a fish-hook attached to a horsehair line or fishing line and this in turn is attached to a rod. The hook slips through the raisin and sticks in the lining of the crop. Or hairs can be attached to the raisin; as the pheasant gobbles down the bait, the hair will protrude from his beak. As it gulps and wipes its beak on the ground it becomes desperate and ends up on its back exhausted.

Netting: A strong net is used, 20–30 yards long and 12–14 feet deep with a 2in. mesh, the top of which is threaded on a rope. On a dark night, preferably with some rain and a bit of wind, the net can be trailed against the wind towards and over the birds where they roost. As they rise the net is dropped. Most often used for partridges.

Snares: Nooses made of the finest catgut are laid in the loose mould where partridges take their morning dustbath, usually near hedgerows where the soil is fine and dry. When the birds begin to scratch in the soil, their feet and/or heads are caught.

Paper cup: Black funnel-shaped cones of paper the size of a pheasant's head are smeared with bird-lime or some thick sticky stuff like treacle and some corn placed at the bottom. These are laid round a wood. The pheasants put their heads in the cone to get the corn, get stuck and, unable to see, are easily picked up.

Sulphur: This is used for pheasants. The sulphur is put in a large tin with holes punched in the sides. On a moonlit night with a good breeze, the tin or tins are placed so that the fumes will carry on the breeze into the trees where the pheasants roost. The sulphur is set alight; in a few minutes the pheasants are overcome by the fumes and they can be picked up off the ground.

Wild fowl

Baited hooks: A poacher describes how acorns are 'split along their length with a fish hook inserted' into the slit with the barb protruding and a short length of line attached to the other end. 'Went down to shallows under oaks where acorns had fallen into water's edge, and there set acorn traps and went some hundred yards up stream. Before long a duck would swim in and splashing of water told me I had made a catch; and I hurried over to put it out of its misery.'[20]

Decoys: Shooting and trapping are facilitated by the use of decoys, solid blocks of wood carved and painted to resemble the real bird or stuffed skins mounted on wooden or bark floats. These are anchored by strings to keep them in place and placed in netted enclosures, held up by wooden structures. The birds can be enticed in by feed and then caught.

Small birds

Remember that it is illegal for unauthorized persons to catch or kill most species of wild bird in Britain today. The following notes are included for historical interest only.

Mouse traps: Gilbert White describes how 'When a boy, I have known twenty [tits] in a morning caught with snap mouse-traps, baited with tallow or suet.'[12]

Lime: This is an archetypal method of catching small birds, still frequently used on the Continent though forbidden here. The lime may be concocted from several different ingredients: from linseed oil boiled slowly until it is reduced by two thirds to a glutinous, sticky mass; from the resin and berries of mistletoe; and from holly or young elder shoots, boiled for up to seven hours, drained of its water in a cloth and then

> laid in heaps in pits dug in the ground, where it is covered with stones, and left for two or three weeks to ferment. But less time than this is required if the weather be hot. It is watered from time to time, if necessary. In this way, it passes into a mucilaginous state; and is then pounded into a paste, washed in running water, and kneaded till it be free from dirt, chips, etcetera. Lastly, it is left for four or five days in *earthen* vessels, to ferment and purify itself, when it becomes fit for use. It ought to be greenish, sour, gluey, stringy, and sticky. It becomes brittle when dry, and may be powdered; but, on being wetted, it becomes sticky again.[19]

The lime is often mixed with goose fat and spread on twigs; these are then set in trees. When the bird alights on the twig its feet stick fast; the twig is then dislodged and falls to the ground. Lime may also be spread on sedges, ears of corn, thistles and teazels – wherever small birds alight to feed.

Nets: It is illegal to net birds in this country. A fine, almost invisible net is strung up against a dark background of trees and shrubs so that the birds are unable to see it until it is too late. The Italians construct what they call *bressana* – a wooded glade the size of a tennis court, enclosed by a double rank of trees and with decoy birds in cages hung among the branches. The trees are swathed in mist netting and the birds are attracted by the singing of the caged birds.

Killing and Preparing Birds

Birds are killed by breaking their necks. Hold the bird in your left hand, put the right over its head with the index finger down one side of the neck and the other fingers down the other. Then, catching the legs with the left hand – and, if possible, the wings so that they do not flap – allow the bird to drop and bend the neck up, at the same time stretching the neck slightly. Larger birds such as geese should be killed by holding them by the legs with the back towards you and their head resting on the floor. Lay a strong stick over the neck, stand on it and pull the bird's legs upwards until you feel the neck break.

Unless otherwise stated, all birds should be plucked, preferably while still warm, before cooking. Put them on damp newspaper and, starting at the breast, pluck out the feathers, one or two at a time with large birds, more with small, pulling them upwards but being careful not to tear out the skin at the same time. Any residue of down is singed off over a flame. The head is then cut off, an incision made at the vent and the entrails removed.

To skin birds, slit along the backbone and peel off the skin and feathers, cutting round the leg and wings. Soaking seabirds in vinegar and water helps reduce any fishy flavour in their meat. Hanging, by suspending the bird by the neck for up to a week in a larder, matures the taste.

Bread

Early bread was unleavened. It was the Egyptians who discovered that if dough is left to ferment it forms gases which make a lighter bread. Later yeast was usually added to produce carbon dioxide to make the dough rise. However, the addition of yeast is by no means universal. In Ireland soda bread is made of coarsely ground flour mixed with sour milk; Thoreau, in *Walden*, finds yeast

> not an essential ingredient . . . Neither did I put any salt, soda or other acid or alkali, into my bread. It would seem that I made it according to the receipt which Marcus Porcius Cato gave about two centuries before Christ . . . 'Make kneaded bread thus: Wash your hands and trough well. Put the meal into the trough, add water gradually, and knead it thoroughly. When you have kneaded it well, mould it, and bake it under a cover', that is in a baking kettle. Not a word about leaven. But I did not always use this staff of life. At one time owing to the emptiness of my purse I saw none of it for more than a month.[1]

But in the main, the theory that bread without leaven is good for no man carries the day.

Around 1577 we are told

> The bread throughout our land is made of such grain as the soil yieldeth, nevertheless the gentility commonly provide themselves sufficiently of wheat for their own tables, whilst their household and poor neighbours in some shires are forced to content themselves with rye or barley, yea and in time of dearth many with bread made out of beans, peason or oats and some acorns among.[23]

Also grasses, nuts, roots (particularly of fern, angelica and silverweed) and the inner layer between the wood and bark of pine and birch trees can be, and have been, ground into flour mixed with water and baked.

Flours and the Breads They Make

Grass seed

The earliest form of flour, eaten by primitive man, was made from grass seed. It was collected, pounded and ground into flour, mixed with water, formed into flat cakes and baked. Though any wild grass seed is edible, the seeds of floating sweet grass (*Glyceria fluitans*), found growing in ponds and streams, have most often been eaten; during the eighteenth century in Germany they were eaten 'at the tables of the great on account of their nourishing quality and agreeable taste'. In Russia they were collected by a peasant who 'takes an old felt hat, and, wading in the water, skims the hat among the patches of *Glyceria* when the grain is ripe'.[23] The seeds of corn spurrey were eaten in the Shetlands, where its local name is *meldi* or meal plant.

Nuts

Every kind of nut has at times been ground and made into flour, – some sweet pastries still include ground chestnuts or hazelnuts in their ingredients. Flour ground from acorns and beechmast is bitter and unfit to eat unless it has been thoroughly soaked in boiling water to extract the tannin; the saturated flour is then squeezed into a cake and dried in the sun or baked. Acorn cake is still eaten by Indians living on the mountain slopes bordering the Pacific Ocean.

Rye

Not an indigenous British plant but one that has been extensively cultivated since the Iron Age and is often found wild. The grain is similar to wheat but with a stronger flavour and may be used for all the same recipes. It is used in Germany for making black bread. The advantage of rye bread is that it will keep indefinitely. In Suffolk

> The bread for storage was usually made of rye or barley meal without any leaven. Some of it was thin as a biscuit or even an ice-cream wafer. Often it was baked in round cakes with a hole in the middle, and then strung on ropes or rods and hung from the ceiling of the kitchen, as we used to hang flitches of bacon.[24]

Its disadvantage is its association with a black parasitic fungus, ergot (*Clavicepts purpurea*), which is poisonous; rye should always be carefully inspected before using. Ergot can cause gangrene, abortion and hallucinations (hence the use of rye in witchcraft).

Barley

Ground into flour and used in the same way as wheat it makes a coarse, dense bread. Barley was often made into 'the round plate bread (the flat loaves that were laid on the table and used as plates)'. Piers Plowman takes 'two loaves of barley bread' and in the book of Judges an Israelite dreams of a cake of barley bread falling on to the Midianites' camp and destroying them. Barley is better employed as an adjunct to broth and porridge, or for malting, than for bread.

Oats

Avena fatua, the cultivated oat, is believed to be derived from *Avena sativa*, the wild oat. Known to have existed in Europe during the Bronze Age, it has been used ever since as cereal, in unleavened bread, oatcakes and porridge, especially in the north where it thrives in spite of the climate. Dr Johnson in his *Dictionary* made the derogatory remark that oats are 'A grain which in England is generally given to horses, but in Scotland supports the people.'

Oatcake

1 lb. oatmeal; 2 tablespoons melted bacon fat (this can be omitted but the oatcakes will be brittle); 1 teaspoon salt; boiling water.

Mix the salt and the oatmeal, add the fat and some of the boiling water. Mix well and knead into a soft dough, adding more water if necessary. Roll out as thinly as possible on a board sprinkled with oatmeal. Cut into circles, squares or triangles and bake in a cool oven or on a girdle until they begin to curl. Finish drying them out in front of a hot fire or in a cool oven with the door open.

Wheat

Bread wheat (*Triticum aestivum*) is unknown in the wild but has been cultivated and hybridized ever since about 6000 BC. Wheat grown in Britain is of the 'soft' variety; it has more starch and less rising power, elasticity and gluten than imported 'hard' wheats. The following recipe for bread is adapted from one by Eliza Acton (1857).[34]

To make two loaves of crusty fresh bread

3½ lb. flour; 1 large tablespoon yeast; 1 teaspoonful salt; 1½ pints water.

Put the flour in a warm bowl, make a well in the centre – not right down, just a 'pokehole amidst'. Take the yeast and rub it gently down into about 1 pint of warm water. If it is tired yeast, a little sugar livens it up, if fresh it should not need any encouragement. Pour this yeast cream into the flour hole, and rock it a little gently with your hand, or a *warm* wooden spoon, so that some of the flour falls down into it, and shake an equal thickness of flour over the top, so that the yeast is embedded warmly in the midst of the bowl of flour. Put a clean cloth over the bowl, and for fear of draughts a piece of blanket over that, and set it to stand undisturbed in a warm place for an hour or a little longer to prove. After an hour the yeast should have grown and permeated the flour and risen up through it in bubbling cracks (thus *proving* the yeast alive). Now pour in another ½ pint warm water, and gently mix in the flour surrounding the yeasty part; go on doing this, sides to middle, with a happy pawing action, like a contented cat, till the dough is all one even mass of warm soft resilience. It will be sticky at first and the moist parts will adhere to your fingers, so keep dipping your hands in the dry part of the flour, and sprinkling dry flour on the damp places, bringing the whole of the dough to one consistency throughout. At the end the bowl should be dry and floury, not sticky. (You may, while working, have to add a little more warm water, but do it gradually, as you cannot remove it and to add more dry flour spoils the consistency of the whole.)

Now you have your dough – knead it. Turn the whole ball out on to the table and press the middle with your fist and work it round and round, sides to middle, folding it in and kneading it down till all is one spongy elastic lump of resilience – no dry lumps of flour, no damp spots of yeast, but an even texture – with a lovely alive elasticity that seems to spring back against your fists.

Gather it up now and put it back into your pan; cut a deep cross over it (the cross should burst open even as you cut it), cover all with the warm cloths again, and set it to rise again for an hour, or until it seems to have stopped swelling up and is as large as it's going to be. The cross will be wide-open gashes now, with the sides glistening and showing the spongy texture within.

Take it up on to the table, cut it into two loaves and shape as you have a mind to do. Put them roundly into large warm bake-pans, set near the stove for another half hour to plump up again and then bake them.

To tell if a loaf is done tap it on the underside: it should sound hollow and dry; the dull thump of a loaf which is still moist in the middle is quite different.

Butter

Butter is the fat of cow's milk, solidified by churning. Churning consists of agitating the cream until the microscopic fat granules clump together as butter granules, separating from the liquid portion called 'buttermilk'. Butter is high in vitamins A and D, food and energy value. It is low in protein and other vitamins. The content of butter fat in cow's milk ranges from 3 to 6 per cent according to the variety of cow (Jersey and Guernsey cow's milk is exceptionally high in butter fat), her health, diet, and the time of year – rich summer pastures produce rich milk. Though you can make butter from any milk, cow's milk is richer in cream than other milks and is so constituted that the cream separates easily from the milk.

To Make Butter

Start with absolutely clean utensils, soused with boiling salted water, rinsed in cold water and air dried. (Soap should never be used – certainly not on wooden utensils as it becomes ingrained in the wood.) Do not use a cloth to dry the utensils as it merely re-contaminates them with germs. Take fresh cooled milk and leave to stand in shallow bowls for at least an hour for the cream to rise. Skim off the cream and put in a separate bowl. Do this every day, adding the new cream to the cream already in the bowl and stirring well every time. Keep in a cool place. Cream should always be allowed to stand for twenty-four hours in a shallow bowl before attempting to convert it into butter. If you have a ready source of milk it is a good idea to make butter twice a week, keeping a bowl of cream ready for the appropriate day. The outside temperature is all-important when making butter: if it is too cold the butter will not form; if it is too hot it goes rancid – 52–66°F is right. Use the cooler end of the scale in hot weather and the hotter in cold.

Butter can be made by simply chomping a wooden spoon around in a mixing bowl of cream, but a churn will speed up the process, especially where larger quantities of cream are involved. Styles of churn vary, but the most common are: the plunger type, where a plunger fitted with holed discs is moved up and down; the paddle type, in which the paddle which agitates the milk is turned by hand; and the barrel or glass jar that is turned end over end, either by hand or with a handle. These can often be bought at country auction sales.

Whichever is used, paddle the cream round until globules of butter begin to form. This should happen in about thirty minutes, if it does not it usually means something is wrong – the butter content of the cream is too low, the utensils are dirty or the temperature is wrong. When the globules are almost half an inch in diameter stop the movement and strain off the buttermilk. Save this; if your cow has been feeding on good herby pasture, it makes a nice cold drink; otherwise use it for mixing up bread, scones and cakes.

Now the butter must be washed to remove any remaining particles of milk. Have a bowl of water the same temperature as the butter and put the globules of butter into this. Turn them over slowly, and as the water goes milky strain it off and replace with fresh. Continue to do this until the water stays clear. Next take the butter from the water and spread it thinly on a wooden board using a flat knife or spatula. Tilt the board so that the water runs off. Fold the butter over and over until all the water is pressed out of it. The less water there is in the butter the better it will keep.

If you prefer butter salt, or want to preserve it, fold the salt in now. Use about 1 part salt to 30 parts butter – if the butter is to be kept for any length of time, add a higher proportion of salt.

To Preserve Butter

The butter must be especially well washed and pressed dry. Then using either a small wooden keg or an earthenware jar, the butter should be 'flung hard' into it and knuckled down so that it is very closely packed. When the bottom of the jar is well covered with no space for air put a layer of salt over it, then another layer of butter, again well packed down, another layer of salt and so on, finishing with a layer of salt. Then ram the top on making sure that there is no air between it and the butter. When the butter is required for use it should be washed again to get rid of the salt.

Butter barrels used to be bound with willow bands which were cut off and the barrel taken apart when the butter was wanted.

In Ireland in earlier times 'Butter was consumed in great quantities, not only fresh but salted. Sometimes it was flavoured with herbs and enclosed in a wooden vessel and buried in a bog to be preserved and matured.'[25]

Another way of preserving butter, one often used in hot climates, is to clarify it or make it into what is called in India *ghee*. *Ghee* never solidifies and its taste is inferior to hard butter, but it is fine for cooking with. Melt the butter, then allow it to simmer for an hour, skimming off the scum as it rises to the surface. When it is clear and free from scum, pour it into airtight containers and store.

Wrapping

The common dock (*Rumex obtusifolius*) is sometimes called 'butter dock' because its large leaves were used for wrapping butter for the market. The juice of the leaves is cooling. (This is why they are used to ease nettle stings: 'Nettle in, Dock; Dock in, Nettle out; Dock rub

Nettle out.' An older version of the saying 'In dock out nettle' was used to describe a vacillating lover.) The leaves of the butterbur were also used for wrapping butter as well as for other purposes. It has the largest leaf of any wild plant in Britain – up to three feet across – and Gerard says that they are 'of such a widenesse, as that of itselfe it is bigge and large inough to keepe a mans head from raine, and from the heate of the sunne'.[26]

Cheese

Cheese-making is thought to be as old as the time when man first took milk from wild or domesticated animals. Since any milk left will in time go sour, the acid curd separating from the whey, cheese-making must have been a natural extension of this process. When the addition of rennet or plant juices to quicken the souring process began is not known. But the common sense of cheese-making as a means of preserving some of the flush or summer milk for winter use must have appealed early on.

Ten parts milk reduce to approximately one part cheese. Cheese contains fat, casein, calcium and vitamin A, and has 2,000 calories to the pound. (Even good beef only contains 1,100 to the pound.)

The quality of the cheese depends on the quality of the milk, which in turn depends on the quality of the pasture the cow, goat or sheep has fed on. The quality of the pasture depends on geography and climate. So regional differences in cheese are not hard to explain. When cheese-making was part of a household's economy all these factors were considered and the cheese was often made only when the animals were feeding on certain herbage.

> For example, a 'moorland' cheese was only made in spring, when the winter, hay-fed cattle went out and grazed the scented alder and new grass on the mountains; this diet cleared their blood, made delicious milk (full of the casein and flavours that make for the best cheeses); and the cheese made from this special milk was 'moorland' – it was blue moulded and light in texture, and had a delicious aroma.[27]

All this ended with the introduction of the Milk Marketing Board, the central collection of milk and the specialized farm.

Whatever your source of milk the following basic recipes give methods which can be elaborated on with practice.

Cream Cheese

Making cream cheese is relatively simple but it does not keep well. Leave the milk in a cool place to go sour and solid, then pour both curds and whey into a muslin, hang in a larder and allow to drip. When this has ceased, remove the cheese from the muslin and either eat it plain or mix with salt and herbs such as chives, or sugar and additional cream. Cream cheese can be eaten with bread or biscuits or with fresh fruit, or it can be used to make cheesecake.

Hard Cheese

This is a much more specialized and involved process. Practice and instinct are all-important for recognizing the changes that occur and the right moment at which to start each stage – a thermometer and an acidmeter will help. First the milk must be ripe. Ideally it should be a combination of the evening and the following morning's milking in equal quantities. This milk will be beginning to go sour but should still taste sweet. You get about 1¼ lb. cheese from 1 gallon of milk.

Warm the milk to about 90°F, stir in about 1 teaspoon of rennet and continue stirring for 5–10 minutes to ensure that the cream is evenly distributed throughout the curd as it sets. To test when this is beginning to happen put your hand in the cream – the milk should cling to your fingers; another way is to pour on a drop of water and see if it stays on top of the milk. Keep the temperature at an even 90°F and leave to set for an hour, or until the curd feels firm when you press it. Then cut the curd with a long knife into squares of about ¾ in. Stir the curds and whey together and heat very slowly to about 100°F, taking an hour to reach this temperature. Stir exceedingly gently all the time in order to distribute the cream evenly, but taking care not to break up the curd. Keep at this temperature for another hour, to allow the lactic acid bacteria to work. It is at this stage that an acidmeter is useful – the reading should be between 0·75 and 0·95. Or take a piece of curd, touch it on a hot iron or stove top and draw it away; if the acidity is right, threads half an inch long will draw off the curd before breaking. If shorter than half an inch leave the curd a little longer, if longer the final cheese will be over-acid and dry.

Next drain off the whey by pouring through a muslin; keep it to drink – 'Water and Whey of drinks are first; They cool, dilute and quench the thirst' (Pope). Tie the curd in bundles about 9 ins. across in cheesecloth and leave on a sloping surface for any remaining whey to drain away. Turn the bags from time to time. Now unite the bundles and break up the curd into walnut-sized pieces, add 1 oz. of salt to every 4 lb. curd and mix well. Then, depending on the kind of cheese you want, squeeze the curds together; the looser they are the more crumbly the cheese will be. Tie them up in clean cheesecloth, and form into round flat cheese ready for pressing.

For this a cheese press is an advantage. These can often be picked up at country sales or even found outside old farmhouses. They are made of two iron or wooden posts with a cross bar from which a stone is suspended and a screw for applying the pressure. If you do not have a press use a tin or other container with holes bored in the bottom to allow excess whey to escape. Make a disc to fit the inside of the container. Place on top of the cheese and use stones or bricks for weights.

Put the cheese in the press and apply about 28 lb. pressure for about six hours. After this remove the cheese, take off the cloth, wring it out in warm water, wrap up the cheese again and put it back in the press with 56 lb. weight on it. Leave for two days, turning once. Then, if possible, apply 112 lb. pressure for two days, turning once.

Remove from the press, put on a clean cloth, pasting it down with flour and water, and leave in a cool airy place for a week, turning every day and brushing off any mould which forms. When the cheese is hard it can be eaten, but it will be better if left to mature for a couple of months, being turned every two or three days. Some people dip the whole cheese in wax to help preserve it. Others soak it in brine for a couple of days. The end result should be a cheese of the Cheddar variety.

Other Cheeses

Goat's cheese (cream cheese)

Take a very thick cream and cool to 65°F in three hours. Hang to drain in a moderately warm place in a draught. Scrape down and turn sides to middle at intervals of six hours. Salt to taste when nearly set. Mould while still sweet.[28]

Boudon cheese

Made with 2 pints buttermilk or sour milk to 1½ gallons whole milk. Heat to 70°F. Add 1 cc (1 ml) rennet to 1 gallon of mixture. Leave to set for about 2 hours. Cut and ladle into cloths for draining. Should be ready in 2 days.

Schabzieger cheese (from Switzerland)

This recipe uses melilot (*Melilotus officinalis*).

The Schabzieger cheese is made by the curd being pressed in boxes with holes to let the whey run out; and when a considerable quantity has been collected and putrefaction begins, it is worked into a paste with a large proportion of the dried herb Melilotus, reduced to a powder. The herb is called in the country dialect *Zieger kraut*, 'curd herb'. The paste thus produced is pressed into moulds of the shape of a common flowerpot and, the putrefaction being stopped by the aromatic herb, it dries into a solid mass and keeps unchanged for any length of time. When used, it is rasped or grated and the powder mixed with fresh butter is spread upon bread.[29]

Cold Storage

'Whoever camps for a week in summer by the shore of a pond, needs only bury a pail of water a few feet deep in the shade of his camp to be independent of the luxury of ice.' So Thoreau idyllically eulogizes in *Walden*.[1] An elaboration on this theme is the 'spring house', frequently found attached to farms, where the butter was set to cool and the milk kept. A small stream was diverted from its course to pass along a slate trough or passage through the 'spring house', larder or dairy, creating natural refrigeration.

In the highlands of Scotland peat was dried and food of all types was preserved in little stone houses called *cliet*, whose design can be dated back to prehistoric times. They are built in the shape of a bee skep using small, flattish stones overlapping each other and meeting in a dome at the tip. This was capped with turves to keep the rain out. Plenty of cavities were left in the walls to let the wind through, thus using nature to advantage.

Ice-houses

More universal was the ice-house, used for the storage of ice and sometimes food. The ice was brought into the house whenever needed to keep food fresh inside, and for making the jellies and ice moulds the Victorians were so fond of. Ice-houses date from the late Middle Ages but it was not until the seventeenth century that they came into general use; their heyday lasted from the mid eighteenth until the nineteenth century. Their demise was caused by mechanical refrigeration and the railway, which meant that even if you did not have a fridge ice could easily be brought in from outside sources.

The ice was cut in blocks in winter and slid into the house on a wooden slide, where it was laid on a bed of crossed wooden planks raised over a drain and covered with straw. More straw was then placed between the layers of ice to make splitting easier. Ice kept in this way lasted a surprisingly long time, often the whole year round, if the insulation was efficient and the ice-house was opened with care.

An ice-house, to be effective, must be dry as well as cool and in this country they were generally built underground on a wooded slope. The main chamber was usually egg-shaped, made either below or above the ground surface and covered with a dome of earth. A passage with steps led from the opening down to the chamber.

Hints for Survival Cold Storage

Keep fish alive in traps until you need them, or store in boxes under water. Pack shellfish in damp seaweed; berries, fruit and roots in wet leaves or moss. Keep food cool in holes in the ground, banks and rocks, or wrap and hang on a tree. A wet cloth put over a hole acts as a cooler. Food stays fresh when buried in sand or snow, but be careful to mark the spot, otherwise you may never find it again.

Confectionery

'And eating awes like sugar plums ere they had lost the May',[30] country children used to eat the young tips of hawthorn leaves just as they began to appear all tightly bunched and pale green. They also ate the seeds of mallow, which have a nutty taste, and called them 'cheeses' and those of the great burnet, caraway and coriander. These were coated with icing sugar mixed to a paste with rose or orange water and allowed to harden; they were called comfits. The following are other sweets which were popular in the past and often still are today.

Marsh-mallow

Bruise fresh or dried marsh mallow roots and boil them either with water, milk, orange or rose water and sugar or honey until thick, then strain off the decoction and leave to set.

Toffees

The roots of restharrow have a sweet sticky juice and they used to be dug and nibbled as a form of rural toffee. The roots of sea holly were made into eryngo toffee. The sliced root was boiled in a little water until it was well flavoured, then this water was added to some sugar and butter and boiled until ready to eat. Then the softened root chips were stirred in and the whole poured into a greased tin to set. The whole plant of horehound was boiled until the juice ran, then this was strained off, sugar added and the mixture boiled again until setting point was reached, then this was left to set into a kind of toffee. Nut toffees were made by simmering hazel nuts in honey for about $\frac{3}{4}$ hour until it thickened or by pouring caramelized sugar over little piles of nuts.

Preserved sweets

All kinds of fruit were candied and preserved in sugar syrup (see also Preserving, p. 124). The roots of elecampane were preserved in sugar coloured with cochineal and made into flat round cakes with a pungent aromatic taste; they used to be sold in London. Angelica was cultivated in and around London for its stem, which was candied for a sweet, and wild plants may still be found in many parts of the city. Bunches of barberry were dipped into sugar syrup, left for several hours, then removed, the sugar boiled again to setting point, then the berries put back in and left until candied. When ready, they were left to dry off and stored in jars. Chestnuts steeped in sugar syrup emerge as the prized *marrons glacés*.

Crystallized flowers

These were more often used to decorate cakes and puddings than eaten as sweets. Primroses, violets and cowslips were collected on a dry day. Sugar was heated with a little water, then taken off the heat and the flowers added a few at a time, the whole stirred until the candied flowers were dry enough to put into jars to store. For rose petals, white of egg was beaten, not too stiffly, and painted on each petal. These were then spread out on a large dish sprinkled with castor sugar and left to dry in the sun or a cool oven for an hour.

Cooking

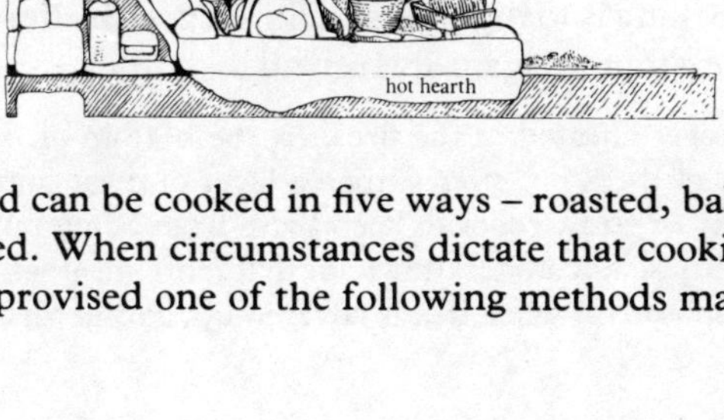

Basically food can be cooked in five ways – roasted, baked, grilled, fried or boiled. When circumstances dictate that cooking arrangements be improvised one of the following methods may be of use.

Roasting

Before the introduction of ovens, which were at first considered a lazy, inefficient method of cooking, food was roasted on a constantly turning spit. In old kitchens the spit – generally with a central claw to hold the meat in place – rested on dogs on either side of the fire and was turned by an unfortunate boy or dog. Often several spits holding different types of meat and fish – small fish were usually tied in place rather than pierced – were set up with a dish underneath to catch the dripping fat. In Ireland

> A spit – made of iron – was an article in general use, and was regarded as an important household implement. But the spits commonly used in roasting, as well as the skewers for trussing up the joint, were pointed hazel rods, peeled and made smooth and white. Meat and even fish, while roasting, were often basted with honey or with a mixture of honey and salt.[31]

If you have no spit, a large flat stone can be stood upright near the fire, with meat hung on this (see illustration below). Turn half-way through to cook both sides.

Baking

One way of baking is to dig a pit and fill it up with alternate layers of meat and hot stones. Again in Ireland

> The stones were heated in the fires. At the bottom of the pit the men placed a layer of these hot stones: then a layer of meat-joints wrapped in sedge or in hay or straw ropes to keep them from being burned: next another layer of these hot stones: down on that more meat: and so on till the whole was disposed of, when it was covered up; and in this manner it was

effectively cooked. The remains of many of these cooking-pits are still to be seen in various parts of the country, and are easily recognized by the charred wood and blackened stones; and sometimes the very pits are to be seen.[31]

Another way, one popular with gipsies, is to wrap the meat in a casing of clay and put it in a fire. After the necessary amount of time the meat is removed and the case chipped off; the meat, having cooked in its own juices, will be most succulent. Vegetables and meat may also be wrapped in leaves, buried in hot ashes and left to cook. On St Kilda and elsewhere the meat would be wrapped in the raw hide of an animal and buried in hot ashes to cook. Francis Galton describes this.

> Sew up as much of the animal as is wanted in its own skin . . . dig a hole in the ground, wall it with stones and make a stone roof to it, all excepting one or two apertures. Then having made a roaring fire in and around the oven, till the stones are quite hot, sweep out the ashes, strew with grass, leaves or bark of any kind that is not bitter, and put the meat in, and over it more grass, etc., now shut up the aperture and continue the fire above the oven for some hours.[19]

A trouble-free but wasteful way of baking is to merely put a large fish or piece of meat in hot ashes, light a fire over it with small twigs and keep it going for about half an hour. Then remove the meat from the fire, wash it in water without letting it cool too much, split it open and spoon out the cooked contents from the burnt shell. An

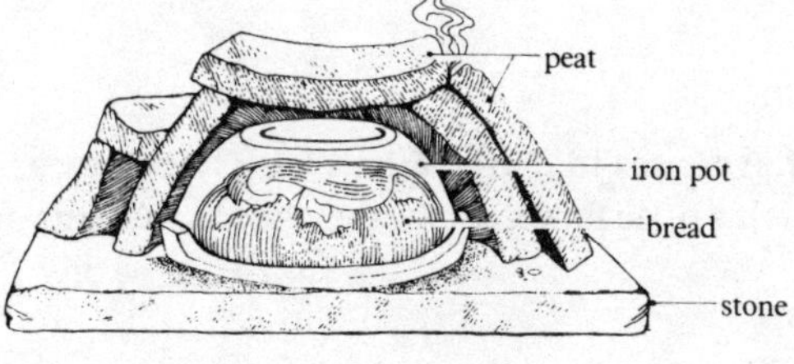

advance on this would be to put the meat in an earthenware dish and cover it with a layer of peat, turf or wood. Robinson Crusoe baked his bread in this way.

Best of all, given time and suitable materials, is to build a brick oven. It should be fuelled with wood and brought to a high temperature. Cooking in it can be planned on the basis of declining heat; bread and cakes baked first, then fruit bottled and firewood and feathers dried last.

Grilling

'Meat and fish were often broiled on a gridion, or something of the nature of a gridion' – what in the twentieth century we would call a barbecue – an iron or sappy wood grill laid on top of a fire made, ideally, of charcoal, which gives a fierce but even heat.

Frying

Heat large flat stones in a fire. When very hot draw aside, sweep off the ashes, melt a little fat on them, then break the eggs or put the meat on to fry.

Boiling

This requires containers, for which see p. 266.

The cauldron was the complete cooker in which the entire dinner would be cooked and often the clothes washed as well. In the eighteenth century:

> A wooden board, pierced with holes, is placed at the bottom of the cauldron . . . Below this board is a piece of bacon, covered with flour-and-water paste and wrapped round with a linen cloth to hold in the fat and juice. It will come slowly to the boil, and stay boiling throughout the dinner, and grow cold, as correct, in the water. On the board stands one jar, packed with fowls resting upon a lubricating piece of suckling pig and held down under their juice by heavy stones, or hard-boiled eggs. To the right we have some birch twigs banked across the bottom to prevent the well-scarified beef from sticking to the pan. The lid is put on, the crack sealed with paste, and the whole top tied down, air-tight, with plastered linen . . . Hanging loose from a string tied to the handle, are an oatmeal pudding and a bag of beans . . . and there is still room for the cook to put in an odd bag for his own dinner.[27]

A boiling range can be constructed as shown. The fire should be lit at one end, with the cooking that requires the most heat placed above it and a simmering stew put further away.

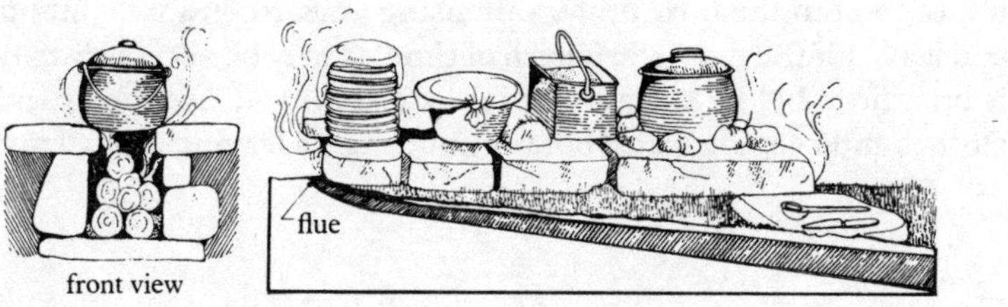

Haybox

When fuel is hard to come by cooking can be begun over a fire and finished in a haybox, on the principle that the food cooks in its own very slowly decreasing heat. A general rule is to cook food for a third of its time on the stove and then, without opening the lid, transfer it quickly into the haybox and leave it there for the other two thirds of the time, or longer. More specific times are:

	On stove	*In haybox*
soup (dried peas)	45 minutes	4 hours
stew	20 minutes	4 hours
bacon	45 minutes	4 hours
beef or mutton	45 minutes	4 hours
fowl	1 hour	3 hours
stewed fruit	3 minutes	1½ hours
porridge	3 minutes	6 hours or all night

To make a haybox start with a stout wooden box which has a close fitting lid. The stuffing may be hay or paper. If of paper, line the box carefully with twenty sheets on the bottom, ten round the sides and twenty again for the lid, pasting them well down and overlapping them at the edges, finishing with a layer of calico material tucked in at the joins and tacked down. Then pack the box really tightly with small balls of paper or hay, almost filling the box, and make two cushions stuffed with balls of paper or hay for the top. They must press well down on top of the filling, and will ensure that the box remains tightly packed when the lid is closed. Finally the lid must fit well and tightly. As a rule four inches of material is required round the sides and six inches at top and bottom. Put the pot of food in the box, preferably using an earthenware container, and leave for the requisite length of time. It may be necessary to heat it up a little before eating. A haybox can also be used for soaking clothes and keeping water hot for morning by leaving it in all night.

Eggs

Though every form of life begins with an egg, only those from birds, fish and insects are eaten.

Birds' Eggs

All birds' eggs are edible. However, with the exception of the domestic fowl and four gulls, the black-backed, lesser black-backed, herring and common gull, all are protected by law. Formerly people living on remote islands like St Kilda ate the eggs of all seabirds, those of the guillemot, fulmar and tern being especially prized. In Iceland the eggs of the goldeneye duck fetched higher prices than any other eggs, and in Scandinavia artificial nesting boxes were built in order that they might be easily collected. In this country plovers' eggs were thought to be the greatest delicacy, 'a joy to which gastronomes looked forward in April'.

Gulls' eggs

Taking gulls' eggs is a recognized way of keeping their numbers down, for they are prolific breeders and predators on other birds. They nest from about April to July in colonies on coastal sites: cliffs, sand and shingle beaches, dunes, marshes and moors. The nest is usually situated on the ground and made of flattened grass, straw, moss, seaweed and sticks. It contains about three eggs, varying in colour from olive green to brown to yellowish buff to bluey grey, with grey or dark brown spots.

Before eating any bird's egg its freshness should be ascertained. Hold an egg vertically in front of a strong light and see how big the void at the top is – the smaller it is the fresher the egg. Another way is to float it in water: if it lies flat it is fresh, if tilted good enough to scramble or fry, but if it sits up it is not worth eating. Egg shells are porous, particularly after washing, when the film which covers all eggs after they leave the hen is removed. Consequently they should not be stored near strong-smelling foods. Eggs should always be cooked slowly and wild birds' eggs are usually best hard-boiled. Geese and duck eggs are richer than hens', and the flavour of all eggs is decided by the food of the bird and almost entirely concentrated in the yolk.

Our consumption of eggs has doubled twice since the beginning of this century, partly because our diet has become lighter and partly because eggs are a cheap form of protein. Like milk they constitute a complete food in themselves; albumen, oil and saline matter are present in the right proportions for sustaining life. There is more concentrated food in an egg than in the same amount of beef steak.

Fish Eggs

Usually called roe, all are edible. Those of the skate and dogfish are the size of a walnut and said to be eaten by the Swedes as a substitute for birds' eggs; others are minute (there are 140 cod's roe to the grain) and are held in bags inside the fish. To remove, split the fish open and take out the bag, which may then be salted, smoked, parboiled and fried or, if cod's roe, made into the ubiquitous taramasalata (smoked roe mixed with garlic, olive oil, lemon, breadcrumbs and sometimes a little onion and parsley).

The eggs of molluscs are usually eaten with the fish, though some use lobster and crab eggs to colour and enrich sauces.

Fats and Oils

An oil is a substance which is inflammable, has a greasy feel and consistency and is practically insoluble in water. As food, oils have more than twice the energy value of carbohydrates or proteins, provide acids essential to life and serve as carriers of fat-soluble vitamins. They are also essential in the making of soap, paint, light, cosmetics and perfumery.

Vegetable Oils

It is safe to say that all plant seeds contain oil, but some have a great deal more than others. They are categorized by their drying capacity: drying oils (linseed) are used for soft soap; semi-drying (poppy, maize, rape) for food, paint and soap; non-drying (almond, olive) for food, soap and perfumery.

Beech (*Fagus sylvatica*)*:* Sound kernels can contain up to 46 per cent oil, unsound as little as 23 per cent. An edible oil, said to be of good flavour, and enjoyed in the USSR.

Cruciferae: The most productive are the *Brassicas*, which include the mustards and rape plants. The oil is edible, though mustard oil has a pungent flavour.

Flax: The oil content varies according to soil and temperature; it is approximately 35 per cent. A drying oil with a high iodine content.

Hazel-nut: Kernels contain up to 68 per cent oil; it resembles olive oil in character and composition.

Oak: Acorns are usually 11–13 per cent oil, though as much as 40 per cent has been extracted. An edible oil.

Pine (*Pinus sylvestris*): Oil is taken from the seeds.

Plum: The kernel yields 35 per cent oil, similar to almond oil in its characteristics.

Poppy (*Papaver somniferum*): The seeds contain 44–50 per cent oil. The commercial return from the oil is said to be about two thirds more than that obtained from opium. (The harvesting of the opium, since it is derived from the sap, does not impair the production of the seeds.)

Walnut: 300–600 tons of walnut oil are made annually in the United States. It is an edible, but drying, oil and is much used as a basis for artists' colours.

Extraction

The oil is extracted from ripe seeds from which all foreign matter has been removed and, if necessary, the shells or hulls. The kernels are then ground to a coarse meal, given a preliminary heating (though cold-pressed oil has fewer impurities) the seeds wrapped in cloth and put in a press. In primitive countries they simply heap the fruit in piles in the the sun and collect the oil as it exudes. An oily fruit, such as the olive, is boiled in water and the oil skimmed from the surface as it rises. The earliest form of pressing was to crush the seeds in a mortar until the oil exuded. The Chinese were the first to grind seeds in stone mills, heat the meal in open pans and then press out the oil using a lever and wedge press. The Romans invented the screw press and this remained in use until the nineteenth century and the invention of hydraulic presses.

Essential Oils

See Perfume, p. 368. Evaporating oils, soluble in alcohol and used as scent and for flavouring.

Waxes

Beeswax is the largest source, obtained from cappings and old honeycomb tied in a cloth and heated in water. The wax floats to the top leaving the impurities in the bag. An aromatic vegetable wax is obtained from the berries of bog myrtle (*Myrica gale*). If these are put in hot water, the wax will float to the surface. Wax is used for candles, polish, bottle coverings and cosmetics.

Fish Oils

These are all liquid, and obtained from fatty sea fish such as herring, mackerel and sardine; from cod's liver; and from sea mammals such as the seal, whale, dolphin and porpoise. They are obtained by rendering down the fish or fat in the manner described for animal fat. Fish oils are used to treat leather, for soap, paint and light.

Animal Fats

Hard fats which come from the fatty tissues surrounding the meat of an animal. The most important domestically are the pig for lard, sheep for tallow and cow for beef tallow. Other animals such as rabbits and deer have a little fat and so do some birds, such as the domestic goose, which has an abundance of semi-hard fat, and many seabirds. Fat can be collected as it drips out of the meat while cooking, or can be cut out of the carcase where the fat is concentrated and rendered down over heat. Then, if it is to be used for anything more than cooking, it should be purified by heating to boiling in water, straining through muslin and leaving to cool. If further refining is required it should be treated in a watery solution of potash or ammonia at a temperature between 104°F and 176°F. The free fatty acids with the impurities will sink to the bottom. The fat should then be washed in water to remove all traces of alkali. Vinegar added to clarifying mutton fat takes away some of the strong taste. Apart from cooking, mutton fat is most used for making candles and for waterproofing leather; beef fat is thought the best tasting and is also used as a supplement or substitute for mutton tallow. Lard is most frequently used as a basis for ointments and in perfumery for enfleurage.

Lanolin

This is the oil washed from sheep's wool. Because it closely resembles our own natural oils it is much used in cosmetic skin moisturizers. Not only is it emollient but it also retains moisture, has no smell and does not go rancid. Lanolin is secreted most thickly round the udders of a milking ewe and it was from this natural lanolin that medieval people prepared their ointments. Two kinds of lanolin are sold. Anhydrous lanolin is prepared without water. It acts as a better moisturizer since it attracts water from the air as well as from the deeper levels of the skin. Hydrous lanolin consists of seventy parts lanolin to thirty parts water.

Fire

According to legend, Prometheus first stole fire from the gods and brought it to earth. According to archaeological evidence fire was first discovered by the Chinese 350,000 years ago and by the Europeans about 100,000 years after that. However, it is probable that the first men to use fire collected it from natural sources. Even in recent times Andamanese and Tasmanian tribes appeared ignorant of how to make fire, relying on carefully tended fire-brands taken from the fires of neighbouring tribes. It is thought that fire was first created, mechanically, from flint and iron pyrites sparks igniting tinder rather than by friction generated by rubbing soft- and hardwood together.

Before the invention of matches these two methods of making fire were in general use, with the flint method being most common in Europe and among the civilized. Once matches were introduced other methods were quickly dropped.

Wood Friction

Fire-making by friction involves a hardwood stick being rotated on a softwood base. Though any sufficiently hard stick will do for the drill, the base must be of a wood with little grain and of middle softness. Pliny says that 'there is heat in the mulberry, in the bay laurel, in ivy, and in all plants whence fire-sticks are made'. The drill will merely dent wood that is too hard; rotation will wear away wood that is too soft before it has time to heat properly. Both woods must be bone dry.

The drill should be held between the palms and rotated rapidly by rubbing them together, while at the same time keeping the drill pressing down on the base (a weight held by another person on top of the drill helps maintain pressure). It is very important to keep the rotation continuous and, since it is quite exhausting, a relief pair of hands will most likely be necessary. As the whirling motion continues a fine wood dust should be produced, becoming charred with smoke rising as it begins to burn. When this happens fire will soon follow and should be nurtured with some dry grass or previously prepared tinder.

There are two other methods which work on the same principle: a sawing motion which can be used on the base with a hard drill or sharp piece of wood and a ploughing motion.

Flints

When steel is struck against a stone flint sparks emanate which, if allowed to fall on tinder, will ignite. This is the best and easiest way to make fire if you have no match. In default of steel, iron, iron pyrites and other stones such as quartz, agate, jasper, a hard piece of china or even another piece of flint may be used. Provided the tinder is dry three minutes is said to be the average length of time taken to make fire from flint and steel. Originally it was thought that fire lay dormant in the flint and was brought to life by the action of the steel. Virgil wrote of 'man learning to strike the lurking fire from veins of flint'.

A flint box containing flint, steel and tinder were essential objects in every household.

> The only way of obtaining a light in times gone by, other than by picking a burning piece of wood from a fire, was by flint and steel and tinder box . . . These circular boxes, formed of iron or brass, in the later shapes had sockets for candles in the top of the lids, and ring handles as means for carrying . . . The tinder lay in the bottom of the box; over it was the damper, a disc with a ring handle, and above this the flint and steel and one or two sulphur matches, which lifted out with the damper. The hook-shaped steel, made of a bit of good metal, was held over the fingers of the left hand and struck by the flint held in the right. A few strokes brought a spark which fell on the tinder; a little gentle blowing would partly ignite the tinder, and the point of the sulphur match then came alight. These matches were thin slips of wood dipped in melted brimstone. Men working in the fields could, at a pinch, get a light by picking up a bit of flint and striking it on the back of a knife; they carried a slip of touch paper in their pockets to act as tinder.[40]

Glass

Glass, preferably lensed glass, placed to catch the direct rays of the sun when hot and focused on tinder will cause it to catch fire eventually.

Tinder

A prerequisite of tinder is that it must be absolutely dry. In wet weather a small amount carried in a cloth bag next to the body will ensure this. If you have no dry tinder in wet weather, the inner fibres of bark from a tree should have escaped the rain. But all manner of other material can be used as tinder. Probably the most effective are charred rags – rags that are lit and allowed to blaze, but the flame extinguished before the rag has burnt to dust – a roll of cloth with frayed ends, hair, dry grass, bark fibre, dried leaves of mullein and coltsfoot, dried fungus, especially puff balls and *Fomes fomentarius* which grows on the stumps of beech trees. If this is stripped of its outer hard layer, the inner spongy mass, boiled in water, and dried till light and brittle, is highly inflammable. It is called 'punk' in Siberia. *Boletus igniarius*, another fungus which grows on oak and beech trees, can be treated in the same way. Remains of this, excavated at Starr Carr in Yorkshire, date from 7000 BC.

Keeping the Fire In

Once the fire was lit it was usual to keep it alight rather than to have to start again. On St Kilda they had only two taxes, one of which, the 'fire penny', was levied every time the one tinder box on the island was used – a rare event as fires were kept in continuously, the embers banked with ashes and the fire revived by raking them up and feeding them with small chips of wood.

Fuel

The fuel burned will be dictated to an extent by the material available and the purpose of the fire. In Scotland, peat is obviously the commonest, cut in summer, heaped and left to dry outside. The fire is then started with thin brushwood from heather. In Suffolk:

> The fuel used was most commonly *whin* faggots – the *bones* of *sere* or dry gorse – bound with elm withes. The process of making them was described by Prissy: 'You tied the whin faggots with green ellum withes. You put your foot on the bottom of a withe then you could rave the top of it like an S.' Broom was sometimes used for fuel: so also was heather. The heather was first stacked and pressed into bundles.[24]

Bones have frequently been used as fuel. Darwin said of gauchos in South America that 'Meat was their diet and nothing but meat, and they used the bones of the animals as fuel for their cooking fires.' At the Upper Palaeolithic site of Kostienki in the USSR 'large quantities of "fuel" bones were found', and in the Russian campaign of 1829 the troops suffered so severely from the cold they were driven to digging up the cemeteries for bones for fuel. Dried animal manure is used the world over, in Canada appropriately called *bois de vache*. Seaweed 'makes a hot, though not a cheerful fire' and travellers often take charcoal with them as it is easily carried and makes a very hot fire. Coal, though not entirely suitable for burning on an open hearth because of the fumes, has been used since early times, dug from places where coal seams surfaced. But the most ancient and universal fuel is wood. Though it has less heating power per pound weight than coal, for fragrance, cleanliness, the properties of its ash and for staying alight all night, wood surpasses all other types of fuel. Generally the denser the wood the better its heating properties and the longer it burns. Heartwood is normally better than sapwood and seasoned wood better than newly felled. Hardwoods burn best, but softwoods make better kindling. Decayed wood is not good as firewood. Logs must be stored in a reasonably dry place, otherwise they rot. The burning qualities of different kinds of wood are listed below.

Good heat, burn well

Ash – burns green or dry
Beech – must be dry
Birch – burns freely
Cherry – difficult to light, fragrant
Elm – smoulders if at all wet
Hawthorn – burns green or dry
Hornbeam – gives intense heat
Maple – second-rate wood
Oak – heartwood burns best
Pear and apple – slightly fragrant
Plane – burns green or seasoned, good for kindling too
Yew and sycamore – tend to spark

Poor heat, burn badly

Alder, chestnut, horse chestnut, lime, poplars, spruce, willow.

Fragrant, but poor heating qualities

Cedar of Lebanon, cypress.

Kindling wood

Larch, pine, plane.

Laying a Fire

There is a country saying that 'one log can't burn; two logs won't burn; three logs will burn; and four logs make a good fire'. To lay a basic fire, first use something easily inflammable like paper or cloth, dried grass or bracken, then a layer of twigs or cones or kindling wood, then dry, not too large, logs placed to allow for the circulation of air but with enough contact to allow the flame to creep from one material to the next gathering strength until, when well and truly alight, the fire may be fed and sustained with larger fuel.

Out of doors, fires should be built on rocks or logs or scraped depressions in the ground, not on the natural earth's surface. Walls of stones placed round a cooking fire reflect the heat. Large logs can be burned by laying them end on, one on top of the other; then as the ends burn away the logs can be pushed together. Here is advice for making a fire when in a hurry:

'For a noonday lunch, or any other quick meal, when you have only to boil coffee and fry something, a large fire is not wanted. Drive a forked stake in the ground, lay a green stick across it, slanting upwards from the ground, and weight the lower end with a rock, so you can easily regulate the height of the pot. The slanting stick should be notched, or have the stub of a twig left at its upper end, to hold the pot ball in place, and should be set at such an angle that the pot swings about a foot clear of the ground.

Then gather a small armful of sound, dry twigs from the size of a lead pencil to that of your finger. Take no twig that lies flat on the ground, for such are generally damp or rotten. Choose hardwood, if there is any, for it lasts well.

Select three of your best sticks for kindling. Shave each of them almost through, for half its length, leaving the lower end of the shavings attached to the stick, one under the other. Stand these in a tripod, under the hanging pot, with their curls down. Around them build a *small* conical wigwam of other sticks, standing each on end and slanting to a common centre. The whole affair is no bigger than your hat. Leave free air spaces between the sticks. Fire requires air, and plenty of it, and it burns best when it has something to climb up on; hence the wigwam construction. Now touch off the shaved sticks, and in a moment you will have a small blast furnace under the pot. This will get up steam in a hurry. Feed it with small sticks as needed.

Meantime get two bed-sticks, four or five inches thick, or a pair of flat rocks, to support the frying pan. The firewood will all drop to embers soon after the pot boils. Toss out the smoking butts, leaving only clear, glowing coals. Put your bed-sticks on either side, parallel and level. Set the pan on them and fry away. So, in twenty minutes from the time you drove your stake, the meal will be cooked.[41]

Bellows

A pair of bellows to keep the fire going can be made out of a goat's skin.

The goat's head is cut off under the chin, his legs at the knee-joint and a slit is made between the hind legs, through which the carcass is entirely extracted. After dressing the hide [see p. 342) two strongish pieces of wood are sewn along the slit, one at each side, just like the ironwork on each side of the mouth of a carpet bag, and for the same purpose, i.e. to strengthen it. Then, after opening these and pulling out the skin, they are suddenly shut, and made to enclose a bagful of air; this, by pushing the skin flat home, is ejected out of the neck, into which a nozzel must be inserted. These bellows require no valve, and are the simplest that can be made; they are in use throughout India.

The tubes to convey the blast may be made of clay or loam, plastered together with grass and moulded round a smooth pole.[19]

Galton says that these goat bellows produce enough air 'to raise small bars of iron to welding heat'. If less heat and more convenient bellows are required the same method might be tried on a smaller animal such as a rabbit.

The young shoots of elder contain a fat pith which is easily removed, leaving a hollow tube. This has been used as a simple bellows or method of blowing up the fire.

Fish

As with any aquatic creature fish are greatly affected by the state of the water in which they live: its movement, pressure, temperature, light, salinity and oxygen content.

The most densely populated region of the sea is that just below the surface, the depth to which light can penetrate. Here plants are able to make their food and in turn feed a large number of molluscs and larvae which are the food of a large number of fish. Fish also take their colour from the water they live in. Thus those of the upper ocean tend to be transparent or blue, those inhabiting lower regions have silver reflecting scales and white bellies and those living where no light penetrates are of dark, gloomy colour. As the type of water has an effect on the fish population so does the type of shore. Rocky coasts have fish with flattened heads and bodies and with sucker-type mouths while sandy coasts suit eel and flat fish. Estuaries where salt and fresh water mix and there is little water movement have grey mullet, flounder, bass and salmon, and eel during their migration.

The habitat of freshwater fish is largely determined by the amount of dissolved oxygen in the water. Trout and salmon parr prefer swift-flowing rivers and streams. Stone loach and minnows live where the flow is less rapid; chub, dace, gudgeon and bleak are found in moderately fast water; tench, bream, carp, roach with their predators, pike, perch and eel, in slow flowing rivers. Lakes in mountainous areas often have steep sides and very deep cool water and, as long as there is some shallow for feeding, these are the conditions preferred by trout and char. Less deep lakes with some shallow water suit pike, perch, trout and sticklebacks; shallow lakes in hilly regions with vegetation growing in them suit bream, carp and tench.

Fish are great travellers. The reasons are many : food, temperature and the urge to spawn, seasonal migrations, pollution and changes in salinity. But no fish follows the same pattern. In winter the mackerel leaves the cold water near the shore and retires to warmer depths; only when the sun has warmed the shallows again in spring does it return. The pilchard follows warm currents north from the Mediterranean up to the coast of Cornwall after its food, the plankton which breed in these conditions. Herring shoals are always on the move after food or going to their spawning grounds. Salmon, eels, lamprey, smelt and shad leave the ocean for freshwater rivers to spawn. Others go in the opposite direction; flounder and other flat fish leave estuaries for the deep ocean and the tunny moves from the Atlantic to the Mediterranean to spawn.

Studying the habits and food of fish is essential if you are to catch them successfully. Experienced fishermen know all about the daily habits and choice of food of their prey, choosing their bait and casting it accordingly.

Eating fish

Except for some tropical fish and jellyfish, none are poisonous. But all fish spoil easily and once caught should be consumed as soon as possible or preserved by smoking, salting or potting. General rules are to beware of fish with flabby skin, slimy gills and sunken eyes. Fish that stink, that dent permanently when pressed with a thumb, that have a naked or bony skin instead of scales, that are covered with spikes, thorns or bristles (which can be poisonous) and fish that puff up as they are taken from the water are all best avoided.

Freshwater fish with their delicate aroma require only the simplest cooking; herbs, if used, should not dominate and should preferably have been picked from beside the pool where the fish was caught. Use thyme for a grayling and watercress for brook trout. Salt-water fish can take stronger accompaniments, pungent herbs and sauces. Oily fish are helped by being dipped in oatmeal before frying, as this absorbs some of the overstrong flavour and grease. Some dry fish, such as pike, are better cooked stuffed with butter or bacon fat. Small fish should always be cooked whole, grilled or fried. Larger fish may be boiled, baked or stewed. Fish soaked in an acid such as vinegar or lemon for several hours become opaque and can be eaten without cooking – much liked by the Scandinavians, Icelanders and William Morris.

Fish from muddy-bottomed water, usually called coarse fish, must be specially treated if a dirty taste is to be avoided. The overlapping scales which keep the mud from the fish's skin while it is swimming against the stream are disturbed when the fish becomes limp and the mud penetrates, affecting the taste.

'Therefore,' according to Dorothy Hartley,

pond fish must never be washed, or even moved, more than can be avoided. Take the fish by the head, and smooth it down towards the tail in clay or paste, and bake it quite flat without turning. For this reason you must roast it, raised up on a grid, or a handful of twigs, anything that will allow the underside of the fish to cook dryly. When done, this crust can be broken off, skin and all, and the fish will be clean-tasting and of very fine quality.[27]

Further uses

Some fish are very oily and the oil can be used for lighting, though it is always rather evil-smelling. Some islanders treat the whole fish, a wick passed down into its stomach, as torches. The thornback is one such. The oil from cod's liver is rich in vitamins A, D and E and helps prevent colds and other winter ailments. In East Anglia the 'eel was much prized for its skin as for its edible qualities . . . for they regarded eelskin as the best and toughest leather for tying the swingel of the flail to the handles.'[24]

Fish are more accessible and easier to catch than most wild animals and not hedged around by so many protective laws. Sea fish may be caught by anyone anywhere, but most stretches of good fishing river are owned by someone who has often paid a lot of money for it and won't be keen on giving much away. Freshwater fish are protected during their breeding season, which for salmon lasts from February to October, for trout from March to September and for the rest March to June. On pages 66-74 is a list of fish which can be caught in British waters. All are edible; some are excellent.

Domestic Fish

When animals could be kept through the winter and improved fishing methods meant abundant supplies of fish from the sea domestic fish ponds were no longer needed. However, with the overfishing that is going on today and the likelihood of all fish becoming scarce, domestic fish ponds may come to have a place again. The commercial farming of trout is already big business, but other types of fish may be kept too. The Romans' knowledge of the breeding habits of fish was extensive and fertilized eggs were collected and placed in special lakes or vivaria. The Assyrians also maintained stocks and used to trade in young fish. In Britain the fish pond or 'stew' used to be an integral part in the economy of the medieval manor, monastery and village. A variety of fish were kept including eel, carp, tench, trout and bream – 'Full many a bream and luce he had in stew' (Chaucer). They were situated wherever there was a gently flowing stream, spring or a marsh. The pond was made either by damming a stream if it ran through a steep-sided valley or by excavating a shallow rectangular basin with two banks parallel to the stream and two others across it, high enough to keep the pond at a moderate depth – 6–8 feet – with a gentle flow of water through it. Too swift a stream might flood and break the banks. Alternatively, with a spring, small trenches were dug to draw off the water into a pond or, with marshy ground, a series of pipes drained the ground into a pond. The banks were strengthened with stones and stakes of oak, ash and elm and had a sluice to cope with flood. The bottom was planted with flote grass to feed the fish and faggots of brushwood staked to the bottom on one side to provide a spawning ground. For eels sods of grass were placed grass-side together. Sometimes a series of ponds were constructed for breeding and keeping different kinds of fish. Then carp, bream and tench were kept together in one, pike, perch, eel and tench in another ('for the Tench being the Fishes Physitian is seldom devoured') and trout in another; in all the ponds there was a good store of roach, dace, loach and minnow 'for they are both food for the great Fishes, and also not uncomely in any good man's dish'. Weeds containing the eggs were often put in a further pond so that when the fry hatched they would be in no danger of being eaten.

If fed for the first few weeks on meal, then as they grow larger on cooked potatoes, cabbage, beans and offal, with an abundance of natural living food, young carp reach 6 ins. in a year and 12–14 ins. in two years, weighing about three-quarters of a pound. Left to fend for themselves they would take five years to reach this size. They are now fit for the table and are improved by being left for a few days without food in a floating cage to purge themselves. Otherwise kill, bleed as soon as caught and leave overnight in salt water. Fish ponds must be kept clean and have to be periodically drained and any build-up of mud dug out. The initial stocks are introduced either as spawn or as grown fish netted from rivers.

The remnants of fish ponds, today often mistaken for moats, can be seen at Fountains Abbey, Glastonbury Abbey and Chilworth Manor near Guildford.

Freshwater Fish

Barbel: Living in swift-flowing, moderately deep rivers with a bed of sand or gravel or mud, it feeds mostly at night on bottom-living organisms: insects, worms, crustacea and molluscs. Introduced into the Severn, Medway and Bristol Avon, they are also found in the Trent and were formerly sold at Nottingham market. The flesh is bony and the roe poisonous.

Bream: Bream inhabit warm, slow-moving or stagnant waters, typically the lowland reaches of large rivers, feeding on insects, worms and molluscs. Large specimens are said to be as good as carp to eat. The French have a proverb that 'He that hath breams in his pond is able to bid his friend welcome.' Good stuffed or baked; place on a bed of chopped shallots and breadcrumbs, cover with more of these, white wine and butter and bake for twenty-five minutes.

Carp: It is found in still waters, marshes and ponds and less frequently in slow-flowing rivers in the lowlands of south-east England, living on plants and animals. It will survive in poorly oxygenated waters where others would die and for this reason has often been raised in fish farms from medieval times to the present day. Izaak Walton said that 'the Carp is the queen of rivers; stately, a good and a very subtil fish'. Golden carp and other kinds are variants of the ordinary carp. It was thought that eating carp conferred longevity, since the carp itself is long-lived.

The following is a recipe for cooking carp. Put a handful of chopped sorrel, some butter, bread, chives, parsley and shallots in a saucepan and simmer for 10 minutes. Add some cream, the yolks of three hard-boiled eggs and the raw yolks of three more, salt and black pepper. Stuff the cleaned carp with this, then sew up and marinate in oil with more chives and garlic, thyme and bay. Grill and serve with a sauce made of chopped mushrooms cooked in butter with parsley, chives, shallots, stock, salt and pepper, and lemon juice or vinegar.

Chub: A disappointing bony fish living in clean running rivers in England except Cornwall, feeding on small fish, caddis and beetle larva and aerial insects.

Dace: Found throughout England, except Cornwall, congregating in shoals, eating algae and other plants, larvae, aerial and aquatic insects. Too small and bony for anything but fish soup and bait, though an old Thameside recipe recommends stewing them with flour, grilling them and serving them with anchovy butter.

Eel: Some eels, like the conger, spend their whole lives in the sea living at all depths, but others, like the common eel, spend much of their lives in fresh water. The common eel is found in most rivers and estuaries, it is nocturnal, lying up during the day in weeds or burying itself in sand and mud. They spawn in the ocean and the elvers enter rivers when about 3 ins. in length. Florence White says that 'a plateful [of elvers] makes a complete meal for a working man'– they are rich in vitamins A and D. They spend from seven to twelve years in fresh water, feeding on bottom-living molluscs, insect larvae and sometimes small fish, and are known as yellow eels at this stage. When the males reach 16 ins. and the females 21–4 ins. they begin migrating back to the sea on dark nights and during floods and heavy rain; in September and October their colour changes to black. They are caught in traps and at river mouths at this time; at other times they are angled for or speared with fork-like implements. They are killed by chopping their heads off or, more correctly, by piercing the spinal cord at the back of the skull with a knife or skewer. We are told that, 'The yellow eels taste muddy; the whiteness of the belly of the fish is not the only mark to know the best; the right colour of the back is a very bright coppery hue; the olive coloured are inferior; and those tending to green are worse.'[36]

Eels may be eaten in various ways. First skin them by pulling the skin back off the body from the head down, like a stocking, then clean and cut in three- or four-inch pieces. Then, if desired, parboil as this removes some of the oily taste, before tossing in flour and frying in fat. Eels are also good stewed in mushrooms, parsley and wine or baked in a pie with onion, herbs, stock and vinegar.

Grayling: Dorothy Hartley thinks that the grayling is the most beautiful fish in the world, 'a fish of silver and pearl'; it inhabits clear, fairly fast, running water though it is sometimes found in mountain lakes. Gregarious; unselective omnivorous feeders on freshwater crustacea, bottom fauna, insect larvae. Distributed throughout eastern and midland England but introduced into some other rivers. Their flesh resembles trout and they are at their best in October and November. They are best simply grilled; thyme goes well with them.

Gudgeon: Tasty flesh, but of small size and more often used as bait than eaten. Found over most of England and Ireland in all types of water, they prefer clear rivers with sandy or gravelly beds; they live in shoals on bottom-living insects and crustacea. Egg and breadcrumb them and fry.

Lampern or lamprey: Look like a cross between an eel and a fish. We have three varieties, two of which are migratory, but all are less common than they were, probably due to pollution and obstructions in their path up river. However they can still be found in river mouths, notably the Severn. Lampreys have two filaments in their backs which are poisonous and must be removed before eating. Henry I had a great liking for them and is said to have died of a surfeit. The sheriff of Gloucester had orders to send as many as he could acquire by purchase or otherwise, as all other fish seemed insipid in comparison. Lampreys are in season from Christmas till June. They used to be potted or made into pies. They are best cut in two-inch lengths and stewed in stock or water for 45 minutes; serve in a sauce made from mushrooms, onions, wine and lemon juice, thickened with flour and some broth from the stew.

Minnow: 'A minnow, a minnow, I have him by the tail,' cried Jeremy Fisher. They are good to eat fried like whitebait or made, as described by Izaak Walton, into minnow tansies 'washed well in salt, and their heads and tails cut off, and their guts taken out and not washed after, they prove excellent for that use; that is, being fried with yolk of eggs, the flowers of cowslips and of primroses, and a little tansy; thus they make a dainty dish of meat.'[33]

They are found over most of Britain except the very north in streams and some lakes and ponds where there is a gravelly bottom and clear flowing water. They live in shoals near to the water surface in summer, descending lower in winter. Minnows over one and a half inches long eat insects, larvae and algae.

Perch: Good eating, though small ones are inclined to be bony and are best made into soup. This is a recipe from Moortown, Co. Tyrone.

Clean the grunts and scale them. Put them in a pot and well cover with water or milk and water. Cook till tender. Lift them out. Carefully remove the bones and skin. To the pot add the chives and boil 15 minutes. Drop in a lump of butter and when melted stir in enough blended flour to thicken. Add the flesh of the fish. Boil 5 minutes.

A distinctively coloured fish, found in ponds and lakes and in slow or moderate-flowing rivers and streams, lying close to objects such as tree roots, landing or bridge piles, large stones. They eat all kinds of small fish and insects such as water boatmen, and beetle larvae.

Pike: The pike is 'the king and tyrant of other fishes, because he not onely devoureth fishes of other kindes, but also of his owne kinde.'[71] The pike is widespread over the British Isles and relatively common in weedy rivers, streams and lakes. It lies concealed in weeds or close to an obstruction until a passing fish comes near enough to grab and then moves at great speed – nine feet per second. Young pike can often be hand-netted from weeds, larger ones prefer a live bait. Though Walton thought pike too good except for anglers and very honest men, most think it a dry, rather coarse fish, much improved by being salted for twelve hours before cooking and then stewed or cut in steaks, breadcrumbed and grilled, and served with horse-radish sauce.

Roach: Very common and found in all types of water up to 3,000 ft, but usually larger lakes and slow weedy rivers. It feeds on animal and vegetable foods. A very bony fish, probably best made into soup.

Salmon: Strongly migratory; salmon tagged in Scotland have been caught as far away as Greenland. They enter strong-flowing rivers all round Britain except the south coast of England, from January on, in order to spawn. The salmon does not eat while it is out of the sea and it is a mystery why it takes a bait. Salmon in the sea have silvery-blue backs and white bellies but in fresh water they gradually lose this colour, becoming greenish-brown, mottled with red and orange – experienced fishermen can tell by the colour how long a fish has been out of the sea. Salmon are now slightly uncommon and highly prized, but at one time were so common that housemaids would have written into their contract that they would not have to eat salmon more than a specified number of times per week. It is indeed a very rich fish and too much can sicken, but a little, simply cooked, is very good. Salmon may be steamed on a bed of herbs, baked, stewed or cut in steaks and fried in butter with a sour cream and vinegar sauce, or boiled. For cold salmon, put in cold water, bring to the boil, simmer for 3 minutes and allow to cool in the same water. For hot salmon, allow 5 minutes simmering per pound up to 5 lb., 4 minutes per pound for 6–8 lb. and 50–60 minutes in total for an 8–10 lb. fish. Serve with mayonnaise or hollandaise sauce.

Smelt: An estuarine and inshore fish; in the east of England some have adapted themselves to freshwater living. They feed on small fish and crustacea. A recipe from 1823 runs:

> When good and in season they have a fine silvery hue, are very firm, and have a refreshing smell like cucumbers newly cut. They should not be washed more than is necessary merely to clean them. Dry them in a cloth, lightly flour them, and shake it off. Dip in egg and breadcrumbs. Plunge into boiling fat for a few minutes.[33]

Tench: Related to the carp and able to live in similar poorly oxygenated waters, it is most often found in still lakes, the lower reaches of rivers and backwaters in southern England. It feeds on bottom-living animals, chiefly insect larvae. A nineteenth-century book says 'They are a firm and good fish to eat; some cooks stew them in wine, but they are by no means bad with parsley and butter.'[35]

Here is a recipe. Clean the fish and cook in stock. Remove the skin, cut in pieces. Make a roux with some butter and flour and add to this some wine; cook for 10 minutes; add the fish and some herbs and cook for another 10 minutes. Blend in two beaten egg yolks, dress with parsley and serve hot.

Trout: They are extremely variable in colour, depending on their surroundings and habitat, and are found all over Britain. There are three main varieties. The rainbow trout was introduced into many rivers and lakes from the USA in the nineteenth century and is able to live in all sorts of conditions from estuarine waters to freshwater lakes and streams. Brown trout are small dark fish living in clean, well oxygenated, fast-flowing waters of the upper reaches of rivers and lakes; they feed on winged insects, aquatic animals, larvae and crustacea. Sea trout have similar migratory habits to the salmon, and a similar, but many think finer, flavour; they feed in estuaries, mainly on crustacea.

All trout have a delicate fine flavour and are best cooked simply. Smaller fish should be fried in butter or grilled, larger ones split open and the backbone removed, then laid flat and either dipped in oatmeal, fried and served with a herb and butter sauce or baked.

Sea Fish

Bass: Migratory from March to October; found in estuaries and round the south and west coasts, particularly near beaches where sand and rock mix. They eat all forms of crustacea and small fish. A large fish, it takes a bait freely.

Cod: All round Britain, migrating in winter to deeper waters. Feeds on worms and small fish. Daylight shoals are found at 16–44 fathoms and may be caught with a rod and line. Traditionally cod should be boiled and eaten with parsnips and a white sauce thickened with egg.

Dab: A flat fish, abundant in inshore waters all round coasts, but particularly off sandy banks at 11–12 fathoms, migrating to deeper waters in winter. Feeds on crustacea, molluscs and worms. Catch with rod and line and with nets.

Flounder: A flat fish, found in estuaries and inshore water, particularly in summer. A bottom-living fish feeding on crustacea and molluscs, especially cockles. Takes a bait freely.

Grey mullet: No relation to the red mullet. Three kinds are found round our coasts. Often forming shoals in estuarine waters during summer, they eat molluscs and crustacea. Difficult to attract to bait, they are more often caught with seine and fixed nets.

Gurnard: Brightly coloured fish forming loose shoals that keep in touch with each other by grunting. Covered with spines and bony, but good to eat. Found all round coasts, migrating in summer to sandy bays and estuaries. Food: crustacea and small fish. Catch with rod and line.

Haddock: Local population living near ocean floor from depths of 16–22 fathoms, mainly in more northerly waters. Feeds on the fauna of the lower depths and on sand eels. Catch with rod and line or in nets. Smokes well and is good baked.

Halibut: The largest of our flat fish, it lives to thirty-five years, and is strongly migratory, living in very cold waters in deep north-westerly waters having sand, gravel and clay bottoms, feeding on crustacea and often quite large fish. Occasionally taken on long lines, more often in trawl nets, it is choice eating.

Herring: Overfishing is reducing the numbers of herring. There are several different kinds feeding mainly on plankton, some crustacea and small fish. Some spawn near the shore, others at depths of 110 fathoms. They are caught in drift nets, ring nets and trawl, and are found all round our coast; migratory. Oily fish, they are best eaten smoked as a kipper, or flattened, filleted, dipped in oatmeal and fried in bacon fat, or just plain grilled.

Ling: Large fish; up to 45 lb. in weight have been caught. Young ling are found in inshore waters at 8–11 fathoms, but adults are commoner at depths of 164–219 fathoms in northern waters. They feed on other fish, and are caught by rod and line or in trawl nets.

Mackerel: Migratory and spasmodically abundant all round coasts in shoals near the surface, they feed on all kinds of crustacea and marine life, and are caught with rod and line, troll lines, drift nets and purse seines. They must be eaten very fresh, the small ones grilled, larger ones stuffed with herbs and baked. Mackerel smokes well.

Pilchard: Migratory and spasmodically common in southern waters, where large shoals appear off the coast, particularly in Cornwall. They are caught in drift and ring nets and offshore at night by means of bright lights. Virginia Woolf remembers rowing out 'early one morning and the sea bubbled and spat with silver. I remember some stranger in the next boat shovelling an armful out of that bubbling mass into our boat.'[32] They feed on plankton and are mostly canned like sardines. An oily fish, formerly salted and pressed, the oil which dripped out being collected for other purposes. They are frequently wrapped in pastry and cooked whole with head and tail sticking out so that none of the oily flavour is lost.

Plaice: An abundant flat fish of shallow water, the plaice frequents sandy and muddy ground down to approximately 40 fathoms. It feeds on crustacea, worms and molluscs all round coasts, and takes a bait freely. It is best filleted and fried and served with a good sauce, as it is relatively tasteless.

Pollack: An inshore fish, found in shoals from mid to bottom water near rocks round the southern and west coasts. It migrates to colder water in winter, feeding on small fish and eels. It takes a bait easily.

Skate or ray: There are many different members of this family of large, flat, long-tailed fish, found close to the bottom on all types of coastline, eating small fish and crustacea. Usually it is caught by trawl nets but sometimes with rod and line – particularly the roker and thornback ray – on muddy, sandy, shingly ground from 1 to 33 fathoms. Only the wing parts of the fish are eaten; they should be marinaded in lemon, vinegar or cider for an hour before being dipped in egg and breadcrumbs and fried.

Sole: Migratory, but found in summer – particularly young ones – on soft ground, sand and estuaries, feeding off bottom-living organisms, worms and crustacea. Sole is usually fished for with trawl nets but some species have been caught with rod and line. It is one of the finest fish to eat – plain grilled.

Turbot: Considered by many the best tasting of all sea fish, turbot is an inshore flat fish found up to depths of 44 fathoms, common on sandy shores from August to October, feeding on sand eels and small fish. Catch with rod and line, seine nets or trawl. Its delicate flavour should not be spoiled by rich accompaniments; turbot is best grilled or steamed and eaten with a parsley sauce.

Whitebait: The young of herring, sprats and sometimes other fish, they are caught in nets in estuarine waters. To cook, wash in sea or salt water, shake in flour, then in a sieve to remove excess flour, deep fry and eat immediately. There used to be a pub at Greenwich where you could eat whitebait caught before your eyes from the Thames.

Whiting: Inhabits shallow, sandy waters, and is common everywhere but particularly in the North Sea, living on crustacea, eels and molluscs. It takes a bait freely. Boswell describes buying some '*speldings*' at Leith and insisting on Johnson tasting them and 'scottifying his palate; but he was very reluctant. With difficulty I prevailed with him to let a bit of one of them lie in his mouth. He did not like it.'[18]

Wrasse: A common inshore fish; there are several varieties which prefer warm water near rocks. A brightly coloured, scaley fish feeding on crustacea and molluscs. The one most frequently found in our waters is the ballan wrasse. Coarse and rather sweet to eat – an acquired taste. Caught by rod and line.

Crustacea

See Molluscs, Crustacea, etc., p. 111.

Capture

Freshwater fishing

Fishing will be most productive where tributary streams enter lakes, rivers or ponds; their waters usually carry food and form gravel beds on which spawn is deposited. Fish come towards lake shores at morning and evening to feed. In streams, deep well-like spots among water plants and still water beneath the shade of overhanging trees are favourite spots. In rivers they like a steady current of well-oxygenated water. Most fish hide during the day, emerging to feed during the early morning, evening and at night, and these are the best times to fish. A falling water is also better than a rising one.

Rod and line: Fishing tackle can be bought relatively cheaply and wherever possible it will be easier to do this than to make your own. However, for centuries fishing was successfully done using home-made rods. The earliest rod-and-line anglers were the Chinese, who started sometime between 1500 and 900 BC, and from this time until the seventeenth century AD all fishing was done with a fixed line. All that was required of a rod was that it should be firm yet springy, tapering at one end and long enough to stretch over any obstructions at the side of the bank in the way of weeds or trees. Hazel sticks about twelve feet long were the commonest, though willow, ash, poplar and beech were also used. Lines were made of greased silk, gut or plaited horsehair, with a single horsehair attaching the hook to the main line. Floats were made of a reed stem or a light piece of wood; weights of small stones or lead attached to the line as shown:

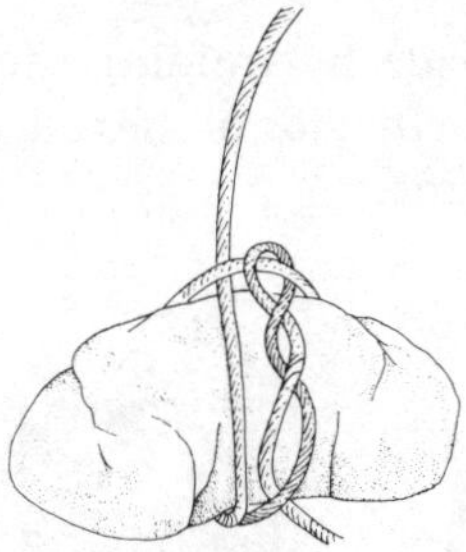

Hooks were anything that the fish would swallow with the bait and not be able to disgorge afterwards: small sharp stones, bones, thorns, and pieces of wood. Carved bones were a later refinement, as were metal hooks with a barb, the point sharpened with a file or stone. Dame Juliana Berners wrote in 1406: 'Ye can not brynge an hoke into a fyssh mouth without a bayte'[36] and the best baits approximate the food of the fish you are trying to catch, placed where the fish is likely to feed. One way of discovering this is to catch a fish, open it up, and inspect the contents of its stomach; general-purpose baits are worms, maggots, larvae, small fish, pieces of meat, mollusc, paste and crusts of bread. Groundbait – a slow shower of bread crumbs, maggots or worms left in a tin punched with holes through which they can escape – creates a genial atmosphere. Regular feeding also encourages a false sense of security in fish, which become quite tame and easily caught. For fish that eat aerial insects the bait should resemble the fly they feed on – made with silk, feathers and hair bound on the back of a hook, using a few feathers rather than a lot. However fish have been known to snap at anything, a wisp of wool (red was thought the best colour) and even individual ears of oats.

Before the invention of the reel, when a large fish was hooked the rod was thrown into the water and kept in sight until the fish had played itself out, and then the tackle and fish recovered. Early reels were made of wood or metal as in this description of 1651:

The manner of his Trouling was, with a Hazell Rod of twelve foot long, with a Ring of Wyre in the top of his Rod, for his line to runne thorow: within two foot of the bottoms of the Rod, there was a hole made, for to put in a winde, to turne with a barrell, to gether up his Line, and loose at his pleasure.[37]

A simple reel can be made by winding the line round two pegs driven into gimlet holes in the side of the rod, or, if trolling, wind the line round a wooden frame.

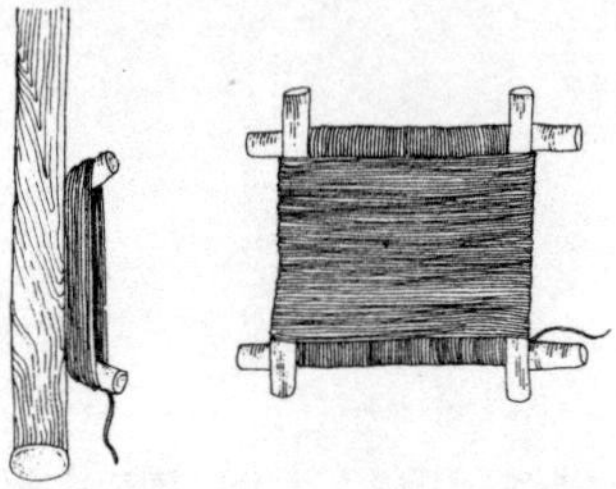

There are two basic methods of angling: using a natural bait sunk to the bottom with a weight or attached to a float or trolled behind a boat; and using an artificial bait such as a fly dropped on the water to resemble a real fly or a spinner dragged to resemble a wounded fish. The techniques and ethics are prodigious and discussed in great detail in many books. As Isaak Walton says 'Angling may be said to be so like the Mathematicks, that it can never be fully learnt; at least not so fully, but that there will still be more new experiments left for the trial of other men that succeed us.'[36]

Liming a pool: If a net is stretched across the bottom of a pool, and a sackful of lime emptied into the water, every fish in the pool will be gasping for breath, its gills full of congested blood, within fifteen minutes, and floating downstream into the net. The seeds of mullein put in water are also said to stun fish with their narcotic properties.

Damming a stream: Wade into the stream. Move stones until they form a barrier at one end. Add turf to plug the holes and gradually build up the dam until the flow of water is reduced to a trickle, when the stranded fish can be grabbed with the hands or caught with a landing net. Best done in a dry spell in summer.

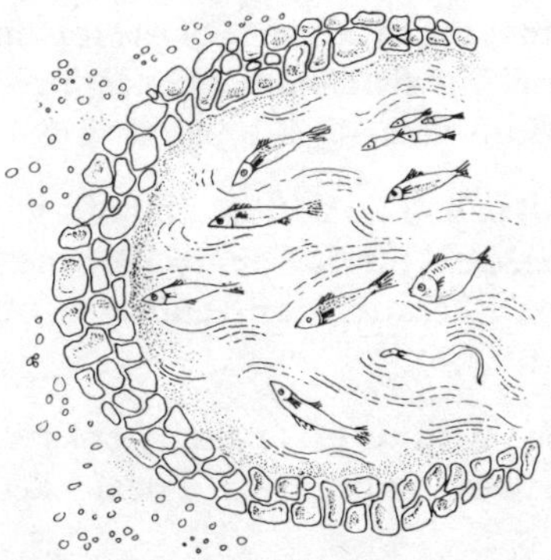

For salmon, put a thick impenetrable barrier of gorse below spawning fish. Drive the fish down by flailing the water with a stick. The frightened salmon should bolt into the gorse driving itself in until it can go no further and can be lifted out with the gorse.

Gaffing: Salmon, trout and eels are attracted to the surface of a pool at night by a blazing torch and can be then gaffed with a fork or spear, or jerked out with a hook tied to a short cord and attached to the end of a long stick. Gaffs were made of carved antler horns attached to sticks – later of metal.

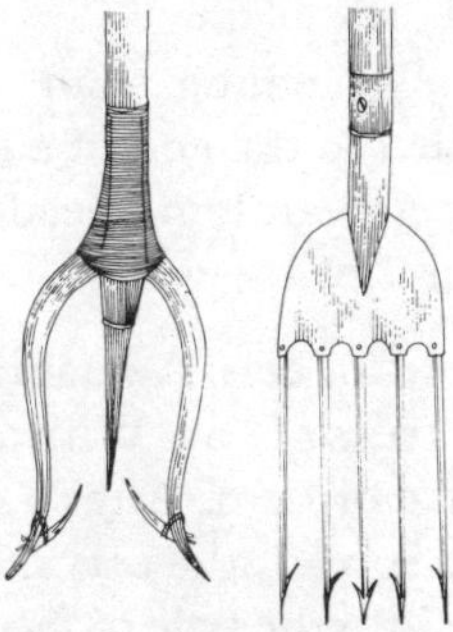

Netting a pool: Only pools of regular shape and depth are suitable for netting. If there are a lot of obstructions these should be removed a week or two beforehand. The net, shaped like a long rabbit net but deeper, about 8 ft square with a 1 in. mesh, has weights along one side and cords down the other. One end is fixed to the bank and the other end taken round by a man wading or in a boat, keeping the bottom of the net moving in advance of the top until the circle of the pool is complete; all the fish should be trapped in the net, if they have not escaped into holes in the bank.

Bottle: For small fish. The bottom end of a wine bottle is broken off, the top corked. Bait put in the neck of the bottle attracts fish which, lacking the wit to turn round and swim out, can be collected with the bottle.

Night lines: A line with several baited hooks is attached to a stake or tree in strategic places in the river. The hooked fish plays himself until exhausted.

Tickling: A very delicate operation, requiring much stealth and practice. The trout must first be located. It has

certain resting places, under rocks, close to but just out of the rush of current. One lies face down on rock; slowly, very slowly, a bare arm is lowered into the cold water; gently, very gently, the fingers brush the trout's side. Suspicious he moves away; but smoothly, confidently, with no sudden movements, the fingers start stroking him again. Reassured, rather enjoying it, he permits them to work up his body to the gills, the only place where a trout can be gripped firmly by a bare hand. A sudden squeeze, and he is held, drawn out kicking and wriggling, knocked on the head and pocketed.[38]

Noose: This method of catching trout also requires stealth. A noose of rabbit wire is tied to the end of a long stick. The noose is slipped over the head of a trout lying head upstream, as far as the gills, then it is yanked out of the water.

Hay bale: Only suitable for eels. A quantity of fish offal is placed in the centre of a bale or truss of hay. With a rope attached, it is cast out or lowered into a lake or dam. After a couple of days, the 'essence' of the hay having spread, the eels should have discovered it and burrowed their way into the bale to feed. The bale is pulled in, with the feeding eels still in it.

Forking eels: This is a fairly common method, as described below:

Carrying a harpoon three-pronged fork fixed to a pole about 12 ft to 14 ft long and perhaps 1½ to 2 inches in diameter . . . we left the town and went up to the River Rother, then at low tide, the banks of the river steep and about 8 ft above water level . . . From the top of the bank he pushed the fork into the muddy bed of the river, and after a time he suddenly said, 'I have caught an eel.' He could tell by the struggling of the eel in the mud that the eel had been caught in the teeth of the prongs. He brought the fish carefully to the top of the water; then, by moving the fork backwards and forwards in the water, cleaned the mud from the fork and the fish, and produced a nice wriggling eel. The mud in the river was at least 2 ft deep and the eels seemed to abound there, for by the end of the evening the sack was well filled. 'Eel spears' of this type can be obtained quite easily from tackle dealers. Usually the eel is seen before it is speared.[39]

Another method of catching eels is by 'babbing'. A bunch of worms is threaded on worsted and let down on a line attached to a short pole. The eels seize hold of the worms and are lifted into the boat before they can or will let go.

Traps: Eel traps made of willow osiers and baited with offal were placed at the outlet of a lake or where there are weirs or hatches in autumn. Often nets were placed across the stream with gaps for the openings of the traps.

Elvers are caught in special cloth nets.

Salmon traps: These are typical of the Severn. Hazel or willow branches are threaded through two circular discs, one larger than the other, the tops of the sticks being rammed into the ground to keep them steady. Two or three rows are woven in and out of the uprights at the point above the largest disc, then another series above that until the top is reached. This framework is then removed from the ground and other lines are woven in. Stakes are set in the river bed with a cross-bar like a football goal and the traps are fastened in lines across the river to these posts. At low tide spikes are let into the traps and these, combined with the force of the current, prevent the fish escaping.

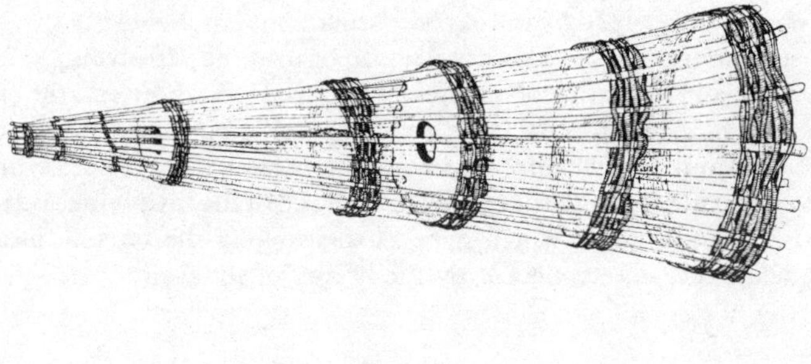

Sea fishing

Good places for sea fishing are in general mouths of streams or rivers, rocks overhanging the sea bed and, for flat fish, sand and gravel stretches. Most sea fish feed as the tide rises, tending to move inland with it and to swim along the shore. It is at this time that the best fishing will be had, but conditions vary with the area; always consult local opinion if possible.

Fish weirs: The power to erect a fishing weir was a privilege given only to important families or religious establishments. The one built at Rhos on Sea in the thirteenth century by Cistercian monks of Conway Abbey is an example; the best ones were to be found along the shores of the Menai Straits and date back a thousand years. They are constructed, as shown,

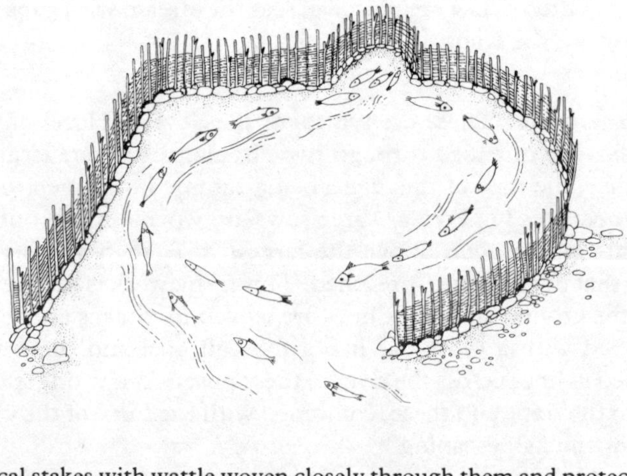

of vertical stakes with wattle woven closely through them and protected by boulders at the base. The long wing stretches from the shore out to low-water mark and is joined by the outside which runs parallel to the shore and then bends shorewards in a shorter length, termed the little wing, so forming an enclosure or garth with an opening between the shore and the end of the little wing. Almost in the middle of the outside a protrusion, called the 'cruive', extends further into the sea. When the water level rises with the tide the fish enter through the opening at the end of the little wing and swim towards the long wing, which deflects them along the outside into the cruive where they are collected by the keeper of the weir.[39]

Another form of weir can be made as in the diagram. Pick the site at high tide and build at low, making it look as much like the scenery as possible and using any natural features such as reefs or spits as part of the trap.

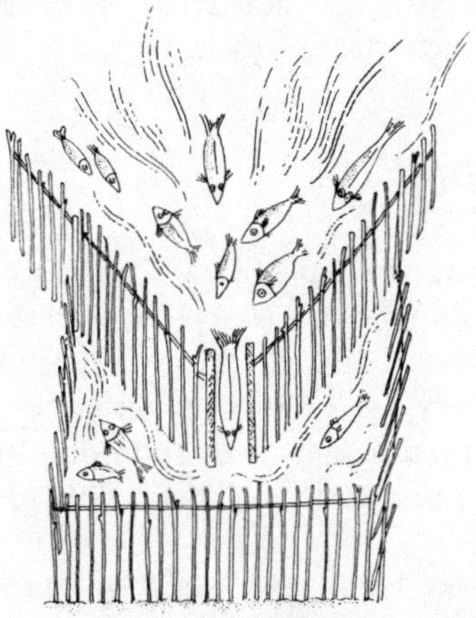

Drift net: This is used for catching herrings and other shoal fish. Row out in a boat until a likely spot is reached with about 50 yards of net having weights at the bottom and floats at the top. Hang it out and watch from one end, periodically rowing down its length to see if any fish are caught. If the floats begin to dip seriously it means a shoal is moving into the net. Haul up into the boat and wait until dry land is reached before shaking the fish out.

Trawl net: This is easily bought and it is possible to obtain nets for small boats. Drag behind the boat. Used for catching all forms of flat fish.

Fixed net: For catching estuary fish. Position a net on stakes across the mouth of the estuary parallel to the shore so that, as the tide rises, it lifts up but, as it ebbs, it closes and catches the retreating fish.

Long lines: Lines with twelve or more baited hooks trolled from the back of a boat will catch mackerel; if laid along the edge of the sea at low tide and left until the next low tide the lines will often catch flounder, dabs, etc.

Spearing: Flounders can be caught at low water or in sandy, muddy estuaries by jabbing with a fork as described for eels, p. 78

Gaffing and harpooning: Using a bright light and a gaff as for freshwater fish, p. 77, shine the torch from rocks into the sea. Basking shark have been harpooned off the Welsh and Irish coasts. (They swim with their dorsal fin in view.)

Killing and Gutting

'I am not of a cruel nature' said Izaak Walton, 'I love to kill nothing but fish.' It is best done with a sharp blow on the head with a stone or wooden implement. This will kill a small fish but may only stun a large one, which will die eventually on exposure to the air. For quickness and completeness its neck should be broken by forcing its mouth open and pressing the top back towards its neck until the neckbone snaps.

Anything but very small fish must be gutted before cooking. Make a slit down the belly from head to vent, scoop out the innards and wash well under running water. Make sure that the line of blood which runs under the backbone has been removed too. Cut off head and tail of larger fish.

Fungi

Fungi are the most neglected source of wild food in Britain. At the right season they are abundant and easily collected; they also taste infinitely superior to any cultivated mushroom. Unlike the French and Italians who eat lots of different kinds we generally leave anything but the ordinary field mushroom strictly alone. The fear of getting it wrong and eating a poisonous variety puts most people off and, indeed, caution is essential. No fungus should be eaten until it has been correctly identified; there are several books which will help with this. The larger, fleshier fungi are easier to identify and also make more of a meal. Woods are the richest source of fungi. Because fungi cannot manufacture chlorophyll they rely on a host plant, usually a tree, to do it for them. The mycelium or thread-like cords by which they spread are in the ground all the year round. Fruit bodies are produced only when conditions are right, usually from August to November, though for morels and some cup species the season is from March to May. Temperature and moisture are the determining factors and a warm summer followed by a damp autumn make ideal conditions.

There are over a hundred edible species to be found in Britain and about forty of these are of good flavour. They should not be picked so young that they have yet to develop any individuality nor so old that they have started to rot. Prone to attack by maggots, all fungi should be carefully inspected before cooking. If you come across a patch in the evening which are almost ready it will be wise not to leave them until the following day in case the maggots get there first. Most fungi can be eaten raw or cooked with the exception of a few, like the blusher, which are poisonous until cooked. All fungi should be eaten as fresh as possible and it is advisable not to eat too many of an untried species the first time as some produce an allergy in certain people. Mushrooms preserved by pickling and drying will keep for a long time (see pp. 133, 129).

If you have no identification book taste is a guide to edibility. Take a small piece and hold it in your mouth. If the taste is bad, peppery or acrid, spit it out, no harm will be done and the odds are the fungus is inedible. Poisonous fungi crop up, like proverbial black sheep, in many families. About 90 per cent of deaths can be attributed to the death cap (*Amanita phalloides*), its close relative the destroying angel (*Amanita virosa*) and the rare fool's mushroom (*Amanita verna*). Symptoms of death cap poisoning do not appear until eight to twenty-four hours after eating, by which time the poison has been absorbed by the body to such an extent that treatment is of no avail. Terrible stomach pains, vomiting and nervous disorder occur and death follows in two to ten days. Toxins in other fungi work in other ways. Extracts of *Coprinus atramentarius*, called Antabuse, are used in the treatment of chronic alcoholism. Eating this and drinking makes the person feel so sick he gives up the drink. The toxin in fly agaric (*Amanita muscaria*) acts as a stimulant. In northern parts of Russia and Scandinavia fly agaric were dried and rolled into balls and swallowed at a gulp – chewing was considered harmful. The narcotic effect, said to be heightened by drinking quantities of cold water, manifests itself in about half an hour with nervous spasms, sometimes followed by vomiting, then a feeling of intoxication and euphoria. One large fly agaric or two small ones are said to make an enjoyable day, though some are unaffected by eating a great deal more. One of the most remarkable features of fly agaric is the effect it has on urine. The urine of a person who has consumed fly agaric has a stronger intoxicating power than the fly agaric itself and the Koryaks would drink their urine to reintoxicate themselves.

It is very difficult to know where to begin recommending even a few edible fungi. They are so fickle, and a variety which may appear in huge quantities in one place will be absent from another.

Grassland

Blewits (*Tricholoma saevum*)*:* The name comes from the bluish colour of their stems. The cap is clay coloured. Found sometimes in woods but more often in fields or by hedges in autumn. Fry or simmer in milk with onion and bacon. Also good in soups and stews. Wood blewits (*Tricholoma nudum*), with a wholly purple stem and a rust-coloured cap, are close relations but are more often found in woods and gardens.

Fairy ring champignon (*Marasmius oreades*)*:* A pale buff in colour, they make the well-known fairy-rings on lawns in autumn. They have a faint smell of sawdust, are good to eat in all the same ways as field mushrooms, and dry well.

Field mushroom (*Agaricus campestris*)*:* Its less tasty relation, *Agaricus bisporus*, is the one sold in shops. The field mushroom grows in pastures, often in great numbers, though recently it has been on the decline, probably because farm horses – the nitrogen in their manure is essential to the development of this species – have been replaced by tractors. Freshly gathered in the early morning, fried in butter or better still in bacon fat, there can be no more delicious breakfast. Though the following recipes are for field mushrooms, other kinds can be used instead.

Champignons à la crème

Heat some butter in a pan and add cleaned and sliced mushrooms; stew for a few minutes; then add some parsley, or chives, salt and pepper and about 4 tablespoons of cream for ½ lb. mushrooms. Stir; in about 5 minutes it will thicken and the dish will be ready to serve, either as a vegetable or on toast as a dish on its own.

Grilled mushrooms

Big, flat mushrooms, going a little over, are best grilled. Brush with oil or butter. First grill them smooth side up, then turn, cover with strips of bacon rind and grill the gill side. Some people grill them on toast so that the juices drip into the toast and make a delicious dish.

Stuffed mushrooms

Melt a large chopped onion and a clove of garlic in 2 tablespoons of fat. Moisten 2 oz. breadcrumbs with milk and mix with ½ lb. sausage meat or minced leftover meat and the onion and garlic; bind with an egg. Stuff the mushrooms and bake for 15–20 minutes in a well-greased dish at 425°F.

Stewed with parsley and garlic

Clean and slice them, pour over a little oil, season and leave to marinate for a couple of hours. Drain and sauté with fresh oil in a frying pan. After 5 minutes of gentle simmering add some chopped parsley, a little garlic or onion and some breadcrumbs. Allow the juices in the pan to be absorbed by this mixture and serve immediately.

Giant puff ball (*Lycoperdon giganteum*)*:* The largest in this family, which includes several edible species, but care should be taken not to confuse them with the earth ball (*Scleroderma* spp.), which is toxic. They can grow to immense size – one in New York State was mistaken for a sheep in 1877 – and are mostly found in sandy pastures in autumn. To cook, cut in slices and fry or bake; some egg and breadcrumb them first. You can also stew them in milk. Also used as kindling tinder and as a razor strop.

Morel (*Morchella esculenta*): Of good flavour, though sinister in appearance, with the cap like a spongy honeycomb. It likes grassy banks and hedgerows, and grows in spring. Needs to be washed well and blanched in boiling water before cooking. Good in soups, stews and for drying.

Parasol (*Lepiota procera*): Found in grassy clearings in woods, this is one of our largest fungi. One cap almost makes a meal and, if stuffed, certainly does. Tall, with white flesh and a flecked fawn cap, it is easily spotted from a distance; August to November.

Shaggy cap (*Coprinus comatus*): Only young specimens with pink gills should be eaten. As the fungus ages the gills go black and auto-digest into a pool of black liquid which has been used for ink (see p. 312). Slice and fry in butter. Found in autumn in fields, roadsides and rubbish tips.

Shaggy parasol (*Lepiota rhacodes*): Same characteristics as the parasol but slightly squatter and not such an excellent flavour. Its flesh reddens when cut and it prefers a richer soil; found in gardens and parks from August to November.

Woodland

Cep (*Boletus edulis*): Several boletus are edible but this is considered the best. Their gills all look like half-covered sponges or, as Varenka remarked in *Anna Karenina*, 'the growth on a dark man's face who's not shaved for a couple of days'. Found in autumn in deciduous woods, especially beech. They should be eaten fresh as they deteriorate quickly. Cook as field mushrooms, but chop the stalk separately as they are inclined to be tough.

Chanterelle (*Cantharellus cibarius*): One of the finest edible fungi. Apricot yellow, with an apricot smell, it likes deciduous woods and grows in the autumn. It dries well but is best cooked in any of the ways given for field mushrooms, or sautéed in butter and parsley with a little stock added at the end to make a sauce.

Horse mushroom (*Agaricus arvensis*): Though most members of this family are edible the horse mushroom is one of the largest and best. White, with greyish gills and a smell of aniseed, it resembles its relative the field mushroom and may be cooked in all the same ways. It is found in woods and pastures in autumn.

Russula (Russula cyanoxantha): Another family with many edible species, of which this is considered the best. Found in autumn in deciduous woods especially beech, it is a pinky brown fungus with the clear-cut crisp gills common to all *Russula*. Cook as for field mushroom.

Wood hedgehog (Hydnum repandum): Blanching before cooking removes the acrid taste that this fungus may have. With curious spine-like gills under a pink, orange cap, it grows in rings in deciduous woods in autumn. Cook as field mushroom; also good in soups and stews.

On Trees

Beefsteak (Fistulina hepatica): It is tongue-like in shape, with a thick fibrous texture, and produces a red juice when cut, hence the name. Found on oak and beech trees in autumn. Rather acrid in taste (like aubergine), it is best cut in thick slices, with the rind peeled off, and stewed with onion and parsley.

Honey fungus (Armillaria mellea): A destructive parasite of deciduous and coniferous trees; it grows in clumps which makes for easy picking. Cook as field mushroom; it has a very rich taste.

Oyster fungus (Pleurotus ostreatus): It is a predator of trees, gradually destroying them, but is good to eat especially when young. Slice and fry or bake with butter. Usually found on deciduous trees, especially beech, but sometimes on conifers.

Underground

Truffle (Tuber aestivum): This resembles in looks but not in flavour the French truffle, *Tuber melanosporum*. André Simon says that 'The only place of truffles in gastronomy is as a flavouring agent, and first of all in *foie gras!* Used any other way or cooked whole it is an extravagance.'[9] They develop underground, especially under beech trees. In the great beech woods of the chalk downs of Gloucestershire and Wiltshire truffle-hunting continues to this day.

Herbs

Under this heading come plants or parts of plants with a strong flavour; they are added to a dish in small quantities to enhance the flavour.

Balm: Lemon-scented leaves used fresh or dried; said to be 'sovereign for the brain, strengthening the memory and powerfully chasing away melancholy'. Can be used in perfume, tea, wine, salad and pies.

Borage: Put in drinks it 'increaseth wit, and memoire, engendereth good blood, maketh a man merrie, and joyfull, and putteth away all melancholie and madness'.[42]

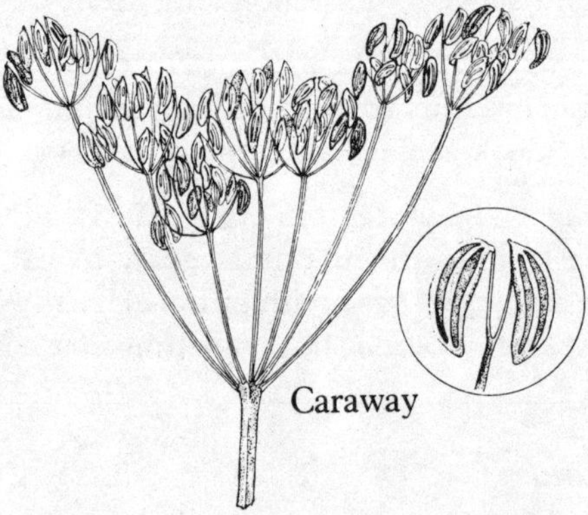

Caraway: The seeds are separated from the ripe fruit by threshing, and dried in the sun or in a warm place. Used to flavour cakes, seed cake, bread, cheese, soups, cabbage and as a table condiment. 'A pippin and a dish of caraways' was eaten by Falstaff.

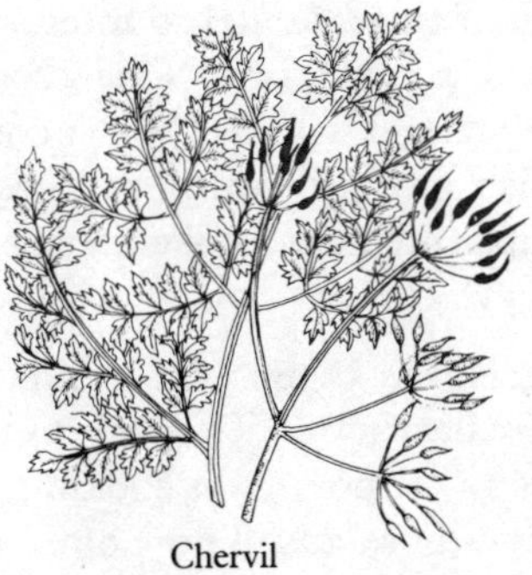

Chervil

Chervil: 'If it be eaten in a sallat, it is good for the stomache and the head by reason of the pleasant smell that it hath';[43] it can also be put in soups and used to flavour fish dishes.

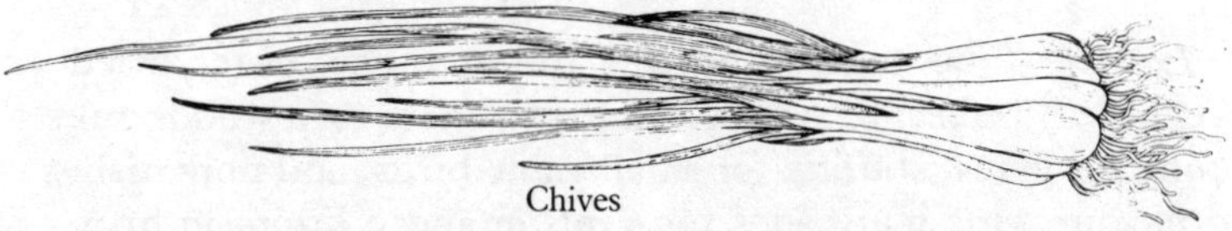

Chives

Chives: A rare plant in the wild; the leaves may be added to salads, soups, cheeses and omelettes.

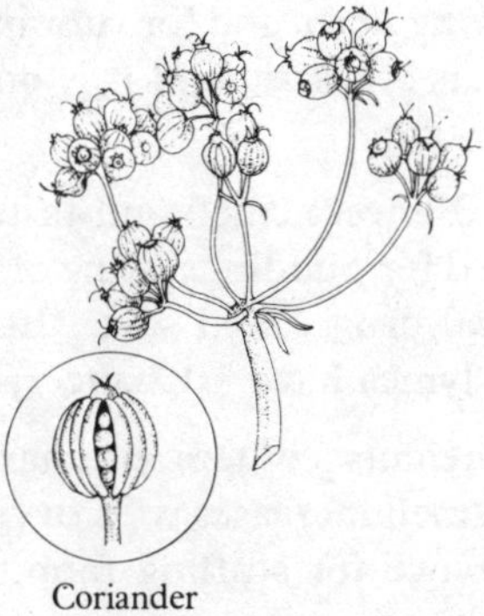

Coriander

Coriander: Len Deighton in a cooking article recommends that you 'hurl crushed coriander seeds into any open pot you see' – stews, chutneys, pickles, pork dishes, sausages.

Fennel: Tasting of anise, fennel counteracts the oiliness in foods, especially fish. As Culpeper says, 'One good old custom is not yet left off, viz. to boil fennel with fish, for it consumes the phlegmatic humour which fish most plentifully afford and annoy the body with.' Salads, soups and meat (cooked on a bed of fennel) all benefit from its pungency.

Garlic: Wild garlic in Britain has a smaller bulb and a weaker taste than the French varieties. The leaves are also garlic-flavoured, though this tends to evaporate on cooking, and are best used as a substitute for chives in salads. The 'onion' mentioned in medieval recipes was often wild garlic. Onions as such do not grow wild and were not introduced into Britain until the sixteenth century.

Herb bennet: The main root has no smell but the stringy side roots taste and smell of cloves and can be used instead of them. They keep well if dried and can also be used as a moth repellent.

Juniper: The berries have a bitter, spicy taste, dried and crushed. Elizabeth David recommends them as 'a wonderful seasoning for pâtés, stuffing for small game birds, and pork dishes . . . to flavour wine marinades for venison and mutton, in brines for hams and salt pork, and in the mixture for curing dry-spiced beef'.[44]

Marjoram: One of the best flavouring herbs for stuffings, soups, stews, beer and tea; it was used by the Egyptians to perfume unguents, as a strewing herb, and for rubbing furniture to perfume it. The whole plant is aromatic and it is one of the few whose scent increases with drying.

Meadowsweet: Flowers smell and taste of almonds, and can be used fresh or dried for puddings, wine or beer. One of fifty ingredients in a medieval drug called save. 'Eek save they drunken, for they wolde here lymes have.' (Chaucer, 'Knight's Tale'.)

Melilot: All melilots contain coumarin, which smells of new mown hay – the smell increases with drying. Used to flavour soups and stews, in France for stuffing rabbits and in Switzerland for Schabzieger cheese.

Mint: Eight different kinds of mint with different flavours grow in Britain. For sauces, cheese, pot-herbs, stuffings and soups use *Mentha spicata* and *M. longifolia*; for toothpaste, *M. piperata*; for strewing and pot-pourris, *M. citrata* and *M. aquatica*; and as a mild antiseptic, *M. rotundifolia*.

Parsley: A garden escape; a common ingredient in all kinds of sauces, stuffings, soups and stews.

Pennyroyal: A kind of mint whose local name of 'pudding grass' comes from the practice of using it as a stuffing, mixed with honey and pepper, for pork.

Salad burnet: A cooling, cucumber-scented leaf which 'gives a grace in the drynkynge', declared Gerard. Also good in salads and, according to Bacon, as a strewing herb: 'perfumes the air most delightfully, being trodden on and crushed'.

Sorrel: Acid leaves which taste of lemon; the young leaves may be used as a substitute dressing in salads. A purée of sorrel cooked in butter makes an excellent sauce or soup.

Spignel: The leaves are reminiscent of celery and can be used in place of fennel. The roots have an even stronger taste and are used as a flavouring spice or grated on salads. Called in the Highlands 'bald money' or 'badminnie' – a name which appears to derive from the type of person who used the herb rather than from the herb itself.

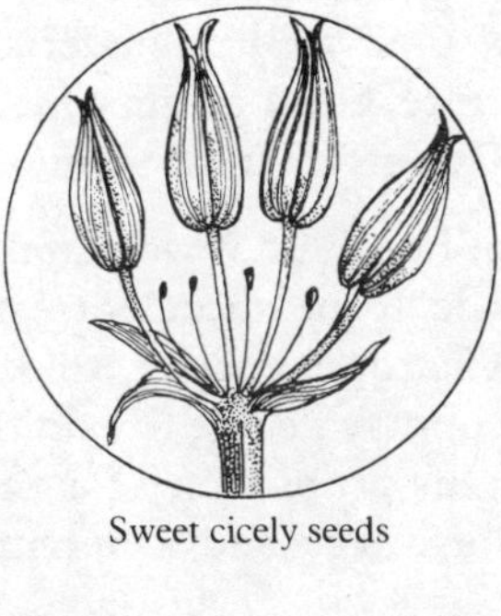

Sweet cicely seeds

Sweet cicely: The large seeds are dried and used in place of cloves or caraway seeds. Used to scent furniture polish in the north.

Tansy: The leaves have a warm, spicy flavour called in the country 'ginger' for this reason. Often used instead of nutmeg and cinnamon in puddings and custards.

Thyme: About forty species of thyme have been identified by botanists in Europe. Some are weaker-tasting than others. Soups, stews, tea, scents and stuffings all benefit from thyme.

Wood sorrel: Also called 'Cuckoo's meate' from the country belief that the bird clears its throat by eating it. The leaves taste extremely acid and may be used instead of lemon and vinegar in salads.

Insects

The idea of eating insects is foreign and abhorrent to most westerners. This is logical in many ways as British insects never attain the size or succulence of their tropical counterparts. However *in extremis* eating insects may become necessary. I therefore include any which have reliable written evidence of their edibility. These are almost all larvae of larger insects and I have to confess to not having tried any, never having been hungry enough to overcome my aversion. However, 'we are what we eat', and we are prepared to consider lobster a delicacy, although it is a filthy feeder, attracted into pots by a bait of rotten fish, so eating a caterpillar which lives on cabbage should be no problem. A rough guide to which insects are edible comes from study of their feeding material: insects that are carnivorous, live on manure, or on plants which are poisonous to man should be avoided. Otherwise most should be safe.

Bees: The larvae of bees and of wasps taken from the comb and baked or fried are said to be succulent eating. The county beekeeping officer for Chard, Somerset, told me that it used to be regular practice for country people to raid their beehives in spring and remove any surplus grubs to fry for their supper. Smoke the bees or wasps from their nests and then remove the larvae, or bake the comb whole.

Caterpillars: Make sure that only those feeding on non-poisonous plants are collected. Then boil them, or fry them, like the Hottentots, in iron pans, stirring them about until cooked. Eaten 'in handfuls, without any flavouring or sauce', they are said to taste like 'sweet almond paste'.

Cockchafer: Also known as the june bug; a brown beetle common in the southern counties. Its grub is eaten. It lives in the soil, feeding for three years on all kinds of roots and growing up to two inches in length. It is a pest to the gardener but, as Darwin observed after watching sparrows and turkeys eating the larvae, it 'might be grateful food, if properly cooked, as the locusts or termites of the East'.

Grasshoppers: Three grasshoppers are indigenous to Britain. According to reports all are well worth eating. This recipe comes from Morocco: 'having plucked off their heads, legs and wings, sprinkle them with pepper and salt and chopped parsley, fry in butter, and add some vinegar'. Pliny says that the eastern nations and the Parthians thought both locusts and grasshoppers choice food. Some prefer males and females after they have cast their eggs; the Greeks preferred them with their eggs. 'Locusts or grasshoppers can be prepared in more ways even than oysters; they may be eaten raw, stewed, and fried in oil, broiled on a gridiron, smoked, or ground up in a handmill and baked into cakes; first boiled in water and then fried in butter they make an excellent dish.'[45]

Meal-worm: 'The meal-worm, the larva of a small beetle (*Tenebrio*), is generally looked upon with disgust, as only fit food for tame birds. Even the strong-stomached and hungry sailor will rap his sea-biscuit on the table to shake out the worms before eating it. Let him shake out the worms, by all means; but let him collect them, fry in lard, and spread the dainty upon his dry biscuit. He will not again throw meal-worms away'.[45]

Moths: These also may be eaten: 'Lately, however, I have done so, to find the dream of my childhood fully realized as to the delights, both in taste and smell, of a fat moth nicely baked.'[45] The inhabitants of New South Wales used to catch moths, remove the grey powder on their bodies and roast them in masses.

Mammals

In the past any animal worth eating was eaten. Now indiscriminate killing and the destruction of their habitat by the pressure of human population has led to a scarcity of some species and all except those classified as vermin (rabbit, rat, grey squirrel, fox, hare, mole, mouse) are protected by law. Some, such as deer, are protected only during their breeding season, but others, such as badger and two species of bats, at all times. However, I have included every animal which is known to be edible.

Most mammals are nocturnal in habit. They hide during the day in vegetation, emerging at dusk to feed through the night, returning home at dawn. It is then, when they are on the move and when there is enough light to see them by, that animals are most easily caught. Mammals are at their fattest and best in autumn, having built up reserves of fat through the summer to sustain them through leaner times in winter or to prepare for hibernation.

Other uses

Always preserve the skin and, with larger mammals, the guts, hooves and fat as well. They have their uses, for leather, clothes, rugs, shoes, glue, string and flooring.

Domestic Mammals

Though it is not the brief of this book to go into the realms of farming, I have felt justified in including descriptions of some of the larger mammals like cows and pigs, because without them we would be deprived not only of a major source of meat but also of leather, glue, fat for light, heat and soap, and also because all domestic species were once wild and it is only through their extreme usefulness to man that they are now domesticated. The following accounts are necessarily brief; HMSO do excellent leaflets on the subject and there are many books on animal husbandry which give greater detail. For the person keeping only only one or two animals of each kind I recommend that he goes for a local breed, which will be hardier, more disease-free and require less upkeep. Modern economic demands have encouraged the breeding of animals which are quick converters of fodder to meat or milk and many are now unable to exist without up-to-date housing and maintenance. As a result the breeds adapted to local conditions are now often scarce. However, if you have trouble you can get advice on the right breeds and where they can be found.*

*Apply to Rare Breeds Survival Trust, The Ark, Winkleigh, Devon.

Cows

Cattle came to Britain during the Neolithic Age in the form of a kind of long-horn cow. Their descendants are the white cattle or Chillingham cattle first mentioned as being enclosed in Chillingham Park, Northumberland, in the thirteenth century and still there today; a thin wiry breed not producing much meat or milk. Your choice of cow depends on which of these two products is the more important. A Jersey or Guernsey gives a rich milk suitable for making butter and cheese. For a continuous supply of milk you will need two cows, so that when one is dry the other is still giving milk. Cows require at least one acre of grassland per head to feed on and one ton of hay in winter; the milk yield will be improved if their diet includes some corn or dairy nuts. The grass they are feeding on has a bearing on the milk too. There is a country saying that 'the hills do feed and the valleys fill' – mountain pastures produce more casein, making good cheese, while rich valley grass increases the quantity of milk. You can eat your domestic cow but, unless she is a dual purpose breed, the meat will not be of the quality of a beef cow and probably by the time you want to kill her she will be too old and tough and too much of a friend. South Devons and Worcesters can be milked and are good eating; a Hereford, Aberdeen Angus or Galloway, or a cross between them, are the prime cattle for beef.

Cows can be mated at fifteen months. Gestation is about nine months, 280 days. A cow should be left alone to calve unless you can see that she is in difficulties and has been for several hours. Then if the calf is in the right position – forefeet first followed by the nose – put a cord round the calf's feet and gently pull when the cow heaves, but not when she doesn't. If the calf is the wrong way round get a vet, if there is no vet, wash your hands and arm in carbolic and delve into her depths to see if you can turn it round. Leave her with her calf for a few hours, then pick it up and take it, with her following, to a cowshed. Let her suckle it for a week and then take it right away to another building. She will howl for a couple of hours and then settle down. Milking twice a day can now begin. The calf should be fed on the skim milk after the cream has been taken off for butter, mixed with 2 oz. ground oats to 2 pints milk, until it can eat grass. A bull calf which is not needed some destroy after a week and eat; others keep for a year or so and then eat them.

Milking: Take a teat in the palm of your hand, press with forefinger and thumb round the top of the teat – this is to prevent the milk in the teat going back up into the cow – then squeeze the teat firmly downwards with your fingers, directing the stream of milk which should ensue into a clean bucket. It takes some practice and the development of some muscles in your hand that you did not know existed. Make sure that the cow has been milked dry at each milking, as any milk left can go rancid and cause disease. When you are a novice this is difficult to judge because the cow may dislike your fumbling and hold back on you and so take longer to milk. Milking should be done twice a day, ideally at twelve-hour intervals, but varying it by a few hours will not hurt.

Goats

Wild goats, descendants of the domestic herds of Neolithic settlers, can still be found in the mountainous areas of Wales, England and Scotland. Modern farm breeds are mostly descended from Swiss goats and if you have a cow you will not need a goat, but if your space is limited, a goat will give up to eight pints of milk a day on rough feeding. Goat's milk is not suitable for butter, being naturally homogeneous, which makes it easily digested and suitable for invalids. Goat's milk, contrary to popular superstition, does not smell or taste rank as long as the billy goat is kept separate from the nanny. The taste will be as sweet as the pasture she is feeding on, which could be your garden. Goats have a tendency to eat anything and everything, are very agile and difficult to contain, and can be a problem. Efficient fencing is required, or tethering; but an animal should never be tethered unless essential, then a running tether should be constructed and moved often. Goats are not as hardy as cows; they need shelter at night and must be kept in during the winter. A goat may be cooked in all the same ways as sheep. 'Good pasture-fed kid is like mountain mutton, old wild goat is more like bad venison.'[27] Milking a goat is the same as milking a cow but trickier as they are smaller. The milk is equally good drunk or made into cheese or yoghurt. The gestation period for goats is 140–52 days.

Horses

The value of the horse as a means of transport and pleasure means that any available flesh is usually old and tough and fit for nothing but dog's meat. However horses up to three years old, especially mares or geldings, are said to make excellent eating if treated like beef, and on the Continent they eat quite a lot and always have done, as many a horse exported from Ireland to Belgium has learnt to its cost.

Pigs

Until, with the population becoming increasingly urban, a law was passed forbidding pigs to be kept near the house, every cottager kept a pig in his back yard. Most cottagers kept only one, probably bought as a weaner from a local farmer at about eight weeks and fattened throughout the summer on vegetable left-overs from the kitchen, with the addition of skim milk, barley and wheat meal. The pig was killed in the autumn and

> salted for home consumption, and not one scrap was wasted.
>
> The head and feet were made into brawn. The stomach was stuffed and roasted. The intestines were stuffed with a mixture of meal, lard, blood, etcetera, and called 'puddings' . . . The liver was fried or boiled with potatoes, forming a sort of Irish stew, or stewed as part of the 'pig's fry'. In preparing the two dishes for salting for bacon, the two undercuts from the sirloin were removed and the two 'pork fillets' were the result.
>
> Then the ribs were filleted off and these gave 'spare-ribs'. Then the sides were neatly trimmed to give them a smooth appearance, and these trimmings, consisting of good scraps of meat, were called 'griskins'. The hind legs produced two hams. The fore legs boned and rolled gave shoulder-bacon, a favourite cut for boiling.
>
> The head was stuffed and pot-roasted or sliced and used for Irish stew with the griskins and spare-ribs.
>
> The lard was rendered and 'slim cakes' made, the remainder kept for frying, bread, etcetera.
>
> In fact, the week the pig was killed was a week of feasting not only on the farm but in the houses of poor people who shared the 'pickings'.[47]

A sow can be put to boar at one year, gestation is 112–120 days and she should be left by herself to produce her piglets – average number ten – preferably in a dry hut. Pigs can be kept inside but prefer the freedom of a field or wood. They reduce everything to the consistency of a ploughed field and a ring through the nose is a good idea if you want to prevent this. It is worth noting that lop-eared pigs are the best tempered.

Sheep

Sheep live exclusively on grass, though in bad winters they need hay and roots or oats. The choice of breed should depend on whether it is the meat or wool or both that is more important, and also on where you live. The South Down is a good all-rounder; large-boned Leicestershire sheep need softer conditions than the hardy Black-face. All mutton is flavoured according to the fodder of the sheep. Mountain breeds give the most succulent meat, which should be simply cooked to do justice to the flavour; lowland breeds need rich sauces to enhance the taste. The strict definition of lamb is that which is milk fed and has not developed its teeth. Present-day lamb is more likely to be castrated male and anything up to two years old. Mutton comes from ewes over four years old whose breeding life has finished.

Once sheep were milked in the same way as cows and it was said that 'a score of sheep would give as much cheese as five cows, while one ewe yields twice as much cream as one cow'. Butter too was made from the milk, and is said to be whitish in colour. The debilitating effect which the milking of sheep had on their lambs led to the gradual dying out of the habit from the Middle Ages on.

A ewe is put to the ram in autumn, gestation is 147 days and timed for the lambs to appear in February or March – later the further north you go. They lamb by themselves but as with cows should be watched and, if in difficulties, helped.

Wild Animals and Pets

Badger: The two hams from a badger's hindquarters, if cured, by salting and smoking are said to make delicious eating, tasting like pork only finer. At a pub in Ilchester, Somerset, they used to have a yearly badger feast, the meat being roasted in front of an open fire.

The guests ate slices of meat off bread and drank ale out of horn cups.

Badgers are found all over Britain but they are rarer in the north and are seldom seen owing to their strict nocturnal habits. They live in communal sets, normally in dry hilly country on sandy or chalky soil. A copse, small wood, embankment or quarry up to 650 ft above sea level is their preferred habitat. A large, tidy entrance in the ground leads to an extensive tunnel system. Some of these sets have been occupied for a hundred years. Badgers are creatures of habit, following the same route every evening, and can be caught with a snare placed on one of these paths. But note that the badger is a protected animal.

Bats: There are over a dozen different species of bat in this country and two are rare and protected – the greater horse-shoe bat and the mouse-eared bat. They are all strongly nocturnal and hibernate in winter. They often sleep suspended upside-down by their legs in roof eaves, caves, rock fissures and trees. To cook: skin and then roast or, better, stew in a good strong sauce.

Cat: Labouchère, who ate cats during the siege of Paris in 1870, said that they were 'something between a rabbit and a squirrel with a flavour of its own. It is delicious. Don't drown your kittens, eat 'em.'

Deer: There are four indigenous species: the red deer, found in mountainous areas in the highlands of Scotland, Devon and Somerset; the roe deer, found in scrubland and woodland throughout Scotland and the north of England, and in Devon, Dorset and Sussex; the fallow deer, a sparse population scattered throughout the country in deciduous woods and pasture land, mostly park escapes; and the reindeer, made extinct in the twelfth century but reintroduced in 1952 in certain areas of the Highlands where their food, the reindeer moss (*Cladonia rangifer*) is found. Gastronomically, the roe deer is considered best, after that the fallow deer, the red deer and last the reindeer. However all may be prepared in the same way, and come under the general heading of venison. The flesh of the male is better than the doe, but none should be eaten if they are over three years old and all are inclined to be tough and dry. Hanging for from twelve to twenty-one days in a cool, airy place, and marinading and larding or wrapping the joint in fat, help to correct this. The best parts are the haunch, fillet, loin and chops. Stew or roast slowly, serving with a gravy made from the juices, with red wine or jelly added. Jelly can also be handed separately; red currant or rowan are traditional. Any herbs used for flavouring should be mountain ones, thyme or sage; some pack the meat in sweet gale (bog myrtle) to flavour and scent it.

Bucks are protected from September to June, doe from December to October.

Dog: From the beginning dogs have been used both for hunting and for food. Pliny mentions roasted puppy dogs as being excellent and Hippocrates thought them light and wholesome. The Chinese used to fatten dogs especially for human consumption. They preferred small dogs fed exclusively on a vegetable diet. Once killed they were scalded in boiling water, and the skin was scraped with a knife to remove the hair as with a pig.

Dolphin and porpoise: The flesh is apparently of a 'very dark red, somewhat oily but not fishy, and that when properly "casseroled" it might pass for jugged hare, and is rich and sustaining.'[9] Porpoise used to be served at the dinners of the Goldsmith's Company and was enjoyed by Henry VIII. Traditionally it is served with a sauce of sugar, breadcrumbs and vinegar. Cookery books from the fourteenth century have many recipes for porpoise, roasted, salted and stewed.

Edible dormouse (*Glis glis*)*:* Distinct from the dormouse (*Muscardinum avellanarius*); it is much larger – up to seven inches long – and has a bushy squirrel-like tail. They were introduced into this country in 1902 by Walter, later Lord, Rothschild at his home in Tring Park, and later spread to the surrounding countryside. They are nocturnal and sleep in hollow trees, preferably oak or beech, in woods; they live on berries and nuts, leaping from tree to tree like squirrels. They hibernate in winter. Regarded by the Romans as a delicacy, large numbers were reared in special oak and beech groves and fed on chestnuts and currants until they were well grown, when they were caught and placed singly in earthenware jars called *gliraria*. In these they quickly fattened until they were usually too big to be got out and the jars had to be broken to release them. They were then cooked and served with sweet sauces. The French still eat them and a farm was started in Cheshire in 1977 to breed them.

Fox: Distributed over almost the whole of mainland Britain, inhabiting burrows, usually those vacated by rabbits or badgers, their numbers are maintained by fox-hunters. The fox preys on all small animals and birds and, left to the farmers, foxes would probably be extinct by now. The flesh is said to be 'ill tasting, rank and disagreeable, and eaten only through necessity'.[8] Skin, then roast or stew.

Hare: We have two kinds of hare, the blue or arctic hare, which lives in heathery, rocky, mountainous areas mostly in Ireland and Scotland and whose coat is white in winter and brown in summer, and the common brown hare which lives in all kinds of rough, open ground up to 2,000 ft. Both types lie concealed during the day in depressions in vegetation called 'forms', emerging in the evening to feed on the surrounding vegetation – often the farmer's turnip field. Shooting is the kindest way of killing a hare, but they are often hunted with dogs such as the beagle and harrier hound or coursed with lurchers, greyhounds and other fast running dogs and caught in traps and snares. Roasting or stewing (jugging) are the most usual ways of cooking, depending on the animal's age. The leveret, small, with little sharp teeth and soft paws and ears, has white meat almost like chicken, does not need hanging and is best roasted as you would rabbit. Older hares should be hung for about a week, then skinned and jointed, saving as much of the blood as possible. Marinading improves the flavour. Hares should be overcooked rather than undercooked and must never be served red.

Jugged hare

Put the jointed hare in a large bowl and pour over a glass of wine vinegar, half a glass of olive oil, salt, pepper, a bunch of thyme and a sliced onion. Leave it for 12 hours, turning it several times. Chop an onion and about 1 oz. pork fat together and put with about 2 oz. butter in a pan. Add the pieces of hare and cook together for about 20 minutes, then sprinkle with flour and simmer for another 25 minutes. Add a ladle of stock and another of red wine. Season with salt and pepper and cook for 35 minutes. Pound the liver to a paste and strain with the marinade and the blood of the hare and add to the hare 5 minutes before serving. Eat now or better still cook it the day before and reheat; the flavour will have deepened and improved.

Hedgehog: Common in most open country, grassy heaths, arable land and in gardens; they hibernate during the winter. The hedgehog is a valuable animal, eating snails and slugs and other destructive insects, and should not be killed wantonly. The flesh is said to taste like a cross between chicken and sucking pig and was a favourite food of gipsies, whose method of cooking was to dig a hole in the ground, line it with stones and light a wood fire on top. When a bed of red hot ashes had accumulated the whole hedgehog, encased in clay, was put in. When cooked, the clay cover was broken open and the spines came away with it.

Mice: Mice have been eaten, and were regarded as a *bonne bouche* by the Eskimos.

Mole: The mole is said to be eaten by some who trap them but they are caught for their fur rather than their meat. Moles live in underground burrows and tunnels in pastureland and deciduous woods; their presence is revealed by their telling, and to gardeners and farmers, infuriating, mole hills. They are caught in traps.

Rabbit:

The first rule about rabbit is: don't ask the people who are going to eat it whether they like it or not. So many people have an idiotic idea that the very thought makes them sick, either because they have never had it properly cooked or because they are well read in Beatrix Potter and can't bear to think of devouring the Flopsie Bunnies. Now if you take trouble and plonk a really appetizing *dish of* rabbit before these people at lunch time, they will eat it up without a murmur, just as they would eat *'bœuf' à la mode* made from their favourite hunters if they were kept in ignorance of the awful truth.[46]

It is worth noting that a doe will taste better than a buck which, especially in season, can be very strong, and a young rabbit will be best of all – you can tell their age by the fragile jaw and ears which tear easily. Very young rabbits are best jointed, brushed with butter or bacon fat and sautéed or grilled. Older rabbits are better stewed or put in a pie and covered with pastry.

Rabbit pie

Joint the rabbit and dust with flour or oatmeal. Fry in a little butter until brown, remove and keep warm. Fry two rashers of bacon and one small chopped onion in the remaining fat. Add 1 dessertspoon flour or oatmeal, ½ pint stock, salt and pepper. Return the joints to pan and cook gently for 1 hour. Put in pie dish and cover with shortcrust pastry made in the proportions of 4 oz. butter to 8 oz. flour. Bake for ½ hour, or until nicely brown on top.

Rabbit casserole

Joint a rabbit and sauté the pieces with some small, or chopped, onions in 1 oz. butter and 3 oz. diced pork until brown. Add thyme, bay leaf and about 1½ glasses white wine or cider. Simmer until tender – about 1 hour. Add about 4 oz. mushrooms which have been fried in a little butter and finish by mixing in a small cup of cream or the yolk of an egg. Sprinkle with chopped parsley and serve.

Rat: Eating rats is a well-known resource for those enduring a siege or in penury. Thoreau in *Walden* says that 'Yet for my part, I was never squeamish; I could sometimes eat a fried rat with a good relish, if it were necessary.'[1]

Seal: the meat should be cut in thin slices and any fat or blubber removed and kept to be rendered down for fat, then the meat soaked for twenty-four hours to remove the blood, which will otherwise give it a fishy flavour. Then stew with bacon fat or fry in pork fat. The most prized part of the seal is the liver, which is cooked without soaking. The Eskimos eat the meat, liver and blubber raw, enabling them to survive long periods at temperatures as low as 58°F below freezing.

Sea-lion: Tougher than seal though similar. After cutting through about an inch of skin there is at least a foot of fat before any meat or bones are reached. Enough fat to fill a barrel has been rendered down from a sea-lion.

Squirrels: The red squirrel, probably indigenous to Britain, lives in coniferous forests but is also found in some deciduous ones. On the decrease since the eighteenth century, due to the destruction of its forest habitat, to disease earlier in the century and to the introduction of the grey squirrel from America in 1876. The latter's success is due to its adaptability; able to survive in woodland, parks and even central London, eating all kinds of fruit, nuts and fungi. The red squirrel is now so rare that it would be immoral to consider killing one, and anyway the grey squirrel makes better eating – it is larger and fatter, and resembles rabbit in flavour, though, as with all species, the taste depends on its food and some can be a bit rank. Squirrels can be shot or caught in traps and snares. After skinning and drawing they are best stewed.

Sautéed squirrel

Wash and then dry the squirrel and cut in quarters. Rub with salt and pepper. Gently fry a finely chopped onion and garlic in butter until golden, then add some chopped ham and the squirrel. Sprinkle with flour and fry until brown. Pour over 1½ cups red wine, put in some thyme, a bay leaf, pepper and some lemon if you have it. Simmer until tender.

Whale: According to Dr F. C. Fraser

provided the whale is young and freshly caught, the steaks are very good eating, in fact much better than much of the beef sold at present (1944). I have had the meat prepared in various ways, of which roasting was the least attractive. We most frequently had it fried with onions, but an alternative, and a very good, dish is to cut the meat in very thin pieces, wrap it round portions of bacon or ham, and serve it with a rather rich gravy like what is called 'Beef Olives'.[9]

Capture

Before any thought of capture an animal must first be found, and since his sense and agility are far in advance of any man's it will be a case of outwitting rather than outstripping him.

Galton says that

A trapper will never succeed unless he thoroughly enters into the habits of life and mind of wild animals. He must ever bear in mind how suspicious they are; how quickly their eye is caught by unusual traces; and, lastly, how strong and enduring a taint the touch of man leaves behind it.[19]

Lord and Baines recommend that the following signs be observed:

Sleeping places, or halts for rest, for food, drink, or other purposes, should be carefully sought for. The condition of the grass cropped by an animal, and the fragments dropped from its mouth, must be examined, as also its dung, the comparative moisture or dryness of which is an unfailing index to the time that has elapsed since it was dropped.[48]

Another set of recommendations:

1. Discover where animals pass. Signs are droppings, tracks, trampled ground. Best areas: water, forest clearings, edges or thickets.

2. Avoid the trail or runway itself once discovered. Prepare to hunt in early morning or dusk.

3. Hide with face to wind or the slightest breeze. If the sun is shining keep it behind you if possible.

4. Keep still.

5. Crawl forward only when animal is feeding, drinking or looking away. As soon as it starts to turn its head freeze.

6. Avoid snapping twigs, brushing aside foliage, silhouetting yourself.[49]

Today, unless you own the land, the authorization of the person who does must first be sought. Methods of capture are also controlled; gin traps and the crueller forms of snares are outlawed. A gun is the fairest and kindest way to kill an animal, a 12-bore shotgun or a ·22 rifle for small ones and a ·275 rifle for larger ones such as deer. The following are methods which were used by poachers, trappers and natives without guns.

Small animals

Snares: a snare of the right diameter, placed at the right height, will catch anything from a small bird to a rabbit and even a deer, the principle being the same for all – a running noose supported by wooden pegs or hung from a tree.

Wire rabbit snares can be bought from any country ironmongers, otherwise they can easily be made from several strands of thin plaited wire, string, horsehair, catgut or even a whippy hazel stick.

For rabbits they should be 2–2½ ins. in diameter, set 4 ins. from the ground and, if possible, just past their jump, set in a hole in the hedge or at the opening of a burrow.

Hares: make a larger loop and place it 7 ins. from the ground.

Rats: a smaller noose placed 3/4 ins. above the ground.

Moles: small nooses set in the mole's run with the holding peg above ground.

Nets: Rabbits, hares and sometimes partridges can be caught by driving them with or without the help of a dog into a gate net. The net should be little bigger in area than a five-barred gate, and used on a night when you can just see the clouds in the sky but with not enough moonlight to see the lines in your palm. Support the net along the top of the gate with half a dozen or so stones and hang it so that the bottom reaches the ground. Block all holes on either side of the gate. The rabbit or hare is driven into the net which falls and entangles him.

Purse nets: Set over rabbit holes and block any entrances not netted. Then put a terrier or ferret or a stick down the hole or light a smoky fire. The rabbits should bolt out into the nets. Rabbits have acute powers of hearing and it is essential to be absolutely quiet and, after the net has been laid, to sit out of sight of the holes downwind. When there is a rabbit in the net act very quickly and quietly. Seize the netted rabbit, shove a foot into the hole to prevent another rabbit bolting out from the same hole, kill the rabbit and put the purse net back into position.

Long nets: Brian Vesey Fitzgerald[50] recommends that long nets are set against the wind along the side of a wood or hedgerow. Rabbits disturbed at night in fields will take shelter in a wood. But the best catches will be made just before dawn. The rabbits are then returning from their nightly travels to fields near their burrows or woods and can be encouraged into a well-placed long net.

However they can also be driven in with dogs at other times. Long nets can be up to 75 yards in length, 3 ft or so in width, with a mesh of not more than 2 ins. and with cords threaded through the top and bottom. The net should be supported on sticks threaded through the net and driven into the ground at intervals of about 12 ft with extra strong sticks at each end. When the net is erected it is tightened with the cords so that as the rabbit strikes the net the meshes bag up and hold him. There should be enough slack to bag all the rabbits. After the drive is complete go along the net with a flash lamp. This dazzles the rabbits and makes them easy to lift.

Jamming holes: Between midnight and two in the morning, steal up to rabbit holes, each marked by a white tag, and push a screwed-up bundle of hay down the length of an arm into each hole making sure it is jammed in tight. Then wait by the holes listening; as rabbits dash down holes the 'work is fast and furious and the haul good'.[20]

Catapults, bows and arrows: These can be made or bought. The most difficult part is hitting anything with them. Arrows may be of wood with metal or bone tips, or use hardened clay pellets. Well-directed stones from a catapult will kill small animals.

Hunting with animals: A lurcher, deer-hound or greyhound will, either in pairs or singly, course and kill a hare and rabbit and even deer. Small terriers, and a ferret if you can get hold of one, are very effective put down rabbit holes to chase them out of their holes into nets. Pole ferrets are the easiest to handle.

Hawks, difficult to manage, will also hunt small game.

Killing and Preparing

Small animals are killed by a sharp blow behind the ears at the back of the neck or by breaking the neck. Richard Jeffries describes the effect:

> It was always a sight to see Little John's keen delight in 'wristing' their necks. He affected utter unconsciousness of what he was doing, looked you in the face, and spoke about some indifferent subject. But all the while he was feeling the rabbit's muscles stretch before the terrible grasp of his hands, and an expression of complacent satisfaction flitted over his features as the neck gave with a sudden looseness, and in a moment what had been a living, straining creature became limp.[51]

Larger animals should be shot with a rifle just behind the eye or, if facing, between the eyes or at a point behind the shoulder blade. With a shotgun spray the pattern as far forward as possible. If you have not got a gun, slit the animal's throat with a knife and the meat will be improved if the veins at the side of the neck are cut and he is bled, preferably strung up by his hind legs.

After this he may be skinned, while still warm if possible as it makes it far easier. Cut a line from the two centre lower teeth down the belly to the vent taking great care not to pierce the abdominal cavity. Then cut a line down each leg from the paw joint to the centre line. Begin skinning with the hind legs, peeling off the hide completely round the paw joints, then release the body, all the time using a scraping movement and leaving behind as much flesh and fat as possible. Release the tail and then the two fore legs, the shoulder joints and the front of the neck and throat. After this turn the animal on its belly and strip the skin off the back.

Small animals are skinned in the same way, though when the skin is to be used as a bag or bottle the following method is useful to know about as it obviates the need for a side seam. Make incisions close to the hindpaws and carry the cut down the borders of the vent, cut round this and the tail. An orifice will now exist large enough to admit the skin being stripped off the animal by turning it inside out. The skin is then stretched on wooden boards rather like boot or glove stretchers.

To gut the animal, saw through the breastbone, cut round the bung or anus and tie off the rectum. After this cut carefully down the belly with a finger against the point of the knife in order not to puncture paunch or bowels, haul out the innards, cut the windpipe and gullet to take out the pluck – lungs, heart, etcetera – and when the carcass is cold joint as required.

Pigs are treated slightly differently: first bled by being stuck with a sharp knife inserted into the front of the throat downwards at an angle of 45°, then scalded by having near boiling water poured over the body, after which the bristles and outer skin are scraped off.

Milling

There are three distinct stages in the conversion of grain into flour. First the grain must be separated from the straw, then the chaff separated from the grain, and finally the grain milled into a powder. The methods and implements employed at each stage vary according to the materials available but the more sophisticated they are, the easier the work becomes.

After the corn has been cut and dried, it is ready to be threshed. For a small amount of grain the heads of corn may be banged over a barrel or the back of a chair – on the Aran Islands they simply beat the straw against a large stone until the grain fell to the ground.

For a larger amount it can be piled on the floor and hit with a flail. In Suffolk threshing was done in the barn the floor of which

was paved with *clay-daub* – clay beaten down until it became as hard as concrete. The threshing was done with a flail, a *frail*, or a *stick-and-half* as it was called in Suffolk. The *half* part of the flail was called the *swingel*, and was made of very tough wood like holly or blackthorn; the handle was made of ash. The handle has a swivel on its top; then the swingel was attached to it by thongs of snake- or eelskin, the underside of a horse's tail or sometimes just pigskin . . . When using the flail the thresher swung the handle over his shoulder and brought down the swingel across the straw just below the ears so that the grains of corn were shaken out without being bruised. Skill was needed to handle a flail: and it was easier for a beginner to hit himself at the back of the neck with the swingel than to get it to fall neatly across the corn. George Messenger, an old Blaxhall man said: 'When I fust used the *frail* I hit myself sich a clout at the back o' the hid! It wholly hurt: the wood was some hard! But the ol' boy along o' me said: "Niver you mind, you'll git one or two of those afore you git used to it. But you'll soon git the swing on it!" And I did, and I used to thrash the corn I growed on my *common yard* for many years arter that.'[24]

The next stage is to winnow the corn – separate the chaff from the grain. The simplest way is to spread a sheet on the ground on a windy day and pour the threshed grain on to it from a height. The wind will blow away the chaff and the grain will fall on to the sheet. In Suffolk, again, the barn doors were pinned back on both sides and

the through draught thus set up helped carry away the dust. After threshing came the sieving: the sievers separated the cavings from the grain and chaff. Then the grain was piled at one side of the middlestead and thrown with a *scuppit* or wooden casting-shovel, high into the air. The heavy grains would fall furthest away, while the lighter and inferior grains, which were often fed to the cattle, would stop short, thus forming a kind of tail. The through draught was often assisted by an artificial draught set up by a hand-turned wheel with sacks fixed on its arms. There was also a hand-winnowing machine or blower for getting rid of the chaff.[24]

Robinson Crusoe milled his corn with a pestle and mortar made out of iron wood. Pestles and mortar can also be made from stone but milling in this way is hard work. Iron Age man put his grain on one stone and rubbed away with another and from this evolved the quern. Though some science has gone into the shaping of the stones querns have largely remained unchanged in design since very early days. They were often worked by horses or by water-power, and many of the water-mills can still be seen today, though few are in working order. A hand-quern consists of two circular stones about eighteen inches in diameter, made of granite or some other very hard stone. A softer stone grinds away and you end up with a certain amount of grit in your flour. The bottom stone is hollowed out to a depth of five inches, with a central pivot on which the top stone rests. The grain is poured through a hole in the top stone, which is turned by a wooden handle. The ground grain works its way out through the sides of the quern. The fineness of the flour is determined by the adjustment of the distance between the stones. For very fine flour a second grinding was often given.

Querns can be made as the diagrams suggest or a new one, made to the old design, can be bought.*

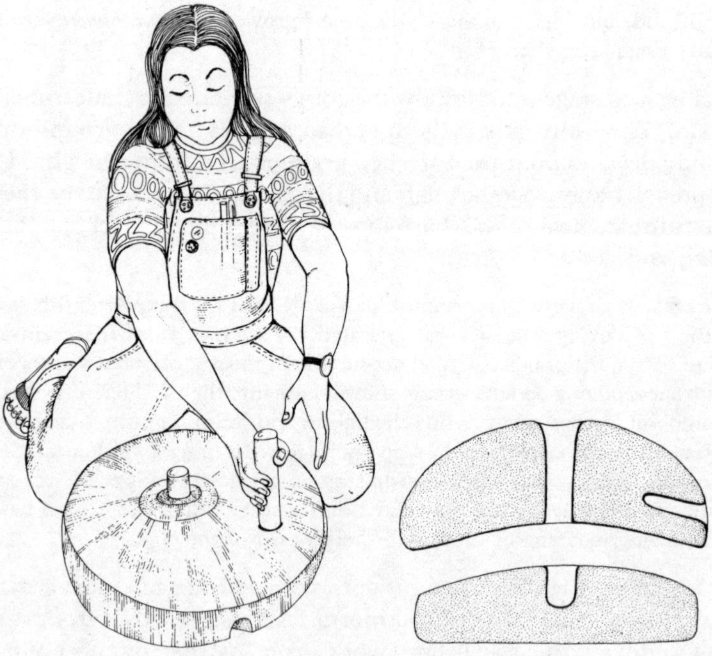

*From Springhill Farm Ltd, 38 Buckingham Street, Aylesbury, Buckinghamshire.

Molluscs, Crustacea, etc.

Molluscs are one of the richest and most available sources of wild food, but they do not occur on every shore, their presence being dictated by the geography of the land and the tide. Therefore if one is going to rely on finding molluscs for food it is as well to understand something of the tides and to learn to recognize different types of shore in order to know when and where to look.

Tides

The tides are at their height when the new moon and the sun are pulling more or less in a straight line, making a 'spring tide'. After this the angle between the sun and moon grows and the strength of their pull on the tide diminishes, making a neap tide. Then the angle closes again (with the tide approximately 50 minutes later each day) until the 'spring' tide returns. Over and above this lunar rhythm is an annual rhythm: the spring tides become progressively higher as the equinoxes are approached on approximately 21 March and 21 September, as only then are the moon and sun in an exact straight line. It follows that the smallest spring tides are in mid-December and mid-June.

Because at spring tides the water comes high up the beach and also retreats a long way down it, this is the best time for collecting the natural life of the beach. The region between these two extremes, known as the foreshore, can be divided into a series of horizontal zones according to how often each is covered and uncovered during the cycle of tidal movements, each zone producing a distinct environment for different plants and animals. These are named as follows:

Upper shore: Uncovered except when tides exceed average range, this has little in variety of species but not necessarily in numbers.

The middle shore: Submerged twice a day by the sea and containing the greatest number of species in the greatest numbers.

The lower shore: Only uncovered when tides exceed their average range.

The sublittoral fringe: Never uncovered; certain seaweeds and marine life live only here.

Types of Shore

Shores are formed by the action of sea and weather on land. According to the rock it pounds against and the force with which it attacks it (east coasts, sheltered coves and estuaries receive less) the result may be rock, shingle, mud or a combination of any of these – rock can be surrounded by sand which may merge into mud.

Rocky shores: Most variable in character, depending on the type of rock. A rich source of molluscs, which occur in seaweed, under rocks, clinging to bare rock, in rock pools, crevices, within clay rock and clinging to pier piles.

Shingle beaches: The instability of pebbles means that no life, whether plant or animal, can survive.

Sand: There is more life on sheltered beaches than on exposed. Vertical zoning takes place here, for animals living in sand are able to move into it and through it – the wetter the sand the easier the passage.

Mud: The clogging effect of mud removes oxygen and prevents respiration at any depth, so most species live on or near the surface – the reason for the large numbers of birds feeding on a muddy shore.

Uses of Shells

Once a mollusc has been eaten its shell can be put to a variety of uses: scallop and whelk can be made into lamps, cups and dishes; oysters polished and used as substitute glass; the earshell used to frighten away birds; the mussel as a knife; all may be burnt for lime and used for surfacing roads.

Condition of Shellfish

Shellfish, though edible all the year round, are out of condition during their breeding season, the reason for the saw about only eating them when there is an R in the month. Most bivalves (those with shells in two halves) feed by pumping water through their shells and filtering out the food particles. Thus if they inhabit dirty water their food and/or they themselves will be polluted. To avoid poisoning do not collect molluscs close to human habitation or where refuse is pumped into the sea. Wash them well outside and in, in clean water. Make sure all specimens are alive before cooking and soak them in clean water for 12 hours so that they may clean themselves. Dead fish are more dangerous than dirty ones as they quickly decompose. A shellfish is alive if its shell when forced slightly open quickly closes once the pressure is released. If the shell is already open, or opens easily and does not shut again it is probably dead and should be discarded.

Edible Molluscs

Cockle (*Cardium edule*)*:* It is found on sand or sandy mud, middle to lower shore, above surface as the tide recedes but it quickly burrows down two or three inches. Abundant in certain areas. Dig with a blunt rake, handle carefully to prevent shells cracking, and take only those measuring more than one inch across. Clean and cook in boiling water for 5 minutes. Strain, remove meat from shells and eat plain, fried with bacon or as a pie.

Cockle pie

Butter a deep pie dish. Boil the cockles, remove the meat and put in a little milk. Strain the liquid and use to make a white sauce with butter, flour and a spoonful of anchovy essence, if available, and some nutmeg. Shake brown breadcrumbs into the pie dish, cover with dabs of butter, then put a layer of cockles on top. Pour over some of the thick white sauce, then another layer of crumbs, butter, cockles and white sauce until the dish is full. Cover with a thin layer of mashed potato and bake for half an hour. Serve with lemon juice.

Fan mussel or sea wing (*Linna fragilis*)*:* The largest British bivalve; occasional on lower sheltered or sandy mud shores, more frequent on bottom at moderate depths. Make into soup or fry.

Gapers: The sand gaper (*Mya arenia*) the American clam, from which clam chowder is made. It is found buried in sand or sandy mud, middle to lower shore. The blunt gaper (*Mya truncata*) is found in muddy gravel and sand from lower shore to littoral level. Clean, boil for 10 minutes, remove meat from shell and take off siphon of black skin and beard. Boil for a further half hour until tender and serve in a white sauce or baked in a pie as for cockles.

Limpet (*Pattela vulgata*)*:* The limpet lives on rocky shores, clinging to the rocks with a powerful sucker; larger species are said to be able to produce a resistance equivalent to the weight of 150 lb. Prise them off the rock with a knife, clean and soak, and boil for 5 minutes. Remove from the shells and cook for a further half hour using any mussel recipe. On the island of Herm, limpets were cooked by being covered with a heap of straw, which was set alight and allowed to burn for about 20 minutes before dinner.

Mussels (*Mytilus edulis*)*:* Middle shore and below; widely distributed on rocky, stony and muddy shores where there are stones for attachment, also on exposed rocks. They are eaten all over the world; in some places special mussel beds are made, either by putting stones between the tide marks or by suspending from wooden piles ropes to which the mussels can cling and grow, the larger the better. Pearls are sometimes found in *Mytilus edulis* but more often in the freshwater mussel (*Unio margaritiferus*). A distorted and deformed shell usually indicates that the mussel contains a pearl; also when 'she [the mussel] sits upright with her mouth in the mud, and her back is crooked'. Suetonius says that Caesar's main motive in coming to Britain was the pearls to be found there. Queen Victoria is said to have paid forty guineas for a Scottish freshwater mussel pearl.

Mussels pump about 10 gallons of water a day through themselves and are easily polluted by dirty water. Clean the shells and leave them to clean themselves in at least two changes of fresh water; make sure they are alive before cooking.

Moules marinière

This well-tried recipe, for which there are endless variations, really is the best way of cooking mussels.

Scrape and brush the shells until clean. For 3½ pints of mussels put a chopped medium-sized onion, finely chopped shallot, parsley stalks, thyme, bayleaf, pepper and 8 tablespoons white wine in a pan. Add the mussels and cover tightly. Put on a fast heat and at the end of two minutes shake the mussels. Do this two or three times more and at the end of 6 minutes the mussels should be cooked. Remove the top shell from each mussel; arrange in a deep dish, keep warm. Boil up the remaining liquor, add some chopped parsley and butter, strain over the mussels and serve.

Oysters (Osterea edulis): Not many uncultivated oysters will be found round English coasts today. Dense beds did occur naturally in creeks and estuaries, especially in the south-east and west of England, but overfishing and pollution have made them scarce. Today most oysters are cultivated in beds round Whitstable, Orford and Colchester, carefully guarded against their enemies, pollution, mud and seaweed. The best oysters are gathered between January and March, the shell prised open with a knife at the hinge and swallowed whole in their own juice or with perhaps a sprinkle of lemon juice. In the days when Sam Weller could remark that 'poverty and oysters always seem to go together' raw oysters were reserved for invalids, and the better off, if they ate them at all, cooked them in various ways. They were dipped in egg and bread-crumbs and fried, put in the traditional steak and oyster pie – the oysters placed on top of the meat just under the pastry – stuffed in fillet steak, and grilled or stewed. Make sure you do not overcook them, otherwise they will become tough.

Periwinkle (Littorina littorea): The largest of the winkle family, found on the middle shore and below, clinging to rocks and weed; very common. Cook by plunging in boiling salted water and simmering for about 10 minutes. Using a pin, 'winkle' out the meat, discarding the black head at the base of the shell. If you like, add pepper and dip in vinegar.

Scallop (Pecten maximus): Occasional specimens are found on the lower shore, but are common off-shore, especially on the south coast. Scallops are the badge of the pilgrim, derived from a legend attached to St James of Compostella. A scallop shell in a coat of arms – such as those of the Duke of Bedford or the Earl of Jersey – shows that someone in the family made the pilgrimage to the Holy Land, went on a long voyage, or had a great victory. Place them on top of the stove and they will open by themselves. Remove the black part and gristly fibre, leaving the red coral, considered a great delicacy, and white meat.

Baked scallops

Remove scallop completely from the shell. Scrub this and line with a layer of fresh breadcrumbs mixed with some parsley, chopped shallot, salt and pepper. Place scallop on top of this and cover with another layer of the breadcrumbs mixture. Pour on melted butter and lemon juice and bake in a moderate oven for 20–30 minutes according to size. Fried mushrooms may also be added.

Scallops can also be dipped in breadcrumbs and fried with bacon, or served in their shell covered with a cheese sauce and a sprinkling of breadcrumbs and baked in the oven.

Slugs: Often eaten by country people as a remedy for lung diseases. Like molluscs and snails they consist chiefly of albumen, which, when raw, is easily digested:

> I have known two gardeners who were in the constant habit of picking up and swallowing any small grey slugs they happened to see. One gave as his reason for so doing, that he thought his chest was weak; the other, that he liked them: both honest enough reasons. The poor might make most nutritious soup and palatable dishes from the common varieties of slug, which, left to themselves, do so much damage to farm and garden crops.[45]

Snails: All snails are edible but the larger varieties repay the work of preparing and cooking them with better dividends. *Helix pomata* is the largest British snail, said to have been introduced to Britain by the Romans expressly for eating and kept and fattened in special snail gardens surrounded by water to prevent escape. The wood snail (*Helix nemoralis*) and the garden snail (*Helix aspersa*) are smaller but just as edible. They used to be eaten as a cure for consumption and for weak chests – in Paris you bought snails from the herbalist, not the fishmonger.

All snails should be made to disgorge their last meal before cooking. Put them in a covered bucket of salt water and change it several times over a period of six hours. Fattening them for a week before eating is also a good idea. Put them in a covered tub or enclosed plot and give them herbs and oatmeal to eat and fresh water to drink. Large snails are best cooked by the traditional recipe for *escargots de Bourgogne*, small ones are better stewed.

Escargots de Bourgogne

Cover snails with water and bring to boil. Simmer for 20 minutes. Allow to cool in their liquid. Then remove the meat from the shells and keep in the broth. Clean and polish the shells. Chop some garlic, shallot and parsley, and mix together with salt, pepper and butter. Push a lump of the mixture into each shell, replace the snail, put another lump on top and smooth off. Put the shells in a fireproof dish, cover the base with water and bake for 5–10 minutes.

Stewed snails

Cover the snails with water, bring to the boil and simmer for 8 minutes, then plunge in cold water, remove from their shells, wash well and drain. Meanwhile put in an earthenware pan some diced streaky bacon, button onions, crushed garlic and red wine in proportion to the number of snails. Add the snails, some salt and pepper and herbs. Bring to boil and cook in the oven very slowly for 2 hours. When cooked they may be finished by adding some butter kneaded into flour and a liqueur glass of brandy.

Whelk (Nucella lapillus): Very common, being often found in association with mussels, especially in rock crevices. In season from August to September. Wash well. Make into soup or eat as cockles, or steam for 1 hour and serve in parsley sauce.

Crustacea

Crustacea are found on rugged rocky bottoms with deep crevices and seaweed.

Crab (Cancer pagurus): Widely distributed along the middle to lower shore, among rocks and under stones and in seaweed. Catch in pots or nets and only keep those over eight inches across and heavy. Bring to the boil as lobster. Boil, discard the innards, remove the flesh from the body, season with oil and lemon or vinegar, or mayonnaise, and serve in its shell. To eat hot, replace flesh in shell, sprinkle with breadcrumbs, dot with butter and bake for 15 minutes.

Crayfish (*Astacus pallipes*): A smaller, freshwater, relative of the lobster. Small ones are found in English rivers in limestone country. Catch in a baited pot. Boil for 10 minutes, and serve in a highly seasoned white wine sauce.

Lobster (*Homarus vulgaris*): Found mostly offshore among boulders and in crannies; widely distributed. Over-fishing has made them less common. Eat only large, heavy specimens, leaving the smaller ones to grow and breed. Catch in baited lobster pots, lowered on ropes to the bottom of the sea. To cook, put in cold water and bring slowly to the boil. Gradual heating desensitizes the lobster and it dies painlessly. Cook for 30 minutes after it has boiled. Split the body down the centre and remove the spinal cord before serving. Crack the claws with a hammer to extract the meat.

Prawns (*Leander seoratus*): Lives at the edge of the sea, especially in seaweed on a flood tide in August or September, along the south-west coasts. Locally common. Catch in nets or pots; cook as for shrimps, but remove the black filament before eating.

Shrimps (*Crangon vulgaris*): Shrimps are found on the lower shore, wherever there is sand, in pools and estuaries. Widely distributed and locally abundant. Catch with a net attached to a pole and scoop them out of the water; or use a baited net. Boil for 10 minutes, fry in oil or pot (see p. 130).

Lobster, crab and shrimp fishing

Using the same pot, baited with offal of fish, you can catch crabs on sand and lobsters on rocks near seaweed.

Shrimps: Shrimps can be caught in finer meshed lobster pots or by dropping a baited hoop netted like a tennis racket and let down by four strings to lie flat on the seabed. Leave for a while before picking it up. Shrimps may also be caught by lowering hand nets into pools where they are seen swimming about or with shrimp nets with a D-shaped rim pushed along sandy bottoms near rocks in low water. Any rocky crevice near to the surface of the sea may also contain prawns which can be driven out with a hook into a net held over the gap. Small pools can be baled out and the shrimps gathered from the bottom.

Other Sea Food

Cuttlefish (*Sepia officinalis*): Widely distributed, especially along the south coast. In sheltered bays or estuaries inshore, often occurring among eel grass. Boil, cut in pieces, season with onion and finally add some vinegar.

Octopus (*Octopus vulgaris*): English Channel, more common after mild winters. Sometimes found in pools or under rocks. Cut in pieces, fry and serve in sauce made from the black pouch, flavoured with garlic and herbs.

Sea-urchin (*Echinus esculentus*): Lower shore; common, particularly in spring. Boil as you would eggs and eat with bread. The flavour is said to resemble crab. Sometimes eaten raw, as are its roe, cut in quarters.

Nuts

Nuts are one of the most nutritious foods, rich in protein, carbohydrates, calories, vitamins and oil. They can be eaten whole, ground into flour, crushed into oil, added to any number of dishes for flavouring and preserve well. Though all nuts are edible, some, like the horse chestnut, are too bitter to eat without treatment and others, because of the damp British summer, seldom ripen enough to eat.

Acorn: The fruit of the oak; though the holm oak produces the sweetest variety, all acorns may be used as substitutes for almonds

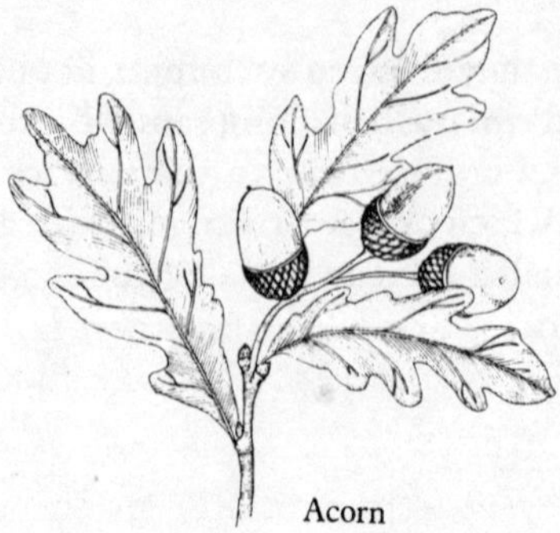

Acorn

or ground for use as flour or a non-caffeinated coffee (p. 182). Acorns should be collected in October, peeled, chopped and dried in the oven, then stored in airtight containers. Raw, untreated acorns are bitter in taste but there are several ways of improving them. Roast them in the oven to a light brown, then grind and roast again; or roast with the addition of some sugar. The Yosemite Indians of California grind them to a meal and make them into a kind of porridge with boiling water, then let them soak before boiling again for an hour. Others have buried them in the ground. Acorns were part of the diet of almost every ancient culture. Buried stores have been unearthed from Neolithic sites all over Europe. Pliny talks of the oak as the 'tree which first produced food for mortal man', though he was thinking of a southern variety which produces sweeter nuts.

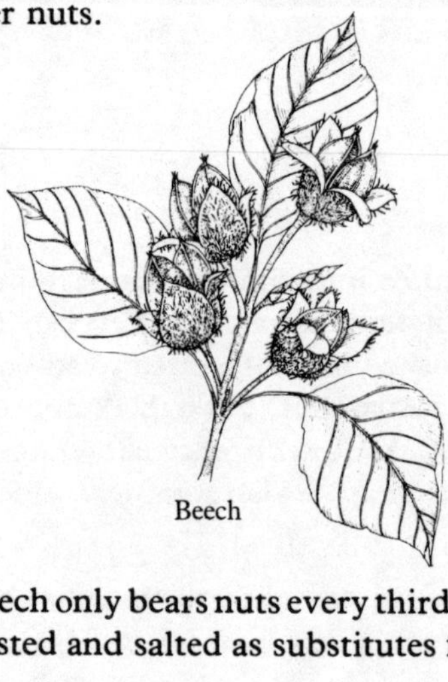

Beech

Beech: The beech only bears nuts every third or fourth year. They can be eaten roasted and salted as substitutes for almonds, ground into flour or crushed into oil – 10 lb. will yield 2 pints of oil. Collect the nuts in September and October and roast in an oven until the skin comes off, then rub between two cloths and shake in a coarse sieve to remove all the hairy down which can cause discomfort if eaten. When quite clean, dry in a cool oven, sprinkle lightly with salt and keep in crocks with well-fitting lids. Another way of treating them before eating is to soak, grind, and boil them in the same way as acorns.

Hazel: A tree said to be protected by the supernatural and yet powerful against its forces. Nut, twig and tree have all been attributed with magic powers since pagan times. In addition the nut has an excellent flavour and contains more protein, carbohydrate and fat than an egg. Hazel-nuts are relatively common, on trees over seven years old which have not been clipped too hard by a hedge-cutter or plundered by squirrels and birds. The nuts are usually brown and ready for picking by the end of September. They are best eaten fresh but will also store. To do this pick the nuts on a dry day, spread them on sacking in a dry place and turn occasionally until the husks fall away. Then pack them in bran, sand or sawdust in an airtight container.

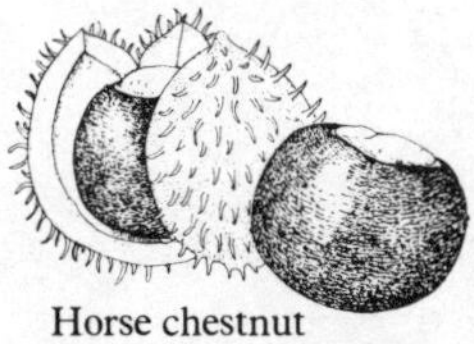
Horse chestnut

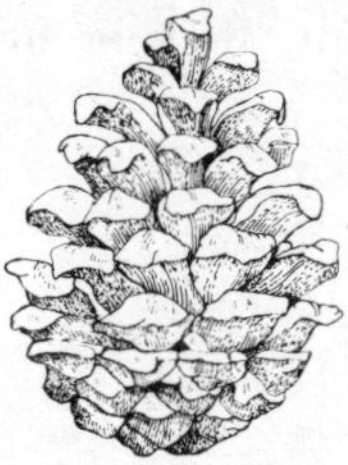
Pine

Horse chestnut: Conkers are not really edible because of their bitter taste. They do however have a high food content and can be made more palatable if ground and subjected to prolonged soaking and boiling. The fruit of a similar species has been eaten by American Indians and the inhabitants of the Himalayas.

Pine: The mature cones of pine trees are packed with seeds which are edible when separated from their husks. They were a delicacy for the ancient Greeks and Romans and are a common condiment in many parts of the world today.

Sweet chestnut

Sweet chestnut: Unfortunately, unless there is a warm spring enabling the tree to flower early and so give the nuts a long enough summer to mature properly, chestnuts do not often ripen in Britain. When they do they should be collected in October, dried and packed in crocks like walnuts. They contain more carbohydrates than any other nut and can be eaten raw, roasted, as a stuffing for game, ground into flour or simmered in sugar for *marrons glacés*.

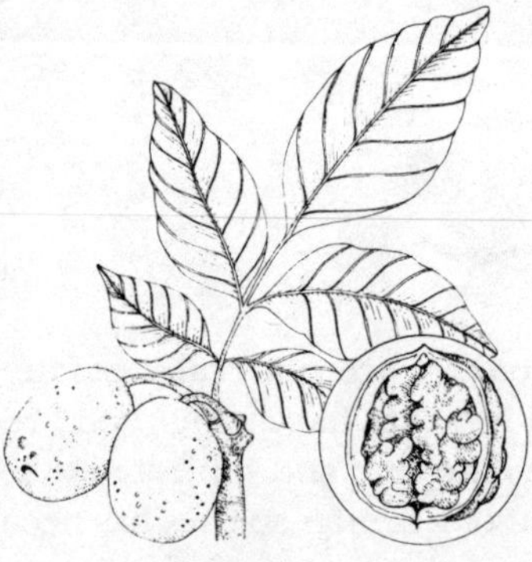

Walnut

Walnut: The tree was introduced into England in the fifteenth century but the nuts seldom ripen properly. However 'green walnuts' are a valuable source of vitamin C, containing even more than rose hips, and can be used for a nut liqueur, to make marmalade and for pickles. The unripe nuts were beaten down from the trees, a custom which probably gave rise to the old rhyme 'A dog, a wife and a walnut tree; the more you beat them the better they be.' Ripe nuts are generally ready by the end of September and should be collected as soon as they begin to fall, then spread in a dry place until the husks fall away. If they are to be stored, clean the shells well with brush and water to remove any traces of the husk which will otherwise grow mould. Spread out and dry again, then store in airtight containers alternating layers of nuts with layers of common salt and sand. Eat plain, grind into flour or crush to obtain oil. It was said that in the Golden Age men lived upon acorns and the gods on walnuts.

Nut Crackers

Nuts can be cracked by hitting them with a wooden mallet or stone or by pressure, applied with a lever or screw. Judging from early literature the hitting method came first; wooden nut bowls accompanied by their own wooden mallet or anvil were a refinement of this method. Levered nut crackers were probably the next development. John Evelyn in his *Sylva* says that boxwood is ideal for nut crackers, and the best old specimens are usually made from this wood, often in the form of elaborately carved heads with the jaws as the crackers. They were constructed with a back lever which passed through a cavity or mortise in the front lever, held together with a wooden or iron pivot pin. Most early examples have jaws only large enough to fit a hazel nut, reflecting the fact that larger foreign nuts did not arrive in quantity in Britain until the late sixteenth century. Screw nutcrackers require more ingenuity to carve; they consist of a wooden cup with a large wooden screw fitted into one side. The nut is cracked by building up pressure on its surface with the screw.

Preserving

No food which contains a high percentage of moisture will keep long in good condition unless special means are taken to preserve it. Dry foods, such as tea, cocoa, rice, barley and sago, keep almost indefinitely without deterioration, since they do not provide a suitable medium for the moulds, yeasts or bacteria which thrive and proliferate in moisture at a moderate temperature. In order, therefore, to preserve such foods as meat, fish, fruit, vegetables, eggs and milk it is necessary either to extract their moisture, or to subject them to such extremes of temperature as will destroy the bacteria which lead to their decay, or to add a substance, such as salt or sugar, which is inimical to bacterial growth.

Since deep freezes became part of every totally equipped kitchen other methods of home-preserving food for winter and out-of-season use are no longer essential. But not everyone has a deep freeze, some foods will not freeze, some taste better or different when smoked or pickled and some last longer done that way. During the voyage made from Ireland to Iceland in 1976/7 by Tim Severin in his leather boat the *Brendan*, he found that dried and smoked food lasted far longer than any of the modern packaged food he took.

Smoking

Most suitable for meat, game and fish. First, some form of smoke house must be constructed. A makeshift smoke house can be constructed as shown in the diagram opposite. The framework of sticks is covered with canvas or any other material available, smeared over with clay to make it smoke-tight. Bricks, stones or slate may be used for the fireplace. The draught is controlled by partly closing the outlet of the grate front. The smoke outlet should be large enough to insert the fish or meat yet capable, afterwards, of being closed to the smallest hole which will allow the fire to draw properly.

Smoking in the fireplace

Alternatively you can hang the bacon to smoke in any large chimney which has an open ungrated hearth: put a layer of straw on the

hearth, then a layer of wood shavings, a layer of sawdust, and a good handful of juniper berries; and over this put wet straw or litter to make the fire smoulder and give a lot of smoke.[33] The smoking must be repeated several times until the hams are quite dry.

Camp fire

If 2-in. strips of meat are hung over the smoke of a camp fire this will smoke them satisfactorily.

Fuel

In all smoking the fuel used is of the utmost importance, as it is this that gives the meat its distinctive flavour. Softwoods should never be used.

Oak lops or the extreme branches of that tree, such as charcoal is made from in the country places . . . Dried fern and short grass, the latter being pared off the heaths and short pastures, very thin, and well dried in the air. Beech and birch chips, or sycamore, are used with all fine goods. Peat of bog-earth must be procured on account of its preservative and deodorizing quality; it imparts a wonderfully mild and truly acceptable flavour mixed with other fuel.

Oak sawdust must be from the dry, old *heart* of oak trees; the outside slabs will not do, as being full of a sour sap. It is needless to say all these should be quite dry when taken into your stock, and kept so, for it is no good to have a damp fume in your chimney.[52]

Time and temperature

The average time taken for a large ham to smoke is 72 hours – 18 for a fish. The temperature of the smoke should always remain cool, 70–90°F, and for this reason the fire must never be lit directly under the meat.

Meat

The following recipes taken from J. R. London's inestimable book on the art and mystery of curing and preserving all forms of meat and game, though for specific joints, can be used for most large joints of the meat in question. If all the ingredients for the brine are not available this will impair only the taste, not the keeping quality, of the meat. The only ingredient which is essential is the salt, and this must be naturally evaporated sea-salt and never commercial free-running salt.

Hung beef – a Shropshire sirloin

Remove the superfluous suet of the underside and when hung a week in cold weather rub it well in every part with coarse sugar, 1 lb.; juniper berries bruised, 1 oz.; shallots minced, 1 oz.; ground pepper, 1 oz. Turn meat and continue the rubbing three days, when you may add rock or common salt, 1½ lb.; bay salt (see p. 146) pounded, 1 lb.; treacle, 1 lb.

Persist in this course four days longer, when it will be sufficient to turn it only every second day, and baste it with the liquid ten minutes each time. When it has thus laid fourteen more days, it may be taken up, wiped dry, and suspended in a quick current of air, and bound with broad tape so that it may be turned upside down occasionally, to prevent the juices settling in one part. When dried sufficiently, rub coarse oatmeal or bran, first well heated, all over the joint, and hang it in your chimney to be smoked, three days only with beech chips, 2 parts; peat, 2 parts; oak sawdust, 2 parts, which will impart scarcely any flavour of the smoke for observe it is 'hung beef'.[52]

Pickling ham

Bay salt 1 lb.; common salt, 1 lb.; moist sugar, 2 lb.; saltpetre, 4 oz.; sal-prunella (saltpetre can be substituted), 2 oz.; juniper berries, ¼ lb.; bay leaves, 3; thyme, sweet basil, marjoram, sweetbrier, tarragon, a sprig of each; a few whole peppercorns and allspice; 1 quart of the strongest ale.

Time: to salt and press 24 hours; in pickle a month.

Method:

1. The moment the hams are cut from the hog they are to be rubbed with common salt.
2. Then placed on a flat board, with another over them and two half-hundredweights placed on the upper board over each ham – under this pressure they must remain 24 hours.
3. They are then taken up and wiped ready for the pickle which must be prepared in readiness.
4. The ingredients for the pickle given above must be prepared as follows: Bruise the juniper berries in a mortar and put them in a pot with the ale, add all the other ingredients except the herbs, and boil for 20 minutes.
5. When this pickle is cool enough to bear the hands the herbs are thrown into the pickling pan.
6. The hams are placed immediately upon them and the whole of the hot pickle poured immediately upon them and well rubbed into them.

NB The brine is soon formed, and the hams are to be turned in it and basted with it every day for a month, when they must be taken out, dried, and smoked.

Welsh mutton hams

Take a couple of legs of prime Welsh mutton, rub them well with treacle made hot, and put them away in a deep pan until the next day.

Make a pickle of: 1 handful thyme, marjoram, bay leaves; 1 oz. saltpetre; 2 oz. black pepper; 2 lb. bay salt (see p. 146); 5 pints water boiled an hour and well skimmed, and when cold to be poured over the meat, and to be rubbed every day, and turned for 3 weeks. Then take them out of pickle, rub them well in all parts with strong vinegar for one hour, then wipe them dry, and hang them up in a current of air until well dry. Then give them a thorough coat of bran or of oatmeal, and smoke them with 2 parts oak sawdust and beech and 1 part peat and turfs or fern for 3 weeks or more. Store in beer barrels with pulverized charcoal and in 3 months they will be very good.[52]

Fish

All fish must be soaked in brine before smoking. A rough estimate of the correct amount of salt to water is arrived at by putting a potato in enough tepid water to cover the fish, then adding rock salt until the potato floats.

Prepare the fish by splitting it from head to tail down the belly. Remove head and tail, guts, gills and, with a large fish, the backbone except for about three inches at the base. Put in pickling brine and leave for twenty-four hours, then remove, wipe dry and fix a stick across its widest part, tie it in place with cord to prevent the fish folding up while smoking. Leave to dry for a day or two, then smoke.

Drying

The process of drying probably began in the Middle East from seeing the effect of wind and sun on fruit and vegetables. This is still the method used in hot climates. However in more northerly climes a lack of sun has to be made up for by using an oven. First prepare the produce. Slice large apples and pears in rings $\frac{1}{4}$-in. thick, submerge them in salt water for 5 minutes to help them keep their colour. Leave small fruit whole. Spread them on trays to allow for a free circulation of air and put them in a very cool oven, slowly raising the temperature to 120°F. Apple rings take about five hours to dry, mushrooms less and fleshy plums much longer. Test by squeezing a piece between your fingers; if there is no sign of moisture the produce is dry. Leave to stand at room temperature for twelve hours then pack between layers of greaseproof paper in wooden or cardboard boxes. Store in a dry place. Soak in water for twenty-four to forty-eight hours before cooking them as though they were fresh. Mushrooms can also be dried by threading them on string with knots in between each mushroom and hanging in a warm kitchen.

Meat: cut in thin slices half an inch thick and dry until hard and leathery. It will keep indefinitely and is good for emergencies. Some people soak the slices in brine first.

Herbs hung in bunches by their stalks in an airy room dry easily and retain their flavour which, in some cases, is intensified.

Eggs dried in a gentle heat and then pounded, keep well.

Salting

The use of salt as a preservative dates back to Neolithic times and is usually confined to meat and fish. Few vegetables, except beans and cabbage, salt well, probably due to the cellular structure and chemistry of the tissues.

Vegetables

Put young fresh vegetables in layers in a container with 3 lb. vegetables to every 1 lb. salt. Pack tightly to exclude the air and cover well. Wash free of salt before eating.

Fish

Take a freshly caught fish, remove dead gills, innards and bones. Scale or fillet the fish, then put in brine made from 1½ lb. salt to 8 pints water for 20 minutes. Drain well, then put on a wooden rack and cover fish with 1 part salt to 4 parts fish. Place a wooden board and weight over the fish and leave it to dry in a cool, airy place for a week or until all the brine has drained away. Hang in a larder until completely dry. Wrap in waxed paper and store in a cool place in wooden boxes.

Fish roe: Can be salted by preparing 'long narrow bags of strong linen and a strong brine. The bags are half filled with the roe, and then quite filled with the brine which is allowed to come through slowly. This being done the men wring the bags strongly with their hands, and the roe is allowed to dry.'[19]

Meat

Pork

2 lb. salt; ½ lb. sugar; ½ oz. saltpetre; 10 pints water.

Put the fresh joint in an earthenware jar with a glazed lining. Cover with the above ingredients. Cover with a plate and weight it to keep the meat submerged. Leave in a cold place. After 7 days take the meat from the brine, stir the brine well, return the meat. Then, allowing 4 days for each pound of meat, continue this process.

Beef, lamb, mutton

Salt; 8 pints water; 1 lb. sugar; ½ oz. bicarbonate of soda; 1 oz. saltpetre.

Place a layer of salt in the bottom of a crock, then layers of meat well rubbed with salt and another layer of salt on top of them. Cover and leave for 24 hours. Then cover with the water, sugar, bicarbonate of soda and saltpetre. Place a weighted plate on top to keep the meat submerged, cover firmly and store in a cold place for 4–6 weeks. The meat is then cured and may be stored in the brine in a cold place.

Potting

Potted meat and fish, while not keeping indefinitely, will, if well covered with fat and stored in a cool larder, keep for a good length of time. Use clarified butter, prepared as on p. 38.

Shrimps, lobsters, crabs

Boil fish and remove from shell. Spread on clean dishes and evaporate moisture in a cool oven so that no two flakes stick together. Season according to taste with mace, cloves, salt, sugar, pepper. Press into pots and dry again in a cool oven. Cover well with clarified butter and paper over.

Potted trout

Scale trout of 1–1½ lb., cut off heads, tails and fins, open the belly and wipe clean. Scatter good moist sugar over the insides, and bring the sides together. Pack backs downwards side by side and leave until the next day. Then mix 1 oz. bay leaves; nutmeg; ½ oz. mace; 2 oz. white pepper; 6 oz. table salt.

Season fish plentifully inside and out and lay them flat in a dish, cover with a coarse meal crust and bake them in a slow oven. Pour off gravy while still warm and leave fish until the next day. Then cut into pieces, fill pots and pour clarified butter over. Cover well, and if they are to be kept for long have the butter at least half an inch thick above the fish. Next day, if all seem firm and safe, paste writing paper over and put away in a cool airy room.

Potted eel

Remove skins, heads, tails and fins, and open at the belly from the head down to the tail end. Clean, wash in salt water and dry. Dust flour over and then for 10 lb. eel prepare a pickle of: 1½ oz. bay leaves (shredded); 2 oz. marjoram; 1 oz. thyme; 1½ lb. bay salt; ½ lb. coarse sugar; ½ pint beer. Lay fish in a deep dish cut up with alternate layers of seasonings, cover and leave for 24 hours, longer if thick. When all are pickled wash with salt water and dry. Dusting with flour, fry in boiling oil until a nice brown, put them to drain and cool. Next day lay in pots and cover with clarified butter.

Potted game

Pluck and draw birds. Cut open at the backbone, wipe clean and wash in salt water. Season well with 1 oz. nutmeg, cloves, bay leaves, pepper and 6 oz. salt rubbed well into the backbone. Leave for a week, turning daily. Put in pots, place a lump of butter inside, cover with paper and bake slowly until cooked. While still warm pour off any gravy and when cool remove any butter and add to the clarified butter. When cold cover the birds with clarified butter to a depth of half an inch.

Potted hare

Hang for 14 days, then stuff with ½ lb. butter, 1 lb. grated bread, ½ oz. thyme, marjoram and ¾ oz. lemon thyme. Bake until cooked. When cold separate the meat from the bones and pound with clarified butter, mace and other spices as desired, plus some red currant jelly and port. Fill pots and top with clarified butter.

Dry Storing

Carefully stored root vegetables and fruit should see you through the winter until the new spring growth is ready.

Fruit

Only the larger, harder types such as apples and pears are suitable for dry storing. Arrange (sound specimens only) on wooden racks in an airy shed or loft, making sure that none touch. This ensures that any fruit which rots does not transmit the fungus and is easily removed.

Vegetables

Root vegetables, cut with one inch of stem, should be packed in boxes between layers of moist sand, which must be kept moist. Store them in a cellar; or alternatively pile them outside. The best method for potatoes is to pile them in a long heap on a layer of straw, and cover to a depth of at least a foot with more straw or bracken, well patted down. Some put earth over the straw.

Pickling

Another ancient way of preserving fruit, flowers, vegetables and eggs. Food boiled in vinegar is completely sterilized and will keep indefinitely.

Eggs

Hard-boil fresh eggs, shell and put in a jar. For 12 eggs boil 2 pints vinegar (either wine or cider) with 2 tablespoons mixed spice for 5 minutes. Pour over the eggs and close the jar. Leave for a couple of weeks before eating.

Fruit

A general recipe is to stew fruit in a mixture of 1 lb. sugar to 1 pint vinegar and spices, such as cloves, allspice, cinnamon and lemon, until tender. Then fill warm jars with the fruit and boil the syrup again, adding more sugar if desired, until it is reduced by a half. Pour over the fruit, make sure there are no air bubbles, and cover well.

Vegetables

Cover the vegetables with a brine made from 1 gallon water to 1 lb. salt, simmer until almost cooked and leave to cool. After 24 hours, drain, pack the vegetables into jars and fill up with boiling hot spiced vinegar. Cover well.

Wild plants

Ash keys: Picked before August. Boil the keys until soft, re-boiling with fresh water if they taste bitter. Drain the keys and cover with boiled white vinegar.

Elder buds: 'Put the buds into vinegar, seasoned with salt, whole pepper, large mace, lemon peel cut small, let them have two or three warms over the fire; then take them out, and let the buds and the pickle both cool, then put the buds into your pot and cover them with the pickle.'[53]

Samphire: Wash and drain samphire well, and pack in a jar with peppercorns. Boil 1 pint cider vinegar with 1 oz. salt for 10 minutes, pour over samphire and put in a warm oven for 1 hour.

Other wild plants often pickled by country people were cowslip flowers (now rare), broom, hawthorn, parsley piert, purslane, rest-harrow, sea sandwort, stonecrop, traveller's joy, vetchling, sycamore keys and walnuts.

Preserving in Syrup

The harder fruits, such as plums and berries, preserve best; they should be ripe without being soft. Steep the fruit, which, if large, should be first pricked with a needle, in sugar or honey. Then cook, pack in jars, completely cover with syrup, add any extra flavouring such as brandy and seal the jars with caps or corks dipped in wax.

Preserved plums

Put fruit in a pan and just cover with water. Simmer for 10 minutes. Drain fruit, conserving the juice and for every pound of fruit strew it with 8 oz. sugar. Dissolve another 8 oz. in the juice and boil for 10 minutes. Leave overnight. Next day add fruit to syrup and simmer for 30 minutes. Pack fruit in jars and simmer juice for another 30 minutes. Pour over fruit and cover well.

Preserved berries

Prick fruit with a needle. To every pound of fruit allow 1½ lb. sugar and strew half of this over the fruit. Leave for a day. Put the rest of the sugar in a pan and add ¼ pint water or juice, stir until dissolved and boil for 10–15 minutes. Add the berries with their sugar and simmer for 5 minutes. Remove the berries and put in jars. Boil syrup again and when cooled pour over fruit. Cover well.

Bottling

Another way of preserving fruit. Special bottles are generally used, though it is claimed that ordinary jam jars can be used if hot mutton fat is poured on top of the contents, which are then covered closely with bladder or parchment papers.

To sterilize fruit, pack the bottles closely with sound, well-graded specimens which have been well washed. Be careful not to bruise the fruit in the process – a silver or wooden spoon is the best utensil to use. Fill the bottles nearly to the top, either with cold water or with syrup made by dissolving 1 lb. of loaf sugar in 1 quart of water, then stand them in a fish kettle or other large vessel such as a clothes' boiler. Protect the bottles from the heat beneath by thick layers of paper or slats of wood. Pour cold water into the boiler till it reaches the necks of the bottles, then bring it *very* slowly to simmering point, and simmer until the fruit is cooked – in about 10 minutes in the case of small berries, 15–20 minutes in the case of gooseberries, and as much as 25 minutes for large plums.[54]

Jam

Originating from the medieval 'marmalade' (a solid fruit preserve eaten as a sweet) and from fruit preserved in syrup, jam first appears in recipe books under its own name in the eighteenth century; by the nineteenth it was being made in enormous quantities to be eaten with bread and used as a sauce for puddings.

For successful jam it is necessary to have sugar, pectin and acid in the correct quantities. Sugar as a preservative, pectin and acid to bring out the flavour and provide the set. Fruits vary in their pectin content: apples, gooseberries, and black currants are all high in pectin; raspberries and plums medium; and strawberries, blackberries, haws, rowanberries are low. Fruits low in pectin need to have it added, in the form either of lemon juice or of fruit or fruit juice high in pectin.

To make jam, first simmer the fruit (with a little water if it is a hard fruit) until soft. Then add sugar, stir until dissolved, bring to the boil again and boil until setting point is reached. To judge this, put a small quantity of the jam on the side of a plate. It should solidify as it cools and wrinkle if you push your finger through. Remove from the heat, take off any scum, pour into hot sterilized jars, cover with waxed paper and store in the larder.

Some guide lines to the proportions are:

Blackberry: ¾ lb. sugar to 1 lb. fruit.
Apple: 1 lb. sugar to 1 lb. fruit and ½ lemon.
Black currant: ¾ lb. sugar to 1 lb. fruit.
Raspberry: Scant 1 lb. sugar to every 1 lb. fruit.
Strawberry: 1 lb. sugar to 1 lb. fruit and the juice of two lemons.

Other wild fruits suitable for jam making are bilberry, bullace, calamint, cherry, cloudberry, crab apple, and the roots of elecampagne and sea holly.

Jelly

Popular from the sixteenth century on, jellies are usually eaten as an accompaniment to meat and are a way of using fruit whose flavour is good but whose consistency makes them difficult to eat in other ways. As with jam, acid and pectin must be present in the correct quantities.

Cook the fruit slowly with any water and lemon until tender. This stage is very important in order to release all the pectin and acid from the fruit. Then strain off the juice through a flannel, or double muslin, suspended over a bowl. Measure the juice, return to the pan and bring to the boil. Then for every 1 pint of juice add 1 lb. sugar and stir until dissolved. Boil until setting point is reached, remove scum and bottle.

Some general quantities are:

Rowan: 1 lb. rowan, ½ lb. crab apple, 1 lb. sugar, water.

Black currant: 2 lb. fruit, 1 pint water, 1 lb. sugar.

Sloe: 1 lb. fruit, 1 lb. apple, 1 lb. sugar, water.

Blackberries: 4 lb. blackberries, ½ pint water, 1 lb. sugar, juice of 2 lemons (optional).

Haws: 2 lb. haws, 2 lb. crab apples, juice of 1 lemon, water, 1 lb. sugar.

Rose hips: 1 lb. hips, 2 lb. crab apples, 1 pint water, 1 lb. sugar, juice of 1 lemon.

For further recipes see Sauces, p. 147.

Herb jellies

These are apple jellies to which herbs are added. The following is a recipe for mint jelly – thyme or other herbs can be used instead.

Mint jelly

Wash 2 lb. green apples or crab apples and cut into quarters. Put in a pan with the juice of half a lemon, enough water to cover and a few sprigs of mint. Simmer till soft and pulpy. Strain through a jelly bag and leave to drain overnight. Add 1 lb. sugar to each 1 pint juice and reheat, slowly stirring until the sugar is dissolved. Boil rapidly for 5 minutes, add a bunch of finely chopped mint and boil until setting point is reached.

Puddings and Desserts

Puddings are eaten much less frequently than they used to be. Leading generally more sedentary lives in warmer houses we are unable to assimilate the sugar, carbohydrates and fat that are the main ingredients in most puddings. Our forebears were more active, and expected at least one pudding with every meal; in wealthy houses there would have been a selection. Originally puddings formed part of the second or third course and were served with the meat, but by the nineteenth century they had evolved into a course on their own.

Bread puddings

Apple charlotte

Probably medieval in origin, but some think 'charlotte' a misspelling of the Hebrew 'schlath' meaning sweet spiced purée, which would make the dish even older.

Stew 1 lb. apples with 6 oz. sugar and, if you like, some lemon rind and a knob of butter, until pulpy. Line bottom and sides of a pie dish with thin slices of bread buttered on the outside. Put in apple and cover with more buttered bread. Sprinkle with sugar and bake for 20 minutes in a hot oven until brown and crisp.

Summer pudding

The apogee of bread puddings, made traditionally with 1 lb. raspberries to ¼ lb. red currants and about ¼ lb. sugar, though others put in black currants and sometimes strawberries too, stewed gently for 2–3 minutes. Line a bowl with slices of day-old white bread with the crusts removed. Fill up with fruit, reserving some of the juice. Cover with another layer of bread and a saucer which fits the top of the bowl exactly and on which you place a 2–3 lb. weight. Leave overnight in the larder. Serve by turning out the pudding on a dish, covering with the reserved juice and eating with cream.

Tansy pudding

Traditionally eaten at Easter. Tansy's other name is 'ginger' from the spicy flavour of its leaves.

Boil ½ pint milk and pour over 3 oz. white breadcrumbs. Leave for half an hour. Beat 2 eggs, add to 1 oz. sugar and a dessertspoon finely chopped tansy leaves. Mix with the breadcrumbs and add ½ oz. butter. Bake in a pie dish in a moderate oven until set. Eat cold with sugar and cream.

Welsh blackberry and bread pudding

Put some blackberries to simmer with just enough water to cover them and throw in torn pieces of bread until most of the liquid is absorbed. Sweeten with sugar, and when the fruit is soft, put into a bowl and allow to cool. Serve with thick cream.

Custard

Custards flavoured with the flowers of elder, meadowsweet, cowslip and acacia were frequently eaten.

Put a few heads of meadowsweet or any other flower in ½ pint milk and bring slowly to the boil. Beat 1 whole egg with 1 yolk of egg and 1 tablespoon sugar and on to this strain the milk, stirring well. Put in a baking dish and stand this in a pan filled with boiling water and bake in a moderate oven for 12–20 minutes or until set.

Fritters

The flowers of elder and acacia and the leaves of comfrey if dipped in batter and then fried in butter make excellent fritters.

Fool

Stew hard fruit with sugar to sweeten and with enough water to prevent it sticking to the bottom of the pan. Sieve, then fold in thick whipped cream. Chill and serve. Soft fruit such as raspberries should be just slightly mashed with sugar before folding into cream and perhaps some brandy.

Fruit tart

All stewed berries can be enclosed in pastry and cooked as a tart. Blackberries are especially good when mixed with apple. Rose-hip tart was a popular dish.

To make a tart of hips

Take hips, cut them and take out the seeds, then wash them and season them with sugar, cinnamon and ginger, close the tart, bake it, sprinkle sugar over and serve.

Frumenty

Very traditional, eaten on its own or accompanying venison or other meat. Recipes vary with the locality and some use wheat and barley instead of oats but the principle remains the same.

Steep three large handfuls of fine oatmeal in cold water for 24 hours. Add the same amount of water again and stand for a further 24 hours. Strain through a fine sieve and add a large spoonful of white sugar and some orange juice, boil until thick, stirring all the time. Serve with wine or honey, cream and sugar. Elder flowers or wild rose leaves may also be used as flavouring.

Junket

Plain junkets are made by warming to blood heat 1 pint of milk with sugar, then adding 2–3 teaspoons of rennet, sprinkling with nutmeg and leaving to set in a warm place.

A more elaborate junket:

Stir 1 dessertspoon of caster sugar into 1 tablespoon of brandy or rum until it is dissolved. Warm 1 pint milk to blood heat, add two bay leaves or a vanilla pod, or a little zest of lemon. Pour the milk on to the sugared brandy, add a good teaspoon of rennet and leave it to set. When it has set run cream flavoured with white wine over the top or powder it with nutmeg or cinnamon.

Porridge

Another form of pudding.

Fill a thick saucepan a third full of water and bring to a fast boil 'bubbling fast as galloping', add salt, then sprinkle the oatmeal 'very lightly down on to the bubbling boiling water, so that every grain falls separately into the boiling water, is instantly sealed up, and so stays crisp, and no grain ever softens to slime'.[27] Stir all the time, and continue to stir vigorously until the porridge thickens. Put on the lid and leave for 20 minutes; the porridge will then be ready. Serve with milk and honey or brown sugar, or as the Scots do, with salt.

Stewed fruit

Fruit which grows wild, and which can be picked, stewed with a little water and sugar or honey, then served with cream or cream cheese are: apple, barberry, blackberry, black and red currants, bullace, gean or wild cherry, cloudberries once they have turned orange, cranberries, gooseberries and the berries of the wayfaring tree.

Syllabub

'During dinner there were French horns and clarionets in the cloister, and after coffee I treated them to a syllabub, milked under the cows, that were brought to the brow of the terrace.'[55] Horace Walpole is describing how he entertained French and Spanish royalty at Strawberry Hill in June 1764. This was one of the ways that syllabub used to be made, though there were numerous others. Here are one modern and two old recipes.

Syllabub

Whip together ¼ pint cream, the juice and rind of one lemon, 4 tablespoons sugar and ¼ pint dry white wine or sherry until thick, but watch as it thickens that it does not go to butter. Chill and serve.

To make a plain syllabub

Take a pint of Verjuyce* in a bowl; milk the Cow to the Verjuyce; take off the Curd; and take sweet cream and beat them together with a little Sack and Sugar; put it into your Syllabub pot; then strew Sugar on it, and so send it to the Table.[6]

To make a whip syllabub

Take the whites of two eggs, and a pint of cream, six spoonfuls of Sack, as much Sugar as will sweeten it; then take a Birchen rod and whip it; as it riseth with froth, skim it, and put it into the Syllabub pot; so continue with whipping and skimming, till your Syllabub pot be full.[6]

* See p. 169.

Rennet

True rennet comes from enzymes in the fourth stomach of a freshly killed young suckling calf. This stomach or 'vell', as it is called in the trade, is then well cleaned with a cloth, but not washed, sprinkled with dry salt and left for a couple of days. Then a salt brine of 2 pints water for every vell is prepared and boiled and cooled; the vell, cut in strips, is then put in and left to soak for five days. The strips are squeezed three times a day to extract the rennet. At the end of this time the brine, which has now become rennet, is strained off and stored in bottles in a cool dark place.

If there is no suckling calf to kill, or no butcher prepared to supply you with the right stomach, you can buy rennet, but it will be about eight times as strong. Alternatively certain plants will act as a rennet or curdling agent. Lady's bedstraw was in general use in many districts up to the end of the eighteenth century and, according to Gerard, 'The people in Cheshire especially Nantwich, where the best cheese is made, do use it in their rennet, esteeming greatly of that cheese above other made without it.' The juice was sometimes mixed with nettle juice, which will also act as a rennet on its own. Nettle rennet is made by boiling the plants in a strong brine and using the juice. Sorrel is another leaf which was used, especially in Lapland. The juice is expressed from the leaves by melting them over a little heat; it is then added to the milk.

Reptiles and Amphibians

Of these we find that many are eaten with eagerness all over the world, and neither want of beauty nor abundance of venom protect them against omnivorous man. In vain they assume all manner of ugly shapes; in vain they move, creeping and hopping and sliding, although they suggest to us by form and motion all that is false and unfair, hideous and horrid; even God's curse of the serpent does not shield it; and from the humble frog of the pond to the colossal crocodile of Egypt, they are all so much food for their master.[8]

The choice in Britain is extremely limited.

Frogs: Though several varieties of frogs are eaten the most esteemed is the green frog (*Rana esculenta*). This was introduced into southern England in the nineteenth century, and small colonies still exist. It is not to be mistaken with the marsh frog which is also green but larger. The common frog is brown and is not known to have been eaten but then it is not known to be poisonous either. As Elizabeth David says: 'It is odd that frogs' legs, which are such delicate little morsels that surely even the most fastidious could not object to them, should inspire such horror in England. Only the green frogs with black markings are considered edible, and the back legs are the only parts ever served.'[56]

In 1977 it was reported that in France frogs' legs are now almost anything but French, a dearth in that country having led to large-scale importations from India, while the importation of Irish frogs' legs has been going on for years. In Britain even the common frog, introduced here by the Normans, is now on the wane. Drainage of the ponds and swamps where it breeds, and the encroachment of human population on the dry land where it spends the rest of the year are to blame. Frogs are considered prime eating when between two and five years of age and the season extends from March to November. They are in best condition in the early autumn but are most easily caught in spring.

> They are taken sometimes by beating them with long poles as they sit on the banks of the streams and ponds. The extreme voracity of the frog is easily taken advantage of, as it will leap after and seize almost anything that floats on the waters near the banks, having the appearance of life, and in action. A hook and line, baited with an insect, or covered with a piece of red flannel, serves as a good tempter to the frog, who will generally seize it without hesitation or difficulty. After being caught, they are preserved in large frog ponds, or froggeries, as they are called, until they are required for the market.'[8]

Before cooking they must be killed and skinned. Put into salt water to stun them, the head is then chopped off and the skin drawn back over the body and down to the feet, which are also chopped off and discarded. As a rule only the hindquarters of the frog are eaten. White and tender, nutritious and of delicate flavour, they are cooked in all manner of ways but usually simply floured and fried in butter. Some people like to blanch the legs first and cook them in a sauce made with white wine, parsley, garlic and lemon juice, or in a *sauce poulette*, a bechamel sauce with lemon and egg yolks added.

Lizards: British lizards cannot really compete as food with their larger, foreign relations and, as they are becoming rare owing to the destruction of their habitat, should not be killed.

Salad Plants

Leaves which can be eaten raw are often also good cooked. But many, like the dandelion, do not cook well, and others such as wood sorrel and hedge garlic are too pungent to make into a salad on their own. These are best added to other leaves to vary the taste and, where there is no dressing available, to act as a kind of substitute. Some leaves, alexanders, chicory and dandelion for instance, become very bitter as they age. To overcome this you can either earth up the growing plant, as you would celery, or put a pot over it, as you would rhubarb, so that they grow in the dark; both have a blanching and sweetening effect.

For a constant supply of winter salad dig up the roots of chicory or dandelion in October, cut off the leaves and leave the roots exposed for fourteen days. Then plant them in deep covered boxes, allowing eight inches of growing space, or put them in earth in an uncovered box in a cupboard or under the kitchen table. Cut the leaves for eating as they grow.

Young leaves are always the best for salads: in a clump the inner leaves will be tenderest and on a stalk the top, newly developed ones. The following are some common wild salad plants:

Alexanders: Brought here by the Romans; the leaves may be eaten but the older stalks are best earthed up.

Beech: The young leaves make a good spring salad.

Burnet saxifrage: There is an Italian proverb which says that 'the salad is neither good nor good-looking when there is no pimpernel' – meaning burnet saxifrage, whose Latin name is *Pimpinella saxifraga.*

Chervil: More useful as a salad flavouring than by itself.

Chicory: Locally common; the young leaves may be eaten straight but the older ones are better blanched.

Dame's violet: Another spicy leaf to be used as a dressing.

Dandelion: Young leaves in spring or, if blanched as described, the older leaves too.

Fennel: An anise-flavoured dressing leaf.

Hairy rock cress: It has a peppery taste like lady's smock; adds bite to salads.

Hawthorn: The tiny leaf buds make a nutty-flavoured salad.

Hedge mustard: One of the first leaves to appear in spring; a crisp, garlicky-tasting leaf best added to others in a salad.

Lamb's lettuce or corn salad: Cultivated in France and called salad Peter as it is eaten in Lent. Has a most subtle and delicate flavour.

Lime: The young leaves are refreshing and succulent.

Oyster plant: The leaves have a consistency of watercress and taste like oysters.

Parsley piert: Culpeper said of it 'it is a very good salad herb'.

Ransoms: The leaves make a good substitute for chives, which are rare in the wild.

Scurvey grass: Bitter tasting but high in vitamin C; it often formed part of sailors' rations as a prevention against scurvey – hence the name.

Sorrel: Lemon-like acid taste, acts as a substitute for lemon dressing in salads.

Stonecrop: Said to be tasty when young.

Valerian: Another plant eaten by the French.

Watercress: Abundant, but since the plant contains a high proportion of water, it is essential that the water it grows in is absolutely clean, otherwise it can be polluted.

Wild celery: Spindly compared to the cultivated kind, and tasting almost too strongly of celery. Earth up if possible.

Wild radish: A widespread weed related to the cultivated radish. The whitish tap root is almost too strong for eating by itself and is best used as you would horse-radish (see p. 149).

Wood sorrel: Acid in taste; a surfeit is said to have killed cows. Best used as flavouring.

Yarrow: Coarse-textured, aromatic, but a good salad plant.

Salt

It is not known when man first started eating salt – there is evidence of Neolithic salt-mining at Lower Halstow in Kent and Heacham in Norfolk. It is thought that originally people ate salt because they liked the taste and only later discovered its powers of preservation. Salt became an emblem of good faith and honour in many countries: we say 'True to his salt' and Arabs place any person who has eaten of their salt under special protection, saying 'There is salt between us.' In feudal England when barons, villeins and serfs all ate together at one long table a large salt cellar was placed in the middle and sitting above or below the salt marked your social position.

There are three ways of obtaining salt from natural resources: separating it from sea water, mining it from rocks and extracting it from plants with a high alkali content. If you are near the sea, the first is much the easiest.

Sea-salt

All sea water is salt. Rain leaches salt from the earth and rocks before it drains down into the sea. Altogether fifty known chemicals have been identified by chemists in sea salt, of which five predominate; sodium chloride 2·60 per cent, magnesium chloride 0·31 per cent, magnesium sulphate 0·22 per cent, calcium sulphate 0·12 per cent, potassium chloride 0·07 per cent. Southern seas are more salt than those of the north, due to the higher rate of evaporation. The ocean round Britain contains about thirty parts salt to 1,000 water; the Dead Sea, the most salt of all, has 11,600,000,000 tons.

The simplest way of making sea-salt is to boil sea water in a shallow pan until all the water has evaporated and only the salt remains. First strain the water through a muslin to filter out any sand or foreign bodies, and watch at the end, when the water has almost all evaporated, to see that the salt does not burn. Finish drying by spreading the salt out on a baking tray and leaving it in a warm place or cool oven. Store in an airtight container.

Bay salt is made by evaporating the water naturally. It is called after Bourgneuf Bay at the mouth of the Loire in France which, by the Middle Ages, was so famous for its salt that the name became abbreviated to bay salt. In Europe most is now produced on the Mediterranean coast. In India they evaporate the water by dribbling it through a series of shallow, clay-lined pools, one leading into the other down a series of steps. A similar method is followed in this country, except that since four months of reasonably dry weather is required to make bay salt, the salt is only made in the summer and the final evaporation is normally done by boiling. Estuaries and backwaters, though less salt, are usually chosen for salt gardens because of their sheltered positions and clay sites. Maldon, in Essex, has been making salt since the Middle Ages and St Augustine spoke of the excellence of the salt at Hayling near Portsmouth.

Rock Salt

At times the sea has come in and covered the land, subsequently receding, or becoming encircled by new land thrown up by earthquakes or volcanoes. Thus inland seas were formed, from which the water gradually evaporated, leaving a layer of salt. Depending on the time of the invasion this salt can be found either on the surface, as in the Great Salt Desert in Utah, USA, or laid down as a layer in the sedimentary rock system. When the salt is still on the surface collection is obviously no problem. However when, as happens in Britain, it is below the surface, holes must be sunk to the salt layer and the salt either dug out or water applied under pressure to dissolve it from the rock. The water is then evaporated by boiling, as for sea-salt.

Sometimes springs rising through the salt layer dissolve the salt and bring it up with them. Brine springs can be found near Keswick in Northumberland, and in the Weaver valley. Here people collect the brine by sinking shafts near the bank of the Weaver and the Wheelock. At Birtley in Durham salt springs occur in the coal formation. Rock salt is of different composition from sea-salt. In England the greatest salt-mines are in the new red sandstone in Cheshire and in the slate rocks of Cumberland. John Leyland recorded that during Henry VIII's reign there were 360 furnaces working at Droitwich, boiling the brine collected from pits dug in the ground, into which the brine had soaked. Salt in a place name, such as Saltford or Salter's Hill, usually indicates an association with a route or place used by salters or salt merchants.

Plant Salt

The extraction of salt from plants is mentioned by the early classical writers and is still practised by certain aboriginal tribes today. The salt is procured from the ash of those plants which have a saline or soapy feel when wet rather than an alkaline taste. The ash is put in a pot and hot water poured on, standing until it has dissolved the salts. This 'lye' is then put in another pot and heated to evaporate the water until only the salt remains.

Sauces

The following are sauces to accompany meat and fish which can be made from the wild.

Berry sauces

These are made with berries which are too tart to eat raw, but which, when cooked and made into a sauce, are an excellent accompaniment to roast meat and game, providing an alternative to the usual red currant jelly.

Cranberry sauce

The berries make an excellent sauce for game, turkey and chicken. Owing to the drainage of bogland wild cranberries are increasingly hard to find. Put 1 pint cranberries with 1 cup of water in a saucepan, cover and simmer until the cranberries have burst open. Remove the lid, add 1 cup of sugar, and simmer gently for 20 minutes without stirring. Crowberries may be used in the same way but will be even harder to find. They are local to the north and west of Britain and to Ireland. Guelder rose berries can also be used in this way, and in North America often were. They are bitter and slightly poisonous when raw, but once cooked they make a good tart sauce.

Rowan jelly

Leave the berries on the tree until about October to allow them to sweeten – the tartaric acid in them is superseded by sugars, citric and malic acid as the fruit ripens. Put 6 lb. rowan berries, stalked and washed, in a pan with 3 pints water and simmer until they are soft. Strain through a muslin bag and for every pint of liquid add 1½ lb. sugar, the juice of 1 lemon or a crab apple for extra pectin. Simmer for about an hour or until it jellies.

Sauce eglantine

Frequently served at Balmoral during Queen Victoria's time with roast mutton and other meats. To every pound of wild rose hips allow half a pint of water. Boil until the fruit is tender and pass the pulp through a sieve fine enough to keep back the seeds. To each pound of pulp allow one pound of preserving sugar and boil until it jellies.

Service jelly

Made from the fruit of the wild service tree (*Sorbus torminalis*) the berries are only fit to eat about October when half rotten, preferably after being subjected to several frosts; then they may be made into a sauce, following the recipe for rowan jelly. In the nineteenth century service berries were sold in Kent and Sussex markets under the name of chequers.

Other sauces

Horse-radish sauce

Thought to have been introduced into this country in the fifteenth century as a medicine for coughs and worms, it is first mentioned by Gerard, who says it 'is commonly used among the Germans for sauce to eate fish with and such like meates as we do mustarde'.[26] Half a century later the use had spread: 'the root, sliced thin and mixed with vinegar is eaten as a sauce with meat, as among the Germans'.[57] Wild horse-radish is a garden escape found in fields, road and stream sides in the Midlands and West Country. To make the sauce mix together 2 tablespoons of grated horse-radish, ¼ teaspoon of made mustard, 1 tablespoon white wine vinegar, 2 teaspoons sugar, salt and pepper. Then when these are thoroughly blended add 1 gill of whipped cream and chill.

Mint sauce

'The smell of Mint does stir up the minde and the taste to a greedy desire of meate',[26] said Gerard. Traditional with lamb, mint sauce is made in the same way as sorrel sauce, using mint leaves. A recipe for mint jelly is given on p. 136.

Mustard

Both black mustard (*Brassica nigra*) and white mustard (*Sinapsis alba*) grow wild though usually as escapes from cultivation. They flower from May to September, after which their seeds, stripped from their pods, can be made into mustard. A mixture of the two, with a higher proportion of black to white, is considered ideal. The black contains a sulphurous volatile oil and the white an acrid crystalline substance called sinalbin; both contribute to the pungency of the mustard. Before 1720, when powdered mustard was invented by Mrs Clements of Durham, mustard seeds were used as a pickling spice or pounded, mixed with honey or vinegar and other spices, made into balls and kept until required. French mustard is still made like this; a mixture of mustard seed, steeped overnight in vinegar, is pounded with more vinegar and spices, wine or honey being added according to taste. Gerard says that 'the seeds of Mustard pounded with vinegar is an excellent sauce, good to be eaten with any groose meates, either fish or flesh, because it doth help digestion, warmeth the stomache and provoketh appetite'.[26] Chico Marx in *Monkey Business* puts it the other way round: 'Mustard's no good without roast beef.' The seeds of charlock, *Sinapsis arvenis*, a common weed of cultivated ground, can also be ground to make an inferior mustard.

Sorrel sauce

Traditional with goose and pork, it adds flavour to bland meats such as veal, and sweetbreads and fish like shad, and counteracts the oiliness of fish like mackerel. Its old name is green sauce; it is made by stripping the leaves of any tough stalks, chopping them with sugar, then adding a tablespoon of boiling water and some vinegar. For serving with hot meat the sauce is made in the same way as sorrel soup (p. 157), without the stock.

Seaweed

Environment

Most seaweeds, like other plants, die down in winter and grow again in spring and, in order to grow properly, need a reliable foothold on a rock or boulder. The best seaweed grounds are therefore the rocky shores of the west and south-west of Britain. However water temperature and light are also important, especially light, as this controls the depth at which a species will grow – a hundred fathoms is considered the limit. The intensity of light is also important and in tropical waters seaweeds grow at greater depths than in British waters, where eight fathoms is the maximum for most species. Concentration of salt and exposure to waves are other determining factors, as seaweeds obtain all their nourishment from the surrounding water. Seaweeds, like molluscs, keep to a certain section of the shore; for definitions of the different shore types and levels, see pp. 111–12.

Seaweeds as food

The general use of seaweeds as food, particularly in Scotland and Ireland, has decreased since the nineteenth century and today, apart from laver and carragheen, seaweeds are seldom eaten. By contrast Far Eastern countries such as Japan, China and Malaysia consume considerable quantities of seaweed, cultivating them in special seaweed beds and treating some varieties as a delicacy. Seaweeds are predominantly composed of carbohydrates and, like green vegetables, supply bulk, vitamins and minerals to the diet. They are rich in iodine and the lack of goitre in the East is partly due to the extensive use of seaweed. In general red, green and blue-green seaweeds are the most edible, brown ones tending to be tough. They should feel firm and slippery; seaweeds with a fishy or putrid smell or seaweeds which are wilted or decaying should be avoided. There is no evidence that any seaweeds are poisonous and they may be eaten raw, though they are more palatable if cooked.

Other uses

Because they contain large amounts of nitrogen and potassium much use has been made of seaweeds as manure. Long fronds of seaweed are regarded by sailors as a sign of the proximity of land and submerged rocks, and an indication of the direction of currents. A frond of sweet tangle makes a good weather forecaster (see p. 331) and the stalk a knife handle or truncheon. Once when bailiffs went to Tory Island off Ireland to collect unjust taxes, it is said that 'the women beat them out of it with slack marrow'.

Kelp, a potash valuable for glass-making, comes from burning seaweed. Agar is the name given commercially to the gelatinous substance obtained by boiling seaweeds such as carragheen (*Chondrus crispus*), *Gigartina stellata* and *Gravilaria*. Boil in water as you would for a plain, unflavoured carragheen mould and leave to set. The mould is then melted down and used as size for paper or cloth, as a weak glue, or a basis for soap, cosmetics and hand lotions. It has also been used as a dressing for wounds, especially in wartime – agar contains a substance which stops the blood clotting and enables wounds to be thoroughly cleansed. More recently it has been used as an insulating material against both sound and heat, and as an ingredient in water-based paints.

Brown Seaweeds

Dabberlocks (*Alaria esculenta*)*:* Long frond with yellowish midrib and slightly wavy, yellow-brown edges. Common on very exposed shores, the succulent sweet-tasting midribs are said to have been eaten raw in parts of Scotland and Ireland.

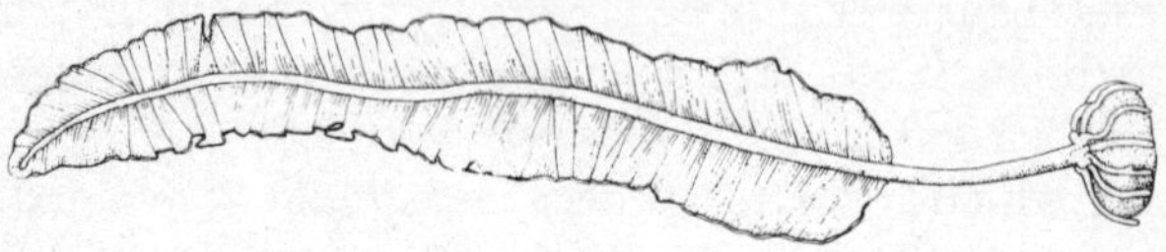

Alaria esculenta

Sweet tangle (*Laminaria saccharina*)*:* A flat frond from eight inches to eight feet long, attached to small stones and rocks from middle shore downwards on muddy sandy flats. Abundant and widely distributed. The young stipes were eaten in Scotland and according to Greville in 1830, were sold in the streets of Edinburgh to the cry 'Buy dulse and tangle.' Tangle has a sweet, peanut taste; a jelly can be prepared from it and in Norway it was dried and powdered and made into a kind of bread. In Japan this and, more commonly, other kinds of *Laminaria* are made into a product that goes under the name of Kan-Hoa and is prepared in the same way as the traditional *kombu*. After washing it is hung in the air until almost dry. It is then rolled up and put in presses to dry out further; it is

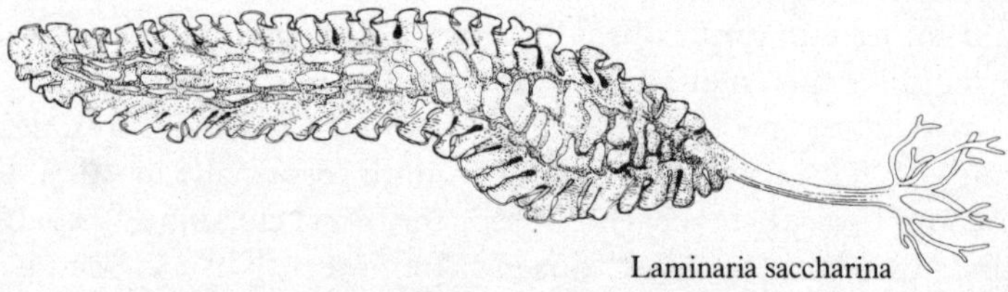

Laminaria saccharina

then shredded with a sharp knife and laid out in the open until the surface is dry, when it should still contain enough moisture to keep it pliable for up to a year and sometimes more. *Kombu* is eaten boiled in soups or as a vegetable with rice.

Green Seaweeds

Enteromorpha intestinalis: Branched, green fronds, found at all levels of the shore, it is especially common in fairly stagnant water where it often forms a carpet. Sold in the markets of China and Japan as a common food but never popular here.

Sea lettuce (Ulva lactuca): Irregular shaped, membraneous, with fronds up to 18 ins. long. Pale, watery-green in colour, darkening with age. Common, but most abundant in July and August on rocky shores, everywhere except the upper levels of beach. Similar to laver, though not as good, it can be served in all the same ways. An eighteenth-century writer commenting on its popularity at fashionable tables says: 'We suspect it to have been originally contrived with a medical intention, for the benefit of scrophulous patients, how numerous alas! in the gay circles of the opulent and great.'[58] Sold in the markets of Peking and Canton as a food and as a medicine to reduce fever.

Red Seaweeds

Carragheen or Irish moss (Chondrus crispus): Most variable in shape of all the red seaweeds, it generally has a shortish stalk, 3–6 ins. long with a wide, flat, branched, tough, dark red frond. Found on middle shore and widely distributed except on mud. Because of its tastelessness and gelatinous properties, carragheen is much used commercially as the basis of ice-cream, pastries, cough mixtures and toothpaste. In 1919 a record harvest of 2,000 wet tons of carragheen were harvested off the coast of Brittany between May and September, using special rakes from small boats. For home use carragheen is best made into a mould which can be flavoured in many ways. Collect clean leathery plants, wash well, dry in the sun, sprinkling occasionally with salt water until dry. Keep until required. See also agar, p. 151.

Carragheen mould

Soak half a cupful of dried carragheen in water for 10 minutes, drain it, simmer for 15 minutes in milk with a flavouring of elder flowers

(2 teaspoonfuls), a bay leaf or sweet spice. Strain it into a basin or mould, sweeten with honey or sugar and leave to set.

A fruit jelly is made by using water instead of milk and adding, for example, the juice of stewed blackberries, red currants or raspberries.

Carragheen moss blancmange (Burton Port recipe)

½ oz carragheen moss; 1½ pints milk; 1–2 eggs, 1 teaspoon sugar; flavouring.

Beat the egg till very light. Add the sugar and flavouring. Trim and wash the moss. Put in a saucepan with the milk. Very slowly bring to the boil. Strain over the egg. Return to the pan and cook for a second or two. Strain into wetted mould. Turn out when cold. Serve with fruit.

Dulse (*Rhodymenia palmata*): Varies in size from 4–12 ins., it may have a single blade or it may be branched. It is a dark purplish red and is found on rocks from middle to lower shore. Used to be popular in Iceland where it is still occasionally eaten with dried fish, butter and potatoes. In times of famine, it has been dried, powdered and made into a kind of bread. It will be leathery and tough unless it is cooked for about five hours. After boiling add butter, salt and pepper, as they do in Iceland.

Stewed dulse (Portaferry recipe at least a hundred years old)

Wash freshly gathered dulse to remove sand and grit. Put it in a saucepan with milk, butter, salt and pepper and stew it till tender. It takes three or four hours. Use it as a supper-dish with oatcakes or brown bread.

Laver (*Porphyra*): There are several very closely related species of porphyra, all edible and all prepared in the same way. It is a long, thin, irregular-shaped, lobed membranous weed, purplish red, becoming greenish brown as it withers, and black when dry. It is found on rocks and stones at most levels on exposed beaches, especially those on which the stones are liable to be covered with sand. It is common and widely distributed and is the seaweed most frequently eaten in Britain. Fried laver cakes are a traditional Welsh breakfast dish.

To prepare laver, wash it well, then steep it in water for three or four hours and boil until tender. Strain off the water, add some salt and beat to a pulp. This mixture may be kept in jars for up to a week, during which time it can be eaten dressed with oil and vinegar as a salad, made into a Chinese seaweed soup, heated with pepper, salt, cream and butter to eat with roast mutton, or made into laver or sloke cakes.

Porphyra

Sloke cakes

Take some boiled laver (sloke), dress it with butter and cream, and season it well. Into it mix enough oatmeal to enable you to form it into cakes. Make these about the size of small fish-cakes. Toss in oatmeal. Fry in the pan after frying the bacon.[47]

Pepper dulse (*Laurencia pinnatifida*): Purplish-red to greenish-yellow with alternate divided branches. Sunny rocks in middle shore. Young plants gathered in spring have a pungent peppery flavour and are used as a condiment in Iceland and as a kind of chewing tobacco.

Soup

Some think of soup as cheap food, a way of stretching a few ingredients (though the French *pot au feu* and *Catalan fabada* are meals in themselves); others emulate the pure standards of Elizabeth David, who states that 'the soup-pot cannot be treated as though it were a dustbin'. Depending on the pocket, or the circumstances, each of these views has its place.

As a way of stretching a few ingredients the dustbin approach is inevitable. Almost anything put in a pan, covered with water and simmered will produce a liquid which can be called soup and which, though possibly wholesome, will probably have little flavour. If you begin by gently sweating some chopped root vegetables in butter or fat for ten minutes, then adding some chopped green vegetables, chopped cooked meat, stock, milk or water, along with herbs, salt, pepper and barley or oats for thickening and simmer the lot for thirty minutes, something quite delicious may emerge.

To make a complete meal, meat and vegetables are all cooked in one pot – a way of using tough cuts of meat or old birds. In peasant economies the meat, once cooked, was often lifted out of the broth to be eaten hot the first day with the vegetables and cold the second. The remaining broth was left to cool and the fat removed from the surface; it was then heated up and served as soup.

First brown the meat in fat, then surround it with root vegetables and cabbage, if available, cover it with stock or wine or cider, add herbs, salt and pepper, bring it to the boil and simmer slowly for about 1½ hours or until the meat is cooked.

With the pure approach, several excellent soups can be made using wild ingredients.

Vegetable Soups

Mallow soup

Popular in Egypt; this is an English version of an Egyptian recipe. Take about 1 lb. mallow (*Malva sylvestris*) leaves, remove the stalks, chop the leaves and boil in 2 pints stock for 10 minutes. Then make a sauce by frying 2 cloves of crushed garlic in some oil, adding 1 dessertspoon crushed coriander, salt and pepper. Then add the mallow, simmer all for a few minutes and serve hot.

Mushroom soup

Any mushrooms can be used in the making of this soup.

Take 1 lb. of mushrooms and chop them finely. Then melt 2 oz.

butter or fat in a pan, put in the mushrooms and soften until the juice runs, then add a piece of chopped garlic, some chopped parsley, salt and pepper and, if possible, some nutmeg; allow all to stew for a few minutes. Soak a thick slice of white bread with the crust removed in some stock, squeeze out and add the bread to the mushrooms and stir until amalgamated. Add about $1\frac{3}{4}$ pints stock and simmer for 15 minutes. To finish, sieve through a coarse mesh, reheat and add cream and more chopped parsley.

Nettle broth

Take 1 pint liquid (milk, water or stock), 1 oz. oatmeal, $\frac{1}{2}$ pint chopped nettle tops, $\frac{1}{2}$ oz. butter, pepper, salt. Put all the ingredients except the oatmeal into a saucepan; when boiling add the oatmeal, and boil for 30 minutes.

Other green vegetables of a similar type may be substituted for nettles – hogweed for one.

Sorrel soup

Melt a good handful of sorrel (*Rumex acetosa*) in 1 oz. butter. Sieve or chop finely and add to it 3–4 tablespoons bechamel sauce or some cream. If you are adding cream, either stir some flour in to the sorrel first or boil the cream, otherwise the acid in the sorrel will curdle the cream. Then gradually add 1 pint stock, or half stock and half milk. Reheat, stirring all the time, and serve hot.

Watercress soup

Take a large handful of watercress, and strip off the leaves. Chop the stalks roughly and put to simmer in $\frac{1}{2}$ pint water. Chop the leaves finely. Melt a tablespoon of bacon fat or butter in a pan and blend with a tablespoon of flour. Strain in the liquid from the boiled stalks and add salt and pepper. Bring to the boil and cook for a few minutes. Remove from the stove, add leaves and some cream.

Fish Soups

I include two recipes which can be adapted for all kinds of dish. Where there are no onions, wild garlic or ransoms should be used as substitute; where there are no potatoes, use flour to thicken.

Shellfish soup

Chop a large potato and one onion and cook gently in 1 oz. butter for a few minutes. Add 2 pints shell fish, 2½ pints fish stock or water, 2 crushed cloves of garlic, herbs and a bunch of edible seaweed, fresh or dried. Bring to the boil and simmer until cooked. Remove the fish from their shells and return to the soup. Reheat, stir in ½ pint cream, sprinkle with chopped parsley and serve.

White fish soup

Put 1 lb. of any white fish with some root vegetables (ideally, onion, leek and celery) into a pan and cover with about 1½ pints water. Simmer until the fish is cooked. Remove this, separate the flesh from the bones, head and skin and put these back with the vegetables and cook for another 20 minutes. Strain, add a glass of white wine, ¼ pint milk, cooked fish and, if possible, fennel, garlic and some grated lemon peel. If desired, this soup can be thickened by adding the stock to a roux of butter and flour.

Starving

Provided you have water, and provided you stay still and use up no energy, it should be possible to survive for up to six weeks without any food. But without water survival time is far shorter, about three days only, depending on the outside temperature. A cool, damp atmosphere will keep you going longer than a hot dry one.

Do not resign yourself to a dismal end too soon, for there are many foods which might not normally be considered as part of a western diet but which are edible and will sustain life. The RAF Survival School insists that almost anything that walks, crawls, swims or flies can be eaten. This includes anything from snakes to slugs to rats – see the appropriate sections in this book. It will be found that food sources which would cause repulsion and nausea under normal conditions become acceptable to the starving man, as in the case of the survivors of the Andes aircrash in 1972 who ate uncooked human flesh cut from their dead companions.

Bones contain nourishment, which can be extracted by pounding the ends between stones and sucking out the marrow in the middle, or by boiling. There are stories of besieged garrisons at Sancerre and at Paris during the reign of Charles IX digging up graveyards and using the bones for food. Untanned skins and hides are also edible, cooked or uncooked. Many a starving man has resorted to eating his shoes and skin clothing. During the retreat from Moscow, Napoleon's troops ate shoe leather, and an eighteenth century missionary reported that 'An eelskin was deemed a sumptuous supper; I had used one for mending a robe, but hunger obliged me to unstitch and eat it.' Candles made from animal fat have also been resorted to *in extremis*.

Rank birds should be skinned rather than plucked, as often much of the offensiveness lies in the skin. People say that watching what birds eat will give a guide to what humans can eat, and that if you examine the crop of a dead bird this will display the safe ingredients. But this is not an entirely reliable guide as pigeons can eat strychnine berries without coming to any harm. However, what is true is that over a period of time the body will build up an immunity to certain food toxins. The natives of any country can often eat large quantities of food which would make the uninitiated very sick.

On the seashore most seaweeds are edible though threadlike ones are best avoided. Plants and fungi vary. Most families contain both edible and poisonous varieties except for the buttercups (Ranunculaceae) which are all poisonous and the cabbage family (Cruciferae) which are all edible. Nettles and bracken are plants which can be found in most places and which give good nourishment.

In northern countries it was customary within the tree limit to supplement food with the ground bark of trees, especially the inner bark of alder, aspen, birch, elm and lime. Beyond the tree limit edible lichens such as iceland moss (*Cetraris icelandica*), reindeer moss (*Cladonia rangiferina*) and rock tripe (*Umbilicaria arctica*) are starchy and, after long boiling, form a gelatinous mass that is digestible, though one of the early Jesuits likened it to 'slime of snails' and another admitted 'that it is necessary to close one's eyes to eat it'. But it must be better than some things, as this sad entry in Sir John Franklin's diary implies: 'There was no *tripe de roche*, so we drank tea and ate some of our shoes for supper.'[41]

The young shoots of grass, before they develop the fibres that take four stomachs of a cow to digest, are disputably edible. In John Clare's description of his escape from the asylum he says that 'on the third day I satisfied my hunger by eating the grass by the roadside which seemed to taste something like bread. I was hungry and ate heartily till I was satisfied and in fact the meal seemed to do me good . . .'[59] The following, more modern, claimant goes further:

> With practical experience extending over five years, I can with confidence assert, that, eaten young and eaten short, grass is not in the least indigestible . . . I am rising sixty-nine, and grass is now as much my staple article of diet, as bread and meat – neither of which I eat at all – are to other folk. To show the energy my (raw) grass diet is capable of producing, I am intending to make my journeys on my pedal bicycle. I know that, given the longer daylight, I can do at least 100 miles a day.

The editor who published that letter felt compelled to add:

> Grass does contain great nourishment but enclosed within tough fibrous cells totally indigestible by normal human beings. The short young shoots are an exception but great care should be taken as unless carefully washed they carry some risk of worm infection and in certain cases cause intestinal irritation.[60]

A general guide for both plants and fungi is to:

1. Avoid anything that is brilliantly coloured, produces skin irritation, contains a milky juice, or has a putrefying or objectionable odour.
2. Test by biting off a small portion, holding it inside the lower lip for a few minutes. It should not cause irritation or produce an acrid, burning, bitter or soapy taste.
3. Finally, consume a small portion, well chewed, and if it does not produce any ill effects within a period of at least eight hours the food should be safe.

Food which passes these tests should be edible in moderate amounts with reasonable safety. There are some well-known exceptions such as figs, safe despite their milky juice, and lemons whose taste is bitter, but it is unlikely that they will concern the reader of this book.

Penultimately, water – for finding and purifying this see the section on water, pp. 188–91. And finally the moral element in survival. Here is an impassioned plea for right attitudes:

> Anyone facing extinction feels the loneliest person on earth. You are alone in the rioting football crowd, squashing air from your lungs, as on a raft at sea.

The anatomy of loneliness is a skeleton. Jerking muscles, scrabbling fingers, shivering marrow, straining sinews – these are the bare bones of panic and initial despair. Survival of the fittest does not mean you have to be physically perfect. Stripped to a clawing puppet by crisis, everyone is reduced to an isolation where survival is all in the mind.

Mental aspects of loneliness

Taking a deep breath and making up your mind to have a really determined go at beating the odds at all costs is the vital factor in survival.

When initial shock brings utter despair it is still possible for that sense of self-preservation to pull you through, though you may be totally disorientated and terrified.

If contemplating giving in or suicide: prayer is a proven help. 'The Lord is my Shepherd . . . Though I walk through the valley of the shadow of death . . . Thy rod and staff comfort me . . .'

Run/drive/signal/swim/make fires/build shelter/signal again . . . all the harder. Don't lie down to die without a fantastic struggle first. Never ever give in.

Tell yourself: Even this will pass.

In unknown environment improvise, improvise, improvise.

Never, never, never never never never never never never give up trying. Out of all the untidiness, quickness and/or dragging slowness of survival, salvage, clutch and spur your vital instinct of self-preservation.[49]

Sugar and Other Sweeteners

Until the introduction of cane sugar from the West Indies in the seventeenth century honey was the only sweetener available and was used for everything (see p. 17). After that cane sugar supplanted honey as the main sweetener both here and on the Continent until Napoleon encouraged the cultivation of sugar beet as a means of boycotting British-controlled cane sugar. It was a German chemist called Marggraf who in 1747 first discovered that the juice of sugar beet contained properties identical to cane sugar. A follower of his, Francis Karl Archard, invented a method of extraction which generated so much interest that the King of Prussia backed the first factory in Silesia. Other countries followed suit and today beet sugar is still commoner than cane sugar on the Continent.

Sugar beet (*Beta vulgaris*)

In its wild state sugar beet is generally found growing near the sea but it is now so widely cultivated, especially in East Anglia, that escapes from arable land will doubtless be found as well. Sugar beet in the wild never achieves the size of root (the part from which the sugar is taken) that its cultivated counterpart does. In looks sugar beet resembles the garden beetroot but its roots are white, about 12–15 ins. long and weigh about 2 lb. A biennial, it produces in the first year a root and leaf tops (which may be eaten as vegetables) and flowers in the second year.

On a small scale sugar was extracted by the following method: first the roots were shredded, then heated in water to extract the sugar. This juice was then strained off and poured into an iron pot over a wood fire, and wood ash and lime were added. These acted as purifiers by creating a scum which was skimmed off until it ceased to rise. Boiling continued until the juice reached a point where it would crystallize when cooled. When this stage arrived the liquid was strained through a cloth and stirred until cool. 'The result was a very excellent raw sugar which can still be recollected and praised by those who go back to the sixties. Very little of the raw beetroot sugar is as good as it was then.'[61]

Sugar was refined by filtering the liquid sugar through a charcoal made from burnt animal bones. The liquor, entering brown, at first comes out white and then, as the charcoal loses its freshness – rather like a cigarette filter – yellow, and finally brown. The different colours are kept separate and the charcoal washed and used again.

Maple syrup

In North America, before cane sugar was introduced, most sugar and syrup came from the sap of the sugar maple (*Acer saccharum*), a source used by the Indians long before colonization and commercialization began. This tree, which looks like a typical maple, is not indigenous to Britain; though it will grow here to as far north as Perthshire, and is to be found planted in some large gardens and arborea, notably Westonbirt. However the field maple (*Acer campestris*) is fairly common in this country and though not so prolific or so good, its sap can be used as a sweetener.

The sap is tapped in spring, just before the leaves begin to appear, by making a cut with an axe in the trunk or by boring a hole two inches deep on the warmest side of the tree about three feet from the ground. Then a hollow twig or curved piece of bark is inserted to channel the sap into a container. The sap should continue to flow for about five or six weeks depending on the temperature, cold nights and warm days being ideal. A sugar maple is expected to produce fifteen to thirty gallons of sap, which is reduced to the right consistency, about a quarter of the original, by boiling. American Indians used to boil the sap in large pans, then pour the syrup on to snow and put it in moulds to crystallize – known as 'sugaring off'. Tapping does not appear to harm the tree, as donating a pint of blood does not seem to harm humans.

Vegetables

Vegetable plants in the wild never reach the size and succulence of their garden counterparts. The competition for survival and the lack of manure and individual attention means that the leaves, roots or stem – whichever is the edible part – always compares unfavourably in size and very often in taste too. Even so, there are an enormous number of plants which can be eaten as vegetables; I list here only those which are reasonably common and which have some gastronomic merit.

Green Vegetables

This is the largest category: unless otherwise stated plants with large, tough cabbage-like leaves should be treated as you would cabbage. That is, washed, then put in a pan with about an inch of water, brought to the boil and stirred occasionally until cooked. Drain, chop if necessary, and add salt, pepper and butter. If the leaves are small and delicate they should be cooked as you would spinach. Wash the leaves and put them in a pan with only as much water as the leaves hold. Bring to the boil and leave for just a couple of minutes, stirring once or twice until mushy, drain, salt and pepper and add a knob of butter.

Caraway: The leaves taste of caraway seeds.

Charlock: A common form of cabbage-type plant.

Chickweed: Very common, tastes of young pea pods, but the leaves are small and a labour to separate from the stems which are too stringy to eat.

Cow parsnip: Common, but rough tasting.

Fat hen: Has more iron, protein and vitamin B than cabbage.

Good King Henry: When an Iron Age Grauballe Man was dug up he had seeds of this in his stomach. Formerly cultivated in East Anglia.

Goosegrass: Pick before the seeds form; the whole plant is cooked.

Ground elder: Has a parsley-like flavour; originally planted as a vegetable, it is now regarded as one of the more persistent garden weeds.

Hedge garlic: Tastes of garlic and is traditionally eaten in Wales with bacon and herrings.

Hedge mustard: Called 'singers' plant' in France, where it is thought to cure loss of voice. A cabbage-type vegetable.

Mustard: Another member of the *Brassica* genus, to which the garden cabbage belongs; all are edible.

Nettles: Pick the first two inches of the top of the plant – the younger the plant the better. After mid-summer nettles become coarse and too tough to make pleasant eating. Wear gloves to pick; the sting disappears in cooking.

Nipplewort: Gets its name from the nipple-like shape of the flower buds. The leaves taste fresh.

Orache: Another member of the Chenopodiaceae family to which Good King Henry belongs – all make good spinach-type vegetables.

Poppy: The young leaves of the field poppy have a nutty flavour said to mix well with sorrel.

Purslane: Thoreau says that he 'made a satisfactory dinner, satisfactory on several accounts, simply off a dish of purslane (*Portulaca oleracea*) which I gathered in my cornfield, boiled and salted.'[1]

Rape: A *Brassica*, with nourishing but rather tough leaves.

Rat-tail plantain: Called 'Englishman's foot' by the natives of America and New Zealand, as it arrived wherever Englishmen settled. Tough mucilaginous leaves.

Sea beet: The midribs drawn from the centre of the leaves are cooked separately and taste faintly of asparagus, while the leaf part is like spinach.

Shepherd's purse: The leaves contain a volatile oil similar to mustard, giving a pungent, slightly bitter taste.

Sweet Cicely: The whole plant may be boiled and eaten – it has an anise taste.

Some leaves, although not poisonous, are too acrid or strong-tasting to make pleasant eating. Added to soups or stews they give bulk and vegetative goodness and their flavour is obscured. Leaves which fall into this category are daisy, dock, marguerite, dead-nettle and ox-tongue.

Root Vegetables

Wild root vegetables compare very badly with cultivated ones. They are best added to stews and soups and, except for a very few, do not really merit eating on their own. Some of the best are:

Bitter vetch: Sweet and starchy tubers, chewed raw in the Highlands as the betelnut is in India.

Burdock: These can be eaten on their own with a sauce.

Cuckoo pint: A potato-like root full of nutrition.

Dandelion: Rather bitter but quite nice to eat. The Japanese chop the roots thinly in rings, fry them in a little oil, add water, then cover the pan and simmer until tender.

Earthnuts (pignuts): Tubers two or three inches down connected by a white thread-like stem to the leaves. They have a nutty taste, good raw or cooked – Caliban in *The Tempest* ate them.

Evening primrose: Boil or slice thinly. The French use them as a form of salad dressing.

Flowering rush: Rhizomes eaten raw or cooked.

Goat's beard: Resembling, though not as good as, salsify. Cook in same way.

Rampion: Thick, fleshy, sweet-tasting root; Rapunzel's mother had a pregnant craving for it.

Salsify: Naturalized in a few places in southern England; scrape the roots down to the inner skin, boil until tender and cover with white or cheese sauce. They are delicious cold if sliced and put in a vinaigrette dressing after cooking.

Silverweed: Tastes like parsnips. Until the advent of potatoes, it formed a vital part of the diet of people in northerly parts of Britain. It is said to have been cultivated as a crop in the Hebrides.

Star of Bethlehem: Can be eaten both raw and cooked, being wholesome and nutritious. Roasted like chestnuts in the East, large quantities of the bulbs were dried and sold in the streets of Cairo and Damascus to people going on long journeys across the desert and to pilgrims going to Mecca.

Wild parsnip: Small roots, but as Gerard said, they 'nourish more than do Turneps or the Carrots'.[26]

Young Spring Shoots

These are mostly cooked like asparagus, by putting bunches of the young shoots in boiling water for about 10–20 minutes, depending on thickness, then draining them and eating either hot with melted butter or cold in a vinaigrette dressing.

Bracken: Pick when the shoots are still curled and no more than three inches in length – the Canadians call them 'fiddle-heads', and tin them. The Japanese eat them by plunging them in boiling water for 2 minutes, then in cold for 2 hours, then in boiling again until cooked and tender. Eat them whole or puréed. A surplus can have a slightly poisonous effect.

Bladder campion: This resembles green peas in flavour and is considered so good that cultivation has been considered.

Elder: The shoots should be peeled before cooking.

Good King Henry: Shoots picked when 5 ins. long and peeled before boiling.

Hops: Cultivated by the Romans for their shoots which used to be sold in English markets.

Rosebay willowherb: Eaten by the Kamchatka Russians.

Samphire: The best samphire has been 'washed by every tide' and picked in June and July; crisp tasting.

Solomon's seal: Excellent; said to have been liked by the Turks.

Stalks

These are all 'celery'-type plants and with most, if possible, the flavour is much improved by earthing-up the stalks for about fourteen days before eating. They may all be eaten raw, boiled for vegetables, baked in a sauce in the oven, or put in stews and soups.

Goat's beard: The bud, with about six inches of stem is cooked like asparagus.

Horsetails: Though all are edible, apart from the water horsetail, they have little flesh and are not worth eating.

Lovage: A northerly plant, better earthed up; tastes rather like celery.

Samphire: When the stalks are old, this is best boiled; the flesh can then be drawn out of the stems through clenched teeth.

Sea kale: The stalks should be eaten separately from the tough leaves. The *Gardener's Dictionary* of 1731 says that 'the inhabitants (of Sussex) gather it in the Spring to eat, preferring it to any of the Cabbage kind'.

Thistles: The young stems of the larger thistles, stripped of their ring, make delicious eating and were sometimes baked in pies. The heads, before they come into flower, can be cooked and eaten like small artichokes.

Vinegar

Vinegar is beer, wine or cider, or something approaching one of these, which has been exposed to the air and attacked by the vinegar bug (*Aceto bacter*). This bug converts the alcohol into acetic acid, making vinegar.

'Vinegar and hard brine are essential for food preservation' wrote Columnella. Vinegar to be used for preserving must contain at least 5 per cent acetic acid; to test this, leave the vinegar exposed to the air, and if it grows mould it is not strong enough. Vinegar also acts as a basis for many sauces; a form of vinegar, verjuice, can be used as a substitute for lemon; and flavoured vinegars, or vinegar in water, was used as a medicine or a refreshing drink – it featured in the rations of Roman soldiers on the march and was given to Christ on the cross.

Malt vinegar

This is made from beer left exposed to the air until it turns sour and becomes vinegar. A rural way of making it was to sprinkle beer on to a bunch of birch twigs previously soaked in vinegar. As the beer trickled through the birch twigs and was exposed to the air, it collected the vinegar bug and emerged as malt vinegar. This kind of vinegar has a pungent taste and is best used for pickling eggs and onions.

White vinegar

Malt vinegar which has been distilled. This takes away the colour and modifies the taste. Good for pickling vegetables.

Wine vinegar

Vinegar gets its name from the French *vin aigre,* which means sour wine and this is what wine vinegar is: wine which has been left to go flat and sour and pick up enough *Aceto bacter* to turn it into vinegar. Sometimes yeast, salt and honey are added to the flat wine to help make the vinegar and act as a flavouring, and sometimes the vinegar is distilled. Whether distilled or not wine vinegar always has a more delicate and subtle taste than other vinegars and goes well with mushrooms and asparagus.

Verjuice or cider vinegar

Verjuice was an important ingredient in the highly spiced sauces that accompanied many medieval dishes. Resembling sharp dry cider in taste, its use declined after it was replaced in the sixteenth century by lemon juice and ordinary vinegar; verjuice can be used as substitute for either, when these are not available.

An imitation is made by mixing cider and white malt vinegar in equal quantities. For the real thing here is a nineteenth century recipe from Lancashire.

> Take some crab apples when the kernels turn black, lay them in a heap to sweat; then pick from them the stalks and rottenness, beat them to a mash, and press the juice through a bag of coarse hair cloth into a clean vessel; it will be fit for use in a month's time. If intended for white pickles, distil it in a cold still. It may be put into a sauce when lemon is wanting.

Fruit vinegars

Usually more medicinal than culinary in purpose, they are drunk hot or cold for the relief of sore throats or as a refresher. Made by steeping fruit – usually one high in vitamin C such as black currants or elderberries, though raspberries and blackberries are used as well – in vinegar for some time. Then the juice is strained off, sweetened with sugar or honey, brought to the boil and allowed to cool before bottling.

Herb vinegars

Fill a container with an aromatic herb – thyme, mint or marjoram are all good – fill up with white wine vinegar, close and leave for several months until the vinegar is infused with the taste of the herb. Strain into a new bottle and use.

Other vinegars

'No store-room should be without tarragon vinegar, anchovy vinegar, French vinegar and white wine vinegar,'[62] advises a cookery book of a century ago, yet many housewives would have added several more to that list. Here are two recipes of the time.[33] Remember not to fill the barrel or container completely full, and to keep it at about 90–95°F for the first six to eight weeks to encourage the vinegar bacteria.

Primrose vinegar

Ingredients: cold water 30 quarts; brown sugar 12 lb.; primroses a peck; yeast (compressed yeast) 1–2 oz.

Time: 10 minutes to boil; a few days to stand; a year to mature in the cask.

1. Boil the water and sugar together for 10 minutes.
2. Before it is cold add a peck of primrose petals and the yeast creamed with a little sugar. Let it work for a few days, stirring often. Then put it in a barrel with the primroses. Keep it close and near the fire. It must stand a year.

Gooseberry vinegar

Ripe gooseberries and to every quart of pulp 3 quarts of water; to every gallon of liquor 1½ lb. brown sugar; *no* yeast.

Crush gooseberries, measure pulp. Boil 3 quarts of water for every quart of pulp. Let the water get quite cold before you put the pulp into it. Stir and stand for 27 hours. Strain through a sieve. To every gallon of liquor add 1½ lb. brown sugar. Stir well until the sugar is dissolved. Put in barrel and finish as before, except that it is not worked with yeast.

Yeast

Yeast is a minute fungus, oval in shape, which if given the right conditions is able to reproduce itself up to thirty times with great speed, creating alcohol and carbon dioxide in the process. The conditions are warmth (the temperature of a warm kitchen or airing cupboard, 65–75°F) oxygen and food. So if a teaspoon of dormant yeast is mashed with a teaspoon of sugar and a little warm water, and left for 20 minutes, the yeast will begin to work. If this mixture is then added to bread dough the yeast will continue working, feeding on ingredients in the dough, and puffing it up with exuded carbon dioxide. If however it is added – usually by spreading on a piece of toast – to wine, beer or whisky it will transform the sugar in the brew into alcohol. This 'working' period, when the yeast is alive and reproducing, is indicated by the hiss of escaping gas and movement in the brew. When working has finished it should be because all the sugar has been used and not because the yeast has become dormant again because of cold or other factors. To test this housewives used to sprinkle a little sugar near the plant and watch the reaction. If the yeast began to hiss and work again the sugar had been used, and the brew was sufficiently fermented. If there was no reaction something else was wrong, and the brew could still be full of unused sugar, which would have a detrimental effect on the drink.

Because yeast is a live organism, keeping it alive but dormant was a problem solved in several ways. Sometimes active yeast was skimmed from the top of the beer, put in a closed bottle and kept in a cold place, such as a larder, or stood in a stream, when it would last a month or even more. Sometimes little bushes of birch twigs were dipped in the yeast, stirred round and left until a quantity of yeast had fastened on to the twigs. The bush was then hung in the open, in a place where it would not get too cold, dry or dusty. 'When your beer is fit to set to work, throw one of these bushes into it, and it will work as well as if you had fresh yeast. You must whip it about in the wort, and then let it lie therein.' After the beer was working well the bush was withdrawn, hung up again, and saved for the next brew. These yeast-covered bushes were also used to revive flat or stale wine. Hence the old saying 'Good wine needs no bush' and the use of a bush to indicate a wine shop. Yet another way of storing yeast was to spread the yeast on a wide board in layers, allowing each layer to dry before the next was applied, to a thickness of about two inches. The yeast was then cut up and stored in airtight containers. When wanted for use a bit was crumbled with sugar and water, whereupon it would start working again. More yeast was grown by putting some in a jar, providing it with air 'let in through the bladder cover of the jar, through a goose quill' and fed with mashed boiled potatoes mixed with honey, treacle or sugar, and left for about a week.

Though yeast was known about and used for centuries, its workings understood by experience and instinct, it was only scientifically identified in the nineteenth century by Louis Pasteur. Since then yeast has been refined and it is now possible to buy yeast specially developed for specific purposes. So there is beer and bread yeast (*Saccharomyces cerevisiae*) and wine yeast (*S. ellipsoideus*), which is again subdivided into yeast for red, white and sparkling wines.

Drinking

The only necessary drink is water. Without water the body becomes dehydrated and dies within a few days in hot weather and a few more in cold. With water, even without food, it can last for about six weeks. If survival alone is the primary aim water is the only drink to worry about. All others must be regarded as luxuries until your state of civilization has advanced several degrees. Even then water is necessary not only for drinking but for making most other drinks and for numerous household tasks. So the establishment of a good natural source, or an artificial one such as a well or pond, is of the utmost importance. We had a stream from which we took all the water needed for washing and general chores and found a spring a quarter of a mile away for drinking water. We would go and collect a few days' supply and bring it back to the hut to store in a shady place.

After water I would place whisky or brandy; both are definitely medicinal and reviving when you feel cold or run down. Tea probably should be in this category too. Though none of our native leaves have the caffeine content of the tea plant leaf, and so do not have quite the same lifting effect, many have other properties of equal benefit. There are those that refresh, others that cool or soothe and others again that have medicinal properties. The coffee plant does not grow in this country either and dandelion, chicory or acorn are poor substitutes and a labour to prepare. You need quite a few dandelion roots to make a good cup and digging them is hard work. When we lived off the land, we gave up coffee in favour of tea. Toadflax was in bloom at the time and we infused a quantity of this. The tea it made was slightly scented and looked pretty too, and I never bothered to strain it. I put the broken-up plant in a cup, poured on the boiling water, left it to infuse for a few minutes and then we drank it, avoiding the bits of yellow and orange flower and green leaves floating on the surface. Herbal teas have no tannin and are therefore better for you than tea. There are many flavours to choose from: raspberry leaf, camomile, thyme and mint are good ones.

We had also had whisky with us. We drank it not only when we were cold and wet but also at times of depression brought on by long periods of rain, or days when there seemed to be no food no matter how far we walked, and at those other times when the boredom and hopelessness of the situation loomed larger than the benefits. Then no 'country' wine can outstrip the hard stuff. But on the days when the advantages outweighed the disadvantages – and these were the commonest – when the sun shone, the country looked beautiful and we had just found a fine patch of chanterelle – we drank dandelion, elderberry and rowanberry wine. The first two I had made before we came, the last happened by accident. I had picked some rowanberries, left them in water in a sunny spot and forgotten about them. When I went back about a week later they had begun to ferment. I added honey as a sweetener and not only did we drink this wine but I used it to flavour stews too. Dandelion-flower wine is a light wine, a moselle, but elderberry is definitely the burgundy of the country wines. It is the only one I have drunk which has anything approaching the body and bouquet of a good French wine; compared to a bad one it (and many others) is infinitely better.

There are many intoxicating drinks which can be made – wines from all kinds of berry, root and flower, as well as cider, mead, gin and liqueurs. Any prohibitionist is fighting a losing battle; there are no people in any part of the world who have not developed an indigenous alcoholic drink. It is just a question of what the local material is and the best way of treating it to induce fermentation; regional differences breed regional preferences. But in this country the days of home-made alcohol are gone; a pot still for distilling wine and perfume is no longer an integral part of a household. The Distillers' Act of 1751 killed all that. It was necessary in many ways, before then, owing to the fact that most water was contaminated and tea and coffee had yet to become everyday drinks, the 'habit of drinking cheap gin instead of beer had led to an alarming increase in the death rate. At the height of the gin era, between 1740 and 1742, the burials in the London region had been twice as many as the baptisms.'[22] Despite the fact that distilling drink is now illegal unless you have a licence, you would need to know how to distil if the bomb had dropped, if only to be able to purify water (see p. 175).

Most spirit for drinking is produced from grains such as barley, wheat and oats, roots such as sugar beet and potatoes, and fruit.

Grain spirits are made by the same process as whisky, the only difference being that a peat fire is not necessary for drying the malt as the flavour is usually obtained during the second or third distillation from herbs or fruits added to the distillate. Vodka is an exception, being a pure spirit made from grain or potatoes with no additions.

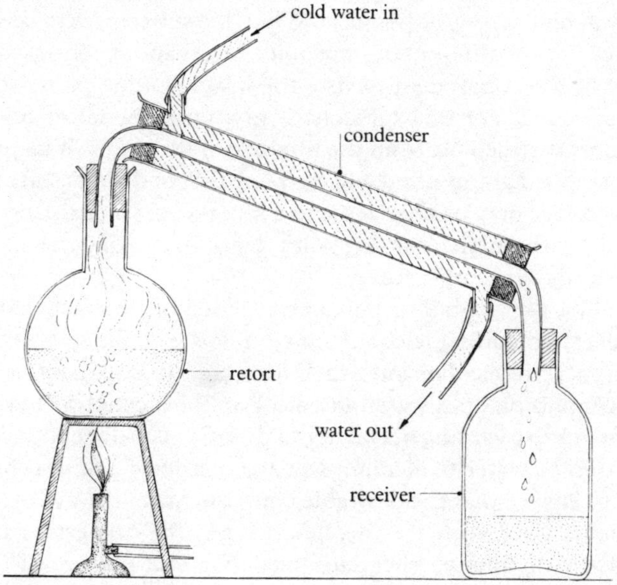

Distilling

Distilling – or the process of vaporizing a liquid and subsequently recovering it by condensation – works on the same principle as rain formed from the sea, when the water evaporated from the sea forms into clouds and eventually falls back as rain.

The apparatus required for basic distilling consists of a retort, a condenser and a receiver arranged as shown. Depending on the purpose they may be made of glass, iron or copper. Heat is supplied by fire, a gas burner, electricity or steam. The condenser is then cooled by air or water circulating in a jacket round the tube. A small still can easily be constructed from any pot which will stand heat. A glass cona coffee pot, for instance, fitted with a cork lid with two holes, one for a thermometer, the other for a plastic pipe to feed the vapours into the condenser. Small glass condensers can be bought from any laboratory suppliers along with the piping and a bunsen burner to heat the retort. If another pipe is fitted to the cold tap and fed through the condenser, it can all be done in the kitchen sink.

The object of distilling is to separate the various components of a mixture as completely as possible. When the substances to be separated have widely different boiling points, the vapour consists almost entirely of the component having the lower boiling point and the distillate consists of this substance only, until the latter has been completely distilled off from the mixture in the retort. The process may be stopped at this point and only one part of the distillate taken, or the receiver may be changed and a second part, consisting of the substance with a higher boiling point, taken by heating the distilling flask to a higher temperature.

Distilling for alcohol or perfume is based on the fact that most substances, including alcohol, have a lower boiling point than water: 172°F for alcohol and 212°F for water. Consequently, with a liquid containing both water and alcohol, the alcohol will vaporize at a temperature varying between 172°F and 212°F depending on the proportion of water to alcohol. But the distiller must also be concerned to ensure that the desirable constituents of the drink or perfume come over with the alcohol, so that the respective liquids retain their distinctive characteristics. (Certain poisonous constituents can also come over and the stages in the distillation should be carefully watched.)

Purifying water

Water can be purified and distilled by merely stretching a handkerchief over a pan of boiling water and squeezing it out periodically as it becomes saturated. Another simple way is to float a basin on top of some boiling water with a large shallow dish on top of the pan containing cold water to keep it cool. The steam will rise from the water, condense on the underside of the large dish and drip down into the basin.

The tradition of distilling goes back through the alchemists to antiquity. The pot stills used in Scotland, France and Ireland today are directly descended in shape and method from the alembics of the ancient Arabs. The continuous distillation used by the large drink manufacturers is comparatively recent, developing only after Coffey patented his still in 1832. Cromwell was the first to see the possibilities of revenue in alcohol and imposed a tax of 2d. per gallon. In 1826 this had risen to 2s. 1d. per gallon, by 1914 to 14s. 9d., by 1948 to £1 1s. 1d. and in 1978 it was £3.28 on a bottle of whisky.

Distilling alcohol is, strictly speaking, illegal in Britain today unless supervised and licensed by HM inspectors. This has the effect of confining it to large authorized organizations. A 'still room' was formerly an integral part of any large household or monastery, scents, medicines and spirits all being made on the premises.

Beer

Brewing is thought to have originated in Babylon, but the first evidence of beer being made from malted grain comes from Mesopotamia in 6000 BC. The Egyptians said that beer was a gift from the god Osiris or his wife, Isis, and taught brewing to the Greeks, who taught it to the Romans, who almost certainly introduced it to Britain, though a form of beer made from corn and honey was probably already in existence. Beer used to be flavoured with all manner of herbs, and a weak brew was drunk by all in preference to the unwholesome water. Hopped beer did not take over until the sixteenth century, introduced by the Dutch, who took the custom from the Germans.

> Hops, Reformation, bays and beer
> Came to England all in one year –

Before this, when people talked of ale they meant a herb-flavoured malt, and when beer, a hopped one. Gerard arguing the case in 1597 says that

> The manifold vertues in Hopes (cleansing and opening the body, purging the blood, etcetera) do manifestly argue the holsomness of Beere above Ale; for the Hops rather make it a Phisicall drinke to keep the body in health, then an ordinarie drinke for the quenching of our thirst.[26]

Modern beer is made from barley and water which should ideally be 'under-chalk' water. This factor helped make Dorchester a great centre for beer and Burton too, its water being rich in gypsum. But any soft water from a 'living' source such as a stream or spring will do and the process for making beer is the same as whisky (see p. 192) up to the draining off of the wort, stage 8. After this, the two methods diverge; to make beer continue as follows:

1. Carefully strain the wort into a pan through a fine muslin. Then add the hops, preferably tied in a muslin bag. The amount of hops depends on the desired strength of the beer: 1 lb. to 10 gallons is average. 'The ingredients of the average cottage brew were: one bushel of malt, costing about 14s.; one pound of hops worth about 1s.; one pint of yeast passed on from a neighbour's brew.'[24] Boil for 1–2 hours.
2. Remove the hops and transfer the wort to another pan to cool. The faster the wort cools the better, as it is at this stage that wild yeasts can attack the mixture and turn it sour. Large shallow cooling pans are often used for this purpose.
3. When cooled to blood heat add the yeast.

> The yeast was added to the beer when it was milk-warm. A couple of clean corks, or a slice of toasted bread, were then placed on top of the beer; the yeast was poured in and as it began to work it collected round the corks. When once she saw this process beginning and the pleasant sight of the mushroom of yeast starting to form round the corks, the wife knew that the beer could now be left to itself. She would say: 'Everything is all right now; the beer is a-smiling!' . . . and after covering the tub with a white cloth, off she would go to bed.[24]

Even better than a white cloth is a thick blanket to prevent the wild yeasts entering.

4. Allow the yeast to work for three days. Skim off the frothy yeast. Keep some, if possible, in a closed bottle in a cool place or in a stream. The yeast will remain active for over a month and can be used for a future brew.
5. Pour the beer into a barrel or jar of some kind and cork; leave it for at least a week before drinking. The beer should last in good condition for up to a year, improving all the time.

Beer Flavourings

Hops

Wild hops are to be found in hedges and bushy places throughout the British Isles but more often in Kent, Worcestershire and other hop-growing areas, escapes from cultivation or relics of earlier days when everyone brewed their own beer and the few hops needed were grown on hedges round fields and not as a main crop. Hops flower in July and August and the cones are ready for picking in September and October. Only the female flowers produce cones and for this reason, and since no one has encouraged their propagation, male hops are seldom found. Female plants are developed from cuttings.

Hops are dried before use, preferably in wood smoke (this is the function of an oast house). They vary in strength according to their freshness and the soil on which they are grown. The fresher the hop the stronger the beer, but hops will keep up to one year and still make a light brew at the end.

Hops are considered superior to other flavouring herbs because of the good bitter taste engendered by the aromatic lupulin they contain and because of their superior powers of preserving.

Herbs

Aromatic, bitter-tasting herbs which were added to the wort instead of hops are bog myrtle, bracken, burnet, coltsfoot, dandelion, eyebright, germander speedwell, ground ivy, heather, marjoram, meadowsweet, mugwort, nettle, scurvey grass, willowherb, wood sage, wormwood and yarrow.

Brandy

'"Ah, Agatha Mikhaylovna," said Oblonsky, kissing the tips of his plump fingers; "what smoked goose you have, what herb brandy . . ."''[21] Though the name brandy is usually associated with distilled grape wine, in its broadest sense brandy can be any distilled fruit spirit. Thus to name a few, you can get myrtille from bilberries, prunelle from sloes, mure from blackberries, kirsch from cherries, calvados from apples, poire William from pears of that name, framboise from wild raspberries, slivovitz from plum (the residue of pips and kernels after the oil has been extracted is distilled, with extra fruit added for flavour) and sorbes from rowan.

Though any fruit can be fermented and distilled into brandy, the finest brandies are made from the finest fruits. Calvados from the luscious Normandy apple, true kirsch from the wild black morello and framboise, described by Cyril Ray as that 'miraculously paradoxical combination of dryness and fruit, austerity and fragrance' from the wild raspberries of the Vosges.

To Make Brandy

First the fruit must be allowed to ferment. Gather the fruit, crush it, and leave it so that the yeast cells clinging to the outer skin of the fruit can get to grips with the sugar in the juice which, now that the skin has been broken, they are able to do. Not only is alcohol made at this stage but carbon dioxide too. Its bubbles keep the fruit moving and the heat given off by the reaction makes it warm. Fermentation continues either until the yeast has absorbed all the sugar or until it has been asphyxiated by the concentration of alcohol; usually the sugar runs out first.

Distilling separates the alcohol, acids and oils from the water. This is the next step – see p. 175. Many fruit brandies are distilled twice to refine the flavour. Only the middle of the second distillation is kept, the first and last parts being put back to be redistilled with the next brew.

The brandy should now be left to mature in wax-lined casks, earthenware or glass jars, or if it is calvados, in wood barrels, in a warm, even temperature. On the Continent brandy is not reserved for drinking when the meal is over but is often drunk as an aperitif or, in the middle of a heavy dinner, as a refresher.

Cider

Cider-making traditionally belongs to the west of England, to great areas of apple orchards: the West Country – Devon, Dorset, Somerset and Cornwall – and the Welsh border counties of Hereford and Worcestershire. And over the years two distinct and hotly defended methods of making cider evolved. In the West Country the crushed apples are packed between layers of straw before being pressed as they believe that minerals in the straw enrich the cider. In the Welsh borders it is thought that the straw 'deadens' the cider and they crush their apples in stone troughs with stone rollers believing that this rough handling releases the aroma in the apple skins and the almond flavour in the pips.

Though any apple can be made into cider the ideal apple has bitterness, sharpness and sweetness combined with a high acid and tannin content. Very few have all these qualities and a mixture of apples is generally used. Recommended varieties are Kingston Black, Tremlitt's Bitter and Sweet Coppin.

Farm-houses in cider-making areas used to have their own presses, and some still do, but the bulk of cider, though made locally, is now done on a commercial basis.

To Make Cider

First spread the apples on racks outside and allow them to weather and rot a bit. Then crush in a clean wooden tub with a wooden mallet or put them through a coarse mincer – though it should not be made of metal – or find some old cider equipment that no one wants any more. Place the resulting pulp on squares made of linen, hessian or horsehair, fold over the sides and stack in a 'cheese' in a press. Weight or screw down the top and collect the juice in a tub as it pours out. Alternatively put the crushed apples between layers of straw in a wooden tub with a hole bored in the bottom to let out the juice. Fill jars or barrels with the juice and leave in a warm place to ferment. If the cider is in a barrel fill it up to the top and keep topping it up.

As the cider ferments the impurities will rise to the surface and overflow. If the cider is in a jar plug it with cotton-wool and keep replacing this with clean cotton-wool as the froth spills out of the neck. When fermentation has ceased plug it properly with cork or wood and leave for three to six months before drinking.

For a sweeter, more alcoholic cider, sugar can be added: 4 oz. to the gallon. If you bottle the cider make sure the bottles are strong, and rack it off from the barrel, leaving any sediment in the bottom. If cider is drunk from the barrel avoid the sediment by not drinking below the tap.

Coffee

'There's an awful lot of coffee in Brazil', but alas none here. Coffee substitutes are the best we can do. Acorns, the roots of dandelion and chicory and the seeds of iris and cleavers make a drink which resembles coffee but never really equals it. However, their advantages are that they possess the tonic and stimulating properties of coffee without the injurious caffeine.

Of them all dandelion coffee tastes the nicest and the nearest to real coffee. Dandelion coffee was a popular drink with gipsies and the roots were sold by herbalists. In a life of Nollekens, the eighteenth-century sculptor, we read of Mrs Nollekens asking Twigg the fruiterer, at Covent Garden, for some dandelion roots, 'an infusion of which had been strongly recommended to her husband by Dr Jebb'. He got the roots from 'that class of people called "Simplers" who sit in the centre of the garden'.[63]

Acorn coffee

Also rather bitter tasting. Chop the nuts roughly and roast in a hot oven. Cool, grind and return to a moderate oven for another roasting before using.

Chicory coffee

The long tap root, dried, roasted, chopped and ground makes coffee. It has rather a bitter taste which is popular on the Continent;

it is often mixed with real coffee to counteract the stimulative effect of the latter.

Dandelion coffee

Dig the roots in early autumn and wash well in running water. (A net full of roots hung under a waterfall does the job for you.) Spread the roots in the open, preferably in the sun, and leave until bone dry. Roast slightly to improve colour and flavour. Grind coarsely and use in the way you would coffee.

Gin

Gin is a grain spirit which has been redistilled over juniper berries. These impart the essential flavour and the name: the Old French word for juniper is *genevre* and 'gin' is a shortening of that. Gin is made first by preparing a spirit from grain – wheat, barley or oats are all suitable. The process is the same as for whisky, but the malt need not be peat dried as the flavour is acquired later. A still is then either half-filled with crushed juniper berries, filled up with spirit and the whole distilled, or the berries are crushed, macerated in water and distilled by themselves, and the result mixed with the spirit. Sometimes coriander seeds are added as well to give extra subtlety of taste. The flavoured spirit is then diluted with water to reduce its alcoholic strength. Gin needs no maturing and can be bottled and drunk straight away.

Liqueurs

Liqueurs are flavoured, sweetened spirits, the basic spirit being either brandy, gin, rum, whisky or a neutral spirit distilled from potato or sawdust. The flavour is derived from a single fruit, flower, root, leaf or seed, though some, such as chartreuse and benedictine, are mixtures and the recipes well-kept secrets. Most brand names are rationalizations of recipes from the days when everyone made their own, when all had their own methods adapted to their likes and resources and when it could be said of French farmers that they 'would distil pretty well anything they could get their hands on, whether from sheer peasant canniness, from enthusiasm, or from a belief that the good God had meant all fruits to be distilled into Alsation *eau de vie*'.[64]

Flavours from the wild in Britain which have been and still are used in liqueurs are:

Angelica: This root has a juniper-like flavour which has been used instead of the latter in gin (p. 183). The dried seeds are an ingredient in several liqueurs, notably vermouth and chartreuse.

Beech: Noyau is thought to be a Buckinghamshire speciality. In a close covered jar steep as many beech leaves as the jar may hold and be covered by gin. Steep for 6 days, strain off the gin (repeat if not sufficiently strongly flavoured). To every pint of gin add 1 lb. sugar dissolved in about ½ pint of boiling water, and a dash of brandy. Mix; bottle when cold. (The leaves of burnet may be treated in the same way.)

Caraway: The basic taste of kümmel comes from oil of caraway, expressed from the seeds. About 6 lb. are needed to produce 4 oz. of oil, which is then mixed with cumin and sweetening and added to a grain- or potato-based spirit.

Juniper: The berries contain a bitter essence called juniperin which gives them a spicy smell and taste, and which they impart to anything made with them, including gin (see p. 183).

Lime: The flowers of lime overflow with nectar, and if these are picked when in full bloom, and left to ferment they make a kind of wine or can be used to flavour spirits.

Mint: The main flavouring of crème de menthe.

Morello cherry: Morello cherries are the correct basis of cherry brandy. Pack an earthenware jar with dark morello cherries, sprinkling crushed brown sugar candy on top. Fill up with brandy and cover the top with a bladder. Keep for several months before bottling.

Sloe: Sloe berries are infused in gin to make sloe gin. Do not pick the sloes until after the first frost as this softens and sweetens them. Put 3 pints of ripe, dry sloes in a gallon jar with 1 oz. sweet almonds (which may be omitted) and 1½ lb. sugar. Pour in 4 pints of gin, and cork. Shake the jar every 3 days for 3 months. Strain off the liquor, bottle and seal the corks. The gin may be drunk now or kept, when it will mature and improve. (You can also use bullace or rowanberries to good effect.)

Walnut: This is an old German recipe for a liqueur made with green walnuts. Chop 1 lb. green nuts into small pieces and cover them with 2½ pints brandy in a large glass jar. Cover and stand in the sun for 2 weeks. Strain the liquid through muslin, pour into a clean jar and add ½ oz. pounded cinnamon and ¼ oz. pounded cloves; leave the jar for another week. Boil 12 oz. sugar with 1½ pints water until the sugar falls in large drops from the spoon, add the nut brandy and strain again.

Wormwood: This is the basis of absinthe. Pepys says – 24 November 1660 – 'I did give them two quarts of wormwood wine.'

Mead

Drunk not only by the ancient British but by all ancient cultures, including the Egyptians, Greeks and Romans. In Nordic areas, before the introduction of wine, mead was the drink for all celebrations, including weddings.

The flavour and character of mead come from the floral essences in the honey and the type of yeast, but the body is determined by the proportions of honey to water. For a dry mead 2–3½ lb. honey to 1 gallon water are recommended and for a sweet one 4–6 lb. It is essential to use soft rain water and a wine yeast such as Maury or Madeira will give better results than an ordinary one. If possible make mead between the end of May and July as this is the time most favourable for the propagation of yeast cells. Correspondingly, bottle mead in February when temperatures are at their lowest and fermentation dead.

Mead

For a general-purpose mead dissolve 3 lb. honey in enough water to make 1 gallon of liquid. Bring to the boil and simmer for 3–5 minutes. Leave until lukewarm, strain through a double muslin into a fermentation jar and add yeast. Plug the neck of the bottle with cotton-wool and leave in a warm place (65–70°F) for 2 days. When the first vigorous fermentation has died down insert an airlock if you have one and leave until all fermentation has ceased. (This will take 6 months or more and depends on the heaviness of the wine.) Stand in a cool place (below 60°F) for a month before bottling. Keep for as long as possible before drinking, but at least six months. (Seven years is best, though.)

Metheglin

This is mead with the addition of herbs and spices. Formerly many variations on the hydromel – honey and water – mixtures were made: omphacomel from grape juice and honey and rhodomel from roses and honey. Sir Kenelm Digby gives twenty-six recipes for mead and twenty-three for metheglin with very slight variations. Here is one.

Another very good white meath

Take to every gallon of water a quart of honey; boil in it a little Rose-mary and Sweet-marjoram: buy a large quantity of Sweet-bryar-leaves, and a reasonable proportion of Ginger: boil these in the Liquor, when it is skimmed; and work it in due time with a little barm [yeast]. Then turn it in a vessel; and draw it into bottles, after it is sufficiently settled. Whites of eggs with the shells beaten together do clarifie Meath best. If you will have your Meath cooling, use Violet and Strawberry-leaves, Agrimony, Eglantine and the like; adding Borage and Bugloss, and a little Rose-mary and Sweet-Marjoram to give it Vigor.[6]

Teas and Tisanes

Tea, since its introduction from China in the seventeenth century, has driven ale, home-made wines, cordials and herbal teas, formerly taken daily, into the background or entirely out of most people's lives. This section deals with herbal drinks or infusions, often called 'tisanes', a name taken from the French. They are made in the same way as tea, and they were frequently used as adulterants when tea was prohibitively expensive.

The list of herbs suitable for making tisanes is long and is divided into several categories: herbs that refresh, cool or soothe; herbs that are aromatic or medicinal (the disease the plant cures being often indicated by its name – feverfew, eyebright, scurvey grass and speedwell); and finally those used as adulterants. We are told that

> A serviceable English 'tea' may be made with hawthorn for bulk, and sage, lemon balm, woodruff (the plant), and black currant leaves for flavour. Do not omit at least three out of four flavouring herbs, but let some flavour predominate. Thus, if currant and sage predominate, the tea will somewhat favour Ceylon; if the lemon balm predominates, it will be more a China cup; if the 'woodruff', it will have the smoky aroma of Darjeeling.[27]

Other adulterants are gorse leaf buds and maidenhair fronds. Cooling teas were made from the leaves of sorrel and the leaves, flowers and root of violet. Refreshing teas came from the leaves of mint, catmint, calamint and holly. Aromatic teas were from the leaves of balm, bilberry, black currant, bog myrtle, sweet briar and woodruff, from the whole plant of marjoram and thyme and from the flowers of primrose, meadowsweet, toadflax and camomile. Soothing all-purpose teas can be made from the flowers of camomile, lime and elm, the leaves and flowers of hop, the leaves of ground ivy, speedwell and wormwood, the root of valerian and the whole of betony. It used to be said of a person that 'He has as many virtues as betony.'

Tisanes can be made from fresh or dried herbs. To dry: pick leaves when not fully developed and flowers when just opened, on a dry, sunny day. Spread them on a wooden table in a shady place and turn twice a day until quite dry. Store in bags or airtight containers.

To make, take half a handful of herb to one pint of water. Boil the water and pour over the herb, cover and leave to infuse for fifteen minutes before straining and drinking. Herb teas are generally drunk without milk but often with sweetening in the form of honey.

Water

André Simon says that

> The best water to drink is spring water, the running water of Highland 'burns' or other mountain streams; also deep-well water. Water from shallow wells, lowland rivers and storage tanks is neither so good to taste nor so safe to drink. Water should never have any colour or smell, but it has a taste which varies according to whatever may be in it beside hydrogen and oxygen: organic and inorganic matter collected in the passage through subsoil strata in the case of spring water, through the sulphurous and sooty air hanging over towns in the case of rain water collected in built-up areas, to say nothing of all the refuse that finds its way into surface water . . . Most natural (other than sea) waters are roughly divided into hard and soft waters. Hard waters are those which have been impregnated with minerals of different kinds. When such waters contain no more than from eight to ten grains of solids per gallon, or at most fourteen grains for water that is impregnated with lime, they are considered as acceptable.[9]

When looking for water in unknown country indications of its presence are:

Caves in limestone country; cracks in rock, moist places, stains.
Cliffs – look at base of limestone faces; in lava country cliffs looking like organ-pipe columns might seep with water.
Valleys may contain springs/streams/seepages – where a valley crosses a lava band, for instance, or a gorge in sandstone leaks water at its sides.
Hillsides first give you a high vantage viewpoint. Look down to lushest vegetation. If green dig a ditch at the base of the lush area and hope it will fill with water. Vegetation on a flat desert area does not mean much, however.
Dry stream beds offer the best chance of water at the lowest point on the outside of a bend. Terraces above dry river beds may yield water.

Shale/sediment/clay areas are often productive if you dig – especially under bluffs if moist.
Sand dunes at the seaside: try at lowest point between dunes on outer edge. If you hit moisture do not dig too deeply; you might reach salt water – stop and let the hole fill with fresh water. Dig a number of holes (some just above high-water mark).
Dry desert islands often produce water in a hole dug in a hollow about 100 yards above the high-tide mark. Do not dig too deep. About 12 ins. is enough following signs of seepage.[49]

Other signs to look for are the fresh tracks of animals, particularly a group of animals at evening. This is the time when, especially in hot climates, they will be going to their water hole to drink. Large flights of birds morning and evening will be making for the same source. Cattle have apparently no instinct for finding water but dogs do.

Water divining is still a totally unexplained phenomenon and all water diviners affirm that the movement of the forked hazel twig is 'as much beyond their control as their heart beats'. Some people subscribe to the 'mineral magnetic' theory and believe that those with a lot of iron in their system make good water diviners; others to the medieval idea of all elements seeking their own level. There are, it seems, 'waters below the earth and waters above the earth'. Thus 'the aqueous molecules exhaled from the soil ascend, and, finding entrance into the stem of the branch, accumulate there' – like sap rising up a tree in the spring season – 'and augment its weight by repelling the air, the ejected matter, returning into the weighted end of the rod, making it dip towards the soil'.

Water for Survival

The best advice during times of water deprivation is to concentrate on reducing loss of liquid from the body to a minimum. Though water does not provide nourishment – its function is to carry food to the body cells and take away waste products – the body's need for water is second only to its need for air and, since it cannot store the material, it is continually having to balance output with intake.

Thirst is relieved by carrying a smooth, non-absorbent pebble in the mouth or by chewing a green leaf, particularly of sorrel. 'The mower gladly chews it down And slakes his thirst the best he may,' says John Clare. Thirst is also greatly satisfied by the skin being wet, even with salt water, and a handkerchief well wetted and tied round the neck allays thirst. When desperate for water one of the first things to do is to keep a watch on the weather and, at the first sign of rain, put out all available clean containers. Most materials can also be made waterproof by rubbing with candle grease or fat and spread out as well. Dam any dry stream beds and strip off clothes so that these can be soaked with water and afterwards squeezed.

Dew is a valuable source of water. Put out any saucer-shaped containers or dig a hollow basin; line it with canvas and scatter with clean stones on which the dew can collect and seep into the basin.

Solid foods, especially fruit and vegetables, often contain more water than liquid ones. A little oil or butter provides energy but needs almost no water for its digestion. It has been claimed that a slit cut in the side of large fish soon fills with a drinkable liquid. Snails contain much fluid, a fact verified by the Institute of Aviation Medicine at Farnborough doing research into desert survival. Sweat can be consumed with advantage, and the water in blisters. There is little benefit in urine except during the first day of deprivation, after which you are merely asking the kidneys to repeat work already done.

Salt water, unless first distilled, builds up salt in the body and, unless there is a flow of urine to take it away, eventually poisons.

> The simplest still is to light a fire among stones near a hollow in a rock that is filled, or can be filled, with the salt water; then taking a hot stone, to drop it in: the water will hiss and give out clouds of vapour, much of which may be collected in a cloth and wrung from it, or sucked out of it. In the same way a pot on the fire may have a cloth stretched over it to catch the steam.[19]

It is wise to treat all unknown water as polluted unless straight from a spring. If possible strain through a cloth of some kind, boil for at least a minute and leave the sediment to settle. Putrid water should be boiled with charcoal or charred sticks, which will help to disinfect it. Bitter herbs are said to have the same effect. Water which has seeped into a hole will be freshest on top but the water underneath will be drinkable. Muddy water can be drunk by taking a good handful of grass or rushes, and tie it roughly together in the form of a cone, 6–8 ins. long; then dipping the broad end into the puddle, and turning it up, a streamlet of partly-filtered water will trickle down the small end. This excellent plan is used by the northern bushmen – at their wells quantities of these bundles are found lying about.[19]

Otherwise drink through your handkerchief – 'either put it over the mouth of your mug, or else throw on the gritty mess as it lies in the puddle, and suck through.'[19]

Ice is a good water producer. Old ice (looks blue, shatters easily and has blunt corners) is better than new (angular, spikey and milky-grey colour). If you are near the sea, old ice will also be less salt than sea water. Making water from snow wastes fuel unless you can melt it in the sun. Here again avoid salt-sprayed snow if near the sea and take all snow from under the surface as it gives more water. Melt it in the hand if you are not afraid of frost-bite, otherwise in a pot over a fire, preferably one with a layer of water already in it – feed in the snow bit by bit.

Storing Water

Where there is a stream water will be plentiful except in times of drought. As an insurance against this, or for convenience, water can be stored in water butts – old wine barrels on bricks with a wooden cover – in tanks or in a pond. Ponds should have a base of puddled clay and, to prevent them becoming stagnant, a constant source of running water passing through from a stream. In streamless areas, such as the chalk downs of southern England, dew ponds were a source of water. Prehistoric in origin, a dew pond lasts as long as its base is intact. It is made by first forming a saucer-like depression on the highest part of the hill, then lining this with a mixture of lime and clay, followed by a closely-packed layer of straw, then a layer of chalk or clay firmly trodden in. The edge should be protected by a chalk rim and a layer of loose flints put in the base. By cutting off the heat of the earth a 'cold spot' is created, and at night moisture from the atmosphere condenses in the pond. Properly made dew ponds never dry out no matter how rainless the season.

Wells are another way of ensuring a continuous supply of water. If spiders crawl out of an old unused well this means the water is still fresh. Otherwise a new one may have to be dug.

Whisky

It is not known when whisky was first distilled, but it is thought that it was probably in Ireland and that monks brought the art with them to Scotland when they first settled in the Mull of Kintyre in the sixth century. The first written record is in the Scottish exchequer rolls of 1494 which lists 'Eight bolls of malt to Friar John Cor, wherewith to make aquavitae.' The Latin term to describe all distilled spirits was *aquavitae*, literally 'water of life', which translated into Celtic became *uiagebeatha* and anglicized and abbreviated 'whisky'. Until 1814, when laws were made which prohibited stills of less than 500 gallons and levied taxes on the drink, every Highlander had his own pot still, producing his own brand of whisky, and consumption of the drink was confined to Scotland and Ireland. 'Freedom and Whisky gang thegither' wrote Burns.

True whisky is made from barley and water, fermented and then distilled. Though two kinds of barley grow wild in Britain, the meadow barley (*Hordeum secalinum*) and the more common wall barley (*H. murinum*) found on waste land, substantial amounts are required for making any quantity of whisky and it will be easier to obtain cultivated barley. For the water, only that which has tumbled icily over peat and granite stones to emerge full of subtle flavours is properly suitable, though as long as the water is not muddy or stagnant and has come from a 'living' source such as a stream or spring it will do.

To make whisky

1. Clean the barley by removing any foreign bodies.
2. Steep it in cold water for two to three days, changing the water several times. A small amount can be put in a sack and left in a stream to soak. This is to make the grain swell.
3. Spread this 'malt' out on a flat clean surface in a warm atmosphere for 8–12 days for the grain to sprout, and allow some of the enzymes in the grain to convert most of the starch to sugar. During this time the grain should be kept moist by sprinkling with water, and turned twice a day. When the sprout is two thirds of the length of the grain – it grows under the skin of the grain – it is ready for the next step.

4. This 'green malt' must then be dried in a kiln at a temperature hot enough to kill the 'malt' but not so hot that the enzymes, which are still needed to continue the process of converting starch into sugar, are destroyed – between 104°F and 122°F. For malt whisky the drying must be done over a peat fire, so that the pungent smoke from the peat impregnates the grain with its smell, eventually giving the spirit its flavour. Other whiskies, grain spirits and beer obtain their definitive flavours at a later stage so any fuel can be used to dry the grain, though many people consider coke essential. Small quantities can be dried satisfactorily in an oven, over a fire, on a perforated iron plate or a sieve with holes small enough to prevent the grain slipping through, but the temperature must be carefully watched. When the grain is brittle it is dry enough – tasting is a good way to test.

5. Next the dried malt must be ground into a meal, but not too fine a meal – coarse coffee grounds are about the right size. For a small amount this can be done with a rolling pin or in some kind of grinder.

6. Mashing is the next process. The meal is thoroughly mixed with hot water (151°F to 154°F), hot enough to extract the sugars but not so hot that the enzymes needed to convert starch into sugar are killed. Country people give 'Three parts boiling water to one part cold water' to get the correct heat, but they usually waited till the steam had lifted and they could see their face in the water and that was the right heat. Mix the mash to the consistency of pigs' swill and leave to soak overnight to allow the water to absorb all the goodness from the grain.

7. The liquid, known as the 'wort', is now drawn off into a vat or barrel and allowed to cool, leaving the barley husks, which are rich in protein, to be fed to pigs.

8. Yeast is now added. Fermentation, lasting for about 48 hours, will then begin. When the wort has become still the name changes again; the mixture is now called 'beer' or 'wash'.

9. Distillation: see p. 195. The result of the first distillation will be of low alcoholic strength, called 'low wines'. Its function is to separate the alcohol from the liquid and eliminate any residue of yeast and unfermented matter.

10. Second distillation: put the low wines in another still and redistil, but keep the first and last part of the distillation separate

from the middle. These two are called feints and contain fusil oils which make a spirit good for removing tar stains but not for drinking. If the mixture turns blue when water is added fusil oil is present. Return the feints to the beer, to be included in the next distillation.

The middle-run spirit is whisky of about 140° and 142° proof, far too strong to drink. In order to dilute it water is added, and in order to smooth the taste it must be matured.

11. Maturing: the length of time necessary for the whisky to mature varies with the character of the whisky and the climatic conditions. In Great Britain the Immature Spirits Act decrees that no whisky, rum or brandy can be sold for public consumption unless it has been matured in wood for at least three years, though most would consider seven even better, and good malt whiskies are laid down for ten years and more. Oak barrels, preferably ones in which sherry has been stored, are ideal for maturing whisky. These allow for the right interchange between whisky, wood and air which all mysteriously contribute to the final taste and colour; they should be stored in a cool warehouse.

Wine

Wine can be made from fruit, flowers, leaves, roots and sap. In times past, when water was often contaminated and before tea became cheap in the nineteenth century, herbal teas, ale and home-made wines were the everyday drinks. Recipes were handed down from one generation to the next:

> Of beverages made from the yields of gardens, orchards, fields and lanes, the kinds hardly could be numbered. Teas brewed from nettles, dandelions and other simples were available everywhere. For superior neighbours they had palatable home-made wines, such as damson, elderberry, currant, parsnip and gooseberry, which sometimes induced nimbleness of speech at nights, followed by a peculiar headiness in mornings. Stronger concoctions of cherry brandy, and similar liquors, served for special occasions of merrymaking.[40]

Licensed beer, imported grape wine and an addiction for tea and coffee have pushed the art of making home-made drinks into obscurity. But they are quite easy, require little time and equipment and are worth reviving, if only to save money as prices constantly rise.

For all wine-making the ingredients should be as fresh as possible and the water as soft as possible. Honey may be used as a substitute for sugar but remember that it is more liquid and therefore add a fifth less water. Lemon and orange are frequently an ingredient in recipes, used to bring out the flavour in some and to supplement a deficiency of acid in others – particularly flower wines. Where these are not available vinegar or verjuice (p. 169) can be used instead. You will need a large bowl capable of holding one gallon of liquid, a gallon flask or glass jar to hold the wine while it is fermenting and a plug for this. Plastic airlocks can be bought, or use fresh cotton-wool: both enable the wine to spill out when fermentation is strong, so preventing a build-up of pressure which could explode the jar. Fermentation has ceased when no foam appears out of the top of the jar, the sound of fizzing has stopped and no bubbles are rising to the surface from the bottom of the jar – it can take from one week to six or nine months. A syphon to suck the wine from jar to bottle in order to leave the sediment behind makes for a clearer wine. Though pouring will do almost as well, the wine may be a bit cloudy as a result. Wine can be matured in cask or bottle though, finally, it is more easily served from a bottle. Where no corks are available, wood, or cloth sealed with wax, will do. For yeast see p. 171. Finally, the enemy of wine-making is the vinegar bug: the cleaner and better sterilized the utensils, and the more the brew is kept covered, the less chance it will have of making a raid.

Space does not allow for a complete list of recipes, so I have tried to categorize the different wines and give a general method for each type with one or two specific recipes. It is hoped that this will be enough to enable the reader without further literature to make all kinds of wine.

Flower Wines

Made by first boiling some water, then adding sugar and lemon, and allowing this to dissolve before putting in the flower heads. Leave to cool to blood heat and then add the previously activated yeast. Allow to ferment for a week and rack off into bottles. The main flowers used for wine are: burnet saxifrage, coltsfoot, clover, cowslip, dandelion, elderflower, eyebright, gorse, guelder rose, lime, may, primrose, sweet violet and wormwood.

Coltsfoot

Coltsfoot

Suitable for dandelion and clover too.

1 gallon coltsfoot flowers; 1 gallon water; 1 lemon; 1 orange; 3 lb. sugar; yeast. Dissolve sugar in boiling water and re-boil for 5 minutes. Add rind and juice of orange and lemon, and coltsfoot flowers. Stir well, squeezing flowers to extract all flavour. Leave to cool to blood heat, add previously activated yeast, cover and allow to ferment for seven days in a warm place. Strain into a jar through butter muslin, cork loosely or insert airlock. When fermentation has ceased, rack off into bottles.

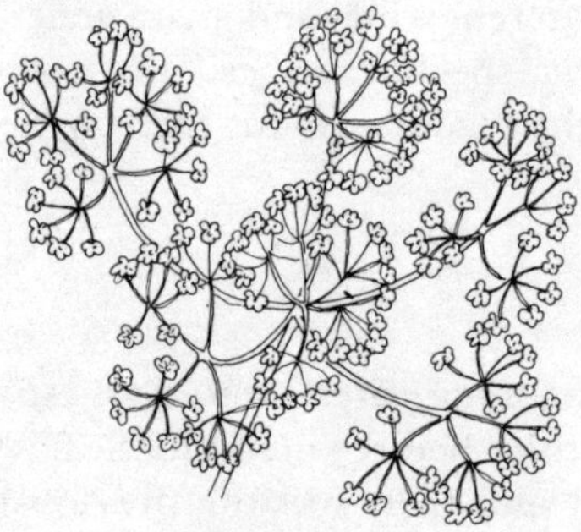

Elder flower

Elderflowerade

This is a concentrate, which is drunk diluted with water, and makes a delicious summer drink.

Dissolve 5 lb. of sugar in 5 pints water and when hot add 2 oz. citric acid (to be bought from most chemists). Pour over 2 lb. elderflowers with the worst of their stalks removed. Stir and press down well. Cover and leave for 24 hours before bottling.

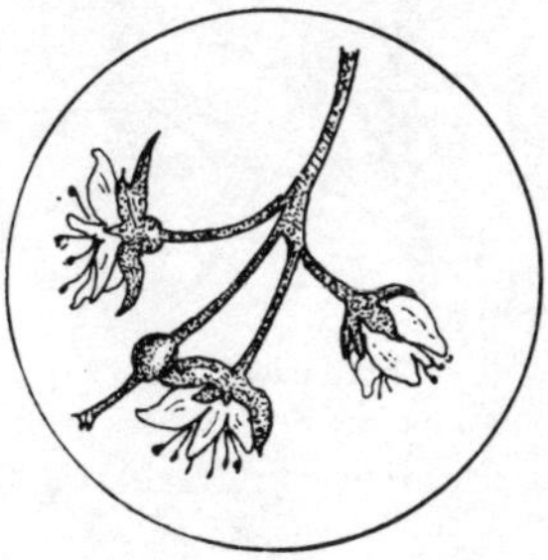

Lime

Lime blossom wine

3 pints lime blossom; 1 gallon water; 1 lb. clean wheat; 1 lb. raisins, chopped (optional); 3½ lb. sugar; yeast.

Dry the blossoms in the sun to bring out the flavour. Boil in water for thirty minutes. Cool to blood heat, add wheat, raisins and sugar and stir until the sugar has dissolved. Add yeast, cover and leave to ferment for 3 weeks. Strain and bottle. Keep for a year before drinking.

May blossom wine

2 pints may blossom; 1 gallon water; 1 lemon; 1 orange; 3½ lb. sugar; yeast.

Boil water then add sugar and lemon and orange rinds. Stir till sugar dissolves, then boil 15 minutes. Pour over blossoms in bowl. Cool to blood heat, add yeast and lemon and orange juice. Stir, cover with cloth, leave in warm place for 3 days, stirring daily. Strain into jar and cork loosely until fermentation ends. Remove to cool place for 2 weeks before bottling.

May, hawthorn

Fruit Wines

In the absence of grapes, the nearest thing to 'wine' is made from fruits. Wines made from fruit require very little water and often no yeast as enough wild yeasts cling to their skin to induce fermentation. Pour boiling water over the fruit and leave to stand for about three days, mashing and stirring the fruit each day. Strain on to sugar and heat until dissolved. Cool to blood heat and add activated yeast if required. Put in a jar, plug or insert an airlock and leave in a warm place until fermentation has ceased. Bottle and leave for at least six months to mature before using. Fruits which make the best wines are: blackberry, black currant, bullace, cherry, crab apple, cranberry, crowberry, elderberry, gooseberry, hawthorn, pear, plum, raspberry, red currant, rose hip, rowan, service tree, sloe, strawberry and wayfaring tree. Recipes for a few are given below, the others to be adapted accordingly.

Blackberry wine

1 gallon blackberries; 1 gallon water; 4 lb. sugar; yeast.

Put berries in bowl, pour over boiling water, cover, leave to stand 7 days, stirring and mashing daily. Strain through muslin on to sugar, stir well. Add activated yeast, put in jar and leave to ferment, loosely corked. When fermentation is finished, rack off and bottle.

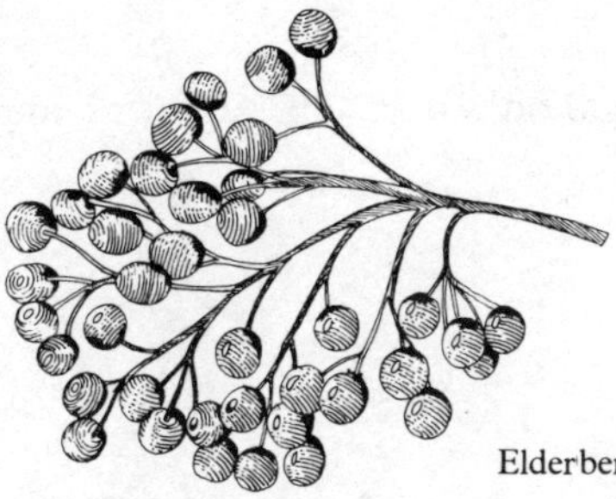

Elderberry

Elderberry wine

Strip 1 gallon of elderberries from their stalks. Cover with cold water, cover bowl and allow to stand for 3 to 4 days, mashing and stirring each day. Strain. To every gallon of liquid add 3 lb. sugar, 2 oz. bruised ginger, ½ oz. cloves and a pinch of allspice. Bring to boil and simmer for 30 minutes. Cool to lukewarm and add activated yeast. Put in jar, allow to ferment, transfer to another jar and leave, tightly corked, for 3 months before bottling.

Hawthorn berry wine

4 lb. berries; 2 gallons water; 4 oranges; 2 lemons; 6 lb. sugar; yeast.

Pour boiling water over the berries, cover and stand for one week, stirring daily. Strain on to rinds and juice of fruit. Add sugar and heat to blood temperature. Add activated yeast, cover and leave for 24 hours. Transfer to jar, cork loosely and leave till fermentation stops. Rack off and bottle.

Raspberry wine

Red currant wine is made in the same way.

4 lb. raspberries; 1 gallon water; 3 lb. sugar; yeast.

Pour boiling water over fruit, leave for 4 days, stirring and mashing well each day. Strain through muslin on to sugar, squeezing all juice from fruit and stirring to dissolve sugar. Add activated yeast, cover and leave for 24 hours. Transfer to jar, cork loosely and leave in warm place to finish fermenting. Transfer to cooler place for 2 weeks. When fermentation has completely finished, bottle.

Rose hip wine

4 lb. rose hips; 1 gallon water; 3 lb. sugar; 1 lemon (optional); yeast.

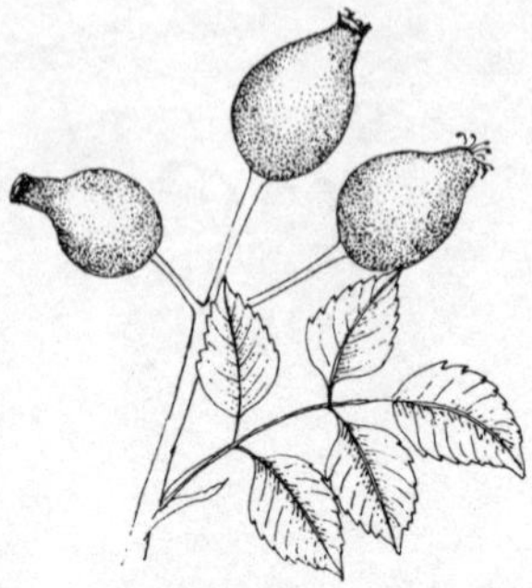

Rose hip

Gather hips after a good frost. Wash and chop finely and place in bowl with sugar and rind and juice of lemon. Add boiling water, stir. When lukewarm add activated yeast. Cover and leave in warm place for 10 days, stirring daily. Strain well into jar. Cork loosely and leave to ferment in warm place. Remove jar to cooler place for one week, rack off into another jar, cork down and leave for 6 months before bottling. After fermentation the storage jar can be topped up with brandy or vodka which greatly improves the wine.

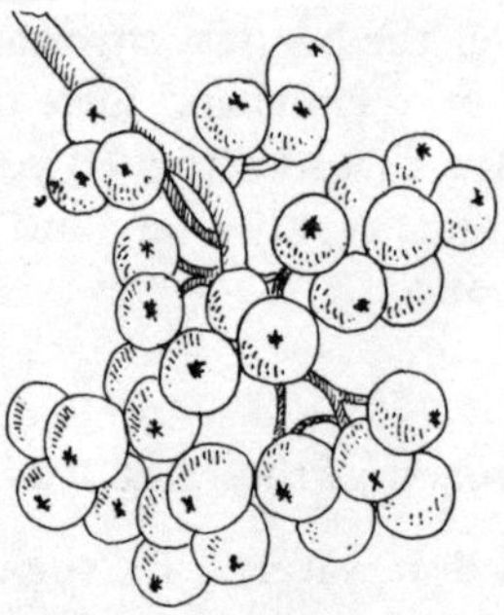

Rowan berry

Rowan berry wine

Diodgriafel is made of the berries of Solus Aucuparta [*Sorbus aucuparia*] by pouring water over the mashed berries and setting the infusion to ferment. When kept some time this is by no means an unpleasant liquor. In Scotland a spirituous liquor is obtained by distillation.[27]

Sloe wine

2 pints sloes; 2 pints water; 1 lb. sugar.

Add boiling water to sloes. Cover, leave to stand for 4 days, stirring and mashing at least once a day. Strain and add to each 2 pints of liquid, 1 lb. sugar. Leave another 4 days, stirring each day. Put in jar or bottles but do not cork down firmly until fermentation has ceased.

Sloe

Strawberry wine

10 pints strawberries; 10 pints water; 5 lb. sugar.

Mash strawberries and mix pulp with water. Cover and leave overnight. Strain off liquid and add sugar, stir well until dissolved. Put in a jar, cork and leave for 6 months; it will then be ready for bottling. (Some people add yeast and raisins to this recipe.)

Root Wines

The oldest and best is parsnip wine.

Parsnip wine

Sugar beet wine is made in the same way.

4 lb. parsnips; 3 lb. sugar – preferably demerara; 1 gallon water; spice according to taste – root ginger, rosemary, lemon; yeast.

Clean parsnips, cut in two, put into water and boil gently until tender. Strain, add sugar and spices, if any, and boil again for 5 minutes. Cool until lukewarm, add toast spread with yeast, leave to ferment for 36 hours, put into fermentation jar and leave for 3 to 6 months before racking off into bottles. Store for a year before drinking; it is said to improve for up to ten years.

Smoking, Snuff

I have added this section mainly because I smoke and the one time I tried to give it up felt that all the pleasure had gone out of life. While living off the land I managed to make quite palatable herbal cigarettes and I know that in any other survival situation I would look around for some weed to dry and roll. While smoking herbal cigarettes you at least have the comfortable feeling that they are better for you as they do not contain nicotine, but because of this they also have less kick. And, as the doctors say, inhaling smoke of any kind into your lungs is bad for you.

Tobacco arrived from the British West Indies along with sugar and cotton and, apart from a period during George III's reign – and then only amongst the fashionable – it has kept its grip from that day to this.

Until the introduction of cigarettes in the nineteenth century, tobacco was always smoked in pipes, usually long churchwarden clay pipes. These early clay pipes varied in length from 3 to 18 ins. according to fashion, but today the only manufacturer left in the country makes them in three sizes: 9, 13 and 18 ins. long.

Clay pipes unfortunately broke easily and they virtually disappeared after the invention of cheap wooden pipes. The first wood or briar pipes were made of the roots of heather (*Erica arborea*) dug out of boggy ground round the Mediterranean.

> The knotty roots are kept in moist sheds until required and are then cut into short lengths while still green and boiled from 8 to 10 hours, which prevents them from cracking. The lengths of roots are then hollowed with saws . . . When polished and finished bruyere pipewood is a pleasant reddish brown and does not burn easily.[65]

But true briar wood is not always available and, as this letter shows, other woods can be substituted; the writer had only his firewood stack and none of the wood was seasoned:

> The first I tried was hornbeam and that smoked about the same pace as the tobacco and when the tobacco had been smoked, so had the pipe! The next was beech which split. Then I found the top of an old oak post the foot

of which had rotted in the ground. This made good pipes which smoke and last well and they are light, but it is not possible to get a fine finish on the outside. Yew does well and is apparently not poisonous, as I have smoked several without any ill effects. Cherry is excellent.[66]

Cigarettes were originally devised by the Aztecs. They stuffed hollow reeds with tobacco. Other South American natives rolled tobacco in crushed oats or other leaves. These 'cigars' were brought back by the Conquistadors to Spain and the smaller cigarette developed as beggars picked up discarded butts, rolled them in paper and called them *cigarillos*. The French collected the habit of smoking these *cigarillos* during the Napoleonic campaign and gave them the name of *cigarettes*.

They weren't always wrapped in paper. In *Lorna Doone*, John Ridd describes Mr Faggus the highwayman

sitting in the great chimney corner . . . And all the while, he was smoking tobacco, in a manner I never had seen before, not using a pipe for it, but having it rolled in little sticks, about as long as my finger, blunt at one end, and sharp at the other. The sharp end he would put in his mouth, and lay a brand of wood to the other, and then draw a white cloud of curling smoke; and we never tired of watching him.[67]

Smoking Mixtures

Though without the narcotic effect of tobacco, herbal tobaccos, formerly called 'smoking mixtures', can be made from several kinds of leaf, either one kind used by itself or several mixed, the recipe being a matter of personal choice.

The main smoking herbs are coltsfoot (picked after all the flowers have gone), eyebright and mullein. Melilot and woodruff are often added to give fragrance. Bogbean, comfrey, beech and chestnut leaves are also commonly used.

The leaves should be dried in bunches in an airy place until soft and turning yellow. Then, after any stalks or tough midribs have been removed, they should be packed down in a wooden box or barrel, mixed with brandy or honey and left to dry again but in a warmer place, such as the kitchen mantlepiece. Finally, while the mixture is still damp, it must be rolled up to get an even texture and pressed under a weight. After this it may be cut up and used.

Snuff

Snuff was prepared from the flowers and roots of Solomon's seal and from the leaves of yarrow which, on account of the pungency of the leaves, used to be termed 'old man's pepper'.

Part Two

Shelter

When we lived off the land our shelter was a wooden hut some Boy Scouts had built a few years before and then abandoned. By the time we found it some of the boards were beginning to rot and a lot of leaves had made a permanent home on the floor; but it was near enough to what we wanted and, more important, in near enough the right place – a valley with a trout stream and surrounded by woods. We had been offered a small cottage in a nearby hamlet but refused it, feeling it was too comfortable, solid and too shut off from the outside world. If you are trying to live off nature then to live at a fairly basic level is the only recourse. You can only enter properly into the mind of your prey if its world is the same as yours. So we opted for the hut, cleared out the leaves, admired the sweep of the valley to be seen from its door and settled in. This did not take long as our possessions were few and there was nothing but a shelf to put them on. We laid bracken as a mattress and then the sleeping bag on top of that. A camp stool completed our furniture, though there was little room for more in the cramped space. Outside, the Boy Scouts had left an old kitchen range dug into a bank. This was our source of heat, our cooking stove and, really, our living-room too. Two stumps of wood served as chairs and every evening we would light the fire, cook a meal and, with the goat nuzzling our legs for heat space too, sit by the range until it was time for bed. Our afternoon room was a rug spread on a bank near the stream which caught all the sun; so in all we had three rooms, though if it rained only one and no cooking facilities either. This was adequate for two months, but had we been going to do it for longer we would have needed something more substantial. A proper wooden hut as described on pp. 228–30 with a fireplace would have done. Fur trappers in the backwoods of America lived in similar ones through harsh winter weather. Survival in more basic accommodation is quite possible: early American colonists lived in dug-out shelters until they built their own cabins. A great number of gipsies throughout Europe live in tents all the year round. Many would have nothing else:

> 'I prefer a tent to a house. With a house it can be very, very draughty. And damp. The old houses up here, they're usually damp. Oh yes. But in a tent – I mean you stay there with the fresh air all the time, all the time. I mean during frosty weather I always keep an extra fire on in the tent. Keep plenty of heat. You can't do that in a house.'[4]

To most people, however, a tent is a temporary shelter only. For a time it may be ideal, since the permanence granted by homes, possessions and too much comfort is conducive to ruts. As William Morris said in an address on 'The Beauty of Life' in 1880 there are too many people to whom

> the attainment of comforts is what makes all the difference between civilization and uncivilization . . . If that is what it is, I for my part wish that I were well out of it, and living in a tent on a Persian desert, or in a turf hut on the Iceland hillside. But however it be, I tell you that Art abhors that side of civilization; she cannot breathe in the houses that lie under its stuffy slavery.[68]

But, like Candide, it is a good idea to settle in due course and be content to cultivate your garden. For this, nothing can surpass a solidly built house fashioned from the best local material.

'The pattern of English building', to quote Alec Clifton Taylor, 'has been determined primarily by geography, but other factors have also contributed their share, among them trading connections and local fashions.'[69] After the Middle Ages, when houses ceased to be made wholly of wood, and until the advent of canals (which meant that the transportation of heavy materials from one place to another was no longer a major operation) all houses, except the grandest, were built of local materials. Flint, granite, cob, sandstone are typical examples – an observant eye can still tell when one geological zone ends and another begins simply by noting the construction of the cottages built before about the eighteenth century. Such an approach was entirely practical and the result very pleasing. Each cottage is built to withstand centuries of wear and fits perfectly into its surroundings. In the south-west cottages were built with rubblestone bases, cob walls and thatch roofs and, in the wooded areas of the west and south-east, of a framework of wood infilled with wattle and daub or later, brick or stones. Stone forms the bulk of the buildings of the central and northern areas of Britain, limestone in the centre giving way to flint in the east and then, as you go north, sandstone, grit stone and finally, in Scotland, the hardest stone of all, granite. W. G. Hoskins describes the building of a wall in a stoneless area to show how the cottages 'look as though they had grown out of the very earth they stand in, so well matched they are and resting so comfortably on it';

it rests on a footing of rubble masonry perhaps a foot or two high, then comes the mud wall itself, and finally it is thatched on top to keep the wet out. Everything in this wall comes from the parish or at the most within a mile or two of it; the stones for the rubble footing are rough boulders, laboriously picked out of the glacial boulder clay that covers the stoneless parishes. They had to be picked up before ploughing could be done in any case, but they were not wasted: they all went into the footings of mud walls, or into the plinths of the old pre-brick cottages. The mortar that binds them so stoutly even now was made from lime burnt in the parish or very near it; the mud was local clay mixed with chopped straw and road scrapings to bind it; the thatch came from wheat-straw grown in the village fields, or perhaps from reeds that grew in one chosen patch . . . Nothing was wasted. Our own civilization, if one may so describe it, has a multitude of unpleasant aspects, but one of the most conspicuous, if not the most unpleasant, is its colossal waste of every mortal thing that grows.[70]

Inside these cottages the rooms, before electricity, were lit by oil lamps or rush lights; the furniture was made from local woods shaped and carved in the forest where the tree was felled, kept clean and shining with beeswax. The floors were made of wood, stone or brick or, in the most primitive, rammed earth. They were carpeted in early times with sweet-smelling herbs or rushes, later with rush mats and, in the grander houses, carpets. These would have been made from wool clipped from the backs of the sheep which grazed outside. Windows, in a peasant's house before the seventeenth century, would have been unglazed and the house protected from the elements only by wooden shutters. The rain would have drained off the roof or water piped into the cottage through wooden, lead or clay drain pipes. All the materials used were therefore simple, appropriate and would have been obtained from within the vicinity.

Modern technology has provided us with superior plumbing, heating and lighting. Where the main construction and furnishings are concerned modern houses are inferior. The following sections will explain why.

Chimneys

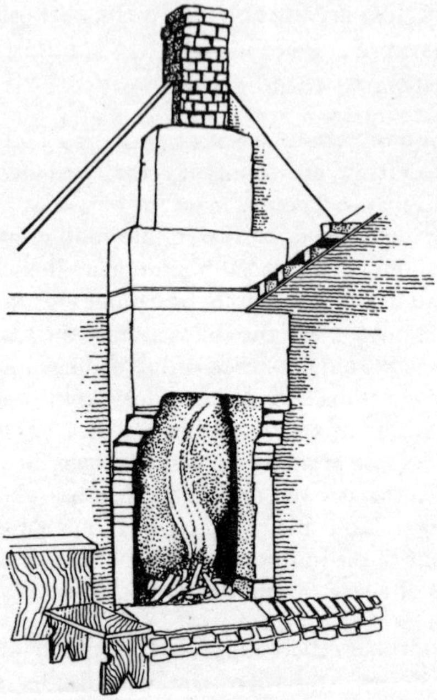

Before the time of Elizabeth I only large houses had brick chimneys. Small houses had crude edifices of unfired clay, which, for structural reasons and in order to make the best use of the heat, were placed in the middle of the building. As time showed that brick resists heat better than any other material it was used increasingly, from the late sixteenth century, for all houses. However, until the seventeenth century it was normal for each fire to have its own chimney stack; it was only after this time that the practice of grouping several flues into one chimney began. This meant that chimneys had to be built at an angle with the resulting problem of draught. Initial improvements were made by tilting two slabs of stone against each other over the top of the chimney shaft, or four thin slabs set against each other or even one slab raised on four corner supports. The chimney pot was largely a Victorian invention.

Cleaning, Household

Housework was a pleasant pastime. When my floor was dirty, I rose early, and, setting all my furniture out of doors on the grass, bed and bedstead making but one budget, dashed water on the floor, and sprinkled white sand from the pond on it, and then with a broom scrubbed it clean and white: and by the time the villagers had broken their fast the morning sun had dried my house sufficiently to allow me to move in again, and my meditations were almost uninterrupted.[1]

Thus Thoreau described his method of housework at Walden. Sharp river sand used as a scouring agent for wood, stone and metal was common practice. Horsetails were employed for the same purpose, being abrasive and, because of the silica contained in their stems and outer skins, cleansing too. Bunches of the prickly stems of madder were favoured by French metal workers for the same purpose. Soap was also used (see p. 372 and, for suitable brushes, p. 274). Furniture was rubbed with the appropriate nut oil (walnut oil for walnut furniture, etc.) or with a lump of beeswax. These not only produced a shine but fed the wood at the same time. Dusters were made of linen or wool, though a lump of dried moss has the same effect.

A primitive form of dry cleaning for woollen cloths was to re-shear them. Chintz hangings were cleaned by being soaked in a bran lye made by steeping bran in water, then boiling it and straining it off; the bran has the effect of levering off the dust by swelling the cotton fibre below. The chintz was immersed in fresh solutions of bran lye until the water remained clear.

Drains and Damp Courses

Early pipes were all made from either wood or clay. These were anything from three to eighteen inches in diameter, intersected and wedged into each other. The earliest were tapered at one end but this led to problems at the ridge and later ones were slotted together in such a way as to make a smooth interior. Runnels of slate were also used as drains and in Scotland field drains were made by filling the base of a trench with old heather plants, then refilling the trench on top of them. Similarly, in Suffolk from pre-Roman times up to the present day they have filled the bottom of drainage trenches with hawthorn and blackthorn bushes.

House damp courses were made in a different way. The floors inside the house were kept dry by being raised above ground level. The ground earth was given a covering of ash or gravel and then porous brick tiles or stones were laid on top. Outside, a damp course was made in the following way:

> Their land drain was set at least four feet down, exactly under the drip of the roof. The base of the land drain was well below the foundation level of the cottage walls, and was set so that it encircled the building, and discharged at the lowest point well beyond it – frequently into a well, if one was conveniently placed. The land drain was filled with loose rounded stones; sea or river pebbles were carried some distance if obtainable, the smaller ones making the cobbled surface close to the wall, the larger ones being placed in the drain. Broken stone was used in default of rounded stone, but rounded were preferred, as they did not pack together, and the object was to keep the drain base as open and loose as possible. Sometimes, cross stones were edged across, making a culvert over the loose drain stones, but the work would be done (preferably) before autumn rains, and once the flow through started the water-way would be kept washed clear by every storm. The drain was then filled in to the surface with large gravel, and the surface levelled with a tilt away from the building. The old thatch usually stood out more than a foot beyond the wall plate, so that every straw or reed on the surface of that thatch dropped its water a foot clear of the house wall. The wide eaves sheltered the top portion of the walls almost down to the first floor level. Below that, the base of the walls sloped slightly outwards and, where the walls were plastered, the plaster was 'run out' over the solid foundation stones or double-walled brick. Beyond this, from the base of the wall, a close packed cobble paving carried the dry ground out, as far as the edge of the deep land drain.[71]

Such ingenious plans are now generally misunderstood: the drains are disturbed or covered by concrete or a flowerbed and the old cottage becomes damp.

Floor Coverings

'A lady once offered me a mat, but as I had no room to spare within the house, nor time to spare within or without to shake it, I declined it, preferring to wipe my feet on the sod before the door. It is best to avoid the beginnings of evil.'[1] For those already corrupted, or with more time and space than Thoreau, the following methods of carpeting are suggested.

Strewing Herbs

Chosen with care both for their scent and for different types of wear, strewing herbs were used as an early form of carpet on all types of floor whether stone, wood or rammed earth. Balm, camomile, feverfew, sweet cicely, tansy and woodruff, the hay-scented ferns and grasses, *Dryopteris cremula*, holly grass and sweet vernal grass were all employed. The mints were used too, of which Gerard said 'the smelle rejoiceth the heart of man, for which cause they used to strewe it in chambers and places of recreation, pleasure and repose, where feasts and banquets are made',[26] and meadowsweet, about which he was even more lyrical: 'The leaves and floures of Meadowsweet farre excelle all other strowing herbs for to decke up houses, to strawe in chambers, halls and banqueting-houses and in the summer time, for the smell thereof makes the heart merrie and joyful and delighteth the senses.'[26] Sweet flag was also freely strewn on the floors of houses, and, at festivals, in churches.

Rush Mats

Rush mats are a development of the use of rushes as strewing herbs. The common rush, prepared as for rush basket work, is that most often used. (The inner bast of lime bark and also strips of rag have been employed in the same way.) The rushes are plaited, about $5\frac{1}{4}$ yards being required for an oval mat measuring 32 × 20 ins. The plaits are laid on their sides and sewn together so that the edge of the plait forms the surface of the mat. Woven rush mats can be made very quickly. The warp threads are of string and bunches of rush are placed between the two sets of alternately raised strings, patted flat with a stick and finished by tying the warp ends together.

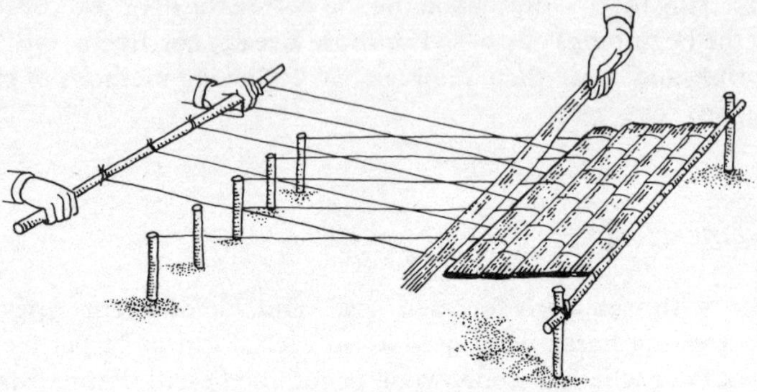

Carpets

Under this heading come all floor coverings woven in textile materials. Carpets can be divided into two classes, pile and smooth face.

Materials

Wool is the material most frequently used for warp, weft and pile. Cotton is often used for foundation and for pile in pure white carpets. Silk, though sumptuous and good for foundation is less satisfactory as pile. Linen, hemp and jute are rarely met in old carpets.

Colour

The warp thread is invariably left its natural colour and the weft usually is. Natural coloured wools make attractive carpets; for a greater colour range dye materials with vegetable dyes, p. 337.

Selvedges

It is usual to have the outermost one or two threads thicker than the others. Easily effected by grouping together two or more threads, then passing the weft round enough times to make up for the lack of knots. The selvedge should not, however, be tighter than the rest of the carpet otherwise it will not lie flat.

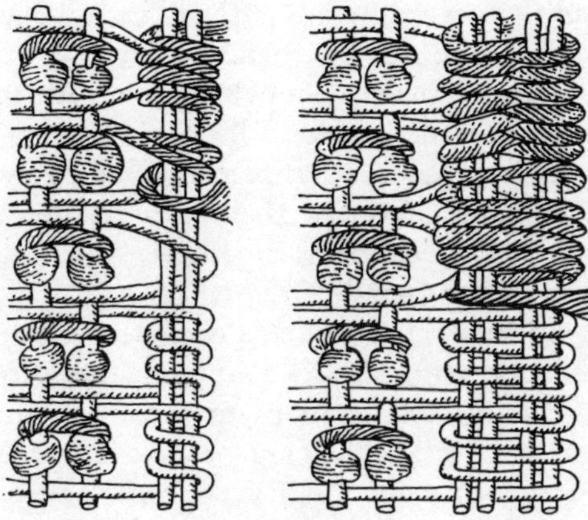

Selvedge

Ends

These may be finished in a variety of ways. For simple woven rugs they can be tied in twos or threes. More elaborately, a band of tapestry can be woven and a fringe made.

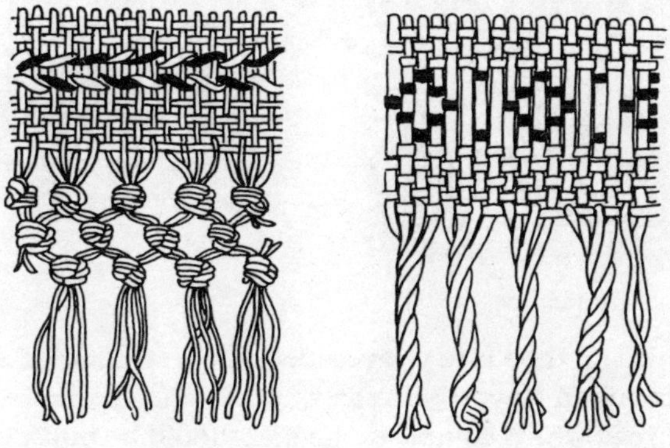

Ends

Pile Carpets

The foundation is the same as for any woven cloth, a warp and a weft thread. In addition, extra threads with cut ends, collectively called the pile, are inserted to stand perpendicular to the woven fabric. A pile carpet, if properly made, should be able to withstand enormous amounts of wear over many years. Pile is constructed in three main ways. In the first short pieces of thread are tied in rows to the warp, interspersed with lines of weft, so that the pile is built up at the same time as the foundation material is laid. This is the method employed in the majority of hand-made Oriental carpets.

In the second method extra warp threads, several times longer than the foundation warp, are woven into the fabric in such a way to form a series of upstanding loops to constitute the pile. These loops are sometimes left as they are – as in a Brussels carpet – and sometimes cut to form a pile. English country hook mats or rag rugs are made by hooking odd strips of rag through a backing of sack cloth, the loops forming the pile.

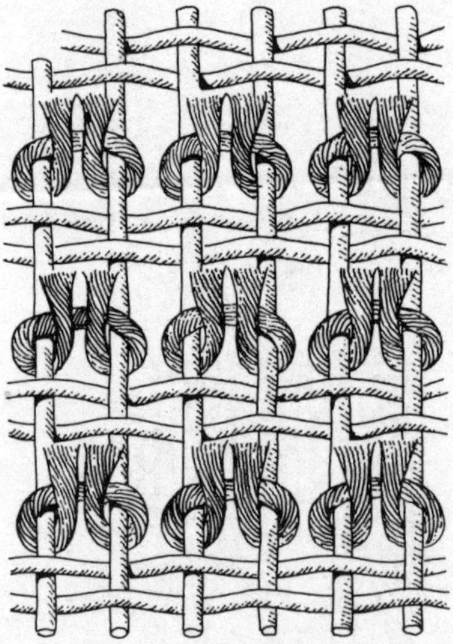

Turkish knots

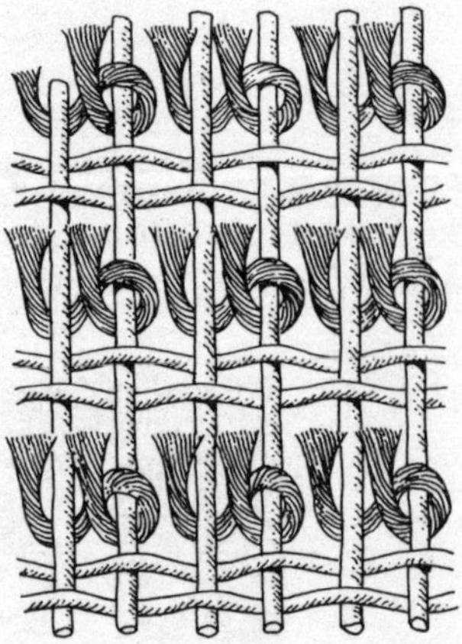

Persian knots

The third method is to weave an extra weft thread raised in loops – a technique in Egypt between the fifth and tenth centuries.

The thread which composes the pile should be bulky and loosely spun and consist of two or more strands. The pile is secured to the warp by a knot, the free ends compacting to form the pile, the ends evenly clipped once the carpet is finished. There are several kinds of knots but the ones shown are the most usual. The first, called a Turkish knot, is that employed in almost all Turkish, Caucasian and English carpets. The second, called the Persian knot, makes a very close pile and is that found in the majority of Persian, Central Asiatic, Indian and Chinese carpets.

To make the knot take a short piece of yarn, or more generally the end of a long piece which is cut afterwards, and tie. Leave no warp thread uncovered and intersperse each row of knots with two rows of weft. The number of knots tied vertically should equal the number tied horizontally. Designs are usually prepared on squared paper. Twenty-five knots to the square inch make a satisfactory carpet, fifty a finer one and a hundred one that will probably be beyond the bounds of most people's patience.

Smooth-face or Woven Carpets

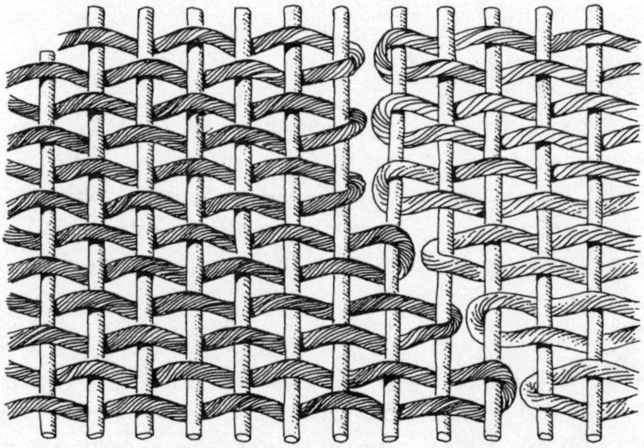

Instead of having pile to resist wear these carpets are woven like cloth or tapestry; they differ in that the materials used are heavier and their design simpler and better suited to the floor. The bulky surface weft – of wool or rags – hides the warp completely. Where there is a design the discontinuity of the weft which occurs when the boundary lines of the design lie parallel to the warp is overcome by avoiding anything but very short vertical patterns, so the designs are typically stepped or diagonal.

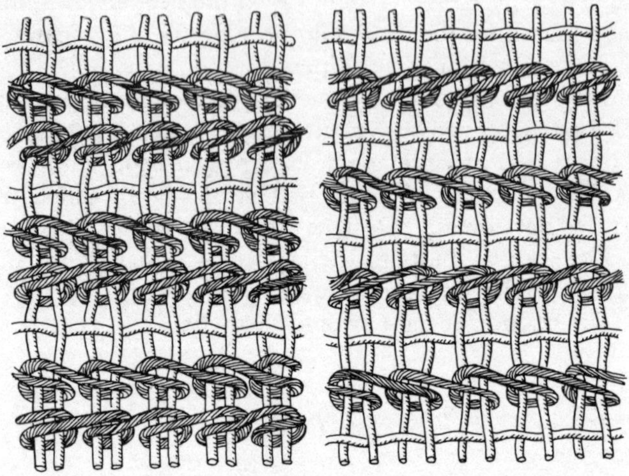

Soumak weaving

Soumak carpets have a weft which 'floats' or goes forward in front of four warp threads and back behind two, making a herring-bone effect. Finer details are achieved by crossing only two warp threads. After every two lines of stitches, a weft thread, subsequently hidden, is put through to strengthen the fabric.

To weave

First set up a loom (see p. 356). The warp thread should be stronger than the weft and generally consists of two threads twisted together and rather tightly spun. Great care should be taken to use an even and very light tension throughout the warping. A guide is that the warp should be tight enough to make the permanent shed perfectly distinct, but not so tight that it is difficult to effect the reverse of the shed. The closeness of the warp threads is the chief factor in determining the fineness of the carpet. The weft is pushed up well, so that the warp is completely hidden.

Floors

For living-rooms, solid well-seasoned oak made the best floors, beech and elm coming a close second. The planks were cut lengthways from the tree and nailed into place on a framework of wooden crossbars or laid flat on the ground. For kitchens slate or stone flags were fitted together and laid on a basis of rammed earth or ash. For outbuildings and huts, well packed ash and clay or rammed earth made serviceable surfaces and in many Eastern countries dried cow dung is used as flooring for this type of building.

Another source of flooring used in the past was animal bones, which were often set into the earthen floor to form a pattern and a good hard surface.

Furniture

The major furniture woods were oak (treated with beeswax and turpentine), which gave way to walnut in the seventeenth century (easily split and carved), which in turn was displaced by imported mahogany in the eighteenth century. However, country people in any century have usually made their furniture out of whatever wood was at hand, often trimmed and turned into shape in the forest where it was cut.

Chest

The chest or coffer was among man's first crude efforts to make his dwelling a home. For centuries, in England, it was his trunk, his treasury, his store for arms, grain, clothing and linen. At a time when it was customary to sleep, eat, and work among skins and rushes heaped on the damp earth floor, the chest offered comparative comfort as seat and bed. It is given literary mention as early as AD 700.[72]

Furniture began with the chest and, really, all other furniture consists of variations on this theme. A table is an elongated chest, a chair a chest with arms and a back; fitted with drawers it becomes a chest of drawers and turned on its side, with a door, a wardrobe. The first chests were literally 'dug-outs', lengths of tree roughly squared with a lid split off lengthwise, the box hollowed out with an adze and bound with iron. From this developed plank chests: single split oak planks, the sides and base attached to upright end boards and held by wooden dowel pins. Later chests were dovetailed together or held by wrought-iron nails or bands of iron. The lid opened with a wooden pin hinge – a horizontal pivot socketed into uprights; strap hinges and iron hinges came later. By the sixteenth century frame (panelled) chests were being made. The invention of panelling meant that furniture became more varied and ingenious; it became lighter in weight and the panels gave greater scope for carving, inlay and gilding or painting. The framework was grooved so that the panels were held in place without nailing, thus allowing freedom for the wood to contract and expand with changes in atmosphere. Chests were mainly made of oak though chestnut and later spruce were also used, with scented cedar wood for linen and blanket chests.

Chests of Drawers

As chests got deeper they were fitted first with internal shelves or boxes and then doors; finally the lower panels were made removable and this led in time to the first drawer. Called drawer chests, the earliest were fitted to marriage chests and are the origin of the 'bottom-drawer'. They first appear in the sixteenth century with one wide drawer and two narrow ones, but by the time of William III they had developed into 'chests of drawers'. Originally drawers had thick sides and were grooved to run on 'bearers' or fillets of wood projecting from the sides of the chest itself. The front and sides of the drawers were nailed together, though later dovetailing became the norm. Mortise and tenon joints held the framework together. Many such chests stood on ball feet.

Cupboards

The first cupboard was an extra-broad chest up-ended so that the hinged lid became a door. Shelves were held by pegs or nails driven horizontally into the cupboard and legs raised it above the floor. Built-in cupboards were made by fixing a door to the front of a hole in the wall, and can still be seen in early churches.

Tables

In Tudor England there were three types of table, one for serving, one for lowly people and one for the master and mistress of the household. Serving tables were crude, sometimes a chest with an elongated top – the side-board – and sometimes a slab of wood mounted on wooden legs.

The lowly ate at long trestle tables, sitting in rows on benches with their backs leaning against the wall; their food was served from the front. These trestle tables were folded away between meals to make more space in the great hall. They were long, made of two, three or four heavy planks often four to six inches thick and mounted on two single folding X-shaped trestles. By the sixteenth century the trestles had become flat vertical boards, the ends either I-shaped or X-shaped, held by a long central stretcher fixed to the upright trestles with a tusk-tenon.

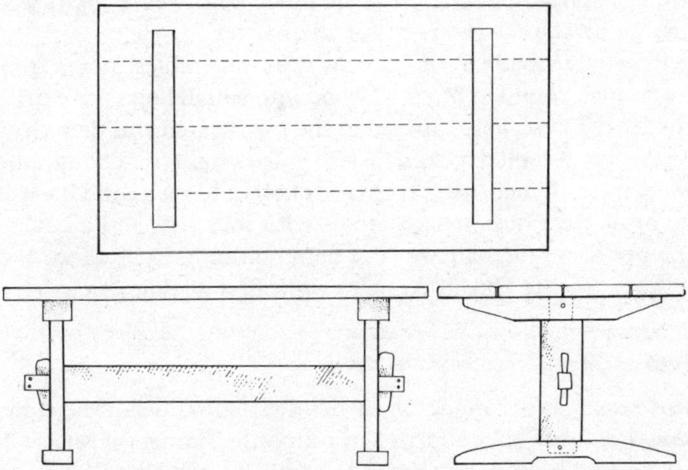

The master and mistress sat at a 'dormant' table on a dais at one end of the room. A design called a refectory table today. Boards formed the table top, which was mounted on four legs held rigid by stretchers. These either directly linked all four legs or consisted of two short bars across the end linked by one running the length of the table.

The rough finish of many of these tables was covered up by rich cloths and carpets.

Chairs

'If you are camping' says Galton, 'for want of a chair, it is convenient to dig a hole or a trench in the ground, and to sit on one side of it, with the feet resting on its bottom; the opposite side of the trench serves as a table for putting things on, within easy reach.'[19] Primitive man sat on the ground; only the ruler sat on a throne or chair. Thus the chair was for many years a symbol of authority rather than comfort. Even today the tradition lingers on: a leader 'takes the chair' and becomes 'chairman'. In the British Houses of Parliament only the Speaker sits on a 'chair' – the Members sit on benches. The old aristocracy have 'seats' in the country and kings, queens and bishops sit on 'thrones'. An inventory of 1594 for Gilling Castle, Yorkshire, shows that the great chamber had twenty-eight stools and only one chair – reserved for the master.

Benches were made in the same way as long tables; stools from a well-seasoned rounded block of wood into which holes were drilled for the legs. These were tapered at the top, heated and then driven in. As the wood cooled it expanded to make a tight fit. Though some early chairs took their form from the chest, adding a solid back and sides, most were designed as stools with four legs and a back.

The upholstered chair was not common until after 1600. Sofas took shape during Queen Anne's reign, first as double chairs.

Seating

A rush seat may be made of rushes twisted to make them firm, joined with a reef knot and woven round the frame, the spaces between top and bottom being padded with extra rushes. String may be used in the same way. Leather seats can be secured with nails or folded right round and sewn. A stuffed seat may be made of horsehair or feathers placed on the wooden base and covered with fabric held in place with nails at the side or with a cushion filled with feathers or other stuffing (see p. 246) placed on the wooden base.

Beds

In the thirteenth century the

> Most important single piece of furniture was the great bed of the lord and lady in their chamber. It consisted of a heavy wooden frame . . . laced with leather thongs or heavy cords, and fitted into sturdy foot and head-pieces . . . On the wooden frame was spread the mattress, preferably of feathers, then sheets, coverlets, and pillows. These were all treasured items which figured regularly in the distribution of goods in contemporary wills.[73]

One of King Henry VIII's beds measured three yards square but his scullion probably had a straw pallet laid on the floor, or at best on a chest or truckle bed frame made like a chair with an elongated seat. Galton says that 'if you want a luxurious bed, make a cartel, which is on the principle of a tennis-player's racket; being a framework of wood, with strips of rawhide lashed across it from end to end, and from side to side'.[19]

Grandiose beds were made of a framework of oak, the sides and end beams pierced and grooved, with cords woven in and out to form a support for the mattress – though sometimes wooden lathes were used instead. The magnificent panelling and bed hangings were originally intended to keep out the draught and give a little privacy. Bed hangings were sometimes suspended from the ceiling and looped up during the day and sometimes hung from a wooden frame as in four-poster beds. It was not until the Regency that couch beds became the norm and until then the best bed was intended for display and the best bedroom was adjacent to the main reception rooms.

Bedding

Sheets were made of fine linen and blankets of wool. Pillows, eiderdowns and quilts were stuffed with feathers, though wool was also often used for elaborately stitched quilts. Mattresses and eiderdowns had interlinking buttons sewn on at intervals on both sides to keep the stuffing in place.

Houses

Housing can take many forms: it may be permanent or semi-permanent, movable or static, able to withstand most climatic upheavals or only some, be comfortable and/or beautiful. The permutations in each category are enormous. I mention only a few, and, because of limited space, with only enough detail to give a good idea of how each is built. They are made, as all houses once were, with very basic local materials.

Movable Houses

Even tents have levels of sophistication. Here are four.

Blanket tent

A simple form of tent may be made at a moment's notice. If the rain comes on, sit upright, joining the hands above the head as if you were about to dive, supporting the blanket on them, and allowing it to hang down on all sides that the rain may run off.[48]

Patrol tent

Our patrol tent was just three yards of double width calico; a small cord was stitched along the middle and loops of tape along the sides. The diagonal pieces cut out of one end were stitched on to form the flaps of the other, and a couple of small sticks for supports . . . seven feet in length, thirty inches high, and nearly thirty inches wide . . . Waterproof material is not required for a tent; oiling canvas or calico would only rot it; stout well-woven canvas is nearly waterproof in itself, and no matter how porous or open the material, the power of a tent to keep out rain depends more on the 'pitch' of its sides or roof than anything else . . . a higher angle than 45° . . . A piece of waterproof is, however, very convenient to lay upon the ground to spread the blankets on.[48]

Robinson Crusoe tent

As for lodging, I kept to the tent except that sometimes, in the wet season of the year, it rained so hard that I could not keep myself dry; which caused me afterwards to cover all my place within my pale with long poles, in the form of rafters, leaning against the rock, and load them with flags and large leaves of trees, like a thatch.[74]

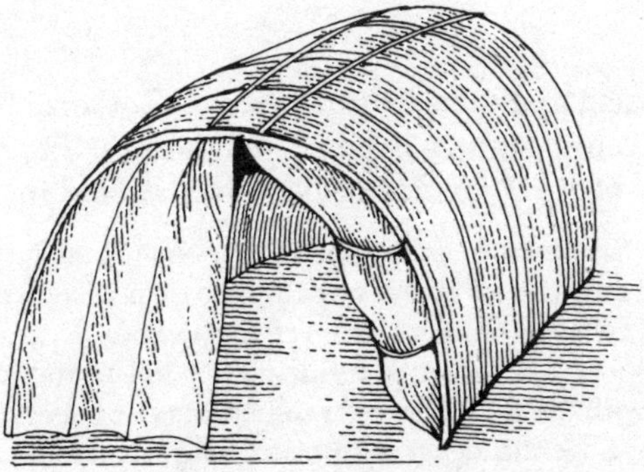

gipsy tent

Gipsy tent

Most of our readers who have visited the by-lanes and breezy downs of England will be familiar with, at least, the exterior of the gipsy's tent. Its mode of arrangement is both ingenious and thoroughly practical. We know of no plan by which a comparatively comfortable resting place can be extemporized equal to it. Blankets, skins, mats, canvas, or old rugs, serve to form a covering. The thicket furnishes the hazel wands or 'benders', of which there are usually eight, seven feet long, and almost any description of tough wood the 'hole piece', and farmers' gate shivers are not infrequently purloined by the Romany Rye to be thus utilized. A red hot poker serves to bore the holes. A few pieces of old cord keep the framework in place, and a set of pegs is readily cut from the nearest hedge. The ends of the benders intended for insertion in the earth are usually fire-hardened, and one set will, with care, last a whole season.[48]

In 1969 between one and two thousand gipsies were still living in tents like these in Britain. Putting them up takes roughly an hour once the boughs are cut.

Semi-permanent Houses

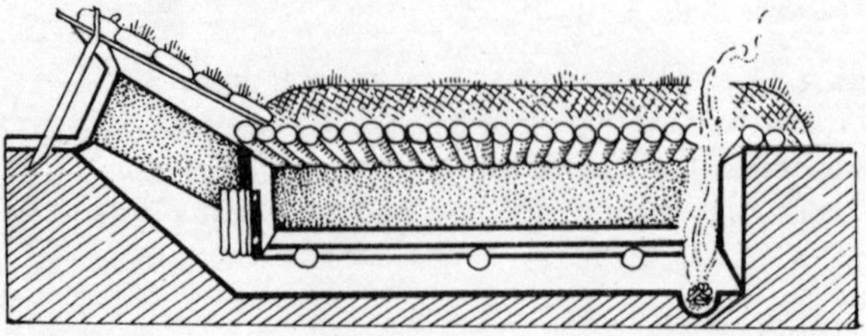

A dugout

Dugout

Palaeolithic man and the first Europeans to colonize New England in the seventeenth century lived in such houses. Thoreau, quoting the secretary of the Province of New Netherland in 1650 says

those in New Netherland, and especially in New England, who have no means to build farmhouses at first according to their wishes, dig a square pit in the ground, cellar fashion, six or seven feet deep, as long and as broad as they think proper, case the earth inside with wood all round the wall, and line the wood with the bark of trees or something else to prevent the caving-in of the earth; floor this cellar with plank, and wainscot it overhead for a ceiling, raise a roof of spars clear up, and cover the spars with bark or green sods, so that they can live dry and warm in these houses with their entire families for two, three and four years, it being understood that partitions are run through those cellars which are adapted to the size of the family.[1]

The bark is stripped from the trees when the sap is up in spring and early summer, the large flakes while still green being placed under timber weights to flatten them. The diagram is of an Upper Palaeolithic dwelling from Timonouka, Russia.

Wood house

Wood is the oldest building material for houses, but of all materials it is the most perishable and was all too often in the past destroyed by fire. By the Middle Ages houses made entirely of wood had largely been superseded. By this time also inroads into the ancient forests were making wood less plentiful. To construct a wood hut of the log-cabin type for

a party who are about wintering in the woods, it is best to construct a log hut of the description represented in the following illustration; its size

must, of course, depend on the number of its proposed occupants; it can be made either oblong or square. When sufficient number of trees of convenient bulk for handling have been felled and logged up into proper lengths, the ends should be notched with the axe, as shown in the illustration. The

Saddle notch

Round notch

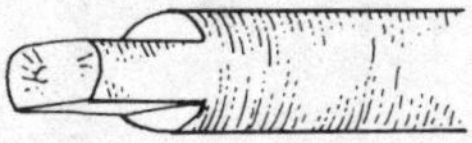

Tenon-shaped end

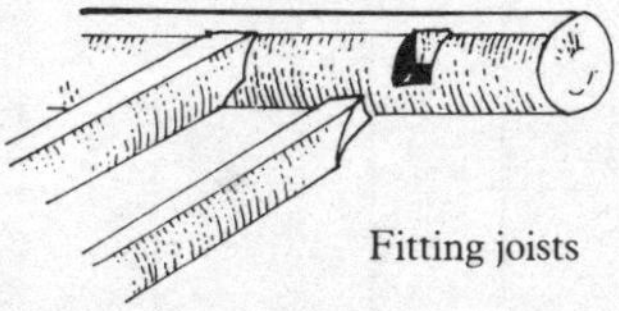

Fitting joists

four ground logs are then laid and keyed together by their notches; the second row are then placed on these, either by the aid of skin bars placed in a slanting direction on the lower logs, or by manual labour. When all the walls are high enough, the doorway must be cut in the following manner: Begin on the upper log and chop through at each end, the exact width of the proposed opening; follow down, cutting log by log until the ground log is reached; cut this nearly half through and then split out the piece, the other portion below forms your threshold. Take a fresh log, and in it split out a space exactly to correspond with that in the ground log, place this as a crowning log with three others, uncut, to form your wall plate, the split-out piece will form the top of your doorway; the square hole for the windows or shutter is chopped in the same way. The gable ends and ridge log must be adjusted at such a pitch as to ensure a free run for rain water or melted snow; the four ends or butts of the gable angles should rest and be firmly wedged in four holes axed out for them in the ends of the upper row of wall-plate logs; where the gable peak crosses, the logs should be notched together and pinned; the ridge log will then rest in the crutches formed by the intersection. Now, after having selected the most convenient spot for a fireplace, chop a hole through the logs, including that on the ground, about 3 ft wide and 4 ft 6 ins. high. There are several ways of forming a chimney and fireback; one is to build a beehive-shaped wall outside the opening, plastering the inside with clay, and forming a round chimney stack with turf and stones. All chinks or crevices between the logs are stopped with clay and moss.[48]

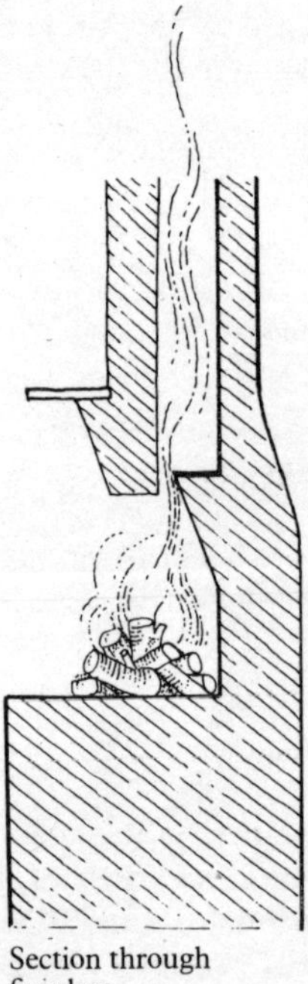

Section through fireplace

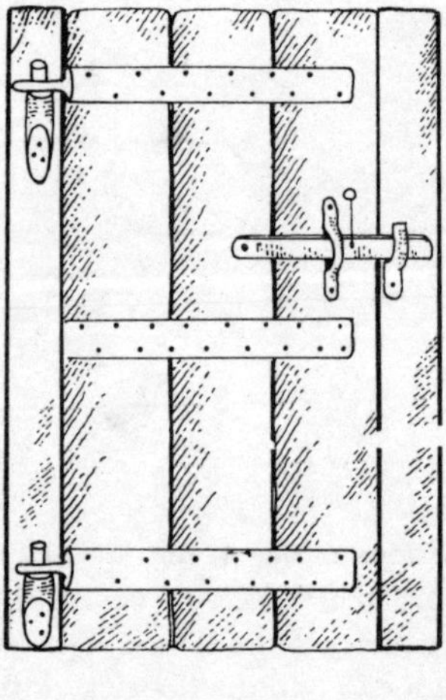

The wood for walls should ideally be light and easy to work (soft pines, spruce and beech), but wood for doors and windows should be strong and durable, and both types cut in spring or early summer and stripped of their bark. Each log should be three feet longer than the inside dimension of the room to allow eighteen inches each end for jointing, and it is a good idea to raise the floor above ground level on piers of flat rocks. A chimney shaped as in the diagram gives the most heat and creates a draught; a wooden door can be constructed and hung on wooden hinges.

Permanent Houses

Timber-framed houses

Developed from the all-wood house and a precursor of the steel-framed skyscraper block of today, a cruck house consists of a wooden frame infilled with a mixture of materials. Oak was considered the supreme building material, for the frame and for the beams, doors and floor as well.

Cruck building remained common in the north and west of England well into the nineteenth century. It is said to have been based

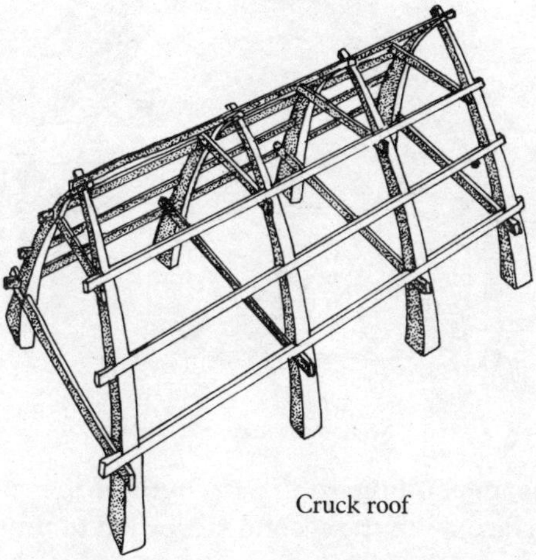

Cruck roof

originally on the idea of an upturned boat; a pair of crucks, either two whole trees with a natural curve or one sliced in half, often charred at the base to make them longer lasting and resting on a slab of stone or turf, were fitted together. The average house consisted of three pairs of crucks or bays. Contemporary records often describe the size of a house as being of so many 'bays' of building each approximately sixteen feet in length and fitted together with a ridge pole. Green, unseasoned wood was often used, being easier to work – this led to warping and sagging of timber, though with no loss of strength, because as the sap dried the wood became harder. Originally of one storey, it was later realized that by resting a floor on the horizontal tie-beams strengthening each pair of crucks a second storey could be fashioned, reached by a ladder through a hole in the floor. The infilling between the crucks was of local material, usually wattle and daub, but bricks, mud and stone were used as well. The parts were all made beforehand and then erected. The roof was of

Section through cruck house

thatch or tiles, depending on the strength of the supporting walls.

Lack of head room in the second storey led to the development of post-and-truss and box-frame houses with a more complex arrangement of beams but the same infilling.

Wattle and daub infilling for frame houses was put in as the house went up. The wattle was made of reeds or flexible sticks such as willow, hazel or ash and later lathes – flat strips of wood such as oak or beech a few inches across. These were fitted into slots in the base of the beams and pegged into holes at the top of the box ten or twelve inches apart. Through them thinner sticks were woven horizontally to make a crude form of basket work. The daub comprised wet clay, or mud mixed with straw, cow hair and sometimes manure and covered both sides of the wattle. The illustration shows an early wattle and earth hut.

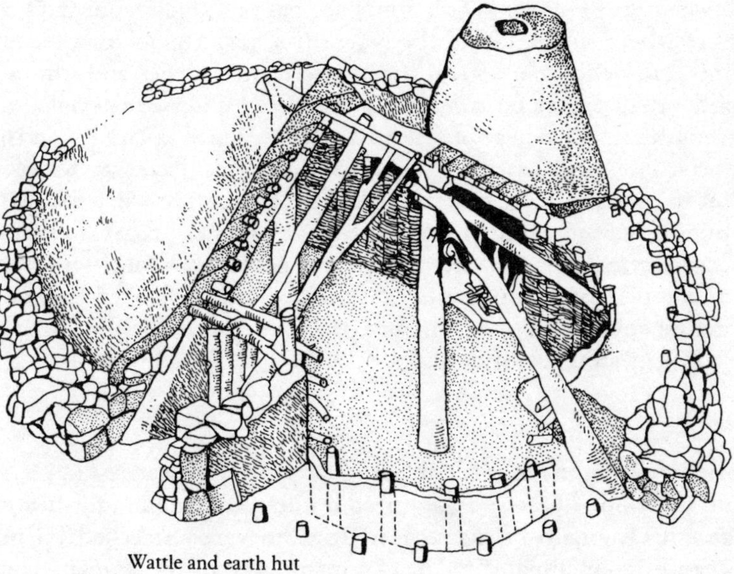

Wattle and earth hut

Stone

Areas of stone, each with its own character, lie in a diagonal pattern across the British Isles. The ideal building stone is one which has good weathering properties, colour and texture. Most stone is deficient in one of these qualities but of them all limestone is the finest, granite the hardest and chalk and sandstone the softest. Most stone buildings are made of rubblestone – hunks of stone, mostly small, sometimes squared, but often left irregular and arranged either at random or levelled to form 'courses' about every twelve to eighteen inches. Many kinds of stone, especially the harder kinds, can only be used in this way and it is certainly the most economical way of building as every bit is used. But since many stones, especially flints, are quite rounded, a lot of mortar is essential in rubble walling.

Flint and pebble

Hard and virtually indestructible, flints are found on the upper layers of chalk formation especially in East Anglia (see Knives, p. 279). Flints can be used whole or split, which makes the building a pleasing grey colour. Whole flints are best gathered from the sea-shore where the action of the waves has made them smooth. All flints and pebbles are small, from two to five inches and, though hard, are therefore far from being the ideal building material. The strength and weakness of a flint wall thus depends largely on the mortar in which they are embedded. Since it is necessary for each flint to be completely surrounded by mortar and this dries slowly, building is impossible in winter; even in summer progress is slow, because after every few feet of wall it is necessary to allow it to dry out completely before another is added. Flint walls are frequently strengthened with other material: boulders or, better-looking, courses of stone or brick.

Brick

Bricks have been made for at least 6,000 years, the earliest in Egypt and Babylon. These were not fired but left to harden in the heat of the sun. Originally bricks made in England were sun-baked too, but because of our climate fired bricks, introduced by the Romans, soon became the norm. Originally bricks were used to strengthen and bind a building rather than for the whole structure.

The best bricks are an amalgam of two clays; one as plastic as possible and the other sandy to counteract any shrinkage on the part of the first. Clays vary in colour according to the area and the temperature on firing – which in early days could not accurately be controlled – and it is this happy accident which gives the richness and variety to old brick buildings.

The clay was in all likelihood dug and fired beside the rising house, leaving a dip in the ground, often filled with water to make a pond. It was always dug in the autumn and left to weather over the winter, then blended and squeezed; water was sometimes added. The right consistency was obtained by treading the clay with bare feet – later it was put in a pug mill turned by a boy or pony. Sometimes at this stage too breeze or coal dust was added to give body and colour. To form the brick, a heap of clay was placed on a bench, sprinkled with sand and kneaded like dough. Next the clay was dropped from a height into a wooden mould so that it filled the mould without forming bubbles or other imperfections. Excess clay was scraped off the top, the brick was then slipped out of the mould and left on wooden boards in the open, protected from the rain and wind, to weather for fourteen days, after which it was fired, the heat being increased to 538°F over two or three days.

Mud or cob (south-west England)

Cool in summer and warm in winter, houses built of cob have much to recommend them. The only rule which applies to all unbaked earths is that they must be kept dry. Subject to prolonged damp they disintegrate, kept dry they last for centuries. There is a Devon saying that 'all cob wants is a good hat and a good pair of shoes'. The hat is provided by the thatch or tiles and the feet by a solid plinth or base one or two feet high of stone, pebbles, flint or brick. The cob consists of wet earth or mud mixed with enough lime to enable it to set (generally in the proportion of 3 : 1) and usually some chopped straw, gravel or small stones, sand and little pieces of slate and chalk. Building is a long business: the mix must be carefully blended and trodden by men or beasts and each layer allowed to harden before another is added. This can take several weeks in bad weather and a two-storey house could take two years to build. The lumps are laid in layers from five to seven inches thick, covered with straw and left to dry. Each course is about one foot high and each lump is trodden into position. The walls are from two to four feet thick. When the wall is finished the loose ends of straw are trimmed and the whole house given a protective covering of plaster or lime-wash or both. No guide lines are used, only the eye, which is why the walls of cob buildings are often, charmingly, far from straight.

Clay lump

Cottages of clay lump, though most frequently found in East Anglia, may in fact be constructed in any clay area. Technically the most advanced of the unbaked earths, the walls need only be half as thick as cob but are just as well-insulated and when one brick is faulty another can easily be substituted. After the clay has been dug, it is watered and as many of the large stones as possible removed. Then chopped straw or spear grass is trodden in. This mix is then pressed into wooden moulds measuring about 18 × 5 × 6 ins. thick and left for several weeks to dry out. The bricks are then mortared together into a wall with puddled clay of a finer consistency than the brick. The wall is finished by giving it a coating of tar or limewash or sometimes a skin of fired bricks.

Mortar

Mortar is used to bond brick or stone. It is generally agreed that mortar should be lighter than the bricks and level with them – not indented, as this encourages damp. The basis of mortar is coarse sand used in the proportion of six or seven parts to one part lime or cement and beaten with water. The colour comes from the sand or hard crushed stone which can be used as a substitute.

Lavatories

When we lived off the land our lavatory was constructed on the army principle. We dug a pit, piled the earth to one side, then covered each layer of excrescence with earth from the pile. Once full another pit is dug. Leaves are used for lavatory paper.

Most old cottages had an earth closet in the garden constructed on the lines of a septic tank. Where the collection of urine was important for bleaching and dyeing these privies would have had two compartments. Even the earliest castles had garderobes, draughty cavities in the wall, the outlet many feet below at ground level. The excreta was cleared once a day by serfs or by large dogs sent round to eat it. Lavatories are a surprisingly modern invention (when Louis XIV built the palace of Versailles none were installed) and did not become widespread until the nineteenth century.

Septic Tank

The tank consists of two chambers: one contains the effluent and the second is filled with coarse gravel or clinkers, with an outlet to a soakaway. Thus the effluent enters the first tank, is attacked by anaerobic bacteria, filters through the second and soaks out through the outlet into the ground.

Septic tank

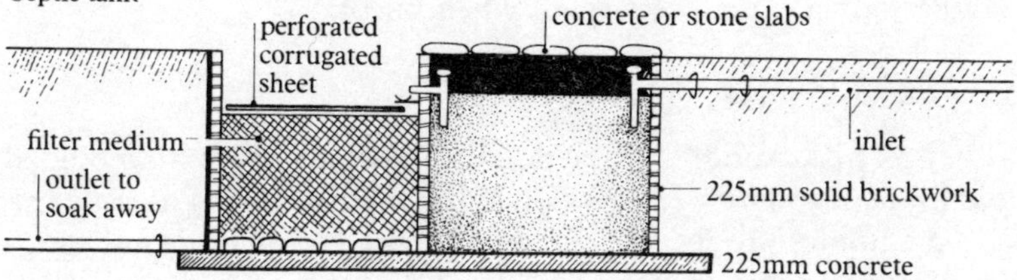

Light

All animal fats, vegetable oils, fish oils, beeswax and resinous woods are inflammable and, depending on their solidifying qualities, will with the aid of a wick produce light of varying degrees of efficiency. The hard fats are obviously more suitable for making into candles and rush lights, whereas the liquid oils are better for burning in lamps and the resinous woods for using as tapers.

Light Fuels

Animal fats

Of the animal fats mutton is the hardest, often the most available, and, therefore, the most frequently used for candles and for dipping rushes. Some people recommend a mixture of beef fat and mutton and most are of the opinion that the addition of some beeswax to any mixture produces a purer and more consistent light, while pure beeswax gives the clearest light of all.

The fat must first be purified otherwise the candle will stink and burn unevenly, 'Base and unlustrous as the smoky light That's fed with stinking tallow.'[75] See p. 55.

Vegetable oils

See p. 52. As a rule vegetable oils never solidify and are therefore only suitable for burning in lamps with a wick.

The berries of bog myrtle (*Myrica gale*) are covered with an aromatic, greenish, waxy secretion which, if collected and made into candles, gives off a sweet smell when burnt.

Fish oil

'They all make candles of the tallow of their beasts, both moulded and dipped; and they all make oil of the livers of fish. The little fish called Cuddies produce a great deal.'[18] So observed the indefatigable Boswell when staying with Dr Johnson on Col during their tour of the Hebrides. For other fish oils see p. 54. Fish oil never solidifies and burns with an unpleasant smell. Suitable for lamps only.

Bird oil

Seabirds are usually rich in oil and the best method of using them for light is to burn them whole, as a torch. It seems macabre, but to Hebridean islanders it was commonplace to catch and dry the stormy petrel, thread a wick through its beak and down into its fatty stomach, stick the feet in a lump of clay and burn it as a lamp. The Danes are said to have done the same with penguins.

Resinous wood

Pine, birch and boxwood are our most resinous woods: they are most suitable for making into torches and splinter-like candles, with or without the addition of extra fat.

Wicks

A wick can be made of all sorts of materials: the pith of a single rush, or several plaited; a strip of bark beaten to separate the fibres; dry moss stretched and twisted; the plaited hairs from a horse or other coarse-haired animal; fibrous plants; strips of linen or string. The last will probably be the most efficient.

Candles

These may be made in several different ways, but dipping and moulding are the most usual. For obvious reasons only fats or wax that set hard are usable. Beeswax candles give the clearest light and burn more smoothly than tallow. The addition of scent to the fat will make a candle that perfumes the air as it burns.

Dipping

To make a candle by the dipping method: take a wick the length you would like the candle to be, dip it in a pot of melted fat, lift it out, allow the fat to harden on the wick and re-dip. Repeat the process until sufficient thickness is attained. It is important to allow the fat to dry before another layer is added otherwise the candle will be spoiled. The method may be speeded up by dipping several wicks at a time – attaching the wicks to the end of a pole so that they resemble the teeth of a rake.

Moulding

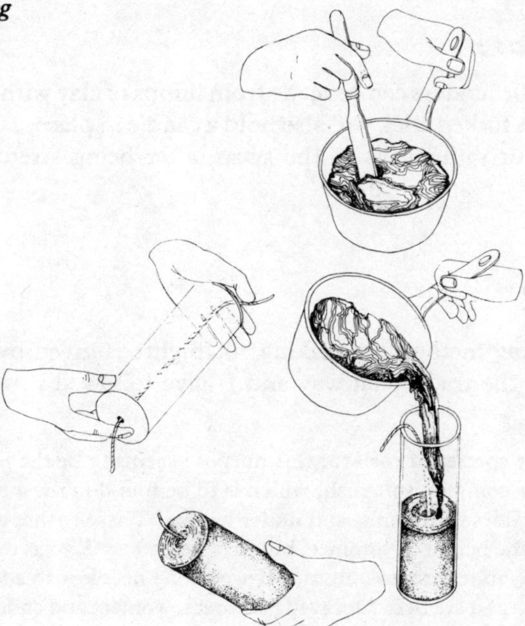

It is less time-consuming to make a candle in a mould in which a wick has been suspended. The mould may be of any size or material. Hollowed wood was frequently used; the stems of the hogweed (*Heracleum spondylium*), after they become hard in autumn, also make good moulds. Another way is to drive a bar into wet sand and fill the imprint with melted tallow or wax. The mould should be stood upright and the wick dipped in fat and secured so that it passes straight down the middle; the fat is poured in from the top. Once the fat has set the candle can be removed, putting it in hot water for long enough to melt the outside of the candle, so that it slips out of the mould.

Snuffing

This is important if the candle is to burn efficiently the whole way down. The burnt end of the wick should be cut off or 'snuffed' before it grows too long and falls into the flame, making it sooty and foul-smelling. A knife will do it but special snuffing scissors were more efficient.

Candle holders

Simple candle holders can be made from lumps of clay with a hole in the centre. A forked stick will also hold a candle in place, as will 'the broad feet, or rather legs of the swan, after being stretched and dried'.[19]

Rushlights

The following method for making rushlights is given by Gilbert White; it is the traditional way and I have followed it with great success.

> The proper species of rush for this purpose seems to be the *juncus conglomeratus*, or common soft rush, which is to be found in most moist pastures, by the sides of streams, and under hedges. These rushes are in best condition in the height of summer; but may be gathered, so as to serve the purpose well, quite on into autumn. It would be needless to add that the largest and longest are best. Decayed labourers, women, and children make it their business to procure and prepare them. As soon as they are cut they

must be flung into water, and kept there; for otherwise they will dry and shrink, and the peel will not run. At first a person would find it no easy matter to divest a rush of its peel or rind, so as to leave one regular, narrow, even rib from top to bottom that may support the pith: but this, like other feats, soon becomes familiar even to children; and we have seen an old woman, stone-blind, performing this business with great dispatch, and seldom failing to strip them with the nicest regularity. When these *junci* are thus far prepared, they must lie out on the grass to be bleached, and take the dew for some nights, and afterwards be dried in the sun.

Some address is required in dipping these rushes in the scalding fat or grease; but this knack also is to be attained by practice. The careful wife of an industrious Hampshire labourer obtains all her fat for nothing, for she saves the scummings of her bacon-pot for this use; and, if the grease abounds with salt, she causes the salt to precipitate to the bottom, by setting the scummings in a warm oven. Where hogs are not much in use, and especially by the sea-side, the coarser animal-oils will come very cheap. A pound of common grease may be procured for four-pence; and about six pounds of grease will dip a pound of rushes; and one pound of rushes may be bought for one shilling: so that a pound of rushes, medicated and ready for use, will cost three shillings. If men that keep bees will mix a little wax with grease, it will give it a consistency, and render it more cleanly, and make the rushes burn longer: mutton-suet would have the same effect.

A good rush, which measured in length two feet four inches and a half, being minuted, burnt only three minutes short of an hour: and a rush of still greater length has been known to burn one hour and a quarter.

These rushes give a good clear light. Watch-lights (coated with tallow), it is true, shed a dismal one, 'darkness visible'; but then the wicks of those have two ribs of the rind, or peel, to support the pith, while the wick of the dipped rush has but one. The two ribs are intended to impede the progress of the flame and make the candle last.[12]

The rush should be burned at an angle of approximately 75° and can either be held in a forked stick or in some kind of clamp.

Lamps

A lamp can be made out of any receptacle which will hold liquid oil and in which a wick can be suspended.

The wick can be made of any of the materials previously suggested and usually the burning end rests on the side of the dish. If it is preferred to have the wick burning in the centre of the oil, it should be attached to a small bag of salt or a small stone. This will weight it to the base of the dish.

Vegetable oils and fish oils are most suitable for burning in lamps though the harder fats may be used as well, especially in hot weather when the solid fats may become too soft to make into candles.

For a good light it is important to have the correct amount of oil in the lamp. Too little can lead to a starved light: 'These eyes/Like lamps whose wasting oil is spent/Wax dim';[76] too much, and the lamp overflows or burns with a smoky flame. Ultimately the quality of light depends on the quality and purity of the oil being used.

Any saucer-shaped dish can act as the holder for the oil; the shell of an oyster, scallop or whelk; snails' shells, several of which can be stuck in a clay base; a hollow stone or a hollowed-out piece of hardwood; the hoof of a beast; or a specially formed dish made from clay. These can be made in a variety of shapes to hold one or more wicks and may be covered or uncovered – the more covered they are the more the side effects of smoking and smelling are eliminated. The following diagrams give examples. To extend the lighted area lamps can be hung from the ceiling or from a holder in twos and threes.

Night Lights

For a light that will burn without any danger of setting fire to surrounding objects, place a candle, or small oil lamp with non-inflammable base, in a small saucer of water.

Torches

Torches, probably the earliest form of artificial light ever created by man, can be made in a variety of ways. Splinters of resinous wood such as pine, birch or boxwood can be bound together with rushes and treated with resin, pitch or wax will make a slow-burning torch. Or a young tree, which will be full of sap, can be cut down, beaten into a fibrous state, then fat rubbed into the fibres and the whole tied together again with rushes. Thick lengths of rope can be treated with oil or fat and held in a torch holder. Ancient wood found in bogs in Scotland and Ireland is full of turpentine; it can be split, dried and used as torches or wood candles, depending on the size. Small splinters of resinous wood coated in tallow, or burnt untreated make a type of candle too.

Roofs

Slates

Limestone

These provide the most beautiful of all roofing materials. For good slates it must be possible to split the stone into thin pieces and not all beds of limestone are suitable. The newly dug stone is spread out on the ground and left for the winter frosts to split it. The stones are watered every evening to help the process. The work nature has begun is finished by splitting the stone into slices. It is then trimmed and a hole is made at a suitable point near the head. The slate is hung by an oak peg, iron nail or even the leg bone of a sheep or breast bone of a chicken over battens nailed across the roof beams. The largest slates are laid at the bottom of the roof over the gutter, becoming progressively smaller in size with the smallest under the eaves. A steep pitch, rarely less than 45°, with an average of 50–55°, is necessary.

Sandstone

These slates are usually sufficiently fissile to split with a hammer without being frosted. As they are thicker, and so heavier, the pitch of the roof has to be lower, about 30–45°.

Slate

Slate is a metamorphic rock – a rock which owes its present composition to some agency such as great heat or sustained pressure over a long period of time. Thus slates from different areas vary not only in colour but also in consistency. Slate is found in abundance in Wales, the Lake District, Leicestershire, Devon and Cornwall. Owing to its formation, slate is easily quarried and splits with no difficulty with the tap of a hammer. It is very hard, close textured and able to withstand great degrees of frost. Damp courses, paving, floors, steps, window sills, shelves, water tanks, cheese presses, salting troughs, mill stones and even gravestones were also made from slate.

Slates come in graded sizes, most with names derived from the female aristocracy descending from princesses and duchesses down to narrow ladies. Two holes are bored in the top of the larger slates and one in the smaller. They are hung over battens in the same way as limestone slates; but the pitch can be as little as 22°. In order to make the roof watertight each course overlaps not only the next course but the one below it too.

Ridges are made from stone chiselled into shape and bedded with lime mortar or from ridge-tiles.

Tiles

The clay is prepared in the same way as for brick but using a finer quality and the mix is more carefully prepared, often with more sand – sprinkled on the mould and the unfired clay to give an attractive texture – and fired at a higher temperature. The pitch for tiled roofs is usually 40–60°.

Tiles are of three types: plain flat tiles, pantiles and Spanish and Roman tiles.

Flat tiles: Flat tiles are made in a mould and laid on the roof in double layers like slates.

Spanish tiles: A half cylinder in shape, they were originally made by the clay being placed over a man's thigh. They are laid in overs and unders bedded in mud or mortar and usually nailed in place as well. Good for roofs with a shallow pitch and straightforward shape. Roman tiles are similar, but larger and flatter.

Pantiles: These are Spanish tiles laid in single overlapping layers, each one hooking over its neighbour, and often on some extra layer of waterproof material, traditionally reeds or hair mortar, in which case the pitch can be as low as 30°.

Thatch

Derived from the old word 'thack' which originally meant any roofing material. Since, in early days, this was usually of vegetable origin thatch later came to have its present meaning. From the fourteenth century, because of the ease with which thatch caught fire its use was discouraged in towns and today it is exclusively a country roofing material.

It is the lightest roofing material, especially suited for unbaked earth walls for which stone tiles are too heavy. It requires only a modest framework of lathes or battens 1½ ins. wide and ½ in. thick, nailed across the rafters at intervals of 5 ins. No gutters are necessary as the water drips off the overhanging thatch into the ground (see Drains, p. 213). The principal thatching materials are reed, straw and heather, though bracken, broom and grass have all been used.

Reed

The common reed (*Phragmites communis*) is found in marshes and fens. Cutting is a cold business, done by hand when all the foliage has died back, in midwinter. Working from the eaves, bundles of reed 2 ft round and 7–8 ft long are put on the roof with the butts facing out, forming the surface of the thatch. The bundles are fixed into position with small pieces of board.

Straw

Wheat, rye, oats or barley. Rye is the strongest with a life of about thirty years, but wheat is more generally available and lasts almost as long. Long-stemmed varieties only are suitable (cut by hand, not mauled by the threshing machine) and applied to the roof in 'yealms' – small flat bundles laid in overlapping courses at intervals of 4 or 5 ins. A pitch of not less than 50° is required to make sure the rain water is thrown off quickly and not given a chance to soak in. (With reed the pitch can be slightly less.)

Wheat reed – actually threshed straw – can be laid in the same way as reed thatch.

Heather

Formerly common, especially in moorland districts. Heather should be cut while in bloom and laid in the autumn with roots entwined and pointing upwards. The ends are sometimes embedded in clay. The thatch is finished by being clipped with shears. Heather thatch is long-lasting but the initial rich brown colour ages to a drab black which can have a depressing effect on a building.

The ridge

The ridge is made in various ways. Sometimes by making a straw crest, arranging the bundles so that they overlap from each side alternately; sometimes clay or turves are used or specially made ridge-tiles.

Stuffing

Pillows to help you sleep should be stuffed with soporific hops; pillows for smelling, with dried, scented herbs – marjoram, thyme, bog myrtle, woodruff, lavender and rose petals. But for comfort pillows should be stuffed with feathers – pure goose down for preference, though other feathers will do as well, after treatment.

> . . . after the bread had been baked and removed from the brick-oven feathers and *dum* (down) that had recently been plucked from fowls were placed in the oven while it was still hot. Baking the feathers killed all the insects that might be in them, and also ensured that they would be dry and not *mat* when they were used. After they had been baked the *dum* and feathers could be stored for years before being used in pillows and mattresses. In addition to the small feathers, *clippings* obtained from the larger ones when they were being shaped into quill-pens, were also treated in the same way.[24]

Sheep's wool was also much used as stuffing and, for small cushions, the down, or silky white hairs that develop as the flower goes to seed, of thistle and coltsfoot. Collect and remove any hard debris before using and it will make a comfortable, light filling. Dried seaweed has also been used as stuffing.

Eiderdowns, as their name suggests, are traditionally stuffed with the small breast feathers of the eider duck, taken from the lining of her nest. Since these are expensive and often difficult to obtain ordinary feathers are more frequently used – preferably feathers from water birds, such as ducks, rather than hens, as these are warmer. For quilts the padding is traditionally lambs' wool, cleaned and used straight from the sheep or in the form of a blanket. This makes a warm, light filling which washes well.

Soft mattresses were stuffed with feathers but for harder ones horsehair was used (only the shorter hairs, as the longer ones were set aside for weaving). It was thoroughly washed, combed and teased to tear the strands and remove any foreign bodies. The newly 'devilled' hair was then twisted into strands, and finally boiled and baked to give it greater elasticity. Rags, wool, sphagnum moss, bracken and straw were also put in mattresses. 'Oat-flight' mattresses, made from oat chaff, were often given to children as they could easily be replaced should a mishap occur. (Sphagnum moss might also be used.) Sweet vernal grass or lady's bedstraw made a sweet-smelling mattress.

Wall Coverings

Paint

See the section on Paint, p. 295.

Plaster

The object of covering a wall with plaster is, to give, outside, additional protection from the weather and, inside, a smoother finish for decoration. The best plaster is made from gypsum, which is now hard to come by. Most plaster is made of one part lime or chalk marl mixed with three to six parts of coarse clean sand. Other substances were once added – chopped straw, hay, animal hair and feathers – to give strength.

Roughcast and Pebble-dash

A way of giving greater protection and of hiding poor quality brick or unbaked earths, it consists of a mix of coarse sand and washed gravel, stone chippings, shingle, shells, slaked lime and, nowadays, cement. The wall surface is first given an undercoat of $\frac{1}{2}$–$\frac{3}{4}$ in. lime and sand or cement and sand and against this the semi-liquid roughcast is thrown with a trowel from a flat wooden board. For pebble-dash small pebbles are thrown on to the cement undercoat.

Whitewash

Its function is to cover the drab colour of plaster or roughcast and to lighten a room. Traditionally made of lime and water – natural stone lime can be bought today – it is porous and allows the damp to come out of a wall. Tallow or glue size can be added to make it more permanent and more waterproof (see Paint, p. 295, for recipes). A new coat was usually applied each year, slapped on to the walls with brushes attached to long poles, its freshness a matter of pride to the owner. Many cottages in the West Country and East Anglia have been whitewashed so often that they look as if they have been plastered.

Care should be taken during slaking to avoid the mix becoming too grey. A tint of powder colour (see p. 296), added during the slaking, brightens the effect.

Windows

The first written reference to window glass in England is in the Account Rolls, 25 of Edward III, which comments on the building of St Stephen's Chapel, Westminster, in the fourteenth century. It remained a luxury, even for the gentry, for a long time and it was not until the seventeenth century that the peasant in his cottage could think of affording glass. As late as 1567 the windows of Alnwick Castle were always removed and stored when the owner was away, to prevent them being damaged by the weather; elsewhere wooden lattices were often fitted outside the windows as protection, or substitutes for glass were found.

Substitute Windows

Ox horn or whale bone frequently made up all, or part of, a window, which probably did not open. (The opening part was fitted with wooden shutters.) The horn was prepared by being boiled or heated in hot sand until quite soft, flattened and then soaked in a pond for a fortnight; it was well washed to separate the pith and boiled again for half an hour. After this it was sawn lengthways and boiled again until it was ready to split into sheets. The sheets were again boiled, scraped to a uniform thickness, pressed into shape and left to dry.

Oiled cloth, preferably linen, framed in wood was also used as window covering; also oiled paper and parchment dipped in gum arabic, honey and white of egg, stretched wet on frames and, when dry, varnished. Woven reed screens, their horizontal lines $\frac{1}{4}$ in. apart and their vertical, 5 ins. apart, or thin slabs of semi-translucent stone such as alabaster or mica are also recorded. Plain wooden shutters were commonest of all before glass, secured inside with wooden or iron bars. In some hotter countries they are still often the only kind of window.

Glass Windows

The first panes of glass were blown in the shape of cylinders. These were then split along their length, placed on heated flat beds and, as they gradually opened, flattened out with an iron or wooden rod and allowed to cool. A medieval development was to blow a bubble of glass, and spin it round, flattening out the glass with a wooden bat. This made a disc anything from three to five feet in diameter, which was afterwards trimmed into shape. Crown glass, as this is called, is always thicker towards the centre, with a bull's eye in the middle known as the 'bullion' or 'knot'. The oldest glass made in this way always has the mark of the blowing iron in the centre. By the eighteenth century this method had been refined and the lumpy piece bearing the mark of the blowing iron was smoothed off and discarded.

Plate glass, the next development, was made by casting the glass in thick moulds. It was initially very expensive and did not become widespread until 1838. It was used in the building of the Crystal Palace.

Setting glass

Initially glass was set straight into the stone, or into lead or iron casings, and windows did not open. Casement – hinged, side-opening – windows came next. The glass was cut in small rectangles or diamond shapes, set in wood, iron or lead frames. When lead was used the size of the panes was dictated by the soft, weak, bendable quality of the lead. Sash windows were first used on a large scale at Chatsworth in 1676.

Containers

Until you are without containers you do not realize how many and various are the ones you need: for storage, mixing, cooking, serving, eating off, washing up, and so on. Obviously some are less essential: you can eat out of the cooking pot; a washing-up bowl was one of the luxuries I easily left behind while living off the land. I used to carry all utensils to the stream and what would not wash off with water was scoured off with earth and grit rubbed in with handfuls of grass and horsetails.

The containers I used were one large cast-iron casserole in which everything was cooked – which meant we ate a lot of stews – two pottery plates, two mugs, a couple of stone jars for making wine, and a willow basket. Thoreau made do with 'a kettle, a skillet and a frying-pan, a dipper, a wash-bowl, two knives and forks, three plates, one cup, one spoon, a jug for oil, a jug for molasses and a japanned lamp'.[1] But, like Robinson Crusoe, I felt a need for a greater variety of containers. Robinson Crusoe chiefly wanted large jars for storing flour and corn. These he made out of clay, giving them a basketwork support. A similar method was used by primitive man, though he probably started by doing it the other way round, smearing the inside of basketwork with clay. Robinson Crusoe also needed fired clay pots for cooking but, like us, he had problems firing anything that remained whole in an open fire.

A selection of baskets is useful: willow baskets for collecting food and for storing wood and other bulky things; rush, lined with leaves, for keeping berries, fungi, roots and eggs. I made rush baskets out of a good supply of rushes which grew near the stream and continued to use them after I got home.

It is thought that the first nets were made for capturing animals; they can also be made into hammocks for sleeping and net bags for collecting leaves and branches or for washing dandelion roots and clothes. (If you suspend these in a fast running part of the stream for a day they emerge reasonably clean.)

Large wooden bowls can sometimes be bought for a price in antique shops. They will have been made from the wood cut from trees growing round the village and carved into shape during winter evenings. They were used as mixing bowls. Plates were made from the same wood and were still in use in country areas at the beginning of this century.

Crafts require more skill and time than knowledge. Anyone can quickly learn the processes involved, though it takes time and practice to do them well – to fit the staves accurately in a barrel, to mould a horn cup or make a leather bottle. Probably because of this specialization began early. Each village used to have a blacksmith, a thatcher, a miller, a wheelwright and a harness-maker while others lived by making baskets and barrels, furniture and fencing, all from local materials.

Baskets

Baskets of osier or willow, rush, cane, heather and oak, and more fragile receptacles of grass can be made in the wild.

I do not propose to go into the variations of basket shapes and patterns of weaving here, but give some basic methods and hope that the ambitious will refer to a book on the subject.

Willow Baskets

Of the nineteen species of willow native to Britain the white willow (*Salix alba*) and the pussy willow (*Salix caprea*) are the most common, growing beside rivers, in low-lying valleys, scrub and wettish woodlands. One-year-old shoots from either of these are suitable for basket-making. They should have finely tapered tops, be free from side shoots and other defects and be long and pliable.

The shoots, called 'rods', should be prepared in the following way. First the colour of the final basket must be decided upon. If white, the rod must be peeled; if buff, the rod must be boiled and then peeled; if brown, not peeled at all. They should then be stored in a dry place until required for use, otherwise they will become mildewed.

Before use the rods should be soaked in water to make them pliable – two or three days for brown rods; buff and white rods, depending on their size and stiffness, may require as little as fifteen minutes or as much as twelve hours.

After soaking they should be stood butt (thick) end down to drain in the open for about half an hour; then laid flat and covered with a damp sack to await use. It is important not to prepare more rods than can be worked in about six hours as if left longer than that under the sack they tend to get greasy and unmanageable.

A round basket

Take six of the thinner rods and make slits in the centre of three.

Through these thread the other three rods. These will form the ribs of the basket round which other rods are woven.

To start weaving take a rod and slice its butt end . Then insert the cut end in the slit made through the first three rods. Cross it over the base, in order to splay out the rib rods evenly. Weave as shown.

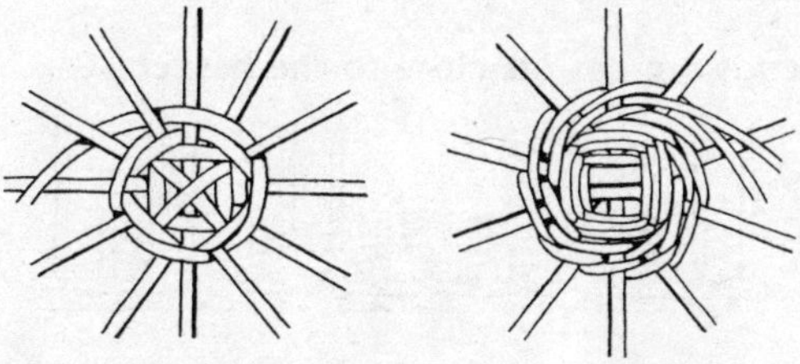

When this rod has been used up, insert another by its butt end. Continue weaving in this way but remember that the article is meant to finish round and concave, so tighten your weaving all the

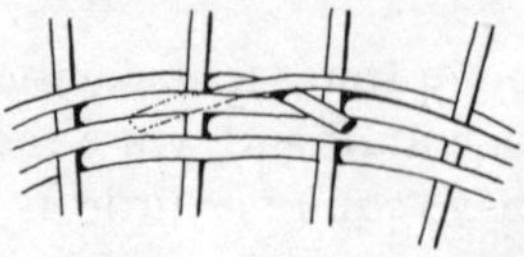

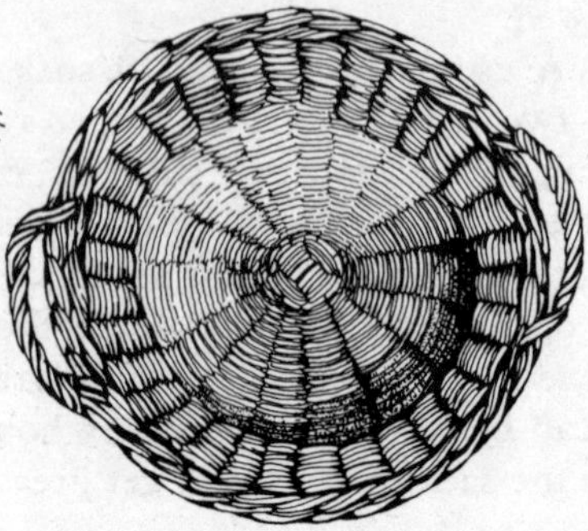

time. Round baskets which require a flat base should have their bottoms woven flat; the ribs are then bent upwards and the sides worked straight.

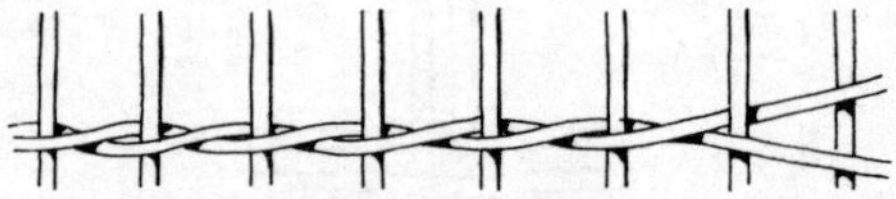

A looser finish can be achieved by pairing or using two or even three rods at the same time. When the sides of the basket are com-

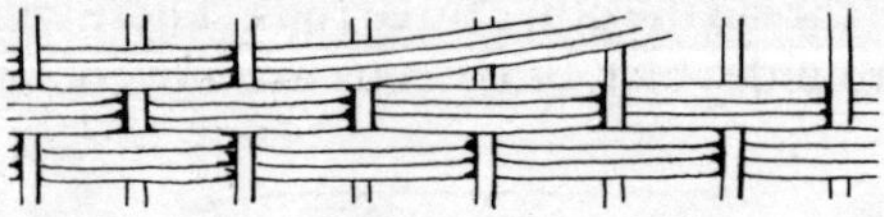

plete, the ribs are woven in to make the top edge as shown. The

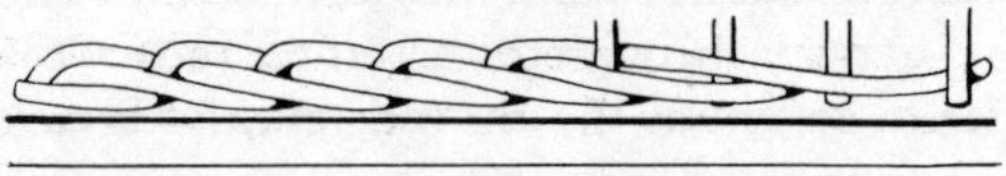

protruding ends are cut off close to the basket.

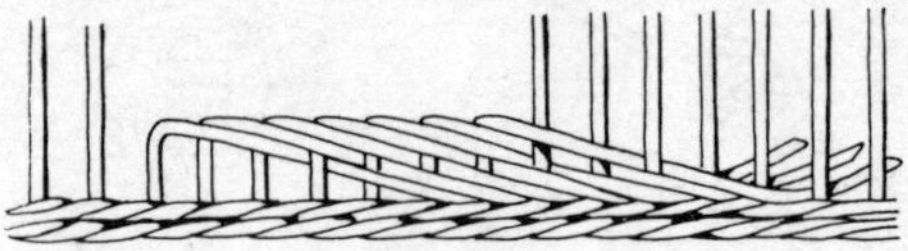

Depending on requirements the basket may be fitted with one large handle or two small ones, one on each side. To fit an overall handle, take three rods and insert them in one side; then take an-

other three and fit them in the opposite side. Take the first three and push them into the second three. Then take the second three and wind them round the first to form the handle, finishing them by inserting them into the opposite base. Or take one thick rod and

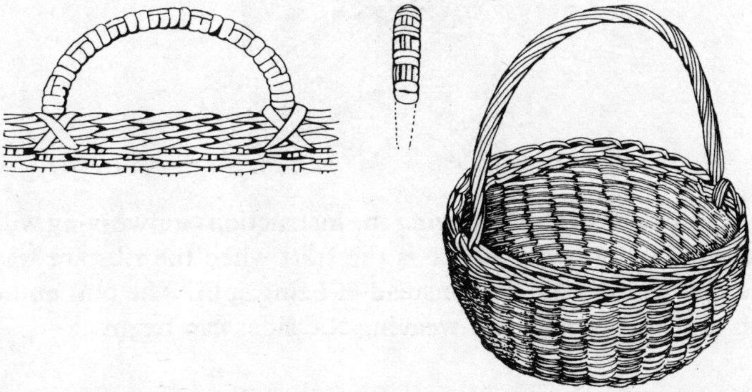

insert one end into each side of the basket. Then take two or three thinner rods and twist them round the edge of the basket and the thick rod to hold it in place. Wind them round the rod to the other end and repeat the holding process.

For two small handles on either side use the same process, but in miniature.

Rush Baskets

The common English rush (*Scirpus lacustris*) found growing by streams, rivers and in boggy places all over the British Isles is the species most suitable for making rush baskets. Because rushes lack the strength of willow only small baskets can be made by the weaving process. For large baskets the rushes must be plaited first into ropes and then sewn into shape.

To prepare the rushes for making into baskets, cut them in July when at their full height and, ideally, the butt end measures about half an inch. Then spread out thinly in the open air, turning occasionally, until they are dry. After this they can be stored in any dry, airy place until required. Before use the rushes must be made pliable by being soaked in cold water for about fifteen minutes, then taken out, covered with a damp cloth and left overnight for the water to penetrate.

Small baskets

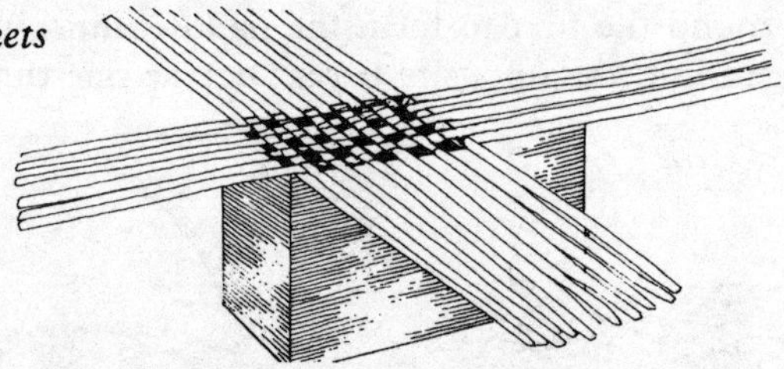

These can be made by following the instructions for weaving willow baskets. The only difference is the start when the ribs are woven together to make the base instead of being split. The butt end of a rush is then inserted and weaving the sides can begin.

Large baskets

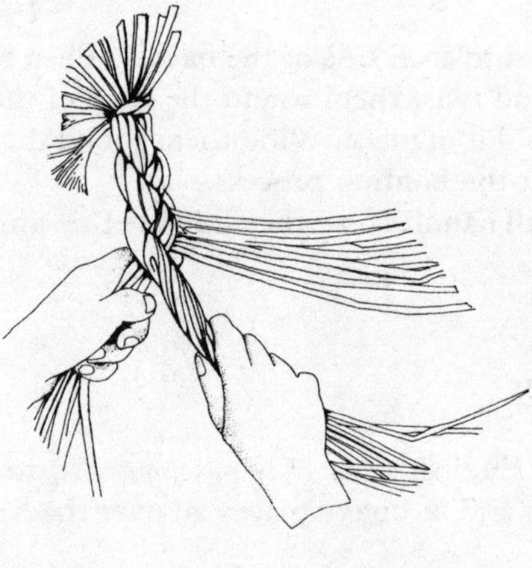

For these the rushes must be plaited together and the plaits sewn into shape. The number of rushes to be used in the plait depends on the size of the finished basket. In a three-strand plait, the strands can be made up of anything from one to a dozen rushes. Tie them all together at the top and attach the end to something firm. Divide the rushes equally and begin plaiting, adding more rushes to the strands as the ends are reached. A successful plait should be uniform in width. To achieve this, new rushes should be put in singly, avoiding an obvious join. Do this by placing each new rush on the inside of an old one and using the two as one for a short way in the plaiting. Also, if in plaiting each strand is given a half turn it keeps the rushes close and makes a firmer plait.

For a log-type basket with a base of 15 ins. and a depth of 12 ins. take 18 yards of plait, 1½ ins. wide, a needle and some strong thread.

First make the plait; allow it to dry out before beginning to sew. For the base coil the plait round sewing tightly as you go with the stitches coming out half-way through the plait. Sewing is made easier if the needle is occasionally passed through a bar of soap. When the base is 15 ins. in diameter continue sewing the plait round vertically to make the sides.

The handles are made from a plait three yards long and should be attached as shown. They may be finished by binding with twisted or plaited rushes.

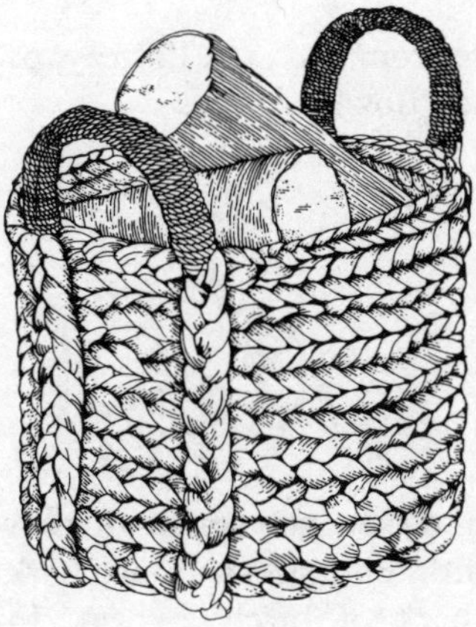

Bowls (Wooden)

For making a wooden bowl hardwood is better than soft and, of the hardwoods elm, ash, beech and oak are best. Wood used for bowls must not splinter, or give an unpleasant taste to the food and must be able to withstand constant washing with no ill effects. A well-made bowl, it is said, should last sixty years.

Most of the directions for making a wooden spoon hold good for a wooden bowl (see Spoons, p. 283) since they are both concave utensils. The timber should be winter felled, then cut into logs of appropriate size. The logs are then hewn into the approximate size of the bowl required and the shape of the bowl roughly cut with an axe. The wood is hollowed out using a knife with a curved blade, the outside of the bowl finished and the base flattened. Finally the whole bowl is smoothed off with sandpaper or the rough skin of a dogfish.

For easy stacking and storing it is a good idea to make bowls of graded sizes. If a branch of a tree is chopped off and cut into lengths for a series of bowls, this will happen naturally.

Containers

For containers made from clay, see Pottery, p. 266; for containers made from wood, see Bowls, above.

Bark

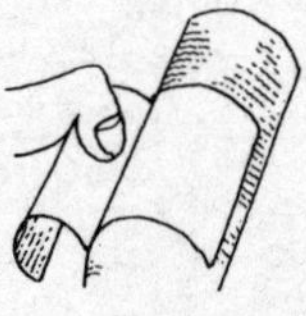

American Indians and backwoodsmen all knew how to make bark utensils of every kind. Though the inner bark of many species of tree will do, the bark of birch is best. First cut a sheet of smooth birch bark (free from holes, cracks and surface eyes or curls) of a suitable size and trim with a knife to the required shape. The bark may be made supple by toasting it over a fire. For a square utensil fold as shown. After folding to shape, either clip the bark

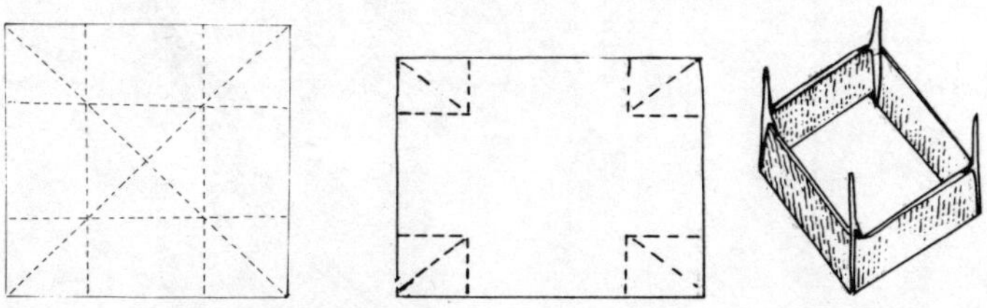

together with a split stick or sew – first punch holes with a sharp twig or awl and then sew, using tree fibres soaked in water as thread or a narrow strip of pliable bark. Buckets are finished by sewing to a rim of hazel; ladles by attaching a wood handle. A trough of the

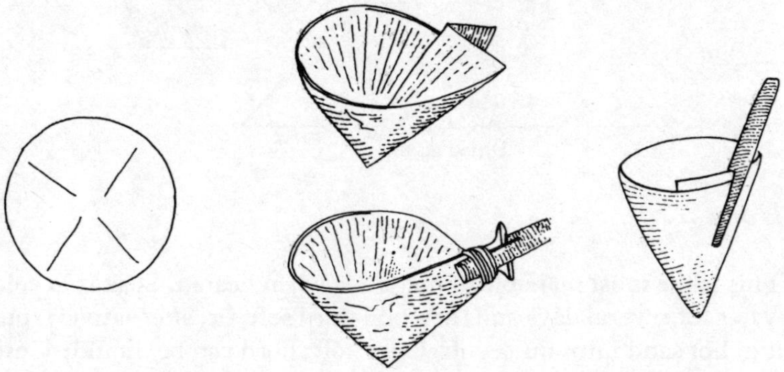

Ladle

shape used by American Indians to collect maple syrup is made by taking a sheet of bark from elm, poplar or any other suitable tree and removing the thick outer bark from each end, folding the ends in overlapping layers, somewhat like the ends of a canoe, and tying them with bark strips. The Indian also made barrels from elm bark; after sewing the seams were sealed with pine resin or spruce gum (see Tar, p. 302), hot grease and oil, and the upper edges stiffened with hoops or splits of pliable wood.

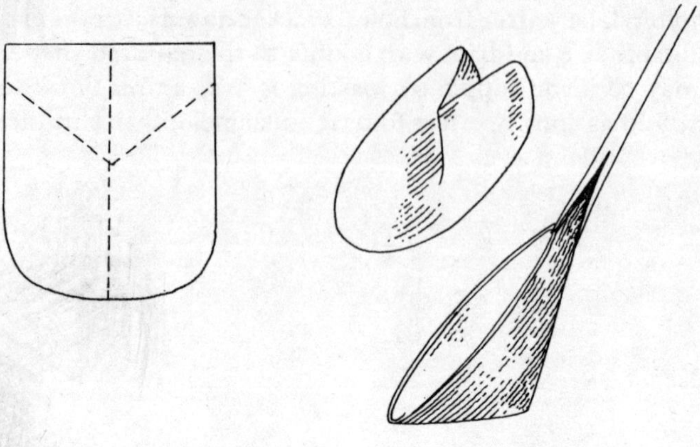

Bark ladle

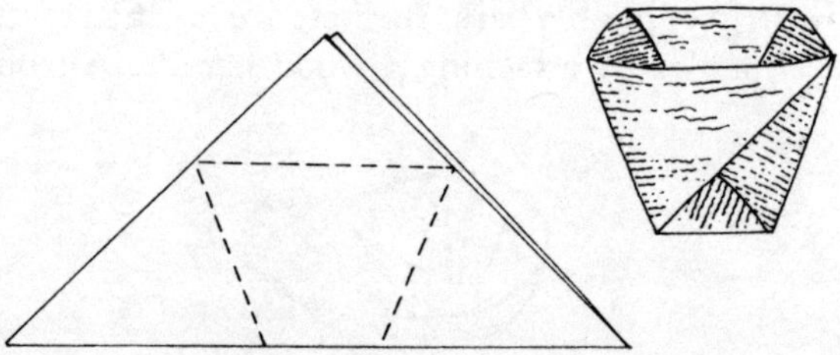

Drinking cup

Horn

This is the most mallable of materials when heated. Soak it in cold water for several days and then boil until soft, or, alternatively, put it in hot sand until quite soft. Once soft, horn can be moulded into any shape which it will hold when cool. Used mainly for mugs, though spoons – especially good for eating eggs, which stain silver – were and still are made from horn. Many people consider horn ideal for drinking beer and cider; tea and coffee too, for it is a poor conductor of heat. Formerly every reaper would carry his horn mug to the fields with him, 'Heo fulde hire horn wid wyn'.

To make a cup, take a cow horn and trim the butt end smooth and even. Then make a groove on the inside near the bottom and into this fit a disc of horn or wood. Alternatively stick the disc to the bottom with glue.

Leather

Leather bottles, cups, buckets and jugs known as Black Jacks and now museum pieces were in everyday use until about the end of the eighteenth century. They were made from a single piece of leather, the sides sewn together and a circular bottom sewn in. The shape was formed by soaking the leather until soft and then stretching it over wooden blocks of the right shape. Cups and buckets were made in the same way; bottles had bottoms sewn in at both ends and a corked mouthpiece inserted in the middle of the main side seam and often a strong cord attached for carrying. Bags for carrying water were made by merely gathering the top of a section of hide with string or a strip of intestine. American fur trappers used to skin a small animal whole (see p. 108), which did away with the need of a side seam. The Bedouin make leather washing bowls with legs and rim of bent wood and a hide lashed to the rim.

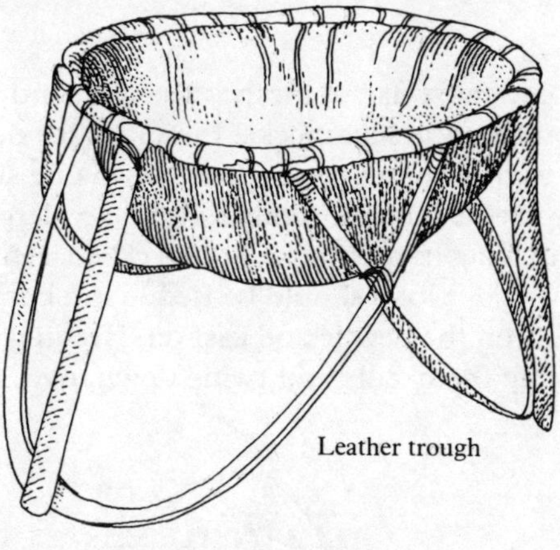

Leather trough

Nets

To begin any kind of netting three items are essential; a mesh stick whose width decides the size of the mesh; a needle – corresponding

Needle

in size to the mesh stick but slightly narrower to allow for the bulk of the thread; and twine, thin for small mesh work and thick for heavier mesh. Cotton or hemp twine is most often used today and is easily bought, but any of the materials mentioned under rope (p. 297) can be used.

The mesh stick can be made from any thin wood, normally about 9 ins. long, $\frac{1}{8}$ in. thick and anything from $\frac{1}{2}$ to 2 ins. wide. The needle, shaped as shown, must be wide enough to pass easily through the mesh but not so narrow that it will carry too little thread.

Diamond mesh

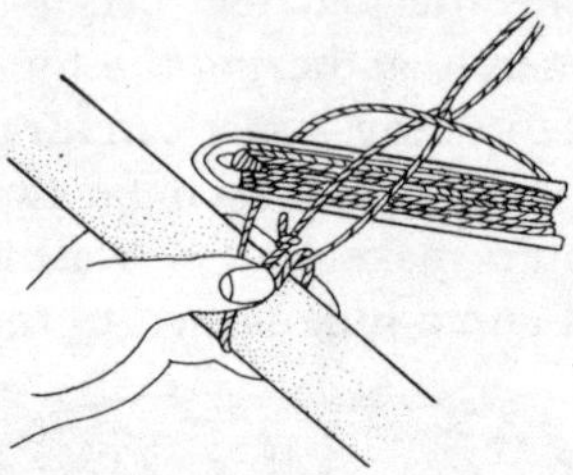

The simplest and most useful mesh is the diamond mesh used for fish nets, rabbit nets and hammocks. First load the needle by winding the twine tightly round the tongue, down one side and up the other until the needle is comfortably full. Make a large loop of some spare twine and hang it on a hook. This is called a stirrup and on to this a second, smaller loop should be tied. Tie a knot to it with the end of the twine on the needle and cast on. Holding the mesh stick lengthways bring the needle and twine down, over the mesh stick

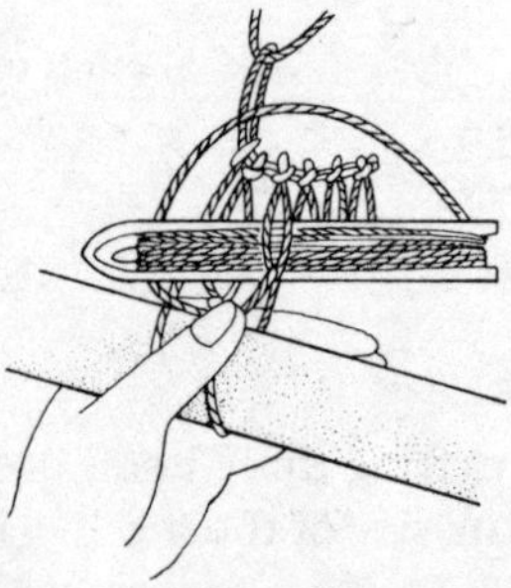

and up through the back of the foundation loop, pull tight and secure against the mesh stick with the left thumb. Then bring the twine round in a circle and put the needle between the whole loop and the circle just made. Tighten by releasing the twine held by the thumb, and the first knot is complete. Repeat until you have the required number of stitches on the mesh stick. If these are more than the mesh stick will hold, allow some to drop off it and hang loose. Very large mesh can be made by winding the twine twice round the mesh stick.

For the next row, pull the mesh stick out of the stitches, turn the work over, so that the last loop of the first row is now the first of the second and work this in exactly the same way. After several rows it should begin to look like the diagram below.

To reload the needle with twine join the ends by using the weaver's knot.

Weaver's knot

Square mesh

Used for tennis nets and many nets for trapping animals. The actual knot is the same as for diamond mesh but the working is different. Tie a foundation knot on the stirrup and cast two stitches on to it. Pull out the mesh stick, turn the work and net into these two loops, increasing one on the second loop by netting two stitches into one loop. Turn the work again and continue netting but always increasing one in the last loop until it is the right size. This is only obvious when you spread the work out and it can be seen that a square is being formed by netting diagonally across the work. When the required width has been reached continue netting but, on the next row, increase at one end and decrease at the other – netting one stitch into two loops. Continue increasing and decreasing on alternate rows, making sure you always have the same amount of stitches on the mesh stick and that all the increase is on one side of the work

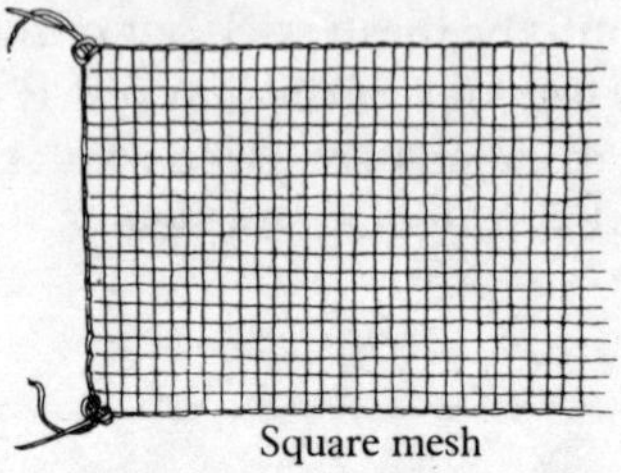

Square mesh

and all the decrease on the other. A marker tied to the side you are increasing on helps to avoid confusion and a zigzag net.

When the increasing side measures the length required, continue netting but decrease at the end of every row until you are down to two stitches again. Tie the loops together and cut those attached to the foundation twine, unpick the cast-on knots and tie these together. The finished net may be somewhat misshapen but pulling and a damp cloth and hot iron will get it right.

To Make a Hammock

For this a mesh stick measuring slightly under 1½ ins. is required. Cast on 32 stitches of diamond mesh and net for 64 rows – each finished row representing two worked rows to complete a diamond. The final row should be netted with double twine for extra strength and when the knots of the foundation row have been unpicked net a

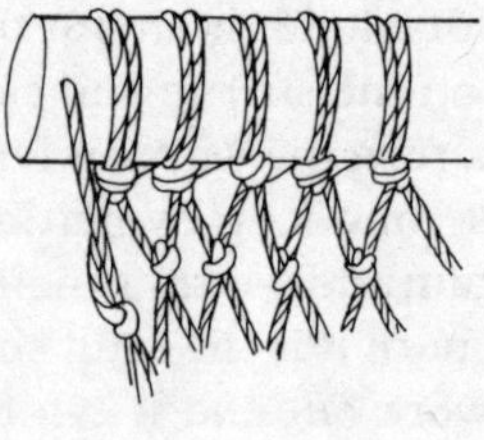

row using double twine at this end too. Take two wooden struts, bore a hole at each end and slip them through the double rows of netting. Cut two lengths of twine somewhat longer than the hammock, thread the ends through the holes in the top strut, then thread them down the sides of the hammock and knot through the holes of the bottom strut. These are to prevent the hammock going flat when someone sits on it but should not be tied so that the weight falls on them instead of the network. Finally take two iron rings, and a length of rope, thread the rope through one ring and attach it to the end of the struts, forming a V. Do the same at the other end and the hammock is ready for hanging.

To Make Purse Nets for Catching Rabbits

Thick and thin twine are required, the thicker used for bordering the nets, also two metal rings, about 1¼ ins., and a wooden peg.

Take a 1½ in. mesh stick and load with the thinner twine. Tie on to the foundation loop leaving a tag end of about a yard – this tag is vital as it is later used for netting into one of the rings. Then cast 18 stitches on to the foundation loop and net 22 rows in diamond mesh. Cut off twine about one yard from the netting. Take one of the rings and, using it instead of the mesh stick, net one more row, using the tag of twine and your fingers instead of a needle, until the whole of

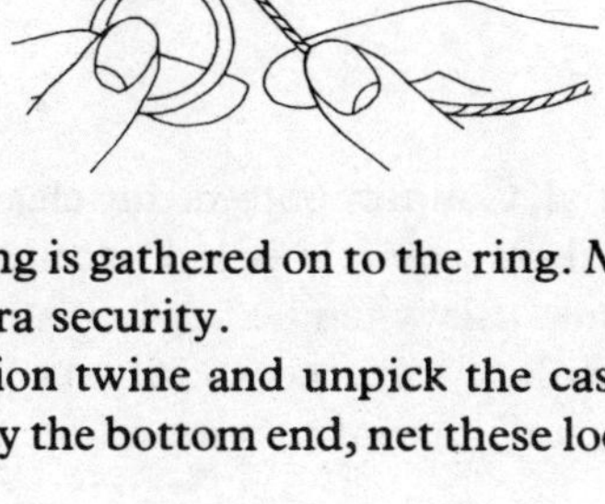

the end of the netting is gathered on to the ring. Make the last knot a double one for extra security.

Cut the foundation twine and unpick the cast-on knots. Then, hanging the work by the bottom end, net these loops into the second ring, in the same way as the other end, using the long tag of twine. Thread the thicker cord through one ring, all down the side of the netting, through the bottom ring, up the other side and back through the top ring. Thread the cord loosely so that the net can be spread out flat and leave about 6 ins. at the top to which the peg should be tied.

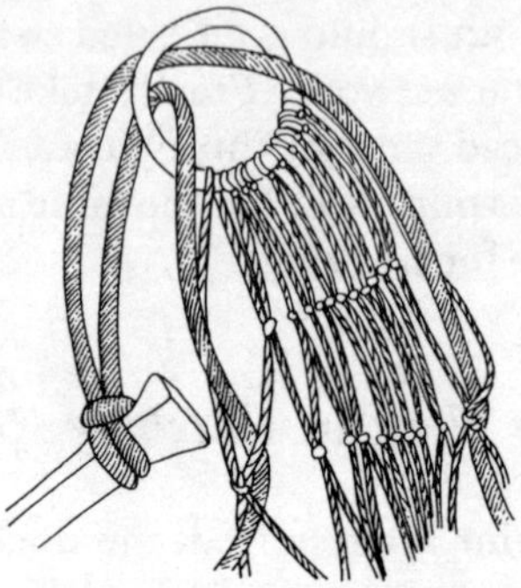

Plates

Plates can be made from hollow stones of a hard granite variety (with soft stones there will be grit in the food), from pottery, see below, and from wood. Wooden plates, or 'trenchers' as they were called, marked a stage in the development of civilized eating – large hunks of bread had previously served to hold slices of meat. Though still in use in country areas until the beginning of this century, wooden plates largely went out with the introduction of pewter and china. They are carved from slices of hardwood (softwood cannot be used as it splinters).

Pottery

Good clay is essential. Country potters dug clean clay in the vicinity of their kilns and their example is still worth following. Bernard Leach was doing just this when he began his pottery in Cornwall. Most clay is the result of the decomposition of feldspathic rock, or crystalline granite, and is found near its mother rock – in Cornwall it occurs in enormous quantities. This clay is able to withstand high temperatures and retain its colour. For local sources of clay and fresh water sand ask at a nearby brickworks, clay pit or mason's. The best clay often comes from below the level of the top soil. For this reason the exposed bank of a river is a good source, the clay being dug from about a yard below the top of the bank. To test whether clay has good pot-making potential, take a small amount, wet and knead it, make into an arch and stand on a flat surface in a warm temperature but away from direct heat. If it dries without cracking or undue shrinkage it probably has the right qualities – enough silica to prevent too much contraction and enough mica to give it plasticity.

Preparing Clay

Clay, ideally, should be dug in autumn and left to weather outside over the winter before using. Then break it into small lumps, remove any stones and soak in water for a day or two. Put it through a fine sieve and leave this 'slip' to settle; the clay should sink to the bottom and the excess water can then be poured off. Next place the clay on a flat slab and leave it to dry out some more. Then, if it is not to be used immediately, keep it damp.

The next process, called 'wedging', is designed to press out any air bubbles. This is done with the foot in Japan. In England a lump of clay is banged down on a firm bench or table, the lump cut in half, the two halves forced together and cut again; the process is repeated until the clay is of an even consistency.

Making Pots Without a Wheel

North American Indians used willow baskets as moulds and, indeed, it is thought that the first pots were derived from baskets which had been given a lining of clay and which, as can happen, caught fire, burning the clay hard. Natives in Africa often use the base of an old clay pot to start a new one and for different shapes use an old pot as a mould. The clay is pressed into the pot or round the outside and left to dry; a sharp tap will separate the two. Without a mould or wheel pots can be formed in the following three ways.

A coil pot: Long, round, even sausages of clay are coiled round to form the base and sides of a bowl. Press the coils well together all the time. Cement with a coat of slip, brushed on if it is a small bowl. With a large bowl, fill the bowl with slip, swill it round and pour it out again.

A pinch pot: Take a large lump of clay and make it into a ball; with your thumb press a hole into the middle and, still using your thumb and your forefinger, rotate the ball while pinching and working the sides with your fingers until the walls are sufficiently thin and even and a bowl is formed.

A slab pot: Roll out the clay as you would pastry on a board, about ⅜ in. thick. Then cut into rectangular shapes with a knife. For a box you will need six, two the same size for the base and lid, two slightly narrower, but the same length, for the sides and two smaller ones for the ends. Leave the pieces to harden a bit before fixing them together with slip. First scratch the surface with a knife, then paint with slip and finally press the sides together. Seal the outside with fine rolls of clay well worked in. To make the lid fit, cut a margin as wide as the top of the walls of the box are thick, and remove this to half the thickness of the lid.

Handles

Handles are made by attaching an end of clay to a shelf and pulling it down and shaping it until the right dimensions are arrived at. Then it is fixed to the pot by looping it over the rim or with both ends fixed to the sides, whichever is appropriate to the outline of the pot.

Throwing Pots on a Wheel

Though, as Bernard Leach says, the 'range of plastic beauty achieved in primitive pottery, made chiefly by the hands of women without a wheel and with tools only of wood or stone, basketry, textiles, leaves of trees or stitched animal hides, is immense'[78] the range and scope of pot making is immeasurably widened with a wheel – basically a revolving wheel, driven by hand, foot or gear. Wheels are known to have existed in ancient Egypt, and their use in Europe can be dated back as far as 2000 BC. In Japan hand wheels have a wooden head with four notches in the edge and, as the momentum slows down, the potter inserts a short stick into one of the notches and gives the wheel a turn. Constant practice is required before pots of any standard are made on a wheel. The principle is to plonk a lump of soft clay down in the middle of the wheel, then set it going at a moderate speed. After wetting your hands, cup both over the clay until you can tell by the smoothness of motion that it is evenly balanced on the wheel. Then begin shaping: press both thumbs downwards and outwards steadily into the centre of the clay. Squeezing the wall between thumbs and forefingers work the clay outwards and upwards, manipulating it until the shape you require is arrived at. For larger pots it will be necessary to keep one hand inside the pot and one out, to draw the clay up. Cut the pot from the board with a cheese wire, leave it to dry for a bit, then return it to the wheel for further smoothing with water if needed. Bernard Leach describes the process:

> A pot thrown on a good wheel with responsive clay, but not too soapy in texture, is impressed and expressed, urged and pulled and coaxed through a series of rhythmic movements, which like those in a dance are all related and interdependent. The spinning wet clay must be kept dead true to the centre of the wheel while it is being hollowed and drawn up, expanded and contracted into a living embodiment of the potter's intention. The preconceived shape will include the mark of each part of the process of throwing, the ribs left by the fingers, the upward thrust of the cylinder from the wheel-head to the major curve of the belly, the fullness or leanness of that curve, the pause and turn on the shoulder, often accentuated with ridge or collar, where convex movement changes to concave, the neck tapering to the lip with a concluding accent and conciseness of finish. Many of the noblest and most spontaneous pots are complete at this point, but others, especially such as are to have a foot-ring or bevelled lip, need to be pared on the wheel when half dry. This cutting off of shavings gives a different and sharper quality of finish: the difference between modelling and carving; and the two surfaces must be brought into harmony with one another.[78]

Firing

Before firing the pots must be thoroughly dried out by being left in a warm place for several days. The object of firing is to heat the clay to a temperature – between 1,500°F and 2,300°F – where the substances in the clay fuse together without melting. Glazed pots need two firings, the first at 1,325°F to 1,685°F to bake or biscuit fire them, the second, after glazing, at 1,685°F to 2,400°F (white heat) to fuse the glaze and make them waterproof. Kilns are chambers fed with flames from one or more fireplaces, with a chimney to draw out the heat and smoke. The construction of the kiln, as well as the method of stoking, helps determine the final composition of the pots. Wood, particularly pine wood, is far superior to any other kind of fuel. A simple up-draught brick kiln can be made as shown, one yard in

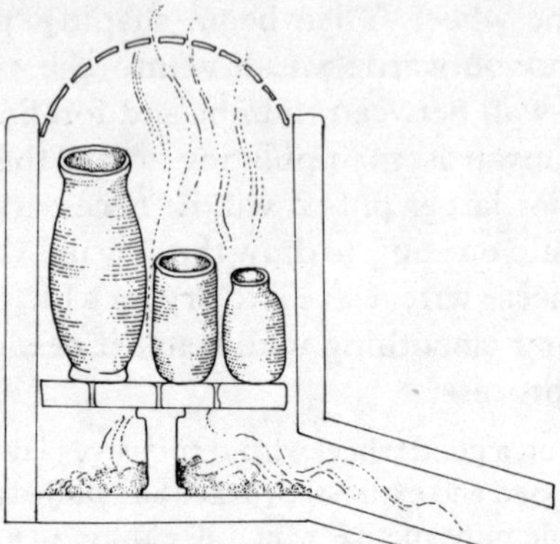

A simple round up-draught kiln

height and one yard in diameter. The more complicated one is taken from Bernard Leach's *A Potter's Book.* The pots are packed on per-

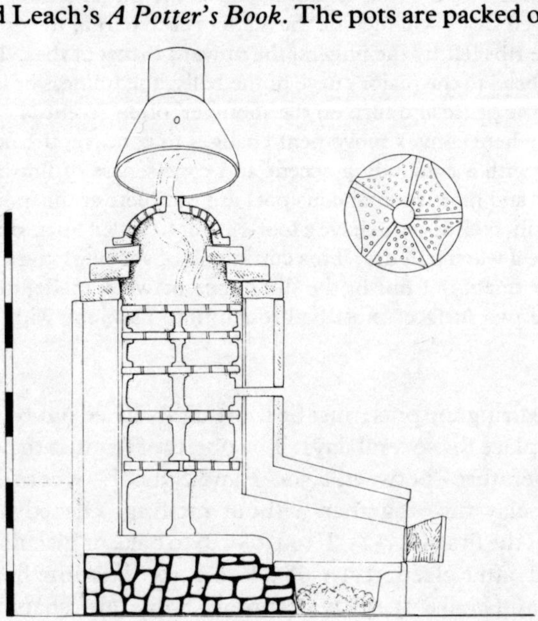

forated shelves, tier upon tier, leaving something like a two-inch gap at the sides for the flames to rise to the top. The temperature at the top will be some 100 degrees lower than the bottom and pots to be biscuit fired are placed here. Stoking the kiln is an art in itself, done in Japan by specially trained men. Big slow burning logs are used first to heat up the kiln gradually; this can take about twelve hours. The fire is then banked down and left for three days to cool slowly. With the second firing more attention has to be paid to the temperature: special cones can be bought which keel over at certain temperatures indicating when to shut down the heat; or rings of clay dabbed with glaze and fished out at intervals can be used to test whether the glaze is ready.

Some African tribes fire their pots in open brush fires and are very adept at it. The fire is kept alight for an hour and a half and then damped down with leaf mould. The pots are carefully stacked and warmed first to help prevent them breaking up in the fire. If this precaution is taken, the clay is well mixed, the pots of even thickness and the joints well fixed, the method does work. But if any of these points have been neglected a pile of chips can be the result.

Glazing

Glazing makes a pot impervious to liquid, protects it from staining and is a means of decoration. When pots were given only one firing they could be glazed by throwing handfuls of salt on to the pots at peak temperature. This was repeated six or seven times, and the fire was then banked down and left to cool. Resins and gums were also used as glazes, applied when the pot was still warm from the fire or before the second firing. Old English slipware pottery was often glazed with slip – made by mixing equal quantities of clay with water. Iron-impregnated clays mixed with powdered rocks were used as glazes long before the art of glazing developed. Glazes vary in character according to the composition and firing temperature: 'As clothes are to the human body so are glazes to pots' – Bernard Leach. The most important ingredient in a glaze is the fluxing ingredient which can be lead, borax, soda, salt, limestone, magnesia or wood ash. To this some heat-resisting silica, in the form of flint or quartz, is added, together with a third ingredient to form the body of the glaze, such as feldspar or clay. The charm of the old glazes was due to impurities and inconsistencies. The great Japanese potter Hamada says that

> In Mashiko the potters obtained clay and kiln materials from near by, and wood from the local forest. Ash and stone for glazes were available in the neighbourhood. Kaki glaze, which is used most, is made from the powder of stone quarried in the neighbouring village; iron powder came from iron dust at the blacksmith's; copper powder from old copper pans, and even brushes from the hair of local dogs. These materials are never first class. Yet, here is purity and harmony as seen in Japanese paper, brush and ink, instead of foreign paper and fountain pen.[77]

Tools and Utensils

For anyone who has had to survive in the wild it is quite easy to see the logic in the statement made by the archaeologist, Kenneth P. Oakley, that 'human progress has gone step by step with the discovery of better materials of which to make *cutting* tools'.[89] Beside the importance of a knife all other tools fade into insignificance. With a knife it is possible to kill and prepare meat to eat, cut wood to build a house for shelter and heat, cut cloth or skins to fashion clothes and even to make sparks to make fire – so providing all the essentials of life. Primitive man did everything with a kind of axe-shaped knife initially made from a sharp flint or other hard stone and later from metal – the Chinese still use an axe-shaped knife for chopping up all their food.

When cast away in our wilderness I had the luxury of a medium-sized steel kitchen knife which I used not only for all the cooking preparation but to cut nettles, scrape bark off trees for dye, cut bracken for bedding, gut rabbits, cut up skins and grub up roots. This knife was obviously more efficient for cooking than for root grubbing and I should have liked to have had Iron Age man's antler or a pick to help me with this. A sickle would also have been better for cutting bracken and it is easier to skin a rabbit if you have a blunt-tipped knife; you are less likely to puncture the innards as you slit down the stomach (see p. 108). We also took with us a large axe, which was invaluable when it came to cutting wood and, had we been intending to split the logs for building, some wedges and a beetle would have been necessary as well (see p. 306). To shape the wood for furniture a lathe, an adze, a small carving knife and some sandpaper or a sandpaper substitute in the form of rough dogfish skin or abrasive stone would also have been necessary (see Furniture, p. 221). For any construction work a hammer would have been imperative – primitive man used a pebble hafted to a wooden handle but we had a metal one – as would something to bore holes with and nails: these can be made from a variety of materials, most coming from bone, wood and metal.

We took a rake for gathering up rushes and bracken laid out to dry, and a spade, though since we did not do any cultivation its main use was for digging the lavatory (see p. 236). We also needed an assortment of brushes for tasks as various as sweeping the floor and keeping our hair from matting and tangling.

For eating we had wooden spoons and wooden forks though the latter were useless as they were not sharp enough to spear anything and the prongs broke, so we ended up going medieval and using just the spoon and our fingers. We took a sieve for straining milk and flour and pegs for hanging out clothes to dry and skins to cure.

The four basic materials of ancient man were wood, bone, shell and stone and from these all his tools were fashioned. Neolithic man made shovels from the shoulder-blades of oxen and adapted bone, horn and antlers into all kinds of tools. (Eskimos still make hammers, wedges and adzes from these materials.) Primitive man tilled his soil with a stone hoe and reaped his barley and wheat with a flint-toothed wooden sickle.

Brushes

The first brushes of which there is pictorial evidence are in the prehistoric cave paintings in Altamira and the Périgord. They are made from hog's bristle. The ancient method of removing bristles from a hog was to coat the skin with resin the moment it was dead and the body still warm. After the resin had hardened, it was torn off, bringing the bristles with it; the resin was melted down and the bristles extracted. The hairs were then washed and sorted according to size, colour and degree of coarseness. Hair from other animals, and the branches of several plants and feathers, can also be used as bristles.

Badger and squirrel hair and feathers are soft and best for shaving brushes, fine paint-brushes and dusting brushes. Horsehair and pig bristle are hard and best for hairbrushes. Birch twigs are harder still and suitable for yard brushes and stiff floor brushes. Rushes, broom and grass are suitable for smooth floor brushes.

The wood for the handle should be well seasoned and preferably of birch, alder, sycamore or willow, though for brushes which will be constantly in water beech should be used. The different types of brush are made as follows.

Hairbrush and Hand Brush

These are both made in the same way though one should obviously be a larger size than the other. There are two common methods.

Sticking

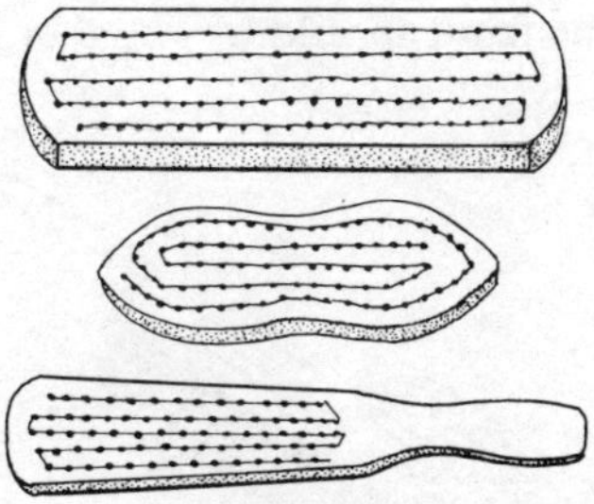

Carve a wooden back to the right shape, then bore holes in it, about $\frac{1}{5}$ in. to $\frac{1}{3}$ in. in diameter and just deep enough to hold the hairs securely. Next take a bundle of hairs – enough to fill one hole and no more – melt some pitch, level the base of the hairs, fan them out and dip one end in the pitch. Bind this end two or three times round with thread and then, while the pitch is still hot, force the hairs into a hole

in the brush, rotating them so that they fan out in the hole. As the pitch cools the hairs will fix firmly in the back. To finish trim the top of the brush.

Drawing

The diagram is self-explanatory. The arrangement of holes is the same as for the glued brush and the thread which holds the hairs in place can be of string, wire or anything else that is fine and strong. To begin, tie a knot round the first bunch of hair. To finish, a back

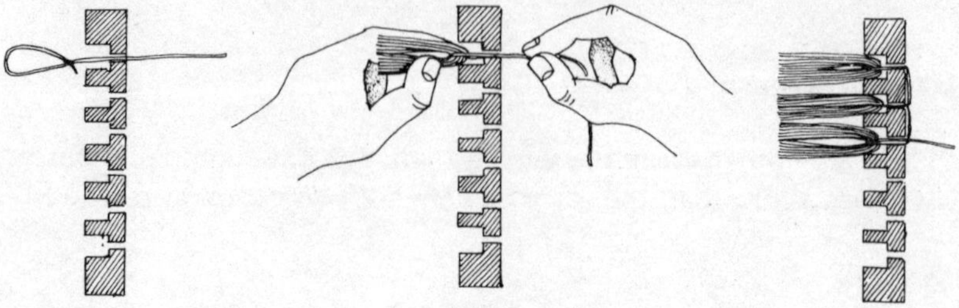

the same shape as the front should be glued or screwed on when all the hairs are in place.

Drawn brush

Shaving Brush or Paintbrush

For a shaving brush take a small log or branch and shape the top as shown opposite. For a paintbrush use a bird's quill – goose is best. Next take the hair or bristle and bind or knot it to hold it temporarily in place. Dip the end of the hairs in warm resin, pitch or glue and stand glue end down on a warm plate for long enough for the glue to penetrate the bristles. Place the bunch of bristles in the handle and bind firmly in place with string or other binding.

Besom

Hard besoms are traditionally made with birch twigs but heather or any other resilient branch will do. For softer besoms use rush, grass or broom. Cut the birch in spring when the sap is rising; cut broom when it is not in flower: 'If you sweep the house with blossomed broom in May; You are sure to sweep the head of the house away.' Tie with rope, string or split willow. Make a point on a pole and drive into the centre of the bundle for a handle. Secure with a peg or nail driven in sideways.

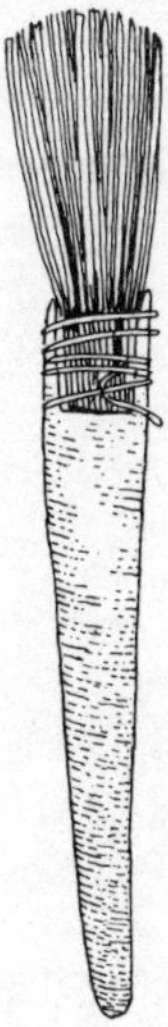

Shaving brush

Besom

Whisk

A whisk for beating up sauces and soups in the kitchen can be made of birch or bog myrtle twigs. Bind round with string as above.

Hare's Foot

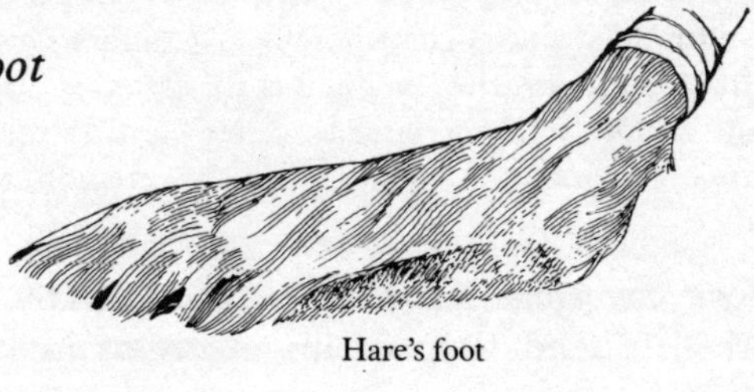

Hare's foot

A hare's pad was cut at the joint, washed thoroughly in soft soapy water and stood bone-end-down in strong disinfectant. It was then dried out and the bone end bound, covered with the finger of a glove or fitted with a handle. These were used as a cosmetic brush for powder and rouge and also in the kitchen to glaze pastry.

Feather Brushes

A bunch of feathers was often used instead of a hare's foot to glaze pastry, having a lighter touch. A bunch of swan's down tied together to form a puff is still the softest thing for powdering face and body. Feather dusters are made of a large bunch of feathers bound to a long hazel or willow wand – for cobwebs, ceilings and walls.

Forks

Forks were introduced into Britain in 1601 by Thomas Coryate, a country squire from Odcombe, Somerset, after a tour of the Continent. In *Coryate's Crudities* a book he published about his adventures on his return he records 'The Italian, and also most strangers that are commorant in Italy, do alwaies at their meats use a little forke when they cut their meat . . . their forke for the most being of yron or steele, and some silver, but those are mostly used by gentlemen. The reason of their curiosity is, the Italian cannot indure to have his dish touched by fingers, seeing that all men's fingers are not alike clean. Hereupon I myself thought good to imitate the Italian fashion by this forked cutting of meats, not only while I was in Italy, but also in Germany, and oftentimes in England since I came home . . .' Coryate's innovation was ill-received by his contemporaries; laughed at for his affectation and satirized on the stage as 'the fork-carrying traveller', and rebuked from the pulpit for the impiety in assuming that God's gifts were unfit to be touched by human hands.[79]

Before the fork, coverings of paper were placed on that part of the joint held by the left hand. (Paper frills on cutlets are relics of this custom.) But by the end of Charles II's reign few self-respecting tables were laid without forks, mostly made of steel and with only two prongs: it was not until the eighteenth century that silver forks with four prongs became common. Forks have to be made of metal to be effective.

Knives

In the absence of an orthodox knife or axe made of steel, cutting can be done with sharp shells and with that staple material of Stone Age man, the flint. Translucent, close-textured and varying in colour from blue-black to red and yellow, flints are to be found all over Britain wherever chalk rocks come to the surface. The softer rock is eroded and the flints, being hard and resistant to weathering, are left behind, forming gravel and shingle on the banks and beds of rivers, in cliffs and on sea beaches, and lying on the surface of arable land. Neolithic man followed good seams of flint underground and remains of his shafts can be found in England in the South Downs behind Worthing, on the eastern downs in Hampshire and on the Norfolk–Suffolk border.

Flint shaping is an art requiring skill and practice. The working of flint depends on its peculiar properties of flaking. If a nodule of flint is struck sharply at right angles to the surface it does not crack or split, but a cone drops out from the point of impact.

Once the flint is mined it is left to dry in the open. Then the flint is quartered. By tapping the flint with his hammer, the flint knapper can tell by the ring where to strike to split the nodule. Then taking a lighter hammer he holds one of the quarters on his padded knee and, beginning with one of the freshly cleaved surfaces, he strikes off a series of parallel flakes from the sides until it becomes a fluted cone. A second set of flakes is then struck from this core, to refine the edge. The flint hand axe was the first standardized implement and was used as a general-purpose tool for felling trees, working wood, skinning animals, etc. Other uses for flints are for striking a light and for fire-arms.

Nails

The strongest and most easily inserted nails are obviously made from metal. But these need not necessarily be the best or most suitable. For furniture wooden nails, or rather thin tapering pegs made from the same wood as the piece, look better and contract and expand with the wood, making it less likely to split. In Scotland pegs made of heather stems and roots were employed for, among other things, fixing slates on roofs.

Animal bones have been used for many implements, including nails. Large bones were carved with knives and shaped by being rubbed against abrasive stones. Small ones such as the leg bones of sheep and the breast and leg bones of birds, especially chickens, were used whole.

In shape these nails were more like tapering pins than a nail with a head; a hole was of course bored in the object first.

Pegs

To make wooden pegs for keeping clothes on the line use softwood only; willow and hazel are best because their long, close flexible fibres can stand being bent slightly without losing their ability to snap back into position. The wood should be cut in midwinter when the sap is low and the wood hard. The peg-maker

would cut a Y-shaped stick about 8 ins. long, having two out-growing twigs at the top. These he would trim off carefully close to the main stem. Then taking a sharp knife, he would make a V-shaped nick at the bottom of the twigs he had removed. The exact angle of this nick in the base of the peg was the hallmark of a master in the art of pegging. For if it was made at any other angle the peg would split clean in two when used. As it was each new peg had to be judged on its own merits, using a similar form of intuition as that used by a diamond cutter splitting a priceless gem.

If the nick had been positioned correctly, the split never went beyond the point where the two knots bound the stem invisibly together, within the wood itself . . . the knotted top of the peg was carved gently into a round white knob, the ends smoothed off neatly and the peg was finished. The bark was never removed from the main stem as this kept the peg weather-proof for years.[80]

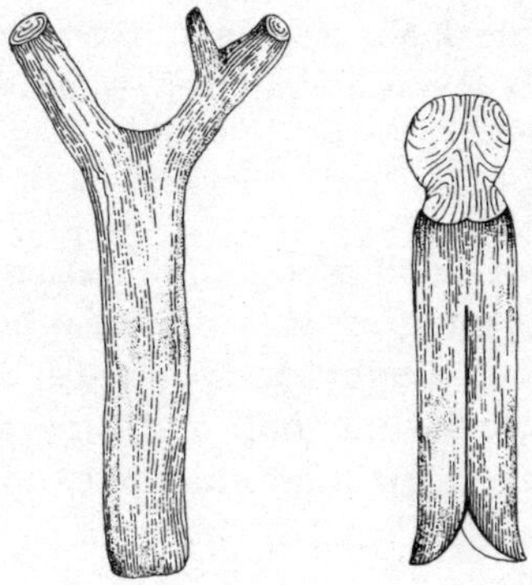

Rakes

Though the general shape remained the same, rakes varied in detail and durability: those designed for raking hay on sloping Welsh fields had short heads set at an angle of 45° to the handle and would last several seasons; those used on lush lowlands had larger heads and were renewed every year. The wood varied too; in Wales they used ash, in Hampshire willow and in other parts of the country pine, birch and alder.

A good rake should be as light as possible and have a handle as smooth as possible to slip easily through the hands.

Handle

For a handle made of ash, take a plank and saw off a strip 3 ins. square; round and smooth the sides. For a willow handle take a stick of the right diameter and straighten out any kinks by steaming and straining in a clamp, then shave and smooth the sides.

Next make the arm of the rake. With ash saw a split down the centre for 14 ins. and bind or, ideally, attach a metal ring at the end of this point to prevent the split travelling any further. With willow, flatten the butt end and then split it for 10 ins.

Head

For an ash rake, take a solid plank and mark and bore fifteen 'tine' holes 2 ins. apart with two holes on the other side for the handle. For willow, take a solid block about 30 ins. in length, shape and bore eleven to fifteen holes about 3 ins. apart, plus two for the handle.

Teeth

These are made from small pieces of wood and are most easily formed on a driving stool, but they may also be carved by hand. They should be long and smooth, and pointed at both ends. One end is then inserted into each 'tine' hole and banged home. Then the bow ends of the handle are pointed and fitted into the rake head and it is ready for use.

Sieves

Sieves can be made from both vegetable and animal materials. A handful of cleavers or goosegrass (*Galium aparine*) was used by shepherds for straining sheep's milk; the sticky hairs of the plant knitting together prevented the passage of foreign bodies. The wood of ivy is soft and porous and slices of this can be used to make a fine sieve or filter. A bundle of reeds tied tightly at the bottom and then more loosely at intervals, to form a cone, makes a coarse sieve. So does wet parchment or rawhide stretched over a wooden frame, left to dry and punctured with holes using a hot iron or sharp instrument. Sheep skins stretched in this way were used for riddling corn or meal in the Scottish Highlands.

Linnaeus describes how in Lapland the shepherds had a way of 'straining milk through plaited tufts of hair from the tails of cows'. Hair sieves, mainly of horsehair, were once a feature of every kitchen. The hair was coarsely woven like cloth and attached to a wooden rim – any flexible stick, such as hazel or elder, bound into a ring and a wooden handle attached. For a free-standing sieve a frame of two circular pieces of plywood is made and the sieve fitted between the two.

Spoons

The best wood to use is sycamore. It is a smooth glossy wood that can be worked while it is still green and, later, will stand constant immersion in water with no ill effects; an added advantage is that it doesn't give a 'woody' taste to food. If there is no sycamore available beech wood has much the same consistency and, failing beech, any hardwood, such as oak or yew, which is smooth and does not have too many knots in the grain. Softwoods are almost all unsuitable as they have a tendency to splinter.

The process of making a spoon begins with the felling of suitable timber in the winter months . . . There is a tradition that sycamore for bowls and spoons should be winter-felled, as this ensures a pale lustrous wood, free of all blemishes and stains. After the sycamore is felled, butts are cut by means of a cross-cut saw into logs, each one approximately twelve inches long. With the aid of a small cleaving iron and hammer, each log is cut in two and the process of shaping the spoon begins. Sitting on a three-legged stool, the craftsman rests the sycamore log on the chopping block in front of him and with a short-handled axe he cuts the log to the approximate shape of the spoon. With a few deft strokes, the handle and the shoulders of the spoon as well as the rough outline of the bowl are cut. For this process the craftsman depends entirely on eyesight and long experience, for the shoulders have to slope at the same angle and the spoon has to be perfectly symmetrical . . . After roughing out with the axe, the half-finished spoon now needs hollowing; this is done with a peculiarly shaped knife known as a *twca cam*. This tool, which has a handle some eighteen inches in length, has a small curved blade, usually made by the craftsman himself from an old file or chisel. It is kept extremely sharp, and to use it he tucks the handle under his right arm and tightly against his body, while the blade is grasped firmly in the right hand. With the tip of the handle acting as a fulcrum, considerable power is applied to the blade, and with a few short sweeping movements the core of the spoon is removed cleanly.

The convex side of the spoon and the handle have to be smoothed next; this is done with an ordinary small spokeshave. This is held in the palm of the hand and is used to smooth away all unevenness. Finally the tip of the handle, the edges of the spoon and the shoulders are cleaned and finished with a short-bladed knife. The whole process in making a broth spoon takes little more than fifteen minutes from the moment when the sycamore log is cleft to the final stage when the spoon is cleaned with the knife.[81]

Ladle

To make the large ladle that is used for a number of tasks in the home and dairy, the process is rather different. Since the ladle will be at least fifteen inches long, the logs have to be larger. Each one is roughed out in the same way as the broth spoon, except that the tip of the handle has to be shaped into a hook. This hook is necessary for hanging the ladle on the edge of a milk bucket or shelf, and it is shaped during the first stage of roughing out with the axe. Since the bowl of the ladle is considerably wider and deeper than that of the broth spoon, something stronger than the *twca* is required to shape it. The roughed-out-ladle is therefore clamped in a vice and a short-handled adze with a 1¼ inch gouge blade is taken . . . all that is required to clear the top part of the ladle is a few sharp knocks with the adze, but since it cannot be used to clear the lower end, nearest the handle, a gouge and mallet are used. A large-sized *twca cam* is then taken and the inside of the bowl cleared in exactly the same manner as the spoon. Finally the ladle is completed with spokeshave and knife.[81]

In country areas up to the end of the nineteenth century it was the custom for a man to show his love for a girl by making her an elaborately carved wooden spoon, many of which are now museum pieces.

Raw Materials

When I began researching the subject of living off the land I was mystified by the constant references to a small number of raw materials a different combination of which seemed to go into the making of nearly everything. The two most common were lime and potash. The first I knew of only as a building stone and the second I had never heard of. Because they were once so common it was never explained what they were – it was assumed you would know. Potash is literally 'ash' which is treated with water to extract the principles in a 'pot'. And lime, used for mortar, paint, treating leather, paper-making, glass and glue to name a few, is made from any material – such as limestone or a shell – which contains calcium carbonate; when ground and treated with water, they will produce lime. Tar, turpentine, charcoal, glue and paint are also easy to make. Metal I would buy if possible. Finding and converting metal into a useful article requires much labour and it would be easier to make do with flints and pebbles (see Tools, p. 273). However, if I was going to have to survive for a long time by myself, I would get round to metal in time, and glass and also rope.

But the most essential raw material is wood and wood, unfortunately, is in increasingly short supply today. It was once used for everything: to build houses, furniture, ships and farm implements; as a cooking and heating fuel; commercially to make charcoal for smelting iron, lead and glass.

Charcoal

Charcoal made in the old way, by the charcoal burners of the Forest of Dean, begins with a rectangular pit. This is usually 12 × 16 ft, and 18 ins. deep, though a smaller hole can be dug. The pit is then filled with piles of wood laid in such a way that a chimney space is left down the middle. Traditionally the wood was cut in 3 ft lengths packed with smaller pieces and placed round a central post which was removed before firing.

Experiments have proved that for charcoal making the order of preference with home-grown timber is beech, birch, hazel, hornbeam, maple, sycamore, oak, elm, white poplar, willow. Softwoods, as far as possible, should be avoided. The order is not hard and fast and depends somewhat on local conditions influencing growth.[82]

When the heap is complete it is covered – except for the chimney space – with turf, loam or clay and holes made for a draught. Then a fire-lighter is dropped down the chimney to set the wood alight and the space covered with a stone. The wood should smoulder, not burn, and the longer it takes for the wood to smoulder into charcoal the better the charcoal will be. Two days to a week, depending on wood and conditions, is normal.

When wood is heated at 200°F without access of air, it remains unaltered, at 220°F it becomes brown, and at 270°F to 300°F it suffers decomposition, torrefied wood or red charcoal being formed. At 350°F it is resolved into volatile products and true or black charcoal.[83]

Any tar in the wood will drain to the bottom of the pit and can be collected and used (see Tar, p. 302). Charcoal is used for many things including pencils, cooking fuel, tooth powders and gunpowder.

Glass

Though today glass has many more components, to add strength, brilliance and purity of colour, it was originally made from a combination of lime, soda and silica sand. The sand had to be pure and free from any of the discolouring iron oxide, which is present in most sand. Certain areas, where there was suitable sand, became centres of glass-making. The finest comes from Fontainebleau in northern France and was probably the reason for the development of the fine stained glass in this area. In Britain, though poor-quality glass was made at such monastic centres as Glastonbury, Jarrow and Monkwearmouth, the centre of the glass-making industry was at Chiddingfold in Surrey. This area not only had the right sand but enough fuel from the surrounding beech woods to fire the furnaces. Local names such as Glass-House and Kiln Copse still survive.

Ingredients

Sand: The main modern supplies come from an area between Southport and St Helen's in Lancashire and from Loch Aline on the coast of Morven in Argyllshire.

Lime: See Lime, p. 289.

Potash: Plants rich in the necessary carbonate of soda are glasswort, seablite and bracken. All are cut and dried; then, as Theophilus says, 'burn it equally and, diligently collecting the ashes, be careful not to mix any dust or stones with them'.[84] The ashes were placed in cauldrons of water to steep and then heated until the water evaporated. The remaining substance, called 'pearl ash', was the ingredient used.

Fuel: Traditionally beech wood, but as forests became depleted other woods, and later coal, were substituted.

Tools

Four were important: a blow-pipe, consisting of a wooden mouthpiece attached to three feet of small-bore iron pipe; a pontee, or rod of iron, four or five feet in length, used for gathering small pieces of molten glass and for holding the glass during manufacture; an implant, with which handles and other appurtenances are attached; a shaping tool, resembling a pair of sugar tongs but with long blades instead of spoons at the end.

Method

A mixture of potash, sand and a small amount of lime were heated until partly fused and then allowed to cool. When cool, the mass, called 'frit', was broken into pieces, put in crucibles or pottery Ali-Baba-shaped pots and stood in a melting furnace. In these crucibles, the frit melted, became fluid and gave off a scum of impurities, removed by skimming. The remaining glass was ladled into pans of water, the water drained off and the glass when dry put back into the crucibles for re-melting. A sample of glass was taken out by dipping an iron rod into the crucible; if the glass when cooled and hardened proved to be of adequate colour and free from bubbles, work began.

The end of the pipe was heated in the furnace and then dipped in the molten glass and a coil of the stuff collected by twisting it on to the pipe as you would thick treacle on a spoon. When enough of the glass was gathered the workman breathed through the mouthpiece, gradually forming a hollow bulb of glass – the first stage in forming any kind of hollow vessel and some flat ones too. The glass was then rolled round on a block of wood while being shaped with the shaping tool. Whenever the glass became too cool for further shaping it was thrust back into the furnace to restore its plasticity by reheating. When the correct shape was arrived at the ends, if it was a bowl or glass, were trimmed with the shaping scissors and lips of jugs and other shapings formed.

The vessel was then plunged in cold water to cool and harden. Handles or stems were put on. These were made from pieces of molten glass, lifted out of the furnace with the pontee and held until elongated by their own weight. Then the hanging end was pressed on to the vessel and, if a handle, the other end fixed in the right place and cut from the pontee. The base of a stem was shaped with the shaping tool and then, after cooling, detached from the pontee by a sharp blow. Old glasses made in this way can be distinguished by their pontee mark – a whirl of rough glass on the underside of the foot.

For flat panes, see Windows, p. 249.

Glue

A variety of materials will make glues of different strengths. White of egg or the leaves of comfrey boiled to a decoction make a thin glue which will stick paper. The slime from the scrapings of bluebell bulbs will do this and more. Geoffrey Grigson says that a notebook mended with bluebell glue withstood another thirteen years use[85] and William Turner in 1568 states that 'The boyes in Northumberlande scrape the roots of the herbs and glew theyr arrowes and bokes wyth the slyme that they scrape of.'[43]

Some seaweeds rendered down produce glue (see agar, p. 151). Isinglass is the name given to the glue or jelly procured from the intestines and stomach of fish, particularly sturgeon. It is made by steeping the innards in water, rendering them down over heat, then straining off the liquid and allowing it to cool.

Extra strong glue is made from hides, tendons, hoofs, and horns of horses, cows, sheep, goats and deer put into a pan with enough water to prevent them sticking to the bottom and simmered slowly. The resulting liquid is drawn off and allowed to set. Lord and Baines recommend the following mixture for a 'fire and waterproof glue:

> Take a handful of well-burned quicklime and mix it with four ounces of linseed oil, rub the ingredients thoroughly together, and then boil the mixture until it is the consistence of ordinary paste. Throw it out on sheets of common tin to dry and harden. When required for use boil it as you would common glue.[48]

Common or otherwise, most of the above glues do need to be melted down before use.

Lime

Although limestone as a building stone was probably first employed in the Stone Age, lime mortar or lime in a prepared form was unknown before the time of Ptolemy, *c.*304–283 BC. Since then it has been used in an incredible number of industries: plaster, mortar, paint, agriculture, paper-making, leather, glass, glue and hair dyes. The process of converting limestone into lime involves the burning of the stone to produce quicklime and the conversion of the quicklime into hydrated lime.

Limestone is a mineral consisting mainly of calcium carbonate mixed with impurities such as silica, iron oxide, alumnina, magnesium carbonate and calcium sulphate. Calcium carbonate is the fifth most abundant substance in the earth's crust, occurring in all limestones, marble, chalk, gypsum, bones, the shells of molluscs and in the waters of the earth.

On burning or calcination, limestone decomposes into carbon dioxide gas and quicklime. Quicklime combined with water produces heat and slaked lime. In the majority of operations excess water is used and the resulting suspension of slaked lime in water is known as milk of lime. When milk of lime is allowed to stand it thickens up into lime putty, the form in which it is used for mortar and plaster.

Quicklime

Burning is a simple process and formerly most lime was burnt on the premises, especially after 1800, when farmers were encouraged to improve their land by using lime as a fertilizer. The lime was transported from the quarries by barge. Horses and donkeys transported the lime from the barge to the limekiln. Here it was cracked into chunks and packed into crucibles, one or two to each kiln. Low-quality coal was used, lit from kindling holes inside the kiln. Finally the lime was taken away by the farmer and the lime ash sold to the poor for flooring. Derelict limekilns can still be seen scattered round the coast above beaches, in creeks up rivers and canals.

Slaking

Quicklime reacts to water with the evolution of great heat to give calcium hydroxide or slaked lime. The exact reaction again depends on the impurities in the original stone. Care in slaking is of the utmost importance not only because of the physical behaviour of the resulting milk of lime but also to prevent the formation of certain harmful compounds. It is essential that the quicklime be thoroughly slaked. Any particles not slaked will slowly absorb water, expanding and cracking any substance it is used for. Even quicklime prepared from marble contains some portions that are over-burnt and others which contain impurities which slake very slowly. During slaking the lime should be given an occasional stir and kept for at least three months before use.

Metal

The first metals known to man were gold, silver and copper, all of which occur naturally in a metallic state and all of which are soft enough to be beaten into shape without heat. The first smelting was probably accidental; even recently prospectors in the Congo have reported seeing globules of copper in the charcoal fires lit by Africans near cupiferous rocks.

Further developments were also probably the result of lucky accidents. Soon after 3000 BC metal workers in Mesopotamia, familiar with tin, found that by mixing it with copper an alloy, bronze, was produced which was easier to cast and gave a harder and better cutting edge than the pure metal. The Egyptians invented the method of moulding it into shape still in use today. An exact model of the article to be cast was made in wax; this was then covered with clay, the clay heated to harden it and, at the same time, melt the wax, which drains off. The mould is then filled with molten metal and allowed to solidify.

By 1400 BC iron was becoming important. Iron does not occur in pure form except in a very few places in Europe and Canada, and in meteorites. Again the method of discovery was probably the result of fires built on outcroppings of red iron ore; the action of the charcoal converting the stones to spongy pieces of iron. At first fires were built against banks of ore and exposed to the prevailing wind, which fanned the flames to a great heat. Later crude rock furnaces were built, their fires fanned by bellows; the sponge iron was put in shallow, clay-lined bowl-shaped hearths with charcoal and iron-bearing stones and intense heat directed at the charcoal through a nozzle. Forges similar to the Catalan forge, *c.*700 AD, on p. 292, were still being used, the design almost unchanged, until quite recently. The bellows were powered by water, hand or animal; although the temperature reached was not hot enough to melt the sponge iron (the melting point of iron is 2,800°F) it did melt impurities in the ore and these combined with the ash in the charcoal to form a liquid slag. After sufficient sponge iron was formed, the hot lumps were withdrawn from the hearth and hammered vigorously to expel most of the slag and weld the pieces of sponge together, the resulting metal being shaped into rods, bars, plates,

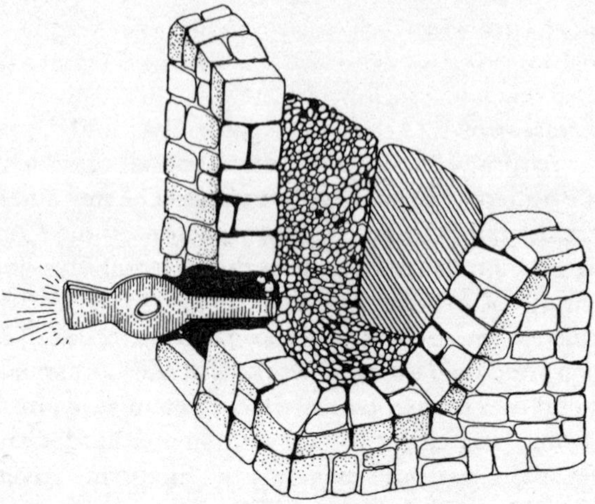

knives and tools. The whole technology of wrought iron took centuries to develop and the knowledge was confined to a few places, China, India, the Near East, Greece and Egypt.

By 1200 BC the process of making steel had been discovered, whereby objects could be hardened by quenching them in water to develop a hard edge for cutting, picking or chiselling. To make steel the carbon content of the wrought iron has to be increased. This is done by keeping the spongy iron in contact with hot charcoal or other carbonaceous material for several hours. The wrought-iron

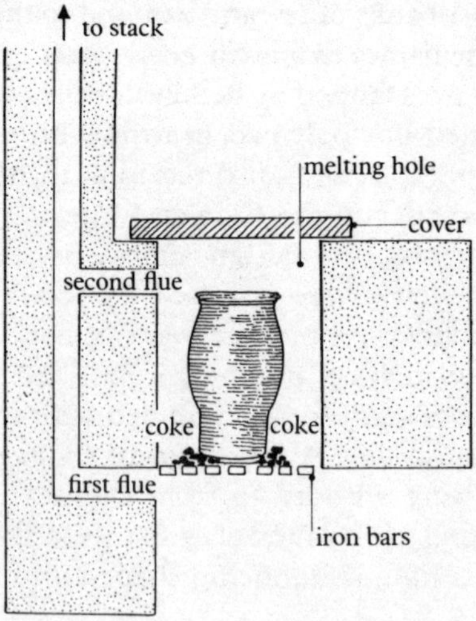

object was packed in a bed of hot charcoal in a clay box or jar and the whole kept red hot for days. This raised the carbon content of the metal surface so that when the object was quenched in water greater hardness was obtained.

The Development of Blast Furnaces

With the passage of time the sides of the smelting hearth grew higher and the bed of ore particles and charcoal deeper. As a consequence the iron absorbed more carbon than it could hold and liquefied, trickling down into the hearth to form a pudding of impure iron which could be cast into articles such as kettles and plates. The first cast iron was probably produced in China in the sixth century AD. The earliest known blast furnace in Europe dates from the fourteenth century (introduced to Britain in the fifteenth) and was still driven by bellows.

The product of the blast furnace was called pig iron because the liquid metal flowing from the furnace was collected on a sand bed shaped like a long trough from which the metal flowed into smaller troughs. The feeder trough was likened to a sow and the side ones to piglets – hence pig iron. The extensive use of charcoal had, by the eighteenth century, led to the almost total destruction of the forests and an alternative fuel had to be found. Coke came into commercial use in 1740 and has been used ever since. Objects were originally worked into shape by hand hammering, then by water-powered hammers which evolved into the enormous rolling mills used today. At first the pieces, after being hammered into shape, were put together with rivets; soldering as a means of fixing was a later development.

Production of Ores

By 1500 BC considerable progress had been made in the mining of ores or minerals. Minerals are chemical elements or compounds which occur naturally in the earth's crust; when a useful metal can be extracted from them in sufficient quantities they are termed ores. Dressing involves the separation of the particles of different minerals, then a breaking down to isolate the desired mineral's elements. In primitive times, crushers were either hand-operated pestles and mortars or millstones that could be turned by horse, man or water power. Some minerals, such as gold and diamonds, require little or no crushing to extract them, but most are in tough rock masses which have to be broken down before the minerals can be released.

Hand sorting then follows. Minerals sorted in this fashion must be sufficiently distinctive for the picker to be able to distinguish the wanted from the unwanted material. Another way of sorting is panning, often used for gold; the heavy particles fall to the bottom of the pan while the lighter material is washed away. Where the valuable material is either finer or coarser than the bulk of the material they can be separated by sifting. Coarse ore was washed in a stream or water to remove the fine sand and clay.

The great expansion of all kinds of mining in Britain – lead, copper, tin and coal – took place during the reign of Elizabeth I. German miners were employed to open up copper mines in the Lake District. The Mendips were found to be rich in lead, and in Devon and Cornwall numerous small tin mines flourished.

Metal Working

An anvil, hammer, tongs, a bench with a vice and a forge are all extremely useful pieces of equipment for the working of metal. The hardness and brittleness of the metal depends on the temperature to which the metal is heated and the rapidity with which it is cooled. The higher it is heated and the quicker it is cooled the more brittle it will be. Metal is heated to blood-red colour for easy bends in steel, bright red for sharper bends and bright yellow for forging wrought iron. For welding wrought iron and most kinds of steel they are heated until white sparks fly off. 'Snowball' heat will weld good-quality wrought iron but will melt steel. Cast iron is hard and brittle and will not stand hammering, while wrought iron is easily shaped.

After the metal is the right temperature, it is taken out of the fire, placed face upwards on the anvil and hammered into shape; if it cools too much before the working is finished, it is reheated.

Paint

For paint to give protection and colour to a house wall the general ingredients are 14 lb. lime to 5 lb. jelly (made by dissolving 1 lb. animal glue in 1 gallon hot water) and, if available, ultramarine blue for extra whiteness or a dye for colouring. Dorothy Hartley gives the following two recipes; as will be seen one is grander than the other.

Recipe used for whitewashing the White House at Washington

From a trade book of 1841:

The following is the recipe for making the celebrated stucco whitewash used in the Whitehouse at Washington, United States. Take half a bushel of good unslaken lime, slake it with boiling water, cover it during the process to keep in the steam. Stir in a peck of salt dissolved in hot water, 3 lb. of ground rice, stirred in while the whole is boiling hot, ½ lb. of Spanish whitening and 1 lb. of clean glue well soaked and melted down and liquid. Add 5 gallons of hot water to the mixture, stir, and let it stand covered several days. Reheat and put on hot.

One pint will cover one square yard and it will retain its brilliance for years.

Whitewash as made for an Anglesey cottage

Collect a bucketful of waste fat, butcher's trimmings, skin scrapings, or any household scraps that have gone bad; a proportion of tallow ends of 'ship's grease' may be added. Chop all roughly with a peat spade (i.e. a narrow blade that will go into a pail). Put the fat at the bottom of an old cauldron, and strew over it twice as much dry unslaked lime broken into pieces. Pour over all the soapy water from the wash tub and cover with a board while it boils. The fervent heat of the slaking lime will entirely melt the fat and more water may be added as long as the heat continues. Next day the cauldron will be full of spongy whiteness; scoop out as much as you need to use into a bucket, wet down to a stiff creamy consistency, and paint it onto the house and walls with a stubby broom of Marrun grass.

If it brushes off, you have not used enough fat.

Modern usage substitutes powdered size for interior whitewashing but it is no use outside, as it melts when wet; fat stands the continuous rain and stays white.[27]

Early pigments were derived from earth minerals, often mixed with ground stones and subjected to heat of varying temperatures. The names of modern paints often betray their origins. So ultramarine blue used to be made with powdered ultramarine and cobalt blue with cobalt. Simple earth colours came from clays stained with different irons. The clay is dug out of the ground and boiled or washed in water, changing the water with each new wash, and then ground, pulverized and used. Black came from lampblack (see Ink, p. 312), bone black from burnt bones and charcoal black from charcoal. Zinc white was oxide of zinc mixed with white lead, though a satisfactory white comes from a lump of white lime bleached extra white in the sun. Sepia came from the ink of cuttlefish, treated with potash or lime, washed in water and dried to a powder.

Medieval monks illuminated their manuscripts with paints coloured with vegetable dyes. A strong solution of dye was used to dye wool or strips of linen. When a particular colour was required, pieces of the cloth were cut off and soaked in the base paint until it became the right colour. The base varied. Sometimes it was a chalky medium mixed with a binding size of animal or vegetable gum, sometimes white of egg or beeswax or even sour milk. The tempera used at this time was composed of yolk of egg mixed with water and vinegar or an oil – linseed, poppy or walnut – and the pigment. Oil paint was developed by Jan van Eyck and his circle and, because of its advantages of faster application and a wider range of colours, superseded tempera. It was made with a basis of oil purified by shaking it with water, lime or vinegar, and then bleached by exposing it to sun and air for several weeks. After this it was mixed with the pulverized colours.

Potash

The *Shorter Oxford Dictionary* defines potash as 'An alkaline substance obtained originally by lixiviating the ashes of terrestrial vegetables, and evaporating the solution in large iron pans or pots (whence the name). Chemically, this is a crude form of potassium carbonate.' Though the ashes of any plant can be burned for potash, some plants contain more alkali than others making them more suitable for glass and soap making. These include bracken and other ferns, mistletoe, gorse and glasswort. Only hardwoods are suitable for potash and of these ash and beech are the best.

Usually the whole plant except the root is dried and then burned on a clean surface, out of any wind which might blow away the ash and reduce the quality of the remainder by burning it white. The best ash is grey or buff. Then depending on its use this may be reduced to 'pearl ash' (see Glass, p. 286), mixed with water to make a 'lye' (see Soap, p. 372) or further refined for glaze (see Pottery – Glazing, p. 271).

Until chemicals were developed to take its place, the major source of commercial potash (and iodine) from the seventeenth century on was seaweed. Both wracks (*Fucus* spp.) and oarweeds (*Laminaria*) are harvested for kelp – the wracks yield more soda and the oarweeds more iodine. The weeds were cut at low tide with billhooks with sawlike edges, then floated ashore on the incoming tide and laid to dry on dunes or low stone walls above high water mark.

Rope and String

Many materials have been used to make rope and string. On St Kilda immensely strong ropes, used to lower men down the cliff sides to collect birds' eggs, were made of horsehair covered with twisted cowhide. These ropes lasted several generations: they were family heirlooms, often given as part of a girl's dowry and were considered to be worth at least two cows. In other parts of the Highlands heather was twisted into ropes called gad ropes, from the Gaelic word *gaid*, meaning rope: light-duty ropes were made from the stems twisted by hand and heavy-duty ones, used for pulling the plough from the roots; but it was thought that the best ropes of all were made from twisted birch twigs. Willows and other flexible sticks and the long stems of traveller's joy have also been made into ropes, being well soaked in water before being twisted into shape. Another material used is the long, stringy, inner bark of lime and elm trees, separated from the outer bark by long soaking in water.

Gerard describes lime bark as being 'white, moyst and tough, serving very well for ropes, trases, and halters'.[26]

Ropes, especially those used for thatching, were also made from straw, rushes and hay, plaited together (see pp. 256–7) or twisted in the same way as hemp rope. It was said that the best 'letter-out' of the straw was a good fiddle player, because the fingers of the left hand through which the loose straw passed had to be continually moving up and down, pressing and packing in the loose ends.

Lengths of marram grass, often extending to thirty feet in length, are easily picked up off the sand dunes they inhabit, for plaiting into ropes. The seaweed *Chorda filum*, common on all shores – it looks like bootlaces – comes in lengths of up to twenty feet; when half dry it was skinned and twisted into ropes and fishing lines.

Leather was cut into strips to make long ropes and into spirals, like a watch spring, for shoe laces and for covering horsehair ropes. Leather must be frequently greased to keep it strong and supple. Catgut, which is the intestine of any animal, is made by soaking the gut in water for a day, then peeling off the outer membrane (this is preserved, twisted and hung out to dry to make threads for sewing leather) and turning the gut inside out by turning over a small piece at the top like a shirt cuff, then dipping the rest in water and so, by scooping water into the gut, allowing it to do the job for you. Scrape any mess from the inner parts and twist up what should be a transparent tube very tightly; stretch it out and leave it to dry. Sinews will serve as string. The longest come from around the backbone of the animal. Dry the whole sinew and tear off straight strips of the required size; wet, scrape to an even thickness and twist together; rub with grease.

But the most usual material for fine ropes and string was flax fibre and for strong string and heavy ropes imported hemp. The method of making them is of great antiquity and has not varied in any substantial way from that depicted in ancient Egypt, except that it has become more mechanical. The fibres to make up the final rope were first spun individually. Though this can be done by hand (see p. 353) it is quicker to attach a few fibres to a metal rope-spinning wheel. This was turned by a boy while a man, carrying a bundle of hemp – or whatever material was being used – round his waist, walked away backwards feeding out the fibres as he went, regulating the quantity with his fingers. This was a process requiring great skill and a long apprenticeship. Once a length was complete, the boy removed the end from the spinning wheel and attached it to a large reel which he wound as the man walked forwards up the rope walk, maintaining tension all the while. Another length was then spun, and so on until enough lengths had been made to make the required thickness of the rope. These lengths were then attached to a wheel with three or four equally spaced hooks and the wheel was turned in the opposite direction to the one used to spin the lengths, so that they would lie evenly together. Then, depending on the function of the rope, it was finished by being either washed in water and treated with size; or waterproofed by winding it from one wheel to another through a vessel containing hot tar and through a hole filled with spongy oaken moss to remove the surplus tar, then hung up to dry.

Ropes were usually made out of doors. The industry was scattered all over the country, most frequently in sea ports; Bridport still has a rope-making industry. Rope walks often ran beside the roadside; the usual length was eighty to a hundred yards and this was the limit of length of the rope. There was an old rope-makers' motto which went 'May rope bind those that honour won't'.

Knots

Much can often depend on knowing how to tie the right knot at the right time. When practising it is easier to use thick rather than thin cord and to follow diagrams rather than written descriptions. Here are some of the most useful knots.

1. A pair of hitches made to run home by pulling the running end.
2. Fisherman's bend, useful for joining two ropes; when the ends are pulled the knots run together.
3. A reef knot for joining ropes and for knotting reef points in sails.
4. A ring-fastening knot.
5. Lark knots for tying up boats, quickly untied by removing the stick.
6. Bowline – a loop which will not run home.
7. Hawser bend for joining the ends of large ropes.
8. For securing a hawser or large rope to a mooring post.
9. Carrick bend – another way of joining two large ropes together.

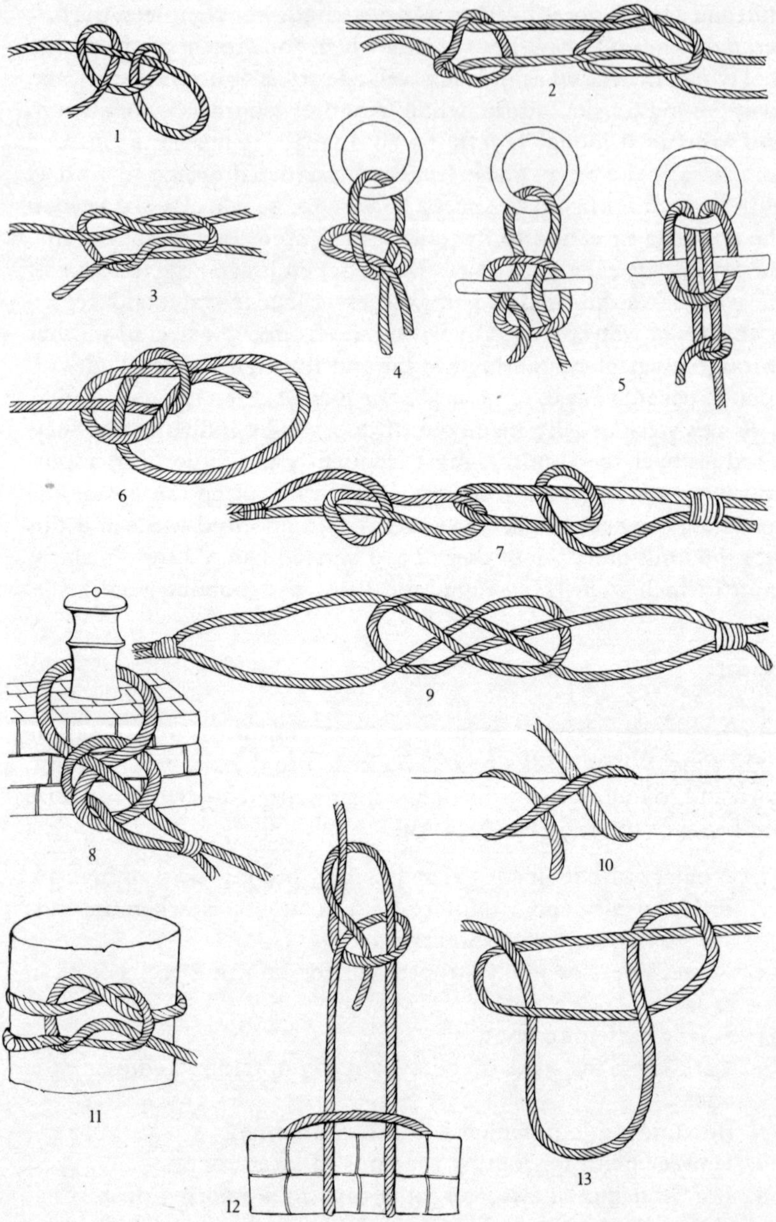
1
2
3
4
5
6
7
8
9
10
11
12
13

14

15

17

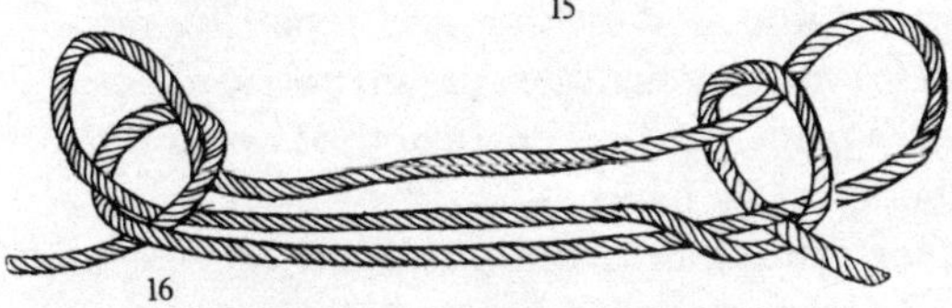
16

18

19

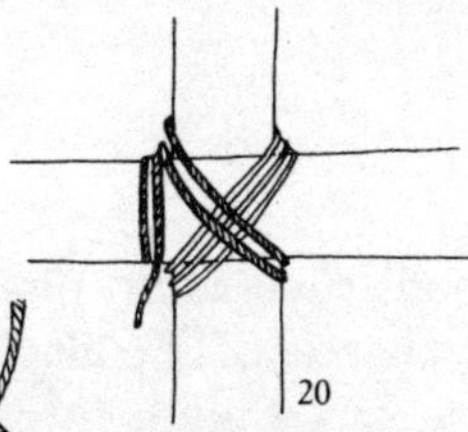
20

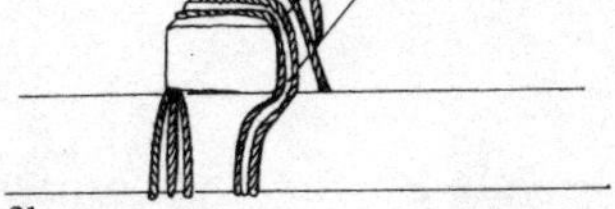
21

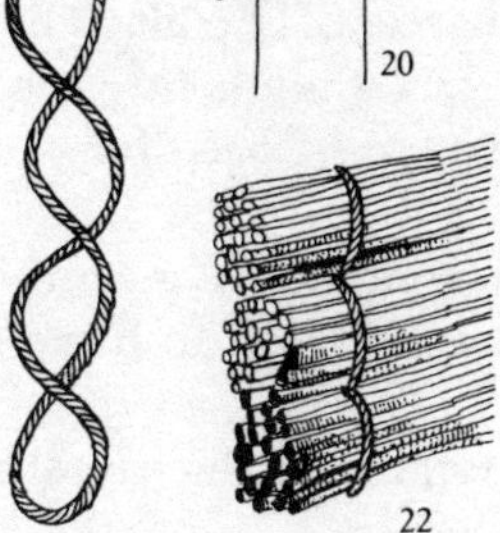
22

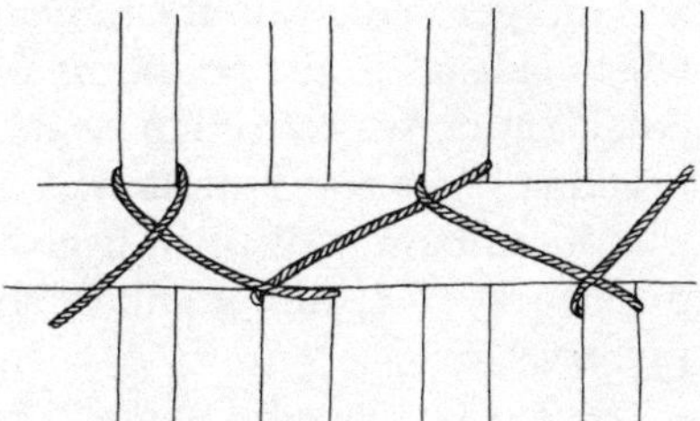
23

10. Timber hitch for holding a round pole.
11. Another (reef) knot for doing this.
12. A sling for raising and lowering goods.
13. Harness loop; several of these tied to a drag rope can be used as shoulder collars for men to drag a heavy obstacle by.
14. Twisted or tril timber hitch for raising or lowering round timber.
15. Preventing a loop from closing on a box lashing by making a knot in the free end.
16. Sheep shank for shortening a long rope, making cutting unnecessary.
17. Loop-slip for uniting two looped ends.
18. Weaver's or netter's knot for making and repairing nets.
19. Tom Fool's knot for making handles for jam pots, etcetera. The neck of the vessel is placed in the centre of the knot and the two ends tied; the loops act as handles.
20. Ledger lashing for tying a horizontal stick to vertical timber.
21. Outlog lashing for tying squared timber to a horizontal pole.
22. Malay hitch, a quick way of putting together grass, reed, etcetera.
23. Paling hitch, used by Indians to make fences, securing small poles to horizontal ones.

Tar

Tar is made by burning coniferous woods such as fir, pine, larch and juniper in a pit, in the same way as charcoal. The black liquid which collects in the bottom is wood tar. If a drain is fitted to the outside it makes collection easier. This tar can be used for waterproofing boats and buildings.

If birch bark is distilled it gives off a tarry oil; in Russia this is purified by redistilling and rubbed on leather as a perfume and preservative.

Pitch is tar boiled down and reduced to greater thickness; it is used for sealing roofs.

Turpentine

Pure turpentine is procured from larch trees by boring holes in the trunk, about four feet from the ground, between March and October, inserting a wooden tube and collecting the liquid which, after straining to remove foreign bodies, needs no further treatment.

Turpentine from the Scots, Corsican and maritime pine and from cedars and cypress is procured during the same months by removing a strip of bark about four inches wide and four feet from the ground and then, with a sharp axe, cutting a thin bit of true wood from the bottom of the strip and inserting a gutter made of a curved piece of bark, or anything else suitable, to collect the juice which the tree secretes. Every few days the cut can be revived by taking off another shaving and, when exhausted, another strip of bark removed above the first. Once collected the juice is distilled and the resulting liquid will be spirit of turpentine while the sticky, solid residue, called rosin or resin, is used by violinists for flexing their bows and may also be used as sealing wax, for sizing paper, dressing rope and as a pitch for sealing the inside of barrels.

Wood

Originally Britain was almost entirely covered with trees. By the thirteenth century there were still over sixty forests and parts of the Midlands were so covered with trees that settlers avoided them but by Elizabeth I's reign indiscriminate felling was fast reducing the supply. By 1880 the indigenous forest had all but disappeared except for the New Forest, Forest of Dean, Savernake Forest and small copses and hedgerow timber. About this time a new type of conifer was introduced by Douglas from America, the quick growing softwoods which form the bulk of our modern forests. But they do not compare in strength, durability or beauty of grain with our indigenous hardwoods.

Until the nineteenth century, apart from a few pines, all indigenous wood was hardwood. The difference between softwood and hardwood is based on botanical classification; hardwoods belonging to a subdivision – dicotyledons – of the angiosperms (their seed is enclosed in a seed case); softwoods are gymnosperms (their seeds have no seed cases) of the conifer group. As a rule softwoods, apart from the yew, are softer and lighter and less enduring than hardwoods, grow faster, and season faster.

In any tree the sapwood is less durable than the heartwood, but the strength of individual trees varies according to the place where the tree grows, the way it is felled, the number of knots in the wood, spiralling grain, and the moisture content – unseasoned or green wood is less strong than seasoned timber.

A tree is composed of a central pith – the heartwood – round which a fresh layer of wood is formed each year, surrounding the growth of the previous year and lying under the bark. As this process continues the heartwood becomes the central column of support and acts as a storehouse for water. Surrounding it, and often darker in colour, are the year rings – called the sapwood; this conducts water from the roots to the leaves. Between the outermost year ring and the bark is a ring of actively growing tissue called the cambium.

Wood when it is felled is therefore full of water and shrinks as it dries out. This is why it is ill advised to use anything but properly seasoned wood – the slower the process of seasoning the better the final wood. As the wood dries the internal cell water disappears first and then, more and more slowly, the cell walls begin to lose water. They never lose their loosely attached water completely unless the wood is heated to a temperature at which it begins to decompose. The aim of seasoning timber therefore is to reduce the amount of water it contains to an average, and as long as this average is sustained, the wood does not crack or warp. In this country the moisture content of timber seldom drops below 18 per cent except in very warm, dry weather. Central heating can bring the level down to 10 or 12 per cent, and this is why it causes so much damage to antique furniture made with wood of a higher moisture content.

When felling a tree with an axe, a broad wedge-shaped cut should be made, keeping the stump surface level – easier than making a narrow cut. This notch is made on the side towards which the tree is to fall. Also, if the tree leans, begin on the side towards which the tree is leaning. A second cut is then made on the other side.

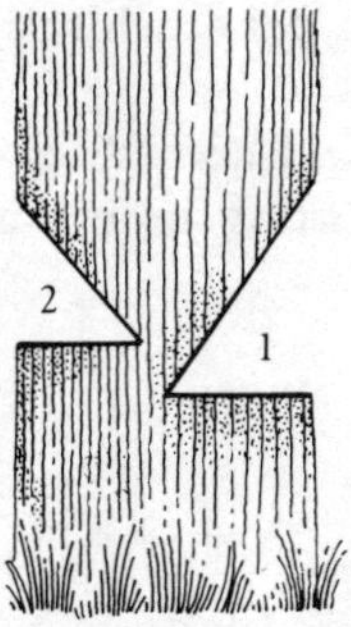

Felling tree

Boggled notch

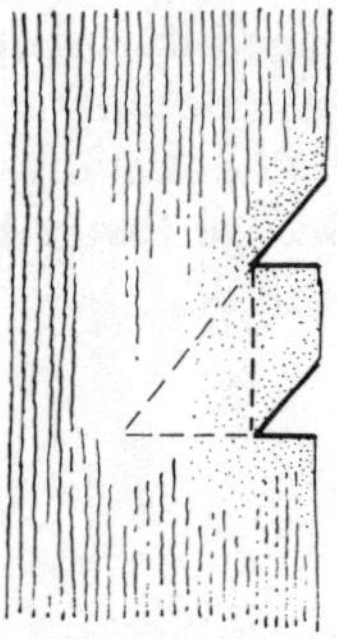
True notch

It is best to fell trees in winter when the sap content is low. When the bark is important, however, the tree should be felled in spring, as bark is only easily removed when the sap is up, in April and May. Bark is stripped by cutting rings right round the tree at intervals from three to nine feet apart and joining them with a vertical slit. Starting from the slit, the bark is prised away from the tree chipping away step by step until the whole cylinder is removed. If it is to be used for building it should be laid on the ground and flattened out by placing stones or logs on it and left to dry for some days. If for tanning it should be stacked up and left to dry for about a week before being used.

Green timber is easier to cut than seasoned timber and it is usual to cut the tree into usable parts before stacking the logs in an airy covered place and leaving them to season, often for several years. Again a saw makes the cutting easier but not necessarily better. In early days timber was cleaved rather than cut – cut in quarters and then split along the lines of dense, non-cellular tissue which radiate

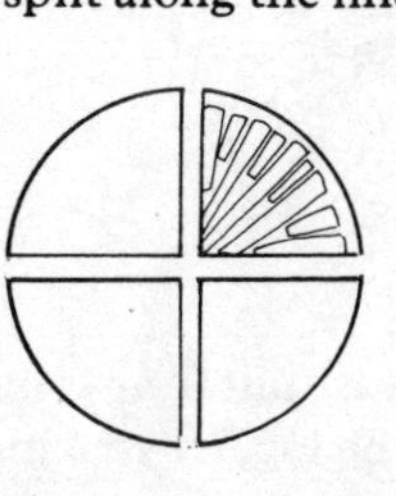

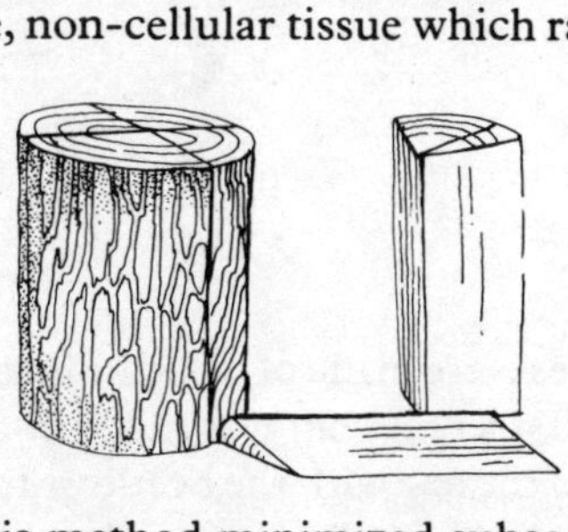

from the centre of the trunk. This method minimized subsequent warping and twisting, but the widths were uneven and had to be planed into shape. In early furniture this was not done, which is why the surface often undulates.

The cleaving was done with a beetle and wedges and, according to George Ewart Evans, these are still used for splitting timber in Suffolk.

A beetle is a heavy banded wooden mallet, its striking surfaces studded with nails. It was made from an *ellum tod*, the twisted knotted growth often found on an elm tree. The sight and feel of a beetle admirably explains Shakespeare's phrase for a nit-wit – *beetle-headed*.[24]

Splitting a log

Wedges were made of wood or iron. The log was split from crown to end; first a cross cut was made in the end of the log, by striking the back of the axe with the beetle until the edge went in deep enough to make a hold for the wedges. Lengthways cuts were then made with the axe. The wedges and beetle do the rest.

Hardwoods

Ash: 'The Ash for nothing ill' according to Spenser; the wood is tougher yet more flexible than any other, it doesn't splinter, has a smooth grain, and can be used for furniture, chopping boards, oars, bows and arrows and, after steaming to bend it, wheels. The stumps and the shoots make good walking sticks, hop piles and fencing. It burns well and makes a rich potash. Evelyn said that 'Every prudent Lord of the Manor should employ one acre of ground with Ash to every twenty of other land, since in as many years it would be worth more than the land itself.'[86]

Apple: Useful for small articles; though it is as hard as oak it decays easily and tends to warp and split while seasoning.

Alder: Not very strong and only durable when submerged in water; then it lasts so well that Pliny talks of it as being 'eternal'. Venice, Ravenna and Amsterdam stand on alder piles. Good for all types of water pipes and drains. A poor conductor of heat. Much used for clogs. Burns slowly; good for firewood and charcoal. The wood has decorative veining and attractive bowls and spoons can be made from it.

Acacia: Rare, but strong and durable and good for fencing and furniture.

Beech: Needs to be carefully seasoned – it is then as strong as oak. Large pieces vary in workability and for this reason it is most often made into smaller articles: furniture, spoons, bowls. Excellent for charcoal. Most durable when kept wet; Waterloo Bridge and Winchester Cathedral stand on beech piles.

Birch: The wood contains oil. The smaller branches were used as torches and for thatching and broom making. The larger branches are strong and hard-wearing; although stiff, it can be bent, with treatment, and is useful for chairs and small pieces.

Cherry: Tough and attractive wood used in high-class furniture work and for pipes and walking sticks.

Chestnut, horse: Soft and easily carved; the wood is absorbent and suitable for racks and shelves for storing fruit, vegetables and drying herbs. Withstands constant scrubbing and is therefore good for kitchen tables and dairy furniture.

Chestnut, Spanish: Requires careful seasoning if it is not to break up; it is then good for furniture, flooring and, as it splits easily, veneer.

Dogwood: Very hard but never large enough to make anything but small articles: pestles, skewers and arrows. According to Evelyn, it is 'of so very hard a substance as to make wedges to cleave and rive other wood with instead of iron'.[86]

Elder: Hard, though inclined to warp and split in seasoning. Never large, it is used for things like skewers, needles and combs. Young shoots contain a fat pith easily removed and the resulting hollow stem can make a pea-shooter or whistle, or simple bellows for the fire.

Elm: Endures extremely well under water; it was often made into drains: sometimes the whole tree was hollowed out, or a tree naturally hollowed by rot might be used. Boat keels, water troughs, basins and piles were also made of elm. The thousand-year-old elm piles on which London Bridge stood have been found in the Thames. It is difficult to saw straight because of its twisted grain and a tendency to warp. It can, nevertheless, be made into furniture and the seats of Windsor chairs are traditionally made from elm.

Elm, wych: Pliant and suitable for bending into wheels – the bows of the Welsh were mostly made from wych elm. Forked branches were used as water-divining rods.

Hawthorn: Strong and tough, but small and often contorted; useful for small things – bowls and tool handles, engraving blocks and walking sticks. Said to generate more heat than any other wood; makes excellent charcoal.

Hazel: Not very strong, durable or large but springy and easily split. Generally only the young whippy shoots are used, cut when seven or eight years old and woven into all kinds of baskets, fish traps, fencing, lathes, barrel hoops, fishing rods, pegs and forked twigs for water divining. The charcoal was made into gunpowder.

Holly: The whitest wood of all, and smooth and strong if kept dry; 'it wor as hard as metal; and would last for a century'.[24] Good for small objects: clogs, brush backs, veneering – stained black it was used as a substitute for ebony – for walking sticks, whip sticks and carving.

Hornbeam: White and finely grained; it lasts better when kept dry and should not be felled under a hundred years old. Used for wooden screws, tools, flooring, furniture and clogs.

Ivy: Soft and porous; thin slices were used as sieves or filters. Its softness and small size limit its usefulness.

Laburnum: Blackens with age, hard and easily worked; made into furniture, musical instruments, knife handles, veneer and, because of its colour, substitute ebony.

Lime: Fine and close grained, rather soft and not very strong; a prime carving wood, used by Grinling Gibbons and his school, notably at Chatsworth, Windsor Castle and St Paul's Cathedral. Holbein's woodcuts are said to be of lime. It was used to make prototype aeroplanes in the Second World War. Also made into musical instruments, toys, handles, bee hives and, as it is easily scrubbed to a clean white finish, dairy and kitchen utensils.

Maple: Needs to be kept dry. It can be polished to a high shine; maple wood with 'bird's eye' markings in the grain is the most prized. Evelyn, in 1664, recommended it 'for all uses of the turner, who seeks it for dishes, cups, trays, trenchers, etcetera, as the joiner for tables, inlaying, and for the delicateness of the grain, when the knurs and nodosities are rarely diapered, which does much advance its price'.[86] A maple harp was found in a Saxon barrow at Taplow, Berkshire, and part of another at Sutton Hoo. The larger pieces make good flooring.

Oak: 'Oak is neither the hardest and heaviest, nor the most supple and toughest of woods, but it combines in a useful manner the average of these qualities.'[69] It was also the most common English tree. Requires long and careful seasoning, but then is strong, close-grained and very durable – examples of thirteenth-century oak are still extant, and for the better buildings of England it was invariably oak which was selected. The English navy sailed in ships of oak, containing men with 'hearts of oak' who had left houses built of oak. Such is the adaptability of oak that it can be used for practically any kind of work.

Pear: A small wood, but one of the most beautiful in colour and with a fine texture. It has a tendency to twist while seasoning, but polishes well and is good for small pieces of furniture, bowls and handles.

Plum: Heavy and hard but not very durable; used for furniture and instruments.

Poplar: Poplar is soft, light, fine, straight-grained but woolly in texture, does not wear well and needs to be kept dry. Its thick consistency makes it excellent for tables, flooring, pencils, matches and plywood.

Rowan: Hard and with a fine texture – useful for furniture, turnery and carving.

Service tree: Similar to rowan.

Spindle tree: White, hard, tough and close-textured wood, traditionally made into spindles – hence the name – skewers and toothpicks. The shoots, with holes bored through them, were made into pipe stems. The charcoal is smooth and easily erased and much favoured by artists.

Sycamore: The wood is fairly hard, with a straight fine grain, but needs to be kept dry; very resistant to fire, strong and with little heartwood. Large flat pieces can be cut from it, and it is much used for furniture and for turnery. As it scrubs well without raising the grain it is often used for dairy and kitchen utensils.

Walnut: Good looking but rather brittle, easily carved and popular on the Continent for furniture, wainscotting, wheels, gun stocks and inlay. Unfit for beams because of its brittleness.

Willow: There is little difference in strength between the various willows, except for the cricket bat willow, which is specially grown for making cricket bats – inferior bats are made from other willows. Light and tough, willow is also made into artificial limbs and, because the wood dents rather than splits, cart bottom flooring. The withies or seven-year-old shoots are made into baskets or hurdles.

Softwoods

Fir, Douglas: The strength of the wood varies with the speed of growth, the slower the stronger – there should be ten annual rings to each radial inch. Seasons well with little alteration; a knotty, splintery, brownish wood best for boxes, props, boarding, boat masts and other rough-hewn work.

Fir, silver: Seasons well and is quite strong and easily cut; it is best used inside unless protected by tar. Silver fir can be made into rafters, floor boards, window and door frames. It also burns well, without sparks, and splits easily into kindling. Long-lived. Before the importation of American firs, the silver fir was the tallest tree in Europe.

Juniper: Durable, strong, easily worked but small. It is used for pencils and turnery, and, as it is aromatic, moth-proof linings and scented firewood.

Larch: Larch is the strongest and most durable softwood grown in this country, and is fairly easily worked. Trees up to twenty years old make good hop poles and fencing material; middle-aged specimens make tougher fencing and pit props. It has the advantage over other woods that it gives warning of imminent collapse by cracking and bending. Wood from mature trees is durable wet or dry, and is made into boats, breakwaters, wheels and piles – some of Venice stands on larch piles. Inclined to warp and split.

Pine, Scots, Corsican and maritime: Straight grain, weakened by too many knots, seasons easily but needs to be treated if used outside. It is used for boxes, barrels, poles and fencing.

Spruce, Norway and Sitka: Tough and elastic, not especially durable even when kept dry, prone to warping; the knots tend to fall out. Glues easily and does not split when nailed; it is made into boxes, furniture, ladders and, as it scrubs well, table tops.

Yew: It is a common saying in many parts of the country that a post of yew outlives a post of iron; certainly posts show little signs of wear after twenty years. It is a long-lived tree, one with many religious associations. The Druids planted them near their temples and the Christians near their churches. The bows of English archers were made from yew; it is also used for furniture, panelling, floors and small articles like bowls.

Writing

The only letter we sent when we were living off the land was written on a piece of cured rabbit skin with a quill pen and the juice of an ink cap mushroom. It was posted with no stamp but was nonetheless delivered safely. On St Kilda they used to put their letters in a box attached to a float, to be carried across to the mainland on the tide, hoping that someone would find the box on the beach and deliver the letter. The classic desert island method is to put a message in a bottle. If a message is attached to the leg of a homing pigeon it will get back to where the pigeon started from.

On the radio programme, 'Desert Island Discs', you are allowed one luxury on an imaginary desert island; one of the most common requests is for an endless supply of paper. I often think when I hear people ask for this that they could have saved the luxury for something else. On a tropical island there should be lots of grasses, barks and skins of animals that could be used for writing material and large birds whose feathers could be extracted for quills; there would certainly be a tree whose bark could be pulverized to make ink, or an octopus whose ink could be extracted, or even wood which could be burnt to make a charcoal pencil.

Ink

Ink can be made from a wide variety of materials. Recipes for ink abound in old books; everyone had their own and some were jealously guarded. Manuscripts can often be traced to their monastic source by analysing the ink. Strong coffee, boiled tree bark, the autodigested ink cap mushroom (the gills of older specimens dissolve into a black fluid), blue expressed from the petals of cornflowers and the dried, powdered roots of the yellow flag iris all make inks varying in colour from sepia to black. To make a lasting ink, not easily erased, some kind of fixative or glue must be added. The sooty bark from winter-blackened blackthorn twigs mixed with milk makes a variety of ink, and if isinglass or glue is substituted for the milk it will last longer and not go sour. Fragonard did his drawings with a mixture of soot and milk, strained before using. Indian ink is mainly lampblack and glue. Printer's ink is lampblack boiled with linseed oil until it is sufficiently thick and sticky. (Lampblack can be collected by holding a piece of tin – or anything else – over an oil lamp.) Invisible ink is made from the juice of lemon or other acid fruit or milk; the words are not revealed until the paper is toasted over a fire or candle. Small hollowed out sheep's horns were often used as ink pots, fitted into a hole in the desk. The following recipe for ink is often given in early books.

For twelve gallons of good ink

Take 12 gallons oak galls, 5 lb. green sulphate of iron, 5 lb. gum, 12 gallons rain water. Boil all together until the right consistency is obtained.

Paper

The invention of paper was accredited to the Chinese Ts'ai Lun, who made it out of bamboo in AD 105, but recent evidence points to an even earlier date for its discovery. Hand-made paper has from the beginning been made from vegetable fibres. Any plant with fibrous leaves or stems will make paper – nettles, cow parsley, flax, rush leaves, coarse grasses, hops, ribwort plantain, thistles and hedge woundwort used singly or mixed are all suitable – but the highest quality paper is always made from rags: linen, perhaps mixed with cotton, the proportion influencing the final paper. Treatment in the initial stages varies according to the material used.

For paper from vegetable fibres begin by collecting a large sackful – a surprising amount of material is required to make even a little paper. This must then be treated to separate the fibres of the plant from other unnecessary matter. The old way was to leave it to ret in a ditch or tank of water (see Cloth, p. 334). A quicker method is to cut the material into half-inch lengths, put it into a non-corrosive saucepan – stainless steel is ideal – cover with water and, depending on the quantity, add about half a cupful of caustic soda. Stir well with a wooden spoon and simmer for about half an hour, until soft and pulpy, skimming off any scum which rises. Strain off the fibres and wash with running water to remove any non-fibrous debris. Then beat and bruise firmly until all lumps and coarseness are removed. A wooden stump with spikes was used for hand-made paper; commercially it is done by pounding with heavy hammers or passing repeatedly underneath heavy rollers.

To make paper from rags begin by soaking the rags with water, pressing them into balls and piling them in a damp cellar to ferment for six to eight weeks, until mould starts to grow. During this time they will become straw coloured, lose nearly a quarter of their weight and grow fragile and foul smelling. Next chop or cut the rags into small pieces, wash them under running water and rub by hand to whiten them, otherwise the paper could be too yellow in colour. Then throw the rags into a trough – usually made from a solid piece of oak or stone and lead-lined – and pound and macerate to a pulp with a hammer over three days.

After this both vegetable and rag pulp are treated in the same way. Transfer the material to a vat, traditionally a barrel made of oak or a stone trough, waist high, five feet in diameter. Dilute the pulp with boiling water – warm pulp works more easily. Only practice will enable you to tell how much water to add, so keep some pulp back in case the mixture becomes too diluted. (If you are able to keep the vat heated, gelatine size can be added at this stage. If not leave until later, see below.) Stir the mixture frequently to keep the pulp from settling.

To make sheets of paper a deckle and mould are now required (a wooden frame – the deckle – and a flat rectangular wire strainer; a flat household sieve could be substituted). All paper was made on laid moulds (thin wires, fifteen or twenty strands to the inch, stretched across a frame, with a stronger raised wire laid across them at intervals) until, in the eighteenth century, John Baskerville, the printer, demanded smoother paper; this was achieved by using fine woven wire instead.

Begin by placing the deckle over the mould, hold it by the short sides and plunge it obliquely four or five inches into the warm pulp. In one continuous movement bring it gradually into a horizontal position one or two inches below the surface. It should be covered with a thick spongy coating of pulp about $\frac{1}{16}$ in. in thickness, enough to make a single sheet of paper. Give the mould a slight shake, right and left, back and front, to cross and mat the fibres, making the paper strong in both directions and uniform in thickness. (If it is now seen that the film of paper is obviously too thin return the pulp to the vat and start again.) Allow the water to drain away, detach the deckle and leave the sheet on the mould to solidify – a distinctive lustre appears on the surface at this stage. Incline the mould for a few moments to allow excess moisture to drain away. Have ready some squares of woollen felt each larger than the sheet of paper and transfer the paper on to one of these by swiftly turning the mould over, rolling it from one long edge to the other, leaving the wet sheet flat and unwrinkled on the felt. Add more pulp, if needed, to the vat and begin another sheet.

Build up layers of felt and paper alternately until the pile is about two feet high. The next stage is pressing, which should be done under a screw press; this expels all excess moisture from the paper and allows the pulp to cohere. From two feet the pile is gradually reduced to six inches. A flat stone or board on which weights are evenly placed could be substituted.

Next remove the felt layers and pile the paper up again, in a different order. Press again to remove more water. Repeat this process until the sheets acquire a smooth finish.

For the final drying hang in fours and fives – single sheets are liable to curl – in a warm airy place. This used to be done in specially ventilated drying lofts, the paper hung on cow or horsehair ropes coated with beeswax or, latterly, merely laid flat on suspended hessian cradles.

Paper at this stage is very absorbent and for writing on with ink it must be sized. Each sheet is dipped in gelatine made from animal residue (see Glue, p. 288). Hold a number of sheets between two wooden sticks, dip them into the warm size and agitate until thoroughly soaked. Excess gelatine is extracted by placing thin polished boards between each sheet of paper and pressing. During sizing paper tears and bruises easily and care should be taken to prevent too much wastage. A mixture of one part milk to nine parts water brushed over the paper and allowed to dry is also said to act as size.

The final process is to 'surface' the paper, that is to close the pores and perfect the surface for writing with ink. Formerly this was done by placing the sheet on a smooth piece of hardwood – which to an extent polished the underside of the sheet – while the top was polished with an agate stone. Paper polished with agate can be recognized by its uneven, streaked look due to the small surface of the stone. By the end of the seventeenth century polishing was done with a glazing hammer; later the paper was passed between rollers. Finally, the paper is held up to the light to inspect it for flaws.

Paper substitutes

These can be made from chips of wood, the inner bark of trees, especially birch, glazed cloth such as calico, lead plates or slate stone or parchment (see Leather, p. 342).

Pen or Quill

To make a quill pen, take for preference a goose feather from the first five on the wing. A wing feather from any large bird will do; the slightly oiled feathers of water fowl are more water resistant, but for general purposes a goose feather is considered to be the most durable and flexible; for very fine writing, however, a crow's feather is superior; and when none of these are available reeds have been used.

To turn the feather into a quill strip off the outer membrane which covers the writing end of the feather. This can be done in a number of ways:

1. The quill end should be heated in a fire for a few minutes to soften the membrane. It should then be laid on a flat surface (ideally an iron plate) and drawn beneath a blunt-edged blade. The membrane should split off without the quill splintering.
2. Some quills can be left overnight soaking in a mixture of turmeric and water and then dried in warm sand. This should soften the membrane so that it splits off easily when drawn beneath a blunt-edged knife on a hard surface.
3. Dip the quills in hot water until the membrane softens and can be removed.

4. Hang a bunch of quills in steam from a boiling pot until the membrane softens.
5. Put the quills in very hot sand until the outer membrane softens and can be stripped off.

The next step is to clean the feathers with a rough piece of cloth or a piece of dogfish skin.

After this the nib may be shaped with a sharp knife and the quill is then ready for use.

Pencil

Originally the name 'pencil' was applied to a very fine paint brush – taken from the Latin *penicillus*, meaning literally 'little tail', and until the late Middle Ages all writing was done with fine brush or quill pen using ink. It is known that Albrecht Dürer used a rod of lead and tin alloy and erased unwanted marks with bread, but the first written description of a pencil is by Conrad Gesner of Zürich in 1565 in a book on fossils. He described an article for writing made of wood and a piece of lead 'called by some *stimmi anglicum*' – English antimony, which referred probably to the great Borrowdale mine in Cumberland discovered about that time, a source of pure graphite. While this mine lasted English pencils consisted of unadulterated graphite. However in 1760 Faber in Germany, reluctant to rely on this diminishing source, developed pencils made of pulverized graphite cemented into solid blocks with resins, gums, glue, sulphur and other similar adhesives. In 1765 Conte began to produce pencils of graphite mixed with certain clays, pressed into sticks and fired in a kiln, and this remains the basis of all pencils. The hardness of the pencil is determined by the ratio of clay to graphite – the more clay the harder the lead.

Makeshift pencils can be made by sawing charcoal into narrow strips and coating them with wax.

Time and Motion

With our reliance on mechanical aids we have lost the sense of time which our ancestors instinctively had, or which they got from noting the progress of the sun or watching the tide.

When we lived off the land we did not even have a sundial. I never wore a watch, and did not miss it, and I do not think that any of the activities which had to be done regularly every day, such as milking the goat, were carried out more than half an hour early or late. When you stop relying on mechanical methods you develop a sense of time. It is something to do with getting hungry; with the position of the sun or, if there is no sun, with the degree of light; the way the birds are singing and behaving as this varies throughout the day; so morning can never be mistaken for afternoon. The longer you live in this state the more your awareness increases and the more accurate your time sense becomes. Time is a tyrant, without a watch time flows rather than jerks. Tasks are continued to the end, without the need to stop for lunch at one.

The same innate sense develops where the weather is concerned. If you are outside all the day you become very aware of changes in the clouds, a breeze springing up or air becoming colder, moister or warmer. In the section on weather I have given some country sayings which help in forecasting the weather.

Sometimes up on Exmoor we wondered where we were but we never really went far enough away from familiar landmarks to feel in any way lost. But had we gone further afield without a map it might well have been necessary to know some of the tips described in the section on direction. We would certainly have needed some help in carrying our goods, and since we were on Exmoor it would have had to have been a tough little Exmoor pony. In other circumstances boats would be useful for transport, as well as for fishing.

Boats

To make a proper wooden boat requires detailed knowledge and experience and is beyond the scope of this book, but boats suitable for travelling and fishing in sheltered waters can be made more simply.

Rafts

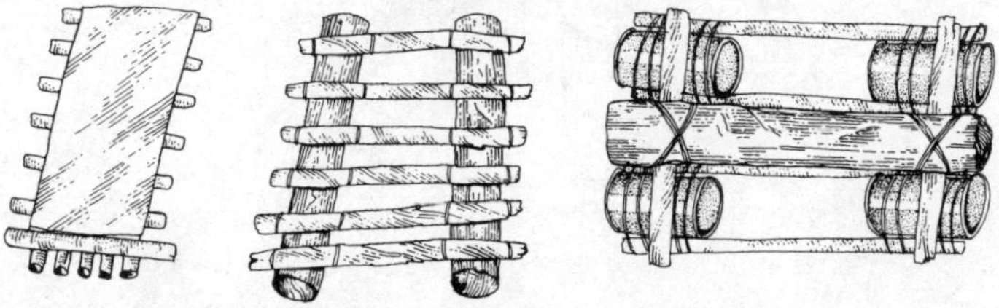

For a successful raft it is essential that the materials from which it is constructed are buoyant. Though all woods but the heaviest float, lighter woods such as pine, larch, fir, elm, willow and poplar are the most buoyant. Smaller trees are preferable to large and the floating power of each log should be tested first. Extra buoyancy in the form of pans, buckets, oil drums, bottles, reeds and straw – packed in waterproof sheets with the seam above water level – inflated skins and anything else that floats well can be fixed round the edges of the raft.

A one-man raft should be about 6 ft wide with logs about 6 ins. in diameter and 10–12 ft long. Rafts should be rectangular in shape and, preferably, pointed at one end. Cross bars are laid over the logs, as shown, and notches are made in the logs to fit the cross bars. Then all is secured with rope, woodbines or other lashings.

Skin Boats

'If the traveller has command of one hide only, he should make a coracle; if of two, a punt.' Skin boats, boats with a framework of willow or other pliable wood over which a skin has been stretched, would be familiar to an ancient Briton. Modern man often has no skin and has to make do with a covering of canvas or denim, waterproofed with tar or even household paint.

Coracle

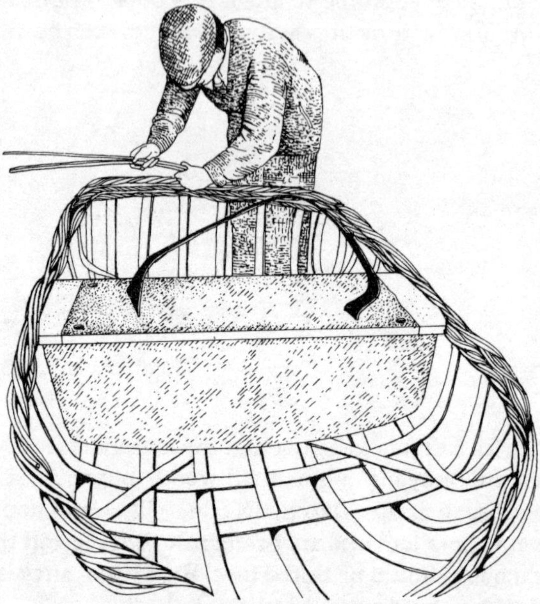

First take twelve or more willow wands. These should then be bent and both ends stuck in the ground in such a way to form the framework of the required boat, bottom upwards. It should be roughly the shape of a half walnut shell but with a flatter bottom. Use a heavy stone to press the willows into shape and tie them into place where they cross. Side pieces are then woven in to make the structure firm. Pull the end out of the ground and weave in more willows to make an edge. (Another way is to lay split willows lengthwise and crossways, then bend them up and secure with plaited hazel rods, as shown.)

When the framework is complete a damp rawhide is stretched over it, sewn in place round the edges and left to dry. Finally the projecting ends of willow are cut off.

Paddle the coracle with an oar; it is quite tricky, so practise in shallow water first. A seat is usually fitted across the coracle, and a leather strap so that it can be carried on one's back.

Punt

Take about ten small willow trees or other flexible wood fourteen feet long. Tie two of the trees together at their thin ends. Cut notches about two feet from the end and bend up. Mark out the

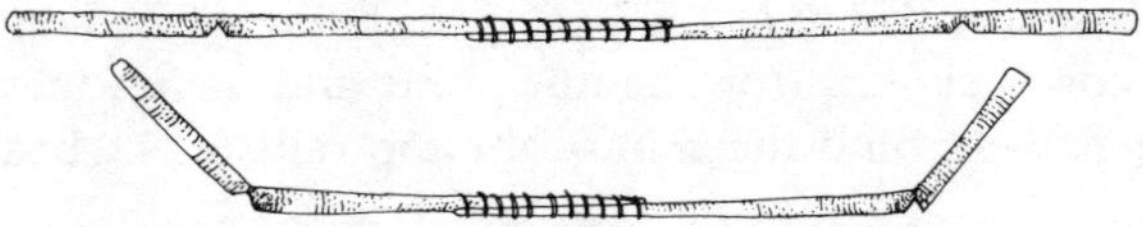

ground according to the size your boat will be with eight strong pointed sticks of wood driven into the ground. To these tie four willows notched in two places for the bottom and sides of the boat.

Bend two other willows to make the gunwhales and two more for the bottom rails. As can be seen each willow is tied in five separate places and the keel in eight.

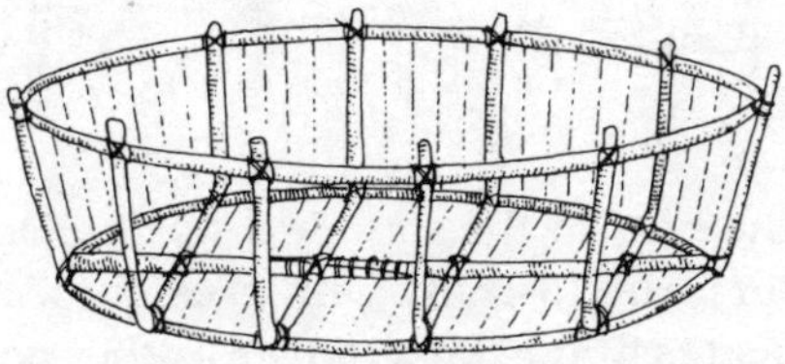

When this main framework is complete, loosen the boat from the stakes and fit in a number of thinner willows (dotted lines in the diagram). If a round bottom is preferred to a square bottom make in much the same way as the coracle. Bend the ends of the willows into holes 10 feet apart, then bend the sides 8 ft apart with a distance of 3½–4 ft between each, using forked sticks where the rowlocks should be.

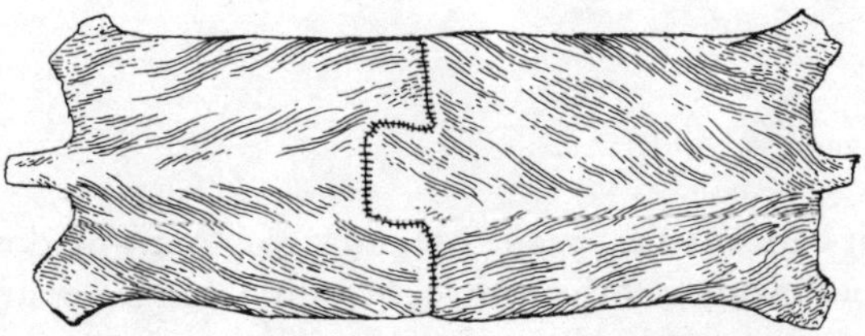

Now the boat is ready for covering. Turn the boat bottom side up and take two ox-skins, or their equivalent in canvas. The skins should ideally be from a freshly skinned ox and they must be damp and flexible (wet earth or dung can be used to achieve this). Cut into shape and sew the skins together at the nape of the neck as shown. The holes for the sewing should not be larger than the size of the thread otherwise the boat will leak. Then stretch the skin, hair side inwards, over the frame of the boat. Cut holes in the edge of the skin, cut cords of skin from another hide and, using these (rope would do as well) bind the skin to the top rails of the boat.

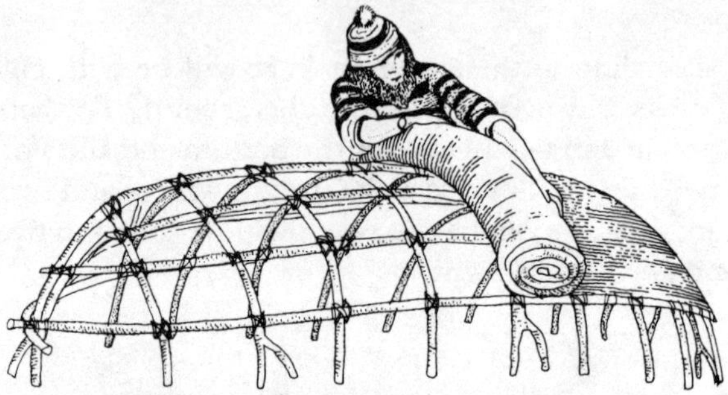

Next, leave the boat in the sun, or a warm place to dry out for twenty-four hours, rub liberally with grease, especially round the seam, and the boat is fit for the water. A leather boat, the *Brendan*, which was sailed by Tim Severin from Ireland to North America in 1976/7 was greased with wool fat and, after six months in the water, was still watertight. Remember to keep the boat out of the water and upside down when not in use.

Instead of using leather, the boat may be planked over, the planks being either nailed in place or, in default of nails, fastened together with strips of hide or woodbines or rope, laced through holes bored in them.

Canoes

A dug-out canoe is best made by cutting or burning down a large tree and hollowing out the centre. Steadiness in the water is achieved by fastening outriggers to the sides. 'To the fortunate possessor of the axe, the adze, the gouge, and the mallet, the formation of a dug-out canoe is a matter of comparative ease.'[48] If, however, you are not among the fortunate, the tree may be hollowed out by lighting a fire in the centre, keeping it within bounds with wet earth or clay and, as the wood becomes charred and ashen, scraping it away with a sharp stone or shell to expose more surface for the fire to work on.

Canoes can also be made of reeds and rushes, bound into faggots pointed at one end, placed side by side and lashed together – see illustration.

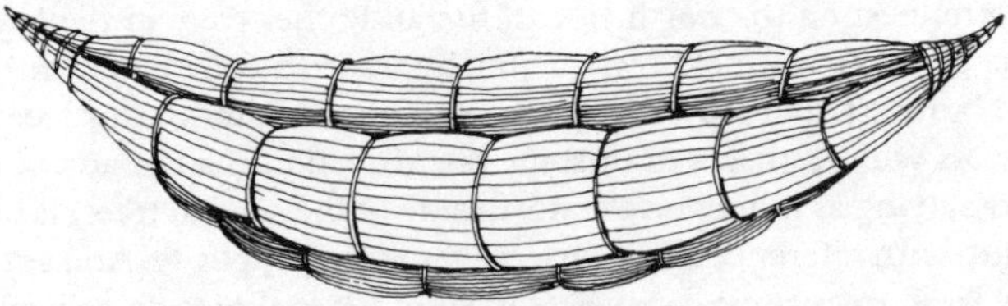

Hints for Anchors, Rudders, Sails, Oars and Paddles

An anchor can be made by lashing two pieces of wood together in the form of a √ and weighting them with a stone. Rudders are best attached to the outside of the boat. Sails can be made of cloth or woven from rushes. A paddle or oar is made with the flat end of a branch or a flat object attached to a branch.

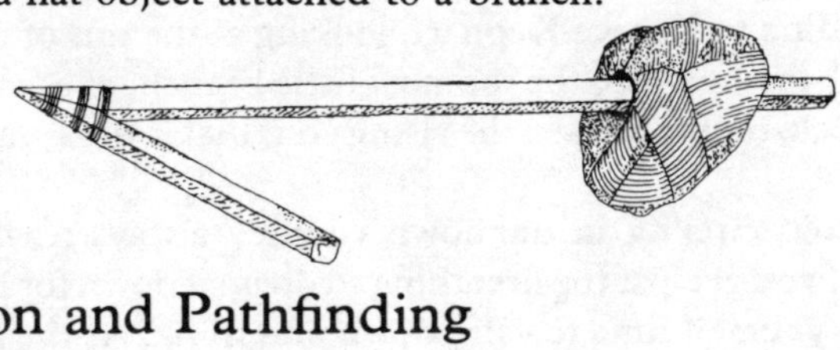

Direction and Pathfinding

The sun is usually the best way of setting one's course by day. To find the sun on a cloudy day, take a knife blade or other flat shiny article and slowly twirl it round. It will cast some shadow unless you are trying it too near noon or the day is very dark. Travelling by the stars is notoriously unreliable since they change their position constantly, but when necessary

select, if possible, those that are far north or south, and as low as possible; or, if the pole be far above the horizon – as it must be in all places far removed from the equator – take the star that is nearest to it, and that consequently revolves with the least possible change of position. In the north the constellation of the Great Bear will serve, but if the pole star can be seen, it is of course, the best – the two stars called Pointers will guide the eye to it, and in the south when the southern cross is vertical either above or below the pole, it is due south.[48]

Francis Galton, among others, advises studying the growth of moss: that it

grows strongest on the north side of firs and other trees in the latitude of Europe, gives, as is well known, a clue by which a course may be directed through a forest. For, looking on the surrounding masses of trees, much more moss will be observed in some one direction than in any other; and that moss, lying as it does on the north side of the several trees, is of course due south with reference to the observer standing opposite. And as he walks on, and fresh trees come constantly in sight, he is able to correct any slight error of direction into which the peculiarities of particular trees may at first have led him.

The Siberians travel guided by the ripples in the snow, which run in pretty fixed direction, owing to the prevalence of a particular wind. The ripples in a desert of sand are equally good as guides; or the wind itself, if it happens to be blowing, especially to a person pushing through a tangled belt of forest.[19]

According to Horace Kephart, looking at the tips of conifers can help: 'the feathery tip, the topmost little branch, of a towering pine or hemlock, points toward the rising sun, that is to say, a little south of east'.[41]

To avoid circling in unknown country always travel by landmarks. If you get lost the first thing to do is sit down for half an hour and give yourself time to calm down and think. As the mind clears start tracing your path backwards, drawing diagrams on the ground, and, if night is coming on, make yourself comfortable and stay put; a good night's sleep always puts a different perspective on things.

Where there is running water finding your way to some form of civilization by following the course of a river downstream should not be too difficult, unless you are in mountainous country where there are myriad streams. In this case be careful that you do not get on the wrong side of a divide that separates two streams which do not run into each other. In country which is very flat take care not to be confused by an oxbow lake.

Time

The principle of keeping time with the aid of a sundial is of ancient origin. The earliest, invented by the Egyptians, was a vertical stick: the time was read by the length of the shadow it cast. A Babylonian astronomer, Berosus, invented the precursor of the sundial in 300 BC. It consisted of a hollow hemisphere of wood or stone fixed with its rim perfectly horizontal, and with a style projecting over the hollow bowl from the rim. The shadow told the time on markings inside the instrument.

Most sundials only mark the daylight hours. Many early ones are to be seen on the outside of churches and often the line denoting 9 a.m. is marked more clearly than the others, this being the 'mass line', the time for the bell to start ringing for church on Sundays and feast days.

A basic sundial consists of a central style hole and a gnomon or style, made of wood or iron, which fits into the style hole and projects from it. The width of style should not be so thick that it confuses, nor so thin that it casts no shadow. Though a fixed dial will always be correct at noon, the time will vary throughout the rest of the year because of the variation of the sun's movement.

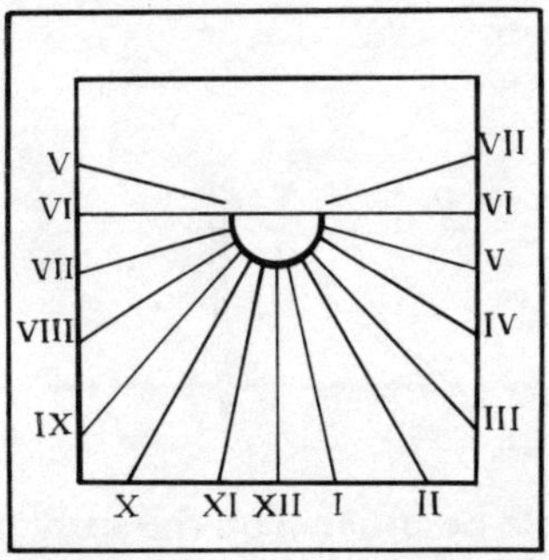

The dial-maker for a church would find a convenient stone on a south wall, make a hole, fix in a straight metal style and cut a line perpendicularly down for his noon line. Then at noon he would bend his style, at the point nearest the wall, to such an angle that the shadow fell exactly on the perpendicular line. It is thought that for greater accuracy styles were often changed throughout the year.

On a horizontal dial the gnomon of a sundial should point towards the noonday line, due north. Check north with a compass, re-

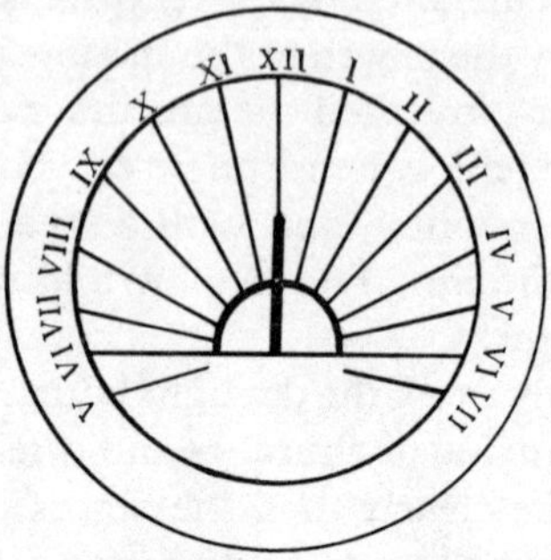

membering to allow for the deviation between magnetic and truth north, as given on a local Ordnance Survey Map. For accuracy, the angle of the sloping edge of your gnomon must be the same as the latitude of your district. Check your latitude on a map and set your gnomon at that angle. (A sundial made specifically for one place cannot be moved to another place of different latitude.)

The gnomon should be situated on the six o'clock base line; if the sundial is vertical the lines should radiate below the six o'clock line and if horizontal above. Sundials made in the southern hemisphere are made in the same way except that the hour lines are inscribed in the opposite direction.

With sundials there is always the problem of telling the time on sunless days. It is likely that a water clock or hour-glass was resorted to. Water clocks, or clepsydras, also invented by the Egyptians, were bucket-shaped vessels from which the water was allowed to escape by a tiny pipe from a small hole at the base. Uniform scales of time, one for each month, allowing for the variation in the length of the day according to the season, were marked on the inside. At the end of the first hour the water would have fallen to the first mark on the scale of the month in question. The difficulty in regulating the pressure of outflow was partly circumvented by sloping the sides of the vessels.

Lord and Baines give the following instructions for making an hourglass:

> An excellent makeshift hourglass can be made from two empty soda-water bottles and a little fine dry sand. A wooden plug of 3 ins. long should be so cut as to fit the necks of the bottles tightly. Through the centre of the plug, from end to end, burn with a red-hot wire a fine even hole, cutting away until the extreme edge of the plug is reached. See that your sand is free from small stones or lumps, pour it into one of the bottles, insert the plug half-way, and test the quantity by letting it run out at the hole. When you have the proper charge to run for fifteen or thirty minutes, place the bottles mouth to mouth in such a way that one half of the plug shall be in the neck of each bottle. A bit of rawhide sewn round the union of the bottle mouths makes all secure. The joined bottles can then be mounted in a wooden frame for use. Two bits of flat square board, with holes in the centre for the bottoms of the bottles to come partly through, pinned at the corners by four bars of wood, is as good a form of frame as any.

And they further say that 'If no watch is to be had the time is obtained by counting the pulsations of an artery. A sound pulse averages from seventy-five to eighty a minute.'[48]

Weather Forecasting

Over the years the close watch kept by country people of the signs which indicate a change in the weather led to the invention of familiar proverbs. With a knowledge of some of these, and a few other natural pointers, a reasonably accurate prediction of imminent weather can be made.

Wind

The south wind always brings wet weather
The north wind wet and cold together
The west wind always brings us rain
The east wind blows it back again.

As Theophrastus said, 'Each wind is accompanied by forces and other conditions in due and fixed relation to itself, and such conditions differentiate the winds from one another.' So, by noting the direction of the wind, certain types of weather can be foretold. A west wind has come in off the cold Atlantic to meet the hotter air over the land which, rising to give way to the cold, meets more cold air above and generally condenses into rain so 'A western wind carrieth water in his hand.' But a north-west wind usually brings cool, clear weather – 'When the wind is in the north-west the weather is at its best'; a north wind is usually cold so 'When the north wind doth blow, Then we shall have snow'; and an east wind in winter coming straight from Siberia is bitterly cold – 'When the wind is in the east, It is good for neither man nor beast'; and a south wind is warm, but full of portent, 'like foggy south, puffing with wind and rain'.

'When the wind do shift agin the sun/Trust 'un not f'r back 'twill run.' Winds blow clockwise round high pressure areas and anti-clockwise round low, so a veering wind will bring good weather and a 'backing' wind – a term used when the wind swings round 'against the sun' – foul. 'A southerly wind with showers of rain will bring the rain from the west again.' However storm winds blow in a curve so 'cruel storms do not blow on a right course' and 'Winds in the daytime wrestle and fight/Longer and stronger than those at night' – during the day the sun's heat causes disturbances in the atmosphere absent at night. The direction of the wind traditionally is told by the weather vane, often a cock, symbolic of the one which crowed when St Peter denied Christ, swivelling round over fixed rods pointing north, south, east and west.

Clouds

The speed of clouds is indicative. If they are moving in a leisurely fashion the weather will be stable, once they begin to scud look out for the wind and rain. If higher clouds are moving in a different direction to lower clouds, or to the prevailing wind, a change of weather is coming from the direction of the high clouds and approaching at the speed with which they are moving.

But the formation of clouds is the most useful guide. Daytime clouds with soft edges that merge into the blue of the sky mean fair weather; clouds with sharply defined edges that bad weather is imminent. If small clouds in late afternoon melt away towards sunset fair weather is assured, if they increase and cover the sky, unsettled weather. 'The higher the clouds, the finer the weather' is not infallible, for at the end of a spell of fine weather small clouds forming very high in the sky often mean that in about two days the weather will change. But the length of warning of any change may indicate how long the change will last – 'Long foretold, long last/Short notice, soon passed.'

Low cloud over hills means rain and has given rise to many local sayings; this one is from Lancashire: 'If Riving Pike do wear a hood, Be sure the day will ne'er be good.' Other indicators of rain are 'When mountains and cliffs in the clouds appear/Some sudden and violent showers are near' or 'A round-topped cloud, with a flattened base/Carries rainfall in its face.' 'Trace in the sky the painter's brush/Then winds around you soon will rush' or 'Hens' scarts and filly tails/Make lofty ships carry low sails'. 'Mackerel sky, mackerel sky/Never long wet and never long dry.'

If a corona, or thin veil of cloud, round the moon grows smaller or is reduced to a halo it means rain is coming, but if larger then the weather is getting fairer.

A lot can be learned too from the colour of the sky and clouds. Yellow is the worst colour, especially at sunset, a forerunner often by as much as thirty-six hours of storms and gales. Copper tints around cloud edges are a sign of electricity and mean that thunderstorms are in the air. Green in the clear spaces between clouds indicates that there is a lot of moisture in the upper atmosphere and showery weather will continue. Dark blue sky also indicates stormy weather, but light blue, settled weather. Violet tints in puffy clouds mean it will be cold and cloudy but dry and so does a yellowish gloom from the east. Ashen grey skies are rain skies. Red sky at night can mean two things: a red glow at sunset evenly diffused across the sky is a sign that a fine day will follow but if the red is reflected in lowering masses of ragged cloud, especially if they extend across the sky from the east, a damp one – 'If the sun in red should set, The next day surely will be wet.' Red in the morning is always bad – 'Red sky in the morning/A shepherd's warning.'

The colour of the moon too should be watched – 'Pale Moon doth rain/Red Moon doth blow/White Moon doth neither rain nor snow.'

Waves

Waves are an indication of how close a storm might be.

Most waves are the result of the action of wind on water. There are exceptions, such as the tidal waves sometimes produced by earthquakes under the sea. But the waves most of us know best are wind waves . . . An observer sitting on a beach can make at least an intelligent guess whether the surf spilling out on to the sand before him has been produced by a gale close offshore or by a distant storm. Young waves, only recently shaped by the wind, have a steep, peaked shape even well out to sea. From far out on the horizon you can see them forming white caps as they come in: bits of foam are spilling down their fronts and boiling and bubbling over the advancing face, and the final breaking of the wave is a prolonged and deliberate process. But if a wave, on coming into the surf zone, rears high as though gathering all its strength for the final act of its life, if the crest forms all along its advancing front and then begins to curl forward, if the whole mass of water plunges suddenly with a booming roar into its trough – then you may take it that these waves are visitors from some very distant part of the ocean, that they have travelled long and far before their final dissolution at your feet.[87]

Birds, Animals and Plants

Forthcoming weather can also be told from the behaviour of birds, animals and plants. Many of the sayings are based more on superstition than fact – cows generally lie down to chew the cud, not because rain is approaching – but some are certainly based on accurate observation. 'Sea gull, sea gull, sit on sand/It's never good weather while you are on land'; gulls regularly fly inland in front of advancing storms. When birds, especially rooks, fly high it is said to mean good weather, when low, bad. 'It will rain much if bats cry much and fly into the house'; 'When black snails on the road you see/ Then on the morrow rain will be'; 'When flies bite vigorously, it is a sign of rain'; and finally 'Before the storm the crab his briny home/ Sidelong forsakes, and strives on land to roam.'

Some flowers close up at the approach of rain; the daisy is one and so is the scarlet pimpernel, often known as the ploughman's weatherglass. The leaves and stalks of lady's bedstraw and the trefoils become inflated when rain is on the way and the white poplar shows the downy undersurface of its leaves. Many people keep a frond of sweet tangle (*Laminaria saccharia*) hanging outside their back door; known as the poor man's weather glass, the frond becomes soft and limp at the approach of rain, brittle and dry in warm spells.

Plants and animals are often good long-term predictors too. A warm, relatively dry, summer often follows when rooks build their nests higher up than normal and a cold winter when migrating birds fly further south than usual, when there is an abundance of berries, when leaves wither on the boughs instead of falling and when branches snap and crack – a sign of a dry atmosphere.

Miscellaneous

'When the dew is on the grass/Rain will never come to pass'; mist in early morning in spring and summer means a fine day will follow, in autumn a bad one. Smoke from chimneys descending to the ground indicates high humidity, as does clarity of vision – 'The farther the sight, the nearer the rain' – and sound – 'Sound travelling far and wide/A stormy day will betide.' If it 'Rains before seven' it will 'Lift before eleven' and 'Rainbow to windward, foul fall the day/Rainbow to leeward, damp runs away.' Regarding frost, 'Hoar frost and gipsies never stay nine days in one place' and 'Moonlit nights have the heaviest frosts.'

Clothes and Clothing

The chief purpose of clothes is to help the body maintain its normal temperature: also to protect it from the weather and injuries. For this primitive man wore skins, as did Robinson Crusoe. When the clothes in which he was shipwrecked wore out he made himself a shaggy outfit from goat-skins, including a goat-skin umbrella to protect him from the sun. We began our survival experiment clothed in jeans and jumpers, intending to replace these with others we had made. In the event, time and lack of energy were against us and we got no further than making a pair of rabbit-skin slippers (using the recipe on p. 346 for curing the skin), which I am still wearing six years later, and most of a wool jumper. This was made from wool picked off hedges and fences from the fields above our valley where sheep grazed. I brought the wool home, picked out any twigs and leaves meshed in it, teased it out and then spun it rather crudely, using a spindle consisting of a stick and whorl, into a wool of about treble knitting thickness. I had never spun before, but did not find it difficult; unwashed wool is wiry, full of oils and each length or 'rolag' twists easily into the others. The most difficult part is getting the wool evenly thick, but I did not bother too much about this thinking, rightly as it turned out, that the result would be more interesting if the wool was uneven. After spinning I wound the wool into skeins and dyed it a soft light brown with oak bark. Then, using four polished hazel sticks, I began knitting. The result was good: thick, of a lovely knobbly texture, and beautifully soft.

Even for primitive man skins and wool were by no means the only source of material for cloth. A piece of cloth made from moss was found in a Bronze Age excavation at Lochlee. At a burial place in Stromness, Orkney, the body of a woman was found swathed in a material made from the rush *Scirpus lacustris* and impressions of woven *Carex* or *Juncus* stems were found in a food vessel buried with a woman at Ballybrew, Co. Wicklow. The waste strips of willow after the tan has been extracted are thought to have been the basis of a strong brown cloth specially woven for windmill sails. In Sweden a fine, strong thread has been spun from the stalks of melilot and a coarse kind of cloth prepared from hop bines – though it is stated that the fibres are so difficult to separate that retting (soaking) takes all winter. All over the north from Russia to Scandinavia and Scotland there is written and material evidence of nettles being made into cloth. In Hans Christian Anderson's 'The Wild Swans' the fairy says to Eliza 'break the nettles with your feet, and you will have flax; of this you must twine and weave eleven shirts of mail with long sleeves. Throw these over the wild swans, and the charm will be broken.' Samples of Bronze Age nettle cloth are to be seen in the National Museum in Denmark and as late as the nineteenth century the poet Thomas Campbell could exclaim 'In Scotland, I have eaten nettles, I have slept in nettle sheets, and I have dined off a nettle tablecloth.' At the Binns near Edinburgh there are curtains still hanging traditionally thought to be of nettle cloth, all that is left of a set of 'hingings for the whole house'. Shortage of cloth led to experiments being carried out in the making of nettle cloth both in Denmark and Germany during the First World War. These were later abandoned owing the special cultivation required to produce nettles of a length to be useful commercially and to the difficulty of separating the fibres from the stalk. I had the same problem though it was partly due to lack of knowledge. They need substantially more time to ret than flax – up to six weeks – and, after the ten days I gave them there was certainly no 'aggregate bundle of fibres' to be pulled from the stem, but rather still woody-looking nettles.

Once spun, cloth fibres, whether animal or vegetable, can be dyed a wide range of colours with plant dyes. Alternatively they can be left their natural colour or, in the case of linen, bleached. Formerly this was done by spreading the cloth outside in a meadow and leaving it for several weeks, watering it each day, until sufficiently faded. Tartans and tweeds were dyed with lichen, some of which had to be steeped in urine to release the colour. Highlanders used to make a living by scraping lichens off the rocks and sending it to Glasgow. 'Cattle on the hills and gold on the stones' is an old Gaelic saying. They also made a living from knitting and still do, especially on the remoter islands. In the Shetland Isles traditional Fair Isle has only three colours, brown, fawn and white, the natural fleece colours of the Shetland sheep.

Cloth is necessary to our lives not only for clothes but for all kinds of household linen: bedding, curtains, carpets, soft furnishings and wall-hangings or tapestries. These were used not only to decorate but to provide insulation from those cold stone castle walls. Leather, linen and wool, the indigenous British materials, are described in the following sections.

Cloth

Nettle

Nettles growing at the bottom of ditches, among brambles and in shady valleys, where the soil is rich and the nettles grow to a height of five or six feet with a stem thickly clothed in lint are most suitable for cloth. Those in other situations have too woody a stem and too many branching stalks. Nettles should be collected at the end of August, or in September, according to whether the weather has been wet or dry. The right time is when the leaves begin to droop and wither, the stems go yellow and the seed is falling out of the pods. The stalks should be cut close to the root being careful not to damage this and so destroy next year's crop. The stalks should be spread in the open air and left to dry for about two days so that the leaves can be easily removed from the stems. Then tie the stems in bundles and put them to ret in slow flowing water. Nettles require long and careful retting in order to dissolve the gummy substance which sticks the fibres to the stem; if the process is not watched the wrong bacterial cultures can develop causing the fibres to rot rather than ret. The stalks should be laid root-end down in the water and covered with sods to keep them submerged. These sods must be trodden down and the treading repeated every day until the nettles are ready – from ten days in warm weather to six weeks in cold. To test whether the nettles are sufficiently retted take a stem out of the water and, holding it by the root end, draw a thumb nail up the stem to the top – if the fibre slips up the stem it is ready. Another test is to lay the stalk to dry for a day and then break the stem – if the fibre leaves the stalk easily retting is complete. The Chinese, who from early times have made cloth from nettles, treated the stalks with lye of ashes and a soap solution to extract the fibres.

Linen

'What department is there to be found of active life in which flax is not employed? And in what production of the earth are there greater marvels to us than this?'[57] exclaimed Pliny. Not only is flax the oldest cloth plant but it is the oldest cultivated plant. By 1200 BC Egyptian Pharaohs were being mummified in linen cloth. Flax likes a rich soil and a warm, moist climate – a combination found in Ireland, where the finest linen comes from. The plant should be pulled from the roots (never cut) as the stem yellows and the leaves begin to fall, usually about August. It is at this stage that the fibres make the finest cloth; later they become coarser. But at this stage the seeds will not be ripe enough to produce oil for which the flax may also be required. Therefore after pulling the flax should be left to dry or 'winnow' in the field for a week, to allow the seeds to mature, propped up against each other like wheat or leant against wooden trestles and turned once to expose both sides to the air. After a week the seeds can be stripped off by hand or by pulling the stems across a coarse comb. (The seeds are then dried further and tied in bags in an airy place until wanted.) The stems are now ready for retting. The flax stem is composed of an aggregate bundle of fibres longitudinally overlapping and held together by a gummy substance called pectose. During retting the pectose splits into pectine and pectic acid; the former is soluble in water and disappears during retting, while the latter remains unless bleached out later on. Retting is done by immersing the fibres in still, soft water for two to four weeks. A pond or sluggish stream or river will do, or flax can be dew retted – that is spread out in a field for six weeks. The stems should be placed in an inclined position, roots downwards, and are sufficiently retted when the stem breaks readily without bending and when it is possible to pull the flax stem away from the fibres without breaking or bending them.

Method (Nettle or Linen)

The next stage is scutching, the object of which is to break the internal pith and remove it completely with as little injury as possible to the fibres. This may be done by hand, by bruising the stem with a wooden mallet or by passing the flax through heavy wooden rollers. Hackling comes next, when the fibres are drawn through heavy combs consisting of blocks of wood set with iron teeth – at first through coarse teeth and then through progressively finer teeth – until all the waste straw is removed and the fibres or 'line' are parallel and even. The short fibres, called 'tow', may be used for stuffing or carded as wool and spun into a heavier yarn. The long fibres should be bunched into a 'horse's tail' and tied to a distaff or rod which will hold the fibres above the level of the spinner so that they may easily be drawn out while spinning. The distaff can be a tall pole, a tripod, a rod which is tucked under the arm or a special rod attached to the spinning wheel.

Wool

Enough wool to make a decent garment can be collected in an afternoon in sheep country by plucking it off barbed wire fences, hedgerows and the ground. Primitive breeds of sheep, such as Soay sheep, shed their wool naturally in summer as their new coat grows in underneath. To prevent the wool being scattered about the moor, it used to be plucked off the sheep's back, often with the aid of a penknife. More modern breeds require shearing. Harry Mason, a Coddenham shepherd recounts how it was done.

> You trimmed the sheep's body first, and you opened the front right up to the neck just as though you were unbuttoning a shart or a weskit. Then you cut down the back legs where the wool hangs over; and you did the same for the front. Do you leave it till later you wouldn't get at the wool that lay just there. Then you set the sheep on its backside and you clipped up one side, just over the backbone. You next twizzled the sheep round and set into your work where you left off . . . Using the old hand-shears you *had* to hev a platform. If you hadn't a board, you couldn't set the heel o' your shears down; it would cetch in the ground. So you'd allus hev to set into your work askew, and you couldn't make a right straight job of it.[24]

Modern sheep are derived from three types. The down breeds which come from the South Down sheep with a short, fine, lustrous-fibred coat; the mountain breeds such as Black Face and Welsh Mountain with medium-length, softish, woolly coats and the Leicester sheep with a long-fibred, strong, coarse inelastic coat. Long-stapled (long-fibred) wool is easiest to hand spin and gives the hardest wear – it is used for carpets; short-stapled wool is fine and most suitable for cloth; while soft, woolly fibres are best for jumpers and blankets. The quality of the wool also varies according to the part of the animal it grows on: the highest quality wool comes from the shoulders and back, fine, felted wool from the belly and coarse wool from the legs and tail.

Wool fresh from the sheep is full of natural grease and lanolin. Some people like to wash the wool before spinning though it is easier to spin if the grease is left in and the skeins washed afterwards in warm, soapy water.

Before spinning the wool must be teased and all foreign bodies removed. This is done by hand or with the aid of carders, flat pieces of wood with handles on one side and the other covered with leather in which bent pins have been inserted. The evenness of the spun wool greatly depends on the thoroughness of the carding. Small pieces of wool should be worked from one card to the other, held so that the teeth point in opposite directions. The wool is carded sufficiently when it comes away easily from the teeth. Then it should be rolled between the backs of the carders into 'rolags' and laid ready for spinning. Hand-teased wool may be rolled into a continuous rope.

Dyeing

Until the sixteenth and seventeenth centuries, when the opening of trade routes to America and India led to the introduction of new kinds of dyes – such as cochineal from the insect *Coccus cacti* – all British dyes were home-grown and of vegetable origin. Roots, stalks, twigs, leaves, flower seeds, berries and bark, all were used for producing the rich subtle colours associated with vegetable dyes. But though many plants will yield a dye, only few give a good, bright colour unimpaired by washing and sunlight (these are listed on pp. 341–2). Also the same plant will yield a slightly different strength of colour according to whether it is young or old, the soil on which it grows, and the time of year at which it is picked. A general rule is to pick whole plants when young, roots in autumn, leaves when just mature, seeds when ripe, bark if resinous in spring, otherwise in autumn, and lichen in winter or after heavy rain – which makes it easier to collect. (Lichen growing on stones gives a better colour than that on trees.) Leaves, berries, barks, roots and lichens may be used fresh or dried but flowers should always be used fresh and not boiled for too long otherwise the colour loses its freshness. Care should be taken when you are collecting large quantities of a plant that you are not denuding the area of its entire population and with bark, that you are not ring-barking the tree, which would kill it.

Vegetable dyes can be divided into two categories, substantive or complete dyes and adjective dyes. The latter require an extra chemical to make the dye stick (called a mordant from the Latin *mordere*, to bite) of which there are many different kinds, complementing different colours. Alum, tin, chrome and iron are the main ones all of which are most easily bought from a chemist though they can be made from available natural materials. Vinegar, salt, lime, tannic acid or gall nuts, oxalic acid or wood sorrel, stale urine and the fir club moss (*Lycopodium selago*) are others.

Dyeing Wool

Before using any mordant or dye the wool must be clean and free from grease. Wash once or twice in warm, soapy water and rinse well. (Use 10 gallons soft water to 3 oz. soft soap and 6 oz. ammonia.) Wool is easier to handle tied in skeins, loose enough for the mordant and dye to penetrate the fibres but tight enough to hold them together. Make sure that the mordant is properly dissolved and that the pot is large enough to take the wool without overcrowding. Stir as little as possible during mordanting and dyeing, just turn over two or three times.

Mordant

Alum: An extract of alunite, a rock found in the Whitby district of Yorkshire, originally procured by soaking the shales in water and stale urine. Use $\frac{1}{4}$ lb. alum to 1 lb. wool. Dissolve the alum in some water, add to a pot of soft water, stir well. Put on to heat and, when the water begins to warm, put in the wool; continue heating until boiling. Simmer coarse wool for an hour, and fine for 45 minutes. Lift out with a stick and drain for a moment before squeezing out excess water. Leave for two to three days in a cool place where the wool can digest the mordant but remain damp for dyeing.

Tin: Used chiefly for bright red and yellow colours in wool. Sometimes as a mordant and sometimes, added to the dye bath towards the end, to brighten the colour. Use ½ oz. tin of crystals to 1 lb. wool, and proceed as for alum.

Chrome: Use ¼–½ oz. of bichromate of potash to 1 lb. wool. Makes wool soft and silky, but an excess can impair the colour. It is light sensitive, so keep the mordant bath covered and the mordanted wool in the dark until dyed.

Iron: Usually ferrous sulphate or copperas but bits of rusty iron – nails or bric-à-brac – can be used, ½ oz. copperas to 1 lb. wool. Its effect is patchy, causing uneven dyeing; too much hardens the wool. With iron wool is often dyed first and mordanted afterwards.

Method

A general guide to vegetable dyeing is to use equal quantities of plant material and yarn. Soak the plants overnight in cold water, then bring to simmering point and keep at this temperature for 30 minutes to 2 hours depending on the amount of colour emanating from the plant. Strain the liquid into a dye bath and make up to 4–4½ gallons per pound of wool. Reheat and put in the wool. (Alternatively the plant material may be tied in muslin bags and simmered with the wool to be dyed.) Simmer the wool until it has acquired the right colour which could take 30 minutes to 3 hours. Leave to cool in the dye bath when it will continue to absorb colour. Stir as little as possible and if anything, such as a mordant, has to be added in the middle remove the wool temporarily. Use soft water and a kettle large enough to accommodate the wool easily. Loosely spun wool takes in more colour than tightly woven wool.

After dyeing is complete lift out the wool with a clean stick, squeeze gently and rinse in, preferably, running water of a decreasing heat until all excess colour has run away. Dry in a warm dark place.

Lichen Dyes

A special and important category of dyes, lichen dyes are substantive but some – crottle, for example – require preparation before they will give their dye. They are used extensively throughout northern Europe for the dyeing of wool, particularly in Scotland, where lichens are the main source of dyes for tartans and tweeds.

Dyeing

Two methods are used:

1. The lichen is put in a large pot (about 1 lb. to 1 lb. wool), which is filled to the top with cold soft water and slowly brought to the boil; it is kept simmering for two to three hours and allowed to cool. The following day the wool, previously made wet, is put in the pot as well, heated up with the lichen and simmered until the wool has taken the required amount of colour; it is then left to cool. After this the wool is removed and washed – the lichen should shake off easily.
2. A layer of lichen is put in the bottom of the pot, then a layer of wool, then another layer of lichen and so on until the pot is nearly full. Fill the pot with cold, soft water, heat over a fire until simmering and continue simmering until the right colour is reached. Allow to cool and wash as above.

Linen

For dyeing linen and cotton the method is the same as for wool but because of their hard tough fibres both mordant and dye penetrate less easily and a good result is difficult to achieve. Linen is more frequently bleached than dyed. Here is a recommended recipe:

To bleach linen

(For 13–15 yards of linen.)

Boil ½ lb. soap and ½ lb. soda in a gallon of water. Put in a copper and fill up with water, leaving room for the linen. Put in the linen and bring to the boil. Boil for 2 hours, stirring occasionally and keeping the linen covered with water. Spread out on the grass for 3 days, watering it when it gets dry. Repeat this boiling and grassing for 3 weeks. The linen should then be pure white.[88]

To bleach linen a cream colour

Boil $\frac{1}{2}$ lb. soda in a gallon of water. Fill up the copper with water and put in the linen. Repeat this once a day for 4 days. The linen should not be wrung out but kept in the water till ready to be put into the fresh bath. Alternatively, steep the linen in sour milk or buttermilk for several days. Wash clean, then spread out on the grass, and repeat the process until the colour is right.

Main British Dye Plants

Unless otherwise stated an alum mordant is used and 'whole plant' includes flowers in bloom.

Yellow
Barberry – stem or root; birch – leaves; bracken – buds or roots; dyer's greenweed – flowers; dog's mercury – whole plant; golden rod – whole plant, with chrome or alum; gorse – whole plant, substantive; heather (ling in particular) – whole plant; lichen (*Parmelia parietina*, *Ramalina scopulorum*, *Peltigera canina*) – substantive; ragwort – flowers; weld – whole plant.

Green
Elder – leaves; ling – tips, with gall apples and iron mordant; privet – berries; reed – pink flower heads.

Brown
Birch – bark, substantive; buckthorn – bark, with iron mordant; larch – needles; lichen (*Parmelia saxitilis*); oak – bark; pine – cones; walnut – green walnut shells steeped in vinegar for several days before adding the wool.

Black
Blackberry – young shoots, with iron; elder – bark with iron; meadowsweet – roots; walnut – shells and husks, put in a cask and cover with water until the right colour is reached, substantive.

Red
Bedstraw – roots with alum or chrome; St John's wort – flower heads with tin; lichen (*Ochrolechia tartarea*) – first soaked in stale urine and powdered chalk; madder – roots.

Blue
Blackberry – berries; buckthorn – berries; sloe – berries; whortleberry – berries, substantive.

Orange
Lichen (*Lobaria pulmonaria*); weld – whole plant, with iron.

Purple
Birch – bark, with iron; elder – berries; lichen (*Ochrolechia tartarea*) – fermented with ammonia and water.

Knitting

Knitting needles can be made from any straight, tough but flexible, smooth and unknotted stick of the right width, wider for loose knitting and thick wool, thinner for fine wool and tight stitches. Polished hazel twigs are excellent for the purpose

The wool is collected from sheep and spun (see Spinning, p. 352) and then either dyed (see Dyeing, p. 337) or left natural. (Wool which retains its own oil is more weatherproof.) Knitting patterns can be found in any of the numerous books and pamphlets on the subject. Or you can invent your own; knitting a trial piece first will help you to deduce the number of stitches needed, which depends on the size of your needles and the thickness of your wool.

Leather

The object of tanning is to convert animals' skins into a strong, pliable material which will last. The methods of achieving this end are various and depend on whether the hair is important, and on your resources. But obviously the more thorough the treatment, especially in the case of large animal hides, the better the leather will be.

Usually hides or the skins of large animals such as cows and horses are used for heavy work, shoe leathers, jugs and harness:

kips, the skins of the young of hide-giving animals, are used for the tops of shoes, bags and light harness; skins from small animals, goats, sheep, pigs and deer, are used for clothes, gloves, book binding, soft bags and shoes.

The quality of any skin is much influenced by the care taken in skinning. It should be done as soon as possible after the animal is killed and leave behind as much flesh and fat as is possible without gashing the hide itself see (pp. 107–8).

To Prepare Tanned Leather

This is the most complete process for preparing leather; during which the skin undergoes a chemical change – it is made supple and soft by breaking up the skin fibres and is then preserved with smoke or with some other agent.

Cleaning

All blood, dung and dirt must first be cleaned from the skins with water. Then the skins are soaked in clean water for two to three days to soften them.

Removing the hair

For this the skins are soaked in a mixture of slaked lime and water. This destroys the epidermis, thus loosening the hair and also filling up the pores of the skin, so preventing shrinkage. A weak solution of lime and water is prepared, making sure that all the lime is in suspension and none sitting on the bottom of the tub. Lay the hides in this, or suspend them from poles, for one to two days; then strengthen the mixture by adding more lime and leave for eight to fourteen days depending on the final hardness of the leather required. Skins and hides for softer leathers should be left up to three weeks in a weaker solution.

Other ways of de-hairing are: burying the skins in the ground for a few days to soften and loosen the hairs; piling the skins up and allowing them to putrefy in a humid temperature for four or five days; or leaving them in salt water. For this the skins are carried down to the sea at low tide, made fast in small piles with ropes, and left for forty-eight hours for the tide to wash over them. They are then put in tubs containing a brine made up of sea water with quantities of additional salt for another forty-eight hours.

Scudding

This requires great skill as a false move can damage the skin irreparably. If possible a rounded beam or a sloping table should be acquired and the skin placed flesh down on this. With a blunt-bladed knife remove the hair, which should come out easily. Turn the skin over and using a sharp knife cut and scrape away any surplus flesh.

Washing and mastering

Heavy hides should now be washed and scudded – scraped with a slate or blunt knife to remove excess lime – if they have been limed. Light hides should be placed in a mixture of either hen, pigeon or, for the lightest leathers, dog manure. The fermentation produced removes excess lime and softens the skin. The manure should be as clean as possible, mixed with warm water to a paste and left to ferment for about two weeks before use. Skins are left in hen and pigeon manure for ten to twelve days but in dog's dung, which is much stronger, for only a few hours.

Wash the skins again in water.

Rounding

Before large skins are tanned, the back and shoulder parts should be separated from the belly. This is because hides are irregular in consistency and thickness and absorb the tan at different rates.

Tanning liquids

A large number of plants contain tannin, but only a few have enough to be of any importance. Of these oak bark leads the way followed by oak galls, acorns, chestnut bark, birch, larch, and pine bark. The bark should be stripped from the trees, ideally in April or May after the sap has begun to rise, and stacked in a dry place – rain leaches the tannin out of the bark – until dry. Then grind into small pieces, add water and allow to soak for a week or so to extract the tannin. Strain off the liquid into a tub.

Tanning

In all tanning it is most important to start the skins in a weak solution of tanning medium and gradually increase the strength in order that the penetration of the hide fibre is accomplished smoothly and completely. Commercially this is done by moving the hides through several pits but something like the same effect can be achieved by simply strengthening the solution in one pit.

First lay or hang the hides in a weak solution, making sure that they do not touch. Increase the strength of the solution every day for ten days. It should be stirred often as the amount of motion influences the rate of penetration and the nature of the resulting grain.

Remove the hides, lie them flat and leave until the creases have disappeared. Then lie them flat in a tub again in a stronger solution, increasing the strength every two or three days for six to eight weeks. At this stage the liquid may be strengthened by adding ground bark instead of solution. For a few days at the beginning the hides should be turned twice a day to help penetration and should be stirred up with a stick.

Then remove the hides again, lay them on a bed of ground bark, cover this with more ground bark and lay another hide on top of this. When the sandwich is complete pour the liquid over the top and leave for six weeks. Then take apart and re-make with fresh bark. Repeat this process for several months or until the leather has absorbed sufficient tan – this could take as long as a year depending on the heaviness of the leather required.

Drying

When the tanning is done wash the hides in a weak solution, brush off any pieces of bark still sticking to them, place over a beam and with a smooth pebble or blunt knife draw the moisture out of them. Next, smooth on a thin layer of linseed oil to prevent them drying too quickly and becoming brittle. Beware of drying too slowly, though, in case of mould. Hang the hides on racks in a dark, dry, airy place for about ten days. They should still be damp at the end. Pile them with sacking between each hide, give them a good beating with a heavy object and then pass a roller over them. The heavier the roller the more solid the leather and the better the surface will be. Repeat the process starting with a layer of linseed oil, etcetera, until they dry out completely.

Currying

In order to finish and soften the leather the hide should be given a further soaking in water, laid on a board and scoured and scraped with an extremely blunt knife while hot water is poured on it. Stack the hides between sacking and, when half dry, wet them again, lay them flat, grain side down and with the blunt knife scrape and stretch. Half dry again and with a hard brush apply a good coating of oil or tallow. Dry completely and scrape off any surplus fat. The hide is now leather and fit for use.

Sheep's Wool Rugs

The skins should first be washed in water to remove all dung, dirt and blood, then thoroughly scoured with alkaline soap solution on both wool and flesh. This removes all dirt and much grease. The next process is to rid the skin of as much greasy matter as possible, which is done by stretching the skin taut, flesh upwards, in a specially made frame and painting the flesh with a paste made of either whiting and water or fuller's earth and water. Leave in a warm room to dry; the grease will be drawn out of the skin and into the whitening and can then be scraped off. Repeat if the skin is very greasy. Next the tawing solution is applied; this is normally a mixture of alum and salt, which is rubbed into the flesh side of the skin. Sometimes the skins are damped down and the salt sprinkled over in a solid state and then well rubbed in by hand; sometimes a strong solution of the salts mixed with a weak solution of soda is used. Then the skins are returned to a warm room to dry out. Next wet the back and, usually after another scouring, remove the grease from the wool and any dirt from the dressing. The wool can then be dyed.

Small Skins

Deer, moles, rabbit and other small skins may be cured by following this recipe from a letter written to *Country Life* in January 1943.

First, by scraping, get the skin quite clean and free from fat, etcetera, and also as thin as possible. To assist in this the skin should be well salted inside with common salt, put aside for a day and then soaked for two days more –

taking it out once or twice in the course of the two days, rinsing in warm water and then putting back again – in a mixture of bran and water (made with boiling water and allowed to cool) of about the thickness of pea soup. When satisfied that the skin is clean and thin, put in a pickling mixture of 1 lb. common salt and ½ lb. burnt alum to 1 gallon boiling water. Put the skin in when the mixture has cooled to the point when the hand can bear the heat. Soak for one day, remove, hang on a line (flesh side out) to dry. When barely dry, knead well over the back of a chair or some hard wooden edge; the longer you knead the softer it will be. Put in mixture again, soak for another day then repeat drying and kneading process. The thinner the skin is scraped and the more industriously kneaded the better it will be.

Parchment

Parchment is made from sheep or goats' skins, vellum from calves', kids' or lambs' skins. Only perfect skins are suitable and after dehairing and liming the skin should be stretched out very tightly between stakes or pegged out or laced to a wooden frame with wooden skewers for tightening. Then the skin is scalded with boiling water and scraped and stretched still further, then dried in a cool room, scraped again, coated with a thick cream of whiting and washing soda to remove the last of the grease and put in a warm room to dry. Then it is scalded and stretched again, and dried slowly, stretching it more each day, removed from the frame and finished by rubbing with flat pumice stones over a wool-stuffed, raw calf's skin.

Sewing

Early man made pins out of polished bones and needles from slithers of bone with a hole bored through the end. The result would be surprisingly accomplished. 'Judging by their exquisitely finished bone needles the Magdalenians were capable of doing quite fine sewing.'[89] Use the right thread for the material being sewn: wool for wool; spun fibres of flax or linen – two or more strands doubled together for strength – for cloth; leather thongs, sinew or catgut for skins. Thread is made stronger and more waterproof if it is waxed before use.

Shoes

In Roman days footwear was dictated by law. Boots worn by the patrician orders had to reach higher up the leg than those worn by plebeians. Common people wore wooden shoes and slaves went barefoot. Scottish Highlanders usually went barefoot in summer until the nineteenth century, and on the island of St Kilda, if they wore shoes at all they were commonly made from the skin of a gannet. The skin was cut close to the eyes and round the base of the neck, then turned inside out so that the feathers were next to the foot; the breast end was sewn up and the heel rested on the crown of the head. These shoes only lasted a few days but they were easily replaced. Bushmen in Africa used a similar technique with the skin from the hock leg of an antelope or zebra. The skin was cut as shown and sewn up; it was then drawn on to the foot so that the heel

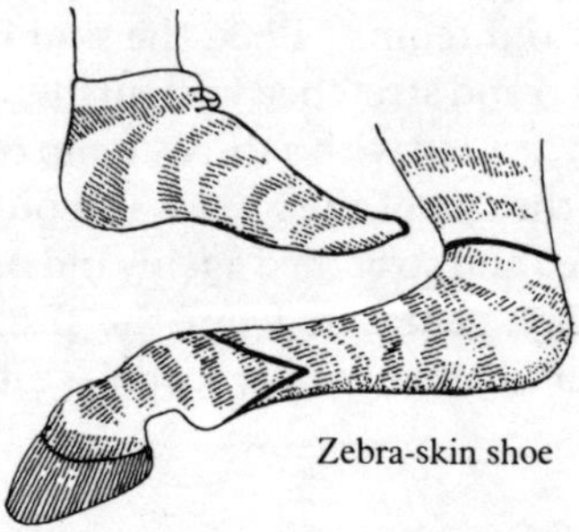

Zebra-skin shoe

rested in the curve of the hock. But they mostly went barefoot too: 'there is no surer sign on the frontier of Cape Colony that the Kafirs intend to make war than to see among them a general preparation of velshoens or sandals'.[48]

To make sandals an outline of the foot is cut out in leather and then two slits are made on either side of the hollow of the foot for a thong of leather to hold the toe strap in place, as shown. The toe strap, which may or may not go round the heel, is fixed by a knot and the sandal finished by attaching an outer sole. Rope sandals can be made in a similar way by using plaited string or thin rope. For the

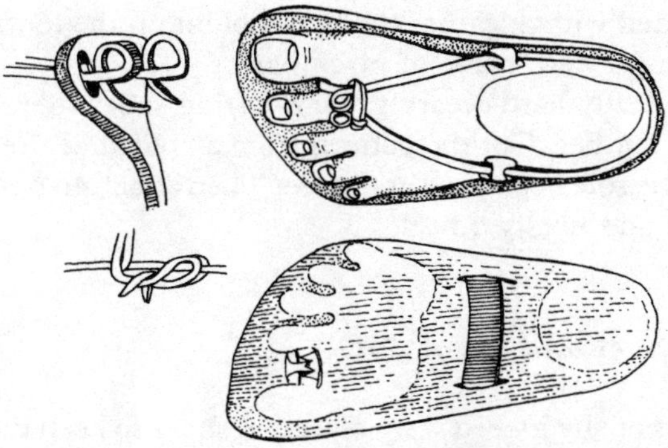

Leather sandal

sole use rope not more than ½ in. in diameter. Thin one end and, beginning with this, start shaping at the hollow of the foot; coil it round six or seven times as shown, finishing at the toe end to make it

Rope sandal

wider than the heel. Espadrilles can be made by stitching a canvas upper to the rope sole.

A wooden-soled sandal worn by the Chinese (which have their familiar modern counterparts in Dr Scholl's sandals) can be made by shaping a piece of wood, preferably light wood such as willow or poplar, to fit the sole of the foot and then attaching a strip of leather across the front with nails.

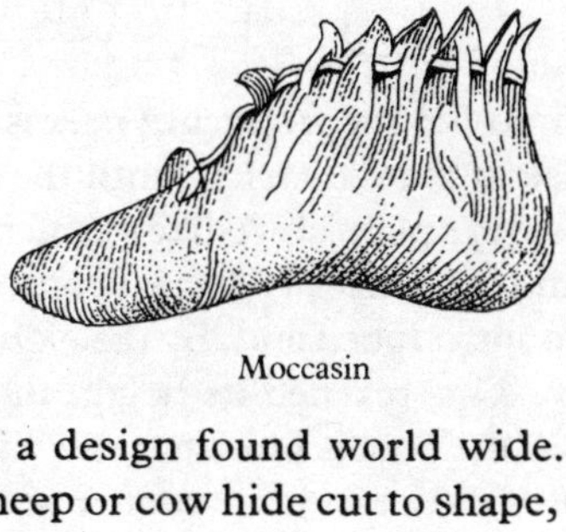

Moccasin

The moccasin is a design found world wide. In Scotland they were made out of sheep or cow hide cut to shape, turned hair side in and threaded with a leather thong to hold it on the foot. In Russia peasant shoes were made of birch bark.

But for really hard-wearing, long-lasting shoes there is no substitute for leather. Cut the pattern from an old shoe. Sew the shoe upper to the sole beginning at the toe. Then attach an outer sole and inner sole and finally a heel.

Feet Coolers and Insulators

The leaves of silverweed were placed in shoes to keep the feet 'cool and prevent a too immoderate sweating of the Feet which causes a soreness in them'[90] and the furry leaves of mullein were placed inside stockings to keep the feet warm and comfortable on cold days in winter.

A Smock

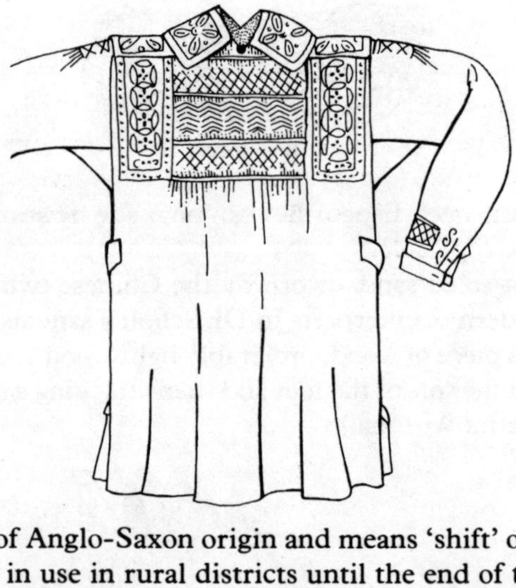

The name is of Anglo-Saxon origin and means 'shift' or 'chemise'. Smocks were in use in rural districts until the end of the last century. Early smocks were plain shirt-like garments without any fullness but, by the time of Charles I, gathers controlled by stitching or smocking had been introduced and, by the eighteenth century, elaborate embroidery. This reached its height in the nineteenth century. The pattern of the panels on either side of the smocking often indicated the trade of the wearer: a gardener would have flowers and leaves; a shepherd, crooks, sheep-pens, sheep and hurdles; a milk-maid, churns, butterpats and hearts; and a grave-digger, crosses. Colours were usually grey for everyday and white for Sundays, though there were regional variations. Deep blue in the Midlands, black in the Isle of Wight and white in the Home Counties.

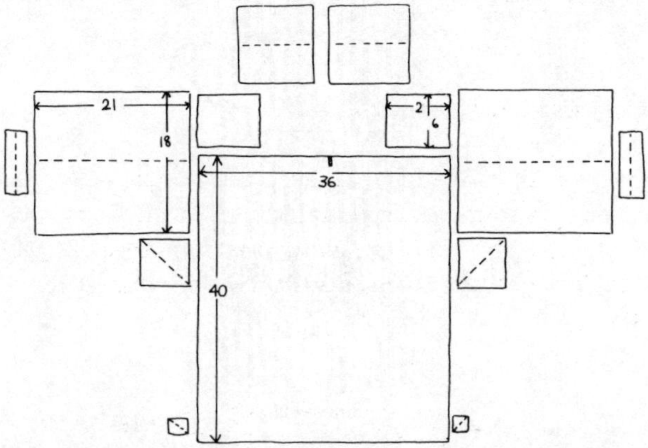

For a man's smock about 4 yards of 36 in. wide material is required, preferably of heavy linen. Practised hands cut them in the following way. The length of material required was three times the length from neck to hem. The material was cut in three equal parts; two were for the front and back of the smock and the third was again cut into three, two pieces for the sleeves and the third for the collar,

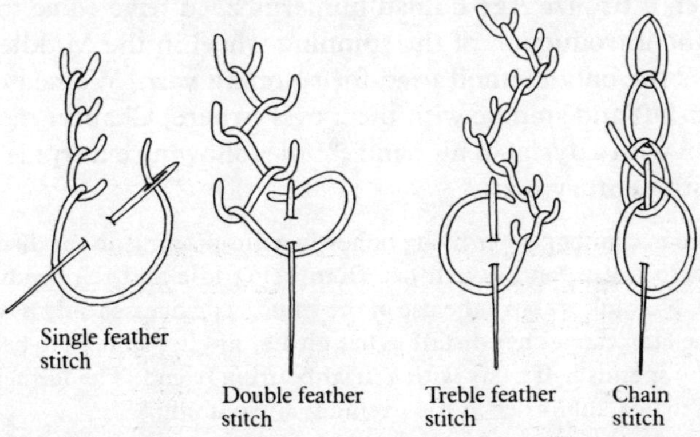

gusset and shoulder pieces. See pattern. The embroidery is done first, using feather or chain stitch. For the smocking the material is evenly gathered in lines half an inch apart to the required width, before stitching as shown. Finally the garment is sewn together.

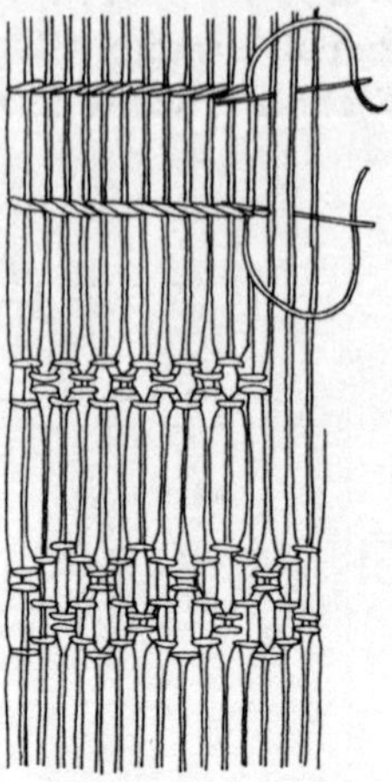

Smocking

Spinning

Spinning with a spindle ranks among man's earliest mechanical achievements. Stones used to weight sticks have been found among Neolithic remains. Others made of pottery, sawn-off femur ends and even a Bronze Age human humerus head have come to light. Until the introduction of the spinning wheel in the Middle Ages, this was the only method used for spinning yarn. Women carried their distaff and spindle with them everywhere; Chaucer mentions 'malpyn with a dystaf in hir hand';[91] the following excerpt is from a sixteenth-century text:

> A woman cannot get her living honestly with spinning on the distaff, but it stoppeth a gap, and saveth her from being idle and the product was needful. No rank is above the use of the spindle; princesses only have them gilt. The lady carries her distaff in her girdle, and her spindle in her hand, when she spends half a day with a neighbouring friend. The farmer's wife has her maids about her in the evening, all spinning.[92]

Feats of spinning were worthy of some early equivalent of *The Guinness Book of Records*: the *Proceedings of the Royal Society* of

1755 record that a spinner in East Dereham, Norfolk, spun a pound of wool into a thread 84,000 yards in length, 480 yards short of 48 miles, a record broken a few years later by a Norwich spinster who managed 168,000 yards. However, reassuringly, a seventeenth-century Duchess of Newcastle was told by her governess that she would 'spoil more flax than get cloth by your spinning'. After the invention of Hargreave's spinning-jenny in 1767 and Crompton's mule in 1775 spinning moved from the cottage into the factory and female hands were freed for other chores.

Spinning

Spinning is done by drawing out a thin fibre from a rolag of wool or bundle of flax (see Cloth, p. 334) and twisting it so that the fibres, which tend to cling to each other naturally, curl round each other. All refinements on the hand-manipulated spindle are designed to facilitate and speed up this basic process. Wool spins more easily when still full of its natural oils. Flax spins more finely when wet – this strengthens the fibres and allows them to be stretched to greater lengths. The water is applied by dipping the fingers in a bowl during spinning.

The amount of twist depends on the final use of the fibre. A hard, twisted thread is strongest. Also the shorter the fibres, the more twist is needed to fix them together. Most yarn is twisted in a Z, or clockwise, direction. To ply threads – make them thicker or stronger – two threads are given an S twist, spun together in an anti-clockwise direction.

The usual spindle consists of a rounded, wooden stick about nine to twelve inches in length, tapered at each end and with a hook at the top. The stick is weighted at its bottom and thicker end by a whorl, which may be of wood, pottery or stone but which should fit well and give an even spin when spun like a top.

To spin, begin by hand-twisting a length of wool fibre about eighteen inches long. Tie it to the stick above the whorl, take it under the whorl, round the stick, back over the whorl and attach it round the hook in a half hitch. Then draw out an even length of wool from the rolag, give the spindle a twist with your right hand, and let it spin until there is a tight twist on the piece of wool. Then, resting

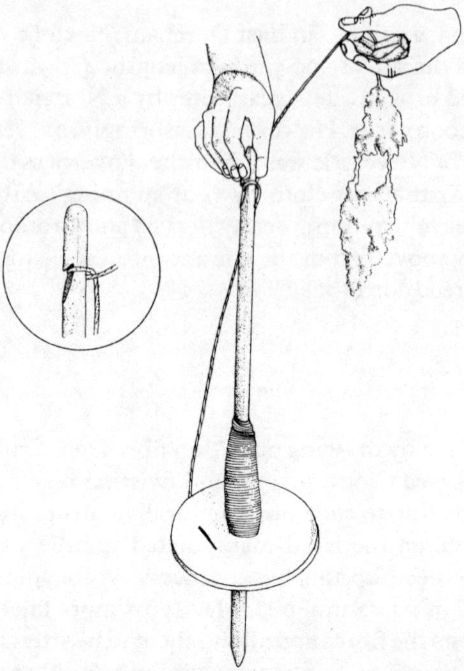

the spindle against your foot, and using your right hand to hold the twisted part, ease out another length of fibres from the rolag, ease your right hand and allow the twist to travel up to where your left hand is holding the rolag. Continue until the thread is as long as your arms will allow. Keep the thread taut by winding it round your fingers. Then take the half-hitch off the spindle hook and wind the thread round the stick just above the whorl. Re-hook the thread for another spin. When one rolag has been used up join another by working the fibres together with your fingers.

Spinning Wheels

If you intend to do much spinning it is much easier and quicker to do it on a spinning wheel.*

* Spinning wheels and spindles may be bought from Dryad Ltd, Northgates, Leicester, or from their showroom in Kensington High Street, London, w8, along with an instruction book.

Weaving

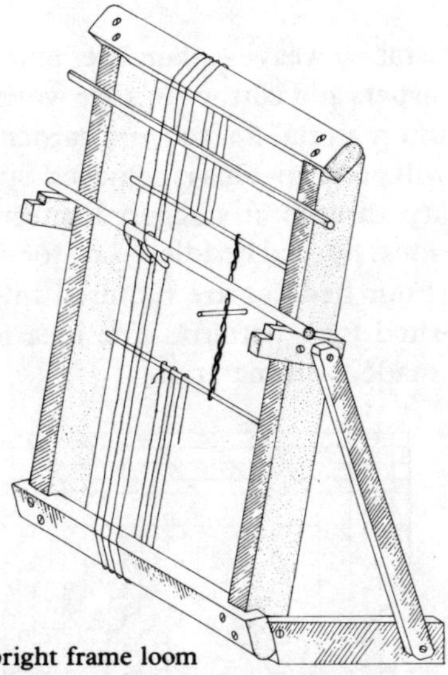

Basic upright frame loom

To weave, a frame is required on which the warp threads can be kept taut while the weft threads are woven in between. This is facilitated by making a shed – this means that instead of the weaver having to pick up each alternate warp thread in turn as he weaves, they are separated by a rod, or loops of thread attached to a rod, so that the weaver merely moves the rod and puts the warp thread through the shed so created. The next development is the heddle, which keeps the warp threads evenly spaced, as well as making the shed. It usually consists of a piece of wood enabling one line of warp to remain fixed while the other moves up or down. The weft thread is

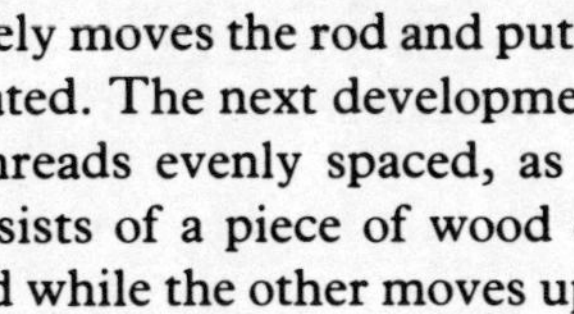

Shuttle

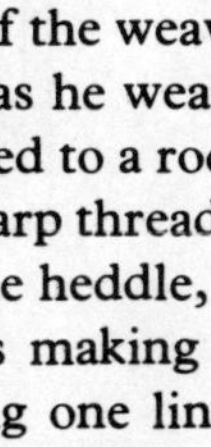

Comb

wound round a shuttle, which is normally long and grooved. A comb or fork, or sometimes even the heddle, is used to beat down the weft threads to ensure a firm fabric.

Patterns

The simplest is the tabby weave – plain over and under as in basket work – and most carpets and cotton rugs are woven in this way. But for linen and cotton material a stronger, harder-wearing fabric is made by using a twill pattern. This is achieved by picking up two or more adjacent warp threads at staggered intervals. The squared diagram gives the idea. Special heddles – one for each permutation – simplify the job. Four heddles are required to give the different sheds for a four-shed twill pattern. The idea is not new – even Bronze Age man made twill material.

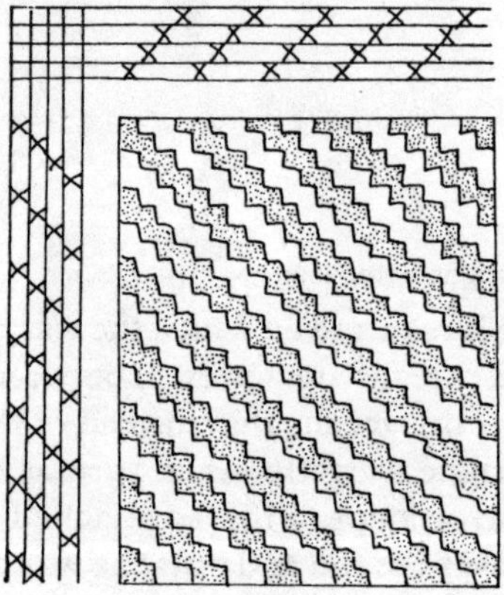

Twill pattern

Looms

Looms come in many different forms. The earliest type, used by Bronze Age man and still in use in remote areas of North Europe in the nineteenth century, is an upright loom with rows of evenly balanced weights attached to the bottom of the warp to keep them taut. The shed is created by keeping a stick permanently in position with alternate threads attached to a heddle rod by means of loose loops or leashes. Thus the two sheds can be opened in turn. This method is adapted for a four-shed pattern by using one shed stick and four heddle rods and the work is woven from the top down.

An adaptation of this method, and one which survived in the Faroe Islands until the last century, was for the loom to be set at an

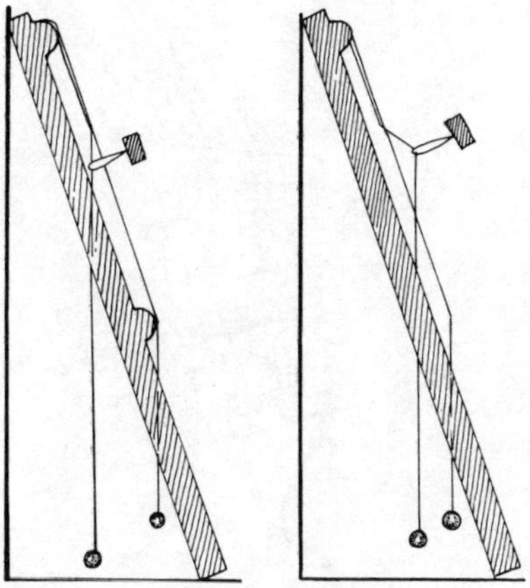

Angled upright loom

angle with every fourth warp thread hung by a separate set of weights and allowed to fall perpendicularly while the others followed the line of the loom, so creating a natural shed. So for this loom only three heddles are required for a four-shed pattern.

The earliest known illustration of a fixed upright loom with a wooden beam at the base instead of weights occurs in a Roman manuscript of the fourth century AD; Bedouins still use a version of it today, but instead of the loom being upright it is laid on the desert floor. The warp is attached to wooden beams pegged to the ground, the distance between them being determined by the length of the item to be woven which, with tent rugs, can be as much as twelve yards. The warp thread is continuous and is wound back and forth round the warp rods. Weaving is generally done by two women who, as the woven part grows, sit on it to maintain tension. The heddle is supported on two stones which are moved up the work as it progresses. The weft threads are continually beaten down with a steel hook or gazelle horn until firmly home and the warp threads are all but obscured.

In parts of South America and Asia they use a back-strap loom (illustration p. 358). The top is attached to a fixed hook and the lower strap to the weaver's waist, who then leans forwards or backwards according to whether he wants to slacken or tighten the warp. The weft is beaten down with a stick.

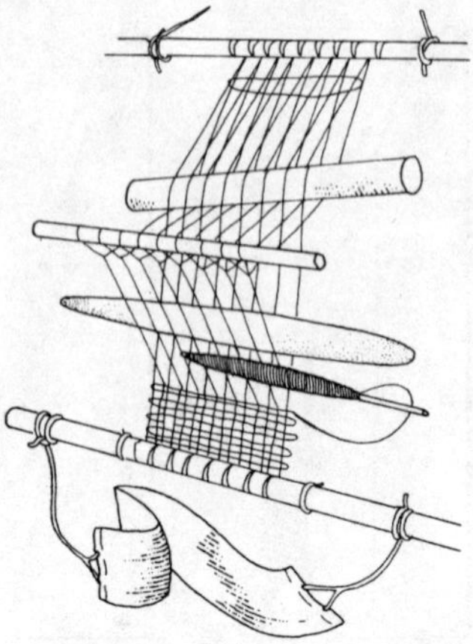

Pre-Columbian back-strap loom

Until the Industrial Revolution the main refinement to these early looms, and one which enabled very long pieces of cloth to be made, were rollers to which the warp threads could be attached; these were unwound at one end to give more warp thread and wound up at the other as the cloth was woven. Another improvement was the operation of the heddle with a treadle. Later machines were invented to do this and to work a 'flying shuttle' which whizzed to and fro.

Until the advent of steam power in the nineteenth century weaving was a cottage industry; the houses the weavers lived in could be distinguished by their second-storey windows, which were arranged in long continuous rows so as to give the weavers as much light as possible – these houses can still be seen, especially on the eastern slopes of the Pennines. But each farm or cottage usually contained one or two looms; the weaving was done by the men while the women did the spinning.

For centuries it occupied men's daily thoughts in town and village, second only to agriculture; our literature and common speech acquired many phrases and metaphors borrowed from the manufacture of cloth – 'thread of discourse', 'spin a yarn', 'unravel a mystery', 'web of life', 'fine-drawn', 'home-spun', 'tease', – while all unmarried women were put down as 'spinsters'.[22]

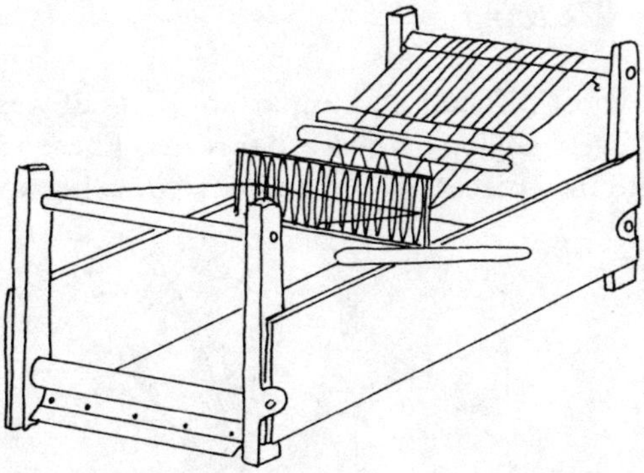

Table loom

The large looms they used were worked with a foot treadle and were elaborations of the small table loom shown in the diagram. These can also be bought commercially (see p. 354 for address) and there are many books on weaving available. William Morris re-introduced the hand-made carpet in the nineteenth century; he used the type of loom, upright and relatively simple, shown in the diagram.

William Morris carpet loom

Hints for Weaving

One of the most difficult and important parts of weaving is maintaining the even tension of the warp threads. These are also inclined to break and new pieces should be inserted, using a weaver's knot.

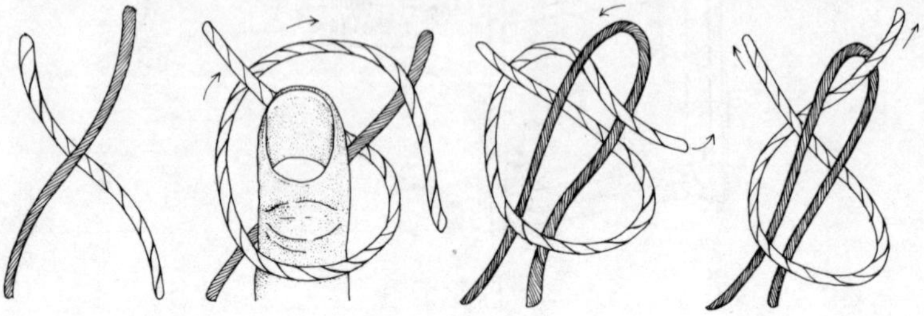

Weaver's knot

Between workings the tension of the warp should be eased. Fraying of the warp can also be a problem and is prevented by starching. Linen thread is stronger when wet and a damp cloth kept lying on the back of the loom helps achieve this. Good, double-ply, well-twisted thread should be used for both wool and linen cloth. To decide on the number of warp threads for a cloth of average thickness, wind the thread round a ruler and count the number which can be placed into a centimetre, then halve the number to get a 'sett'. Multiply this by the desired width in centimetres and add 10 per cent for good measure. Add another six for the selvedge – three for either side which may be doubled over or woven (see Carpets, p. 216) and round up the number to make it even. When calculating the length of the warp threads, remember to allow for the amount taken up in weaving and add on a bit extra.

Grooming

During the two months we spent living rough Brendan had three baths and I none, as the only available source of running water was a freezing stream. I afterwards learnt that, inadvertently, I had been the more sensible. When living rough you should not bathe, on the same principle as not grooming a horse at grass – it removes all the protective oils from the skin. Penelope Chetwoode during two months riding through Andalusia and Dervla Murphy during five months spent travelling in Baltistan studiously avoided bathing for this reason. But, on certain occasions, vanity will overcome expediency. It certainly overcame my fear of cold water whenever I knew a newspaper photographer was about to appear. Then I would dip my hair in the stream and wash it as best I could. For this purpose I used some of the soap I had made before we came. This is very easy to make and it does not surprise me in the least that, before mass production, soap-making was part of the household duties. The only surprising thing is that this odd mixture of mutton fat and potash lye does saponify and solidify and works as well as anything one can buy. But, for the rest of the time, apart from cleaning face, hands and teeth – which I cleaned with salt water and a frayed hazel stick – night and morning, washing played little part in my daily life. But then I do not think I was dirty in the way you become dirty leading an urban existence. I did not feel uncomfortable nor, as far as I know, did I smell. This I am sure must have had something to do with our way of life. We were always in the fresh air, wearing clothes made from natural fibres, eating clean, unspiced food and never coming in contact with dirt other than earth. Earth rubs off leaving the skin smoother, in much the same way as a beauty salon's mud bath, whereas town dirt is sticky and grimy and requires soap and water to remove it.

Once back home, ordinary life resumed, my normal habits of grooming began again. It was then that I really began compiling the information in this section, delving in books written by the great seventeenth-century dilettante, Sir Kenelm Digby, and by those fine ladies who all published herbals at the beginning of this century, Mrs Leyel, Mrs Grieve and Eleanor Sinclair Rohde. The picture their books evoked of summer scenes and still rooms in old country houses, of gardens and meadows full of scented flowers which were collected as they bloomed and, according to their scent and colour, were judiciously mixed into perfumes and pot-pourris, all persuaded me to try for myself. I began to distill perfume, experiment with different herbs in the bath and to make my own cosmetics. I discovered how good and pure they all are and at the same time derived great pleasure from their different textures and essences.

The first peoples to succumb to the use of cosmetics are thought to have been the Chinese, but the first evidence of their use is from Egypt, about 3000 BC. When Tutankhamun's tomb, erected c. 1350 BC, was opened, vases containing still fragrant unguents were found. The Greeks cared about their appearance; the Romans were apparently indifferent until they invaded Greek-occupied southern Italy. By the time of Nero and his wife Poppaea, cosmetics and perfumes played an important part at court. Cosmetics and perfumes were introduced into Britain by the Crusaders, who brought back samples of those prized by the ladies of Middle Eastern harems. They became so popular that, according to G. V. Septimus Piesse, in his *Art of Perfumes* (1770), a Bill was introduced in Parliament with the provision:

> That all women of whatever age, rank, profession or degree, whether virgins, maids, or widows, that shall, from and after such Act, impose upon, seduce, and betray into matrimony, any of His Majesty's subjects, by the scents, paints, cosmetic washes, artificial teeth, false hair, Spanish wool, iron stays, hoops, high heeled shoes, bolstered hips, shall incur the penalty of the law in force against witchcraft and like misdemeanors and that the marriage, upon conviction, shall stand null and void.[93]

The fashion fluctuated and in the Victorian era no self-respecting woman would dream of tinkering with her appearance by the application of cosmetics. However, by the time of the First World War it was permissible for a lady to wear a little powder in public and the upswing has continued.

Some of our obsession with cosmetics may be to do with the awful clarity of the modern mirror, which reflects every defect. It must have been easier to think yourself lovely when gazing at the less defined image mirrored in metal. Until the seventeenth century in England most glass was too defective to give a proper reflecting surface and in general hand mirrors were made of highly polished metal, usually steel. This type of mirror was used by the early Chinese, Etruscans, Greeks and Romans. One part tin to three parts copper was the ideal mix and they were often set in fine frames. Henry VIII's wardrobe at Windsor detailed 'a square loking steale glasse set in blew vellet all over embrowderde with Venice golde and damaske pearles'.

Bathing

To the Romans the bath was a social institution, a ritual to be gone into with science and care. At the great baths of Caracalla there was a choice of over two dozen kinds of bath, among them mineral, steam, massage, friction, herb and oil baths. As a reaction early Christians adopted a puritanical attitude to the bath, still partly with us, though alleviated to some extent when returning Crusaders introduced the vapour bath to this country in the fourteenth century and modified today by our modern obsession with cleanliness and abhorrence of any form of bodily odour.

Until the advent of modern plumbing, a bath usually consisted of a large container into which hot water was poured.

The simplest way of taking a bath is to soak oneself in a stream or river and allow the current to do the rinsing, or, one up, dig a hole beside a stream with a channel leading from it to the hole. Once the bath is full, the channel is blocked and the water heated with stones made hot in a fire.

Cleopatra, among other beauties, had milk baths which are nourishing and soothing to the skin. Catherine the Great and Madame Pompadour believed in herbs: camomile and lovage are cleansing; mint and elder healing; lime and nettle beneficial to the skin. Any of the fragrant herbs mentioned in the section on perfume (p. 368) impart a scent. Tie the herb in a muslin bag and infuse in the bath or hang over the running hot-water tap. Oatmeal or bran put in the bath and a handful rubbed over the body cleans and softens the skin. Nut oils help replace the body oils removed by soap. Some other oils also smell nice.

> Here first she bathes, and round her body pours
> Soft oils of fragrance and ambrosial showers.[94]

Sea-salt tones, as does an infusion of pine needles. Boil the needles for twenty minutes or infuse in boiling water and leave for twenty-four hours. Cider vinegar is reviving and restores the acid mantle of your skin. Lovage, sage, cleavers and lavender act as deodorants. But most body odours come from toxins in food, the wrong clothes and cramped conditions; if your diet contains a lot of green vegetables, and if you wear clothes of natural fibres which allow your skin to breathe and lead an open air life, you should not smell.

Combs

The jaws of the skulls of large animals have been used by primitive people as combs. Darwin during his voyage on the *Beagle* noticed that the Fuegian women combed their hair with the jaws of a porpoise. Traditionally combs have been made from bone and wood. Though plastic is the commonest material for modern combs, the best combs from the most expensive shops are still hand-made from tortoiseshell, bone or horn. Borde said 'Comb the head with an ivory comb, nothing refreshes the memory more.' The following is a seventeenth-century list of combs and materials.[71]

Combes – Wood combes be made of light and close wood as blackthorne.
Box combes be made of Box tree.
Horn combes be made of ox and cows horns (also deer horn may be used).
Ivory combes be made of elephants teeth.
Bone combes be made of the shank bone of horses.
Tortoise combes be made of sea or land tortoise shell and the counterfeit of this sort are horn stained with tortoise colours.
Crocus combes be made of crocus wood.
Lead combes be used by such as have red hair and to make it of another colour.

Bone combs and wood are carved into shape with a knife or sawn and smoothed. For horn combs, the horn must first be melted down (see p. 260) and then cut into shape.

(For Brushes, see p. 274.)

Cosmetics

The best aid to beauty is a healthy life based on a balanced diet, exercise, and fresh air, but cosmetics can help stay the inroads made by hard water, weather and generally grimy conditions. Mary Quant, when asked which cosmetic she would take to a desert island, replied:

> I would like to have Tearproof Mascara or Lash Tint Mascara and have lots of it, because all other cosmetics could be made from nature's own products. Dyes from vegetables, flowers and tree bark would make colours to put on eyes, lips and cheeks. Oils – coconut, almond, walnut, peanut, sunflower seed, olive and fish – to be used as moisturizers and conditioner for hair. Oils mixed with vegetables and fruit – beetroot, carrot, avocado – to make nourishing creams. Oils mixed with wheatgerm or oats to make a face pack, together with eggs, if there happened to be a hen there! Eating vegetables and fish for vitamins. Salt water for cleaning teeth. Spring water for washing hair.

The following are some more specific recipes.

Cleansing cream

This is an adaptation of the recipe given by Galen, the Greek physician.

Melt ½ oz. white wax and 1 oz. anhydrous lanolin in a double boiler. Slowly add 3 oz. oil, preferably almond, and 1 oz. rosewater, stirring all the time. Remove from the heat, add some perfume and pour into a jar.

Facial mask

This is useful for deep cleansing the skin.

Beat up the white of an egg and mix with finely ground oatmeal. Apply to the face with cotton-wool soaked in rosewater, elder-flower water or witch hazel. Allow to dry, rinse off with warm water and then splash face with cold water or astringent lotion.

A more thorough mask

Melt $\frac{1}{8}$ oz. beeswax with 1 oz. lanolin in a double boiler. Add $\frac{1}{8}$ pint rosewater and stir thoroughly. (Some agar, perfume or linseed oil may be added, if desired.) Stir in 4 oz. fuller's earth (an absorbent clay) and work to a smooth paste. Apply to face, allow to dry and rinse off as above.

A healing mask

Mix $\frac{1}{3}$ cup oatmeal with 3 teaspoons of honey – or enough to make a paste – and 1 teaspoon rosewater. Spread on the face for half an hour.

Astringent lotion

Used to tone and cleanse the skin, astringent can be made from an infusion of herbs in water or better, the herb distilled in water. Rosewater and witch hazel mixed in equal quantities, or with a greater proportion of rosewater if the skin is dry, is a recipe which often appears in old books and in the small print under various well-known commercial labels. Witch hazel is an American plant and where it is not available, elder flowers, camomile, nettle and yarrow and sage are all plants with astringent qualities and can be used instead, or cider vinegar diluted with rosewater in the proportions 1:8.

Moisturizing creams

Elder flower ointment

This also heals blemishes and softens the skin.

Melt 8 oz. lard in a pan, add a small cup of water and stir well. Simmer with the lid on for an hour and then with the lid off until all the water has evaporated, i.e. no water should rise when the mixture is stirred. Cool; strain through a muslin. Add some bundles of elder flowers and simmer in the lard for 1 hour. Strain and allow to cool.

Lily root nourisher

Lily and narcissus roots are well-known skin foods.

To one cup of water add 2 tablespoons pulverized lily root. Simmer in a covered pot for 30 minutes. Strain, add 1 tablespoon honey and 1 oz. anhydrous lanolin melted in a double boiler. Add ½ teaspoon rosewater; store in a jar.

Hand creams

For a general-purpose hand cream take some oatmeal moistened with a little milk or almond oil and make a paste with a yolk of egg, a few drops of cider vinegar and a large spoonful of honey. If the hands are very chapped bathe the hands in a mixture of linseed and almond oil. A barrier cream is made by mixing together a teaspoon of fuller's earth, almond oil and an egg yolk, then working it into your hands and allowing it to dry.

Lip salves

Lip jellies which help prevent chapping can be made from gelatinous seaweeds (see agar, p. 151); if soaked with the cut root of alkanet (*Pentaglottis sempervirens*) they will absorb its red colour. Lanolin can also be used, or the following recipe.

Pomade rosat

Melt 2 oz. white wax with 4 oz. almond oil and leave to soak with cut alkanet root. Strain and add 12 drops of otto of roses to scent.

Eyes

The eyes are very delicate and need special attention.

Eye cream

Melt 4 tablespoons of anhydrous lanolin in a double boiler. Add a beaten egg yolk. In another double boiler melt 2 tablespoons beeswax and 2 tablespoons safflower oil. Add to lanolin with 1 tablespoon cold water. Beat until frothy and put in a jar.

A compress to restore tired eyes

Soak cotton-wool in an infusion of the whole plant of eyebright.

Culpeper said of eyebright that 'If the herb was but as much used as it is neglected, it would half spoil the spectacle maker's trade and a man would think that reason should teach people to prefer the preservation of their natural before artificial spectacles.'

Hair

For fair hair: an infusion of camomile lightens and brightens.
For dark hair: an infusion of rosemary or sage.
For greasy hair: an infusion of nettle used by itself or added to shampoo – the sulphur in the nettle dries the grease.
For dry hair or hair out of condition: mix 1 part olive oil to 2 parts honey and massage a generous amount into the hair. Wrap in a warm towel and leave for 20 minutes before washing off.
For dandruff: add vinegar to the rinsing water. This also gets rid of any remaining shampoo and makes hair easier to comb out and shiny.

Hair dye for fair hair

An infusion of rhubarb root or mullein leaves is said to be effective.

Hair dye for dark hair

Walnut shells make a dye which progressively adds colour to the hair. Before the nuts are ripe crush the green outer shells in water. Cover with water, add a good pinch of salt and stand for 3 days. Then add 3 cups of boiling water and simmer for 5 hours, adding more water as it evaporates. Strain and press out all liquid from the shells, then reduce by a quarter over heat. Add some perfume, alum to act as a fixative and some glycerine to soften the hair. Use as a shampoo on clean hair. At first it produces a yellowish effect, but this darkens to give the hair a good deep black colour.

Perfume

Though toilet waters are usually derived from a single plant smell most perfumes have compound origins, since for a perfume to be rich in odour, have body and lasting power, other ingredients beside the basic flower smell must be added. As Theophrastus remarked 'perfumes are compounded from various parts of the plants; flowers, leaves, twigs, root, wood, fruit and gum; and in most cases the perfume is made from a mixture of several parts'.[94]

To begin, the different smells have to be extracted. This smell, or essential oil, as it is called in perfumery, is normally at its most intense when the plant is ready to be fertilized and may be contained in the petals, stems, leaves, bark or even the root of the plant. A dry season and a hot climate develop greater amounts of oil in a plant – this is the reason why so much perfume is made in the south of France. There are three basic methods of extraction.

Distillation

This is the most usual process (see Distilling, p. 175). Direct heat or steam heat may be used (except in the case of roots, wood, bark and seeds when steam heat is best) and the vessels must be made of glass or earthenware – never metal. As a rule a more perfect oil is obtained from a larger rather than a smaller amount of material and it is advisable to macerate it in the water in which it is to be distilled for twenty-four hours beforehand. The more rapidly the distillate is sent over the better. The resulting liquid should be sent over several supplies of fresh leaves in order to obtain a strong smelling liquid. The result, depending on the part of the distillate taken, may be a fragrant water or toilet water, refreshing and lovely to use but without great depth, or an essential oil which may be used by itself or blended. The following two methods demonstrate the difference: other flowers may be adapted in the same way.

Elder-flower water

Macerate 1 lb. elder flowers in 1 pint water for 24 hours. Distil.

Rose otto

Traditionally said to have been discovered in the sixteenth century during the Moghul rule in India at the marriage of the Emperor Jehangir. While walking with his bride in the garden he noticed an oily film on the canals which had been filled with rose petals for the ceremony – produced by the action of the sun on the rose petals. The royal couple were so entranced by the smell that they ordered it to be bottled – the first otto or attar of roses. Bulgarian rose otto is thought the finest in the world, its excellence due to a combination of the climate and soil of that area. The damask and cabbage or Provence roses are the main species used and the flowers are picked in May and June just before they begin to open and before sunrise while still covered with dew. Those collected later in the day emit a more powerful fragrance but of less delicacy. All foreign matter is freed from the petals, which are then placed in twice their weight of water in great stills. The first distillation yields a water with a green oil floating on the surface. This is skimmed off and the remaining water returned to the still with a fresh charge of petals. The second distillation yields a water on which a yellow oil floats. This too is skimmed off and mixed with the green oil to form the base of rose otto. The remaining water is used as toilet water or for any of the things requiring rosewater. To the attar minute amounts of civet, a drop or two of musk, certain gums and resins such as benzoin, storax and balsam are added and finally ambergris to fix and make the perfume long-lasting – but it should smell only of roses.

Maceration

Some plants, such as violet, have such delicate smells that distillation is too violent a method of extraction. For these the best results are obtained by maceration in oil, lard or beef suet, purified by melting, skimming, straining through a flannel and finally washing with alum solution. The grease is then melted in a bath or a jar to a temperature of 140–160°F, the flowers added, stirred for a period and left for twenty-four hours. After this time the exhausted material is drained off and replaced by fresh matter until the fat becomes thoroughly charged with the required odour. This is one of the earliest methods of extraction. Unguents, used by the Egyptians and, according to Homer, by Aphrodite to anoint the dead body of Hector, were made in this way.

Enfleurage

As old a process as maceration, and particularly suitable for flowers with elusive smells. Two grooved sheets of glass are spread on one side with purified fat (see maceration). The flowers are laid on the fat on one glass and the second placed over them and left for one to three days for the fat to absorb the scent. Fresh petals are then substituted for the exhausted old ones and so on until the fat has absorbed the scent of the flower. The result is called pomade.

Other Processes

Scented alcohol

If scented fat is treated with alcohol the scent transfers from the fat to the spirit. To do this the fat is either macerated and shaken in alcohol until this has absorbed the scent of the fat, or the fat is spread on a cone of paper and the alcohol poured on and allowed to filter slowly through the fat, collecting the scent on its way – in much the same way that filter coffee is made.

Tinctures and essences

For a tincture a solid, scented substance such as orris root or saffron is agitated in alcohol and allowed to stand in a warm place for 2 weeks. Rough quantities are 1 oz. orris powder to 1 pint alcohol. For an essence, the essential oil of a plant is agitated with alcohol. For thyme essence use 4 drachms oil of thyme to 1 pint alcohol; for lavender 4 oz. oil of lavender to 1 pint alcohol.

Blending Perfume

After the essential oil has been obtained by one of the above methods, it may then be blended with other ingredients chosen to complement, give depth and fix the main smell. The most important fixatives in perfumery are ambergris, obtained from sickly specimens of the sperm whale; musk from the sac of the musk deer, a native of China and Siberia; civet from the African civet cat; and foreign barks and resins such as patchouli, sandalwood, camphor, cumin and benzoin. There are also some native vegetable fixatives which, though not as good, do work. The lichen oakmoss (*Evernia prunastri* and *E. furfuracea*) grows wild; orris root (the root of *Iris germanica*, *I. pallida* or *I. florentina*) and clary sage (*Salvia sclarea*) are easily grown garden plants. Other plants with strong, definite scents which can complement each other or be used by themselves are listed below. Once their essential oil has been extracted they may be blended according to the nose of the perfumier.

Wild plants used for blending

Cedar wood, cypress wood, marjoram, bog myrtle, thyme, valerian, male fern, juniper berry, saffron, coriander seed, wild parsnip – flowers, seeds and roots.

Wild plants used on their own

Wild plants which have been used to make scents in their own right are: balm – leaves; bog myrtle – leaves; broom – flowers (by maceration); camomile – flowers (mainly to scent soap and shampoo); clover – flower; elder – flowers; gorse – flowers (by maceration); hawthorn – flowers (by maceration); honeysuckle – flowers; marjoram – whole plant; meadowsweet – flowers; melilot – flowers; mint – whole plant (different varieties are used for scent or to perfume soap or toothpaste); pine – needles; wild rose – flowers (by maceration); sea holly – whole plant; sweet cicely – leaves and flowers; thyme – whole plant; valerian – root; violet – flowers of *Viola odorata* (by maceration); woodruff – whole plant.

Some garden plants used for blending and by themselves

Origanum, camomile, scented geranium leaves, lavender, bergamot, rosemary.

Soap

Soap arrived in this country in the Middle Ages and until the nineteenth century, when commercial production got under way, every household made their own soap from their own recipes. Even after it was made commercially it was the habit to buy cheap soap, melt it down and add your own scent and finishing touches.

If oils are treated with an alkali in the presence of water they become saponified. By varying the type of oil or alkali soaps of different quality and softness can be made.

Oil: Animal fats are the most important for soap-making – some vegetable oil is often added to give softness. Pure mutton tallow produces a hard soap and pure lard a soft one.

Alkali: Since they have to be water soluble this restricts the choice: sodium – caustic soda, lime or salt; ammonia – urine; and potassium – potash. Potash makes a soft soap and soda a hard one.

Scent: This is added in the form of essential oil or scented herbs put in the lye.

To Make Soap

Rough-and-ready soap can be made by boiling ashes in some soft water, allowing them to settle, then decanting the clear liquid. Evaporate this by boiling until it is strong enough to support an egg and, while still hot, add melted animal fat. Simmer until it is the consistency of thick porridge and pour into a flat vessel to cool. This makes a soft soap which can be made harder if salt is added, in the proportions of ¼ pint to 5 pints of soap, just before it is put to cool; adding resin to the melted fat will make it firmer.

A better soap but one which takes longer is made by first making a 'lye'. Using a barrel or large container, preferably one with a tap at the bottom, put in a layer of straw, twigs or scented herbs, with an extra amount to plug the tap. Then scatter on some lime if liked, and fill up with potash. Pour on a bucket of cold water and leave for a couple of hours until the action of the lime has subsided. Then fill the barrel with water and leave to stand, stirring at intervals, for about five days. Experienced soap-makers can tell when the lye is thick enough, but a rough guide is that it will support an egg floated on the top. Drain off the lye through the tap into a bucket. Lyes of different strengths can be prepared and, once the first has been strained off, the barrel refilled to make another, weaker, lye. Next prepare the fat. It is important that this is as smooth as possible; free fatty acids make the soap gritty. Warm the fat just enough to enable it to be thoroughly mixed with a wooden paddle, but not so much that the fat is injured (about 100°F). Then pour on the lye in the proportion of approximately one part lye to two parts fat. Mix until a mark made on the surface remains for a short time and the soap, when examined on a spoon, looks homogeneous. This should take from fifteen to forty-five minutes. Any perfume is now added. After this, pour the soap into frames, preferably wooden ones as if soap is cooled too rapidly it has a deleterious effect. Leave for two or three days and cut in pieces with a cheese wire.

Shampoo

Shampoo is usually a soft soap to which some alcohol is added to make it liquid. The following recipe is a guide to proportions.

3½ oz. soft soap made from olive or linseed oil, dissolved in 9 fl. oz. alcohol with 1 teaspoon lavender oil, scant ½ teaspoon rosemary oil and ½ teaspoon rose geranium oil. Mix 2 fl. oz. solution of potash with 1 pint water and add gradually to the soft soap mix.

Shaving Soap

Peppermint oil is added to shaving soaps to give a cooling effect on the skin. Make soap from 1 lb. lard, 3 oz. tallow, 3 oz. potassium hydroxide and 7 fl. oz. water. When saponified and cool knead in 2 dessertspoons alcohol, 1 dessertspoon peppermint oil and 1 dessertspoon bois de rose oil.

Soap Powders

Soap powder for washing clothes is made by flaking hard soap and adding extra soda ash or soda crystals if liked.

Stains

These are removed by soaking in a strong lye of wood ash or in ammonia (in the past this would often be urine). The juice of sorrel leaves, sold as 'salts of lemon', was also used for the removal of stains.

Starch

'The most pure white starch is made from the root of cuckoo pint (*Arum maculatum*), but it is most hurtful to the hands of the laundress as it blistereth, and maketh the hands rugged and withall smarting.'[26] The root was crushed, washed in running water and dried, and mixed with boiling water; the liquid strained off to use as starch. This is what kept Elizabethan ruffs and collars stiff. Starches for fine lace were made from milk, for net from gum arabic and for the veils that floated from medieval steeple headdresses from parchment size. The seeds of ribwort plantain are coated with a glutinous substance which comes away if they are soaked in hot water and this has also been used as starch.

Soap Plants

Certain plants contain substances which have soapy qualities; soapwort (*Saponaria officinalis*) is the best known. The crushed root used with water will produce a lather, or if some of the crumbled root and leaves are boiled and the liquid strained off this will serve as soap. Ragged robin (*Lychnis flos-cuculi*) is also said to contain saponin and used to be added to the potash lye. Crushed horse chestnut conkers contain about 10–12 per cent saponin and will make a crude kind of soap. If the stalk of the cuckoo pint is soaked in water for about three weeks and the liquid poured off carefully each day, the glutinous sediment which collects in the bottom of the bowl makes a quite efficient soap. However it is better known as a starch.

Teeth

Hard bristles, soft bristles, medium bristles, short brushes, long brushes, used with toothpaste or without it, brushed up and down or round and round: fashions in tooth hygiene seem to follow each other almost as frequent as fashions in clothes. The salient facts appear to be three. First diet: too many sweet things do rot the teeth, but even a sensible diet is not proof against decay. Primitive people living exclusively on raw meat, nuts and fish have less trouble but do not escape completely. Some Bronze Age skulls show evidence of tooth decay; bits of grit eaten with their food have worn away the teeth to such an extent that bacteria have penetrated the pulp of the tooth, causing abscesses.

Second, some form of brushing is beneficial. An orthodox toothbrush can be made with pig's bristle as described for the hair-brush on p. 275 or a stick of green hazel with one end frayed can be used – this is said to have been the method used by the ancient British and seemed effective during the two months that I used it. Rags or feathers have also been used.

The cleansing agent is also important. The usual one is salt, or a strong solution of salt and water. Soot or potash are also said to be good cleansers, especially when mixed with lemon juice or vinegar. Avoid the old-fashioned recipes for toothpastes with their large quantities of pumice stone and coral; though these have an initial whitening effect they remove the enamel along with the stains. A sixteenth-century writer recommends that you 'Take honey, salt and rye meal: mingle them together and froth the teeth with them.'[95] *A Lady's Toilet*, published in 1808 suggests that 'to give firmness to gums which are soft and liable to bleed, make use of brandy and a small quantity of common water'.[96]

Health

Except for a time, right at the beginning, when it rained continuously for ten days and, feeling continuously damp, cold and miserable, I felt as though I had a slight chill – which I treated with whisky and honey drinks – I cannot remember feeling anything but well while living off the land. Underfed yes, but ill no. Probably the lack of food, had it gone on indefinitely, would have led to illness, but in the short term the life we led was conducive to health. We were always in the fresh air, always active, had no stress and a good clean diet. Nothing happened which required either first aid or expert medical attention, and since we were always careful to identify any unknown plant or fungus before eating it, we were never poisoned. We maintained daily hygiene by cleaning our teeth night and morning and washing face and hands; though we seldom bathed properly we did not feel the normal social need for it.

The conditions that killed our ancestors, especially our peasant ancestors, at an early age were lack of hygiene of house and body, too long hours of physical work, a defective diet and diseases such as tuberculosis. If they managed to survive their youth they lived to a good old age as can be seen by looking at old gravestones. It is interesting to note that the 'allotted' life span in Shakespeare's time was 'three score years and ten'. We survive the early hazards but die off in large numbers in middle to late middle age from illnesses connected with stress, obesity and lack of exercise. We should be able to use our increased knowledge of medicine, hygiene and the way the body functions to ensure that we eat the right food and take adequate exercise and so lead long and healthy lives. But it does not happen like that. Given enough food, most of us eat the wrong foods –too much sugar and starch; we smoke and drink to excess; and the fear of cholesterol would never have arisen if we did not lead such sedentary lives. After all Eskimos only survived their harsh conditions by eating blubber, which is raw seal fat; I am sure cholesterol never silted up their arteries. We have tended to cast aside all herbal cures as being 'folksy' forgetting that some of the drugs we rely on most are derived from plants. The painkiller morphine comes from the sap of the opium poppy, antabuse, used to cure alcoholics, from the fungus *Coprinus atramentarius* and digitalis from the foxglove. This was the herb taken by country people as a purge and for colds and dropsy. Most herbal treatments work on the principle of 'cleansing' the blood, as herbalists believe that many illnesses come from bad or poisoned blood. By cleaning the blood they aim to cure the source rather than the result of the disease. As a consequence herbal cures often work slowly.

The following sections are designed to give a general guide to the right herbs for first aid and general hygiene; for remedies for specific ailments consult one of the reference books on the subject, such as Mrs Grieve's *A Modern Herbal* or *Potter's Cyclopaedia of Botanical Drugs and Preparations*, edited by R. C. Wren (see Bibliography).

Disinfectants

Commercial disinfectants are designed to kill bacteria and prevent their multiplication; other materials possess these qualities to some extent; though they will probably not be as potent.

Soap: This is of value to prevent superficial infection, since washing the skin results in a diminution of bacteria.

Alcohol: Pure alcohol, somewhat diluted with water, makes an excellent skin disinfectant.

Tar: This possesses antiseptic qualities. Amputated limbs used to be painfully dipped in tar to seal and disinfect the wound.

Salt: Good antiseptic qualities. Bathing in salt water is recommended for all wounds.

Lime: Dissolved in water lime acts as a disinfectant, especially good for use in cleaning rooms and walls.

Garlic: The bulbs make an excellent antiseptic for use both internally and externally. During the First World War it was grown for medicinal use. The expressed juice, diluted with water and put on swabs of sterilized sphagnum, saved many wounds from gangrene.

Mint: Oil of mint acts as a mild antiseptic, particularly that from the apple-scented mint (*Mentha rotundifolia*), which contains thymol.

First Aid

Without cotton or linen bandages, dressings can be made from leaves and moss as in this gipsy remedy:

> Cuts for instance. She'd take a dock leaf with the spine out of it and put it on, then some bread soaked in hot water, then another dock leaf and tied all up tight. It heals a cut quick and clean. Same with a burn, only she'd do that with a cabbage leaf and keep it on two or three days and then if it wasn't healed then she'd put on a hot bread poultice.[97]

Poultices for boils can be made by filling a large bag with finely chopped cabbage or comfrey and placing it over the boil to draw out the pus. A poultice for gangrene and indolent ulcers is made by simmering the powdered bark of willow in cream. The crushed seeds of flax and the powdered or crushed root of marsh mallow are also well known as effective poultices.

Sphagnum moss was much used as a dressing, as it is far more absorbent than cotton-wool – a 2 oz. dressing will hold up to 2 lb. of discharge – and with its deodorant and iodine content, it is perfect for wounds. During the First World War sphagnum moss dressings were frequently used instead of cotton-wool and often the only antiseptic used was garlic juice. A Gaelic chronicle of 1014 says that the wounded from the battle of Clontarf 'stuffed their wounds with moss'[57] and again, after Flodden, the Highlanders filled their wounds with moss and soft grass, and wounded deer are known to drag themselves to beds of sphagnum moss. After gathering, the moss should be squeezed as dry as possible and any foreign bodies removed, then shaken out and dried completely in a well-ventilated place. To make a dressing put about 2 oz. in a sterilized muslin bag large enough to allow for expansion, then bandage into place. Honey is an ancient cure for skin diseases and wounds.

Boils

Correct diet by increasing consumption of green vegetables and fruit and foods high in vitamin B. Decrease consumption of carbohydrates, especially sugar. Apply a cabbage or comfrey poultice.

Bruising, severe

Apply cold compresses.

Burns

Douse with cold water immediately, if possible cold running water. Apply a sterilized dressing and leave until the skin is healed.

Cramp

Try to extend the muscle by stretching against the cramp. Hot, wet compresses should be applied. Massage the muscle, working towards the centre of the body.

Earache

Heat a bag of salt – about 2 lb. – in the oven. The patient should then lie with the affected ear against the salt bag. This relieves suffering and should draw out any pus or blockage in the ear. Warm oil inserted in the ear also helps loosen a wax plug, which can be the cause of temporary deafness.

Fainting

Place the head in a position lower than the body: if sitting, put the head between the knees; if lying, raise the feet. Keep the patient warm.

Fractures

These may be recognized by the loss of movement of the limb, pain and acute tenderness over the area of the fracture, unnatural movement, deformity, swelling and bruising at the site of the fracture and grating when the ends of the bone rub together. Though broken arms and legs are usually easily recognizable, broken or incomplete breaks of fingers and wrists may not be unless the patient is Xrayed. First the patient should be made as comfortable as possible, then any wounds should be treated and shock allowed for. Cold compresses may be gently applied to the area of injury. Then, according to where the injury is, splints or some form of support should be applied until expert help can be reached.

Nosebleed

Rest head back, breathe through mouth, apply cold compresses or ice bags over nose and back of neck.

Poisoning

The patient must be able to breathe, so keep the airway clear. A cold compress round the neck can help. Try to identify the poison. Then, if the patient is conscious and the poison non-corrosive, try to make him sick. Otherwise a doctor and hospital are needed fast. Strong salt water or tickling the back of the throat with two fingers can help. If possible, dilute the poison in the stomach with milk or other liquids, such as warm vinegar or mustard and water.

Resuscitation when breathing has stopped

Of the three methods – mouth to mouth, Silvester and Holger, the first is considered the most effective and is the one described here. In all cases speed in starting is paramount. Lay the patient on his back. Tilt the head as far back as possible and until the nostrils are facing upwards. Pinch the nose shut. Open the patient's mouth, clear out any obstructions. Take a deep breath yourself, seal your open mouth over the whole of the patient's mouth, breathe into the patient firmly and fully and, as you blow watch the patient's chest to see if it is rising and filling with air. Lift off your mouth and allow the patient's chest to empty naturally. Take in another good breath yourself and repeat.

Give the first five breaths rapidly to replenish the patient's blood with oxygen then continue steadily at the rate of twelve breaths a minute. If the patient vomits, turn his head to one side, clear mouth when finished and resume blowing (this is not a task for the weak stomached as the patient can be in a very repulsive state) until the patient breathes for himself. If and when he does, watch to see if he needs further help.

Shock

This is a state of collapse resulting from severe haemorrhage, pain, injuries, burns. The symptoms are rapid, shallow breathing, expressionless face, pallor, dilated pupils, sweating, absence of pulse. Treatment: lie the patient down with the feet above the level of the head with the head to one side to make sure that he doesn't swallow his tongue. Keep warm. Don't give anything to drink except in cases of mild shock where no injury is involved. **Never** give alcohol.

Snake bites

In Europe the only snake whose bite is poisonous is the adder, identified by its brown colour, yellowish zigzag markings and length – about thirty inches. It tends to inhabit mountainous areas, moorlands and the edges of woodland. The bite is painful and reactions to it can be swelling, sweating, vomiting, diarrhoea, stomach pains, loss of consciousness and, in rare cases, death. Treat the bitten limb as though it were broken and immobilize it. Cover the bite with a dry dressing. Relieve pain with a pain-killing drug. Get expert help.

Stings

Minor stings can be treated by placing the affected part under cold running water. Half a raw onion placed cut side down on the affected area will allay irritation and reduce swelling. See a doctor if there is any undue swelling.

Strained muscles

Alternate hot and cold compresses applied to affected area to increase circulation. If there is undue pain on movement immobilize the area by strapping with crêpe bandage and, if possible, get a doctor.

Toothache

Apply cotton-wool soaked in spirits, peppermint, or the resin of virginia creeper dissolved in vinegar.

Wounds

Clean with soap and water and remove any foreign bodies unless they are embedded, like a nail, in which case leave for a doctor to deal with if possible. Apply antiseptic ointment. Dress wound with fine cotton or linen or gauze. Pad with cotton-wool and bandage. Suspect severe internal damage if the victim has bruise mark patterns on his skin from his clothes.

Insecticides

Opinions vary as to the effectiveness of vegetable insecticides. Bunches of mint hung about a room drive away flies who are repelled by its strong smell. The Swedes say that if toadflax is boiled in milk and the infusion stood in a room it makes an effective fly poison. The melilots ward off moths; if packed between clothes, the chemical coumarin contained in them scents the clothes and keeps the insects away. An infusion of feverfew in wine sponged on to the skin is said to be an effective insect repellent; oil of lavender, rosemary, bergamot or citronella are also effective, especially if mixed with an oil to give them body. A well-puffed cigarette is also effective against insects; incense and perfumes were burned to keep off mosquitoes.

Select Bibliography

Allaby, Michael, with Marika Hanbury Tenison, John Seymour and Hugh Sharman, *The Survival Handbook, Self-Sufficiency for Everyone*, Macmillan, 1975.

Andrews, Edward Deming, *The People called Shakers – A search for the perfect society*, 1953.

Arber, Agnes, *The Graminaea, A study of cereal, bamboo and grass*, CUP, 1934.

Ark, Journal of the Rare Breeds Survival Trust, Vol. IV, Nos. 1 to 12, 1977.

Armes, Alice, *English Smocks with Directions for Making Them*, Dryad Press, Leicester, 1971.

Austin, Thomas, ed., *Two Fifteenth Century Cookery Books*, OUP, for the Early English Text Society, 1888.

Barrett, John, and Yonge, C. M., *Pocket Guide to the Sea Shore*, Collins, 1974.

Barry, G., *History of the Orkneys*, London, 1805.

Bennett, H. G., *The Manufacture of Leather*, Constable, 1920.

Blunt, Wilfrid, *The Compleate Naturalist: A Life of Linneus*, Collins, 1971.

Blythe, Ronald, *Akenfield, Portrait of an English Village*, Allen Lane, 1969; Penguin Books, 1972.

Boswell, James, *Journal of a Tour to the Hebrides with Samuel Johnson*, London, 1887.

Boulger, G. S., *The Uses of Plants*, Edward Arnold, 1889.

Boulger, G. S., *Wood: A Manual of the Natural History and Industrial Application of the Timbers of Commerce*, Edward Arnold, 1902.

Boulton, E. H. B., and Jay, B. Alwyn *British Timbers: Their properties, uses and identification*, A. & C. Black, 1944.

Bradbury, Fred, *Flax Culture and Preparation*, Pitman, 1920.

Brothwell, Don and Patricia, *Food in Antiquity*, Thames & Hudson 1969.

Buchman, Dian Dincin, *Feed Your Face, A complete herbal guide to natural beauty and health*, Duckworth, 1976.

Carson, Rachel, *The Sea Around Us*, Staples Press, 1953.

Carter, H. R., *Modern Flax, Hemp and Jute Spinning and Twisting*, 1967.

Carter, H. R., *Rope Twine and Thread Making*, 1924.

Chapman, V. J., *Seaweeds and Their Uses*, 2nd edn., Methuen, 1970.

Clapham, A. F., Tutin, T. G., and Warburg, E. F., *Excursion Flora of the British Isles*, 2nd edn., CUP, 1968.

Clifton-Taylor, Alec, *The Pattern of English Building*, 3rd edn., Faber, 1972.
Cook, W. E., *The Art and Craft of Glassmaking*, London, 1934.
Cooper, C., *The English Table in History and Literature*, Sampson Low, 1929.
Cornwell, John, *Coleridge: Poet and Revolutionary 1772–1804, A Critical Biography*, Longmans, 1973.
Country Life , 1930–74.
Cowper, A. D., *Lime and Lime Mortars*, London, 1927.
Curtis, A. T., and Speakman, F. J., *A Poacher's Tale*, G. Bell, 1960.
Danaher, Kevin, *In Ireland Long Ago*, Mercier Press, Cork, 1962.
David, Elizabeth, *French Provincial Cooking*, Michael Joseph, London 1960; Penguin Books, 1964.
David, Elizabeth, *Spices, Salt and Aromatics in the English Kitchen*, Penguin Books, 1971.
David, Elizabeth, *Summer Cooking*, Penguin Books, 1967.
Defoe, Daniel, *Robinson Crusoe*, 1855.
Dickinson, C., *British Seaweeds*, Eyre & Spottiswoode, 1963.
Digby, Sir Kenelm, *The Closet of the Eminently Learned Sir Kenelm Digby Knight Opened*, 1669 (reprinted Philip Lee Warner, 1910).
Drummond, J. C., and Wilbraham, Anne, *The Englishman's Food*, Cape, 1958.
Dryad Press, *Chair and Stool Seating*; *Hand-Weaving on Two-Way Looms*; *Netting*; *Rug Weaving*; *Rush Baskets and Mats* and *Spinning Wool*. (A series of leaflets published by The Dryad Press, Leicester.)
Ealand, C. A., *Insects and Man*, Grant Richards, 1915.
Eckey, E. W., *Vegetable Fats and Oils*, New York, 1954.
Encyclopaedia Britannica.
Evans, G. Ewart, *Ask the Fellows Who Cut the Hay*, Faber, 1956.
Falkus, Hugh, and Buller, Fred, *Freshwater Fishing*, Macdonald & Janes, 1975.
Fitter, R. S. R., *Finding Wild Flowers*, Collins, 1971.
Galton, Francis, *The Art of Travel*, Murray, 1860.
Gifford, Isabella, *Marine Botanist*, London, 1853.
Green, Albert R., *Sundials, Incised Dials or Mass-Clocks*, Macmillan, 1926.
Greenbank, Anthony, *The Book of Survival*, Wolfe Publications, 1974.
Grieve, M., *A Modern Herbal*, Cape, 1931; Penguin Books, 1976.
Grieve, M., *Wild Vegetables and Salads*, Whins Cottage, Chalfont St Peter, Bucks, 1926.
Grigson, Geoffrey, *A Herbal of All Sorts*, Phoenix House, 1959.
Grigson, Geoffrey, *The Shell Country Alphabet*, Michael Joseph and Rainbird, 1966.
Grigson, Geoffrey, *The Englishman's Flora*, new edn., Hart-Davies, 1975.

Grigson, Jane, *Fish Cookery*, Penguin Books, 1975.
Halbaek, Hans, 'Studying the diet of ancient man', in *Archaeology*, Vol. 14, 1961.
Hald, Margrethe, *The Nettle as a Culture Plant*, Folk-Liv, 1942 T. VI.
Harrison, S. G., Masefield, G. B. and Mallis, Michael, *Book of Food Plants*, OUP, 1969.
Hartley, Dorothy, *Food in England*, Macdonald, 1969.
Hartley, Dorothy, *Water in England*, Macdonald, 1964.
Hawker, James, *Journal: A Victorian Poacher*, OUP, 1961.
Heath, Ambrose, *From Creel to Kitchen*, Adam & Charles Black, 1939.
Heath, Ambrose, *Haybox Cookery*, Jenkins, 1961.
Henshall, Audrey, S., 'Textiles and weaving appliances in prehistoric Britain', in *Proceedings of the Prehistoric Society for 1949*, Vol. XV.
Henslow, G., *The Uses of British Plants*, London, 1865.
Hill, Jason, *Wild Foods of Britain*, A. & C. Black, 1939.
Hoeher, Siegfried, trans. Winwood Reade, *Birds' Eggs and Nesting Habits*, Blandford, 1974.
Holt, Vincent M., *Why Not Eat Insects?*, E. W. Classey, Hampton, Middlesex.
Hoskins, W. G., *Midland England, A Survey of the Country between the Chilterns and the Trent*, Batsford, 1949.
Hoskins, W. G., *The Making of the English Landscape*, Batsford, 1955; Penguin Books, 1970.
Hughes, Therle, *Old English Furniture*, Lutterworth Press, 1949.
Hutchinson, R. C., *Food for Survival*, Melbourne, 1959.
Huxley, Aldous, ed. Harold Raymond, *Selected Essays*, Chatto & Windus, 1967.
Irwin, Florence, comp., *Irish Cookery Recipes*, Belfast, 1937.
Jekyll, Gertrude, and Jones, Sydney R., *Old English Household Life*, Batsford, 1944–5.
Joyce, P. W., *A Social History of Ireland*, Longmans Green, 1906.
Kephart, Horace, *Camping and Woodcraft*, Collier-Macmillan, 1947.
Knock, A. G., *Willow Basket-Work*, Dryad Press, Leicester, 1965.
Labarge, M. W., *A Baronial Household of the Thirteenth Century*, Eyre & Spottiswoode, 1965.
Lange, Morten, and Hora, F. Bayard, *Guide to Mushrooms and Toadstools*, Collins, 1970.
Leach, Bernard, *A Potter's Book*, 2nd edn., Faber, 1945.
Lekai, Louis J., *The White Monks: A History of the Cistercian Order*, Wisconsin, 1953.
Leno, John Bedford, *The Art of Boot and Shoemaking*, London, 1915.
Leyel, C. F., *Herbal Delights*, Faber, 1937.
Leyel, C. F., *The Magic of Herbs*, Cape, 1926.

Loewenfeld, Claire, *Nuts*, Faber, 1957.

London, J. R., *The Art and Mystery of Curing, Preserving and Potting All Kinds of Meats, Game and Fish*, Chapman & Hall, 1864.

Lord, W. B., and Baines, T., *Camplife, Travel and Exploration*, London, 1876.

Lovell, M. S., *Edible Mollusks of Great Britain and Ireland, with recipes for cooking them*, Reeve & Co., 1867.

Mabey, David and Rose, *Jams, Pickles and Chutneys*, Macmillan, 1975; Penguin Books, 1976.

Mabey, Richard, *Food for Free*, Collins, 1972.

Maclean, Charles, *Island on the Edge of the World: Utopian St Kilda and its passing*, Tom Stacey, 1972.

McNeill, F. M., *The Scots Kitchen*, rev. edn., Blackie, 1974.

Mairet, Ethel M., *Vegetable Dyes*, Faber, 1940.

Markham, Gervase, *The English Housewife*, London, 1688; ed. Dan Lucid, Robson Books, 1976.

Marshall, N. B., *The Life of Fishes*, Weidenfeld & Nicholson, 1965.

Martineau, G., *Common Commodities of Commerce, Sugar, Cane and Beet*, Pitman, 1910.

Mason, John, *Papermaking as an Artistic Craft*, Twelve by Eight Press, 1963.

Mauduit, Vicomte de, *They Can't Ration These*, Michael Joseph, 1940.

Maxwell-Hudson, C., ed., *Kaleidoscope of Beauty: Recipes and treatments of 3,000 years*, Octagon Press, 1968.

Mead, William Edward, *The Englishman's Medieval Feast*, Allen & Unwin, 1931.

Ministry of Agriculture, Fisheries and Food, *Beekeeping*, HMSO, 1972.

Mitchell, Alan, *A Field Guide to the Trees of Britain and Northern Europe*, Collins, 1974.

Moorhead, Alan, *Darwin and the Beagle*, Hamish Hamilton, 1969; Penguin Books, 1971.

Niall, Ian, *New Poacher's Handbook*, Heinemann, 1960.

Nicholl, Lucie G., *The English Cookery Book*, Faber, 1936.

Nixon, Marion, *Book of Vertebrates*, OUP, 1972.

Oakley, Kenneth P., *Man the Tool-maker*, British Museum (Natural History), 1972.

O'Dea, W. T., *Social History of Lighting*, Routledge, 1958.

Ormerod, W. T., *Wool*, Constable, 1918.

Owen, R., Jones, *The Practice of Perfumery*, Houlston & Sons, 1870.

Patons, *Woolcraft, a basic guide to knitting and crochet*.

Peterson, Roger, Mountfort, Guy, and Hollom, P. A. D., *A Field Guide to the Birds of Britain and Europe*, Collins, 1974.

Pirie, N. W., *Food Resources, Conventional and Novel*, Penguin Books, 1969.

Poucher, W. A., *Perfumes, Cosmetics and Soaps*, Vols. 1 and 2, Chapman & Hall, 1925–6.

Powell, H. J., *Glassmaking in England*, London, 1923.

Pratt, Anne, *The Green Fields and their Grasses*, London, 1854.

Pyke, Magnus, *Science and Scotch Whisky*, The Distiller's Company.

Ranson, F., *British Herbs*, Penguin Books, 1949.

Ratton, J. J. L., *A Handbook of Common Salt*, Madras, 1877.

Rohde, Eleanor Sinclair, *Rose Recipes*, Longmans Green, 1939.

Sandford, Jeremy, *Gypsies: Interviews with British Gypsies*, Secker & Warburg, 1973.

Seymour, John and Sally, *Self-Sufficiency*, Faber, 1973.

Simmonds, P. L., *Animal Food Resources of Different Nations*, London, 1885.

Simmons, W. H., *Soap, Its Composition and Manufacture*, Pitman, 1936.

Simon, André, L., *Guide to Good Food and Wines – A concise encyclopaedia of gastronomy*, Collins, 1956.

Sitwell, Edith, comp., *A Book of Flowers*, Macmillan, 1952.

Tattersall, C. E. C., *Notes on Carpet Knotting and Weaving*, Victoria and Albert Museum, 1969.

Thoreau, H. G., *Walden*, Boston, 1884.

Thurston, Violetta, *The Use of Vegetable Dyes*, Dryad Press, Leicester.

Tibble, J. W. and Anne, *John Clare, A Life*, Cobden-Sanderson, 1932.

Trench, C. Chenevix, *The Poacher and the Squire*, Longmans, 1967.

Trevelyan, G. M., *English Social History*, Longmans, 1944; Penguin Books, 1964.

Tyler, Keith, *Pottery without a Wheel*, Dryad Press, Leicester, 1968.

Underhill, T., *Heaths and Heathers*, David & Charles, 1971.

Urquhart, Judy, *Food From the Wild*, David & Charles, Newton Abbot, 1978.

Urquhart, Judy, *Keeping Honeybees*, David & Charles, Newton Abbot, 1978.

Vaughan, J. G., *The Structure and Utilization of Oil Seeds*, Chapman & Hall, 1970.

Vesey Fitzgerald, Brian, *It's My Delight*, Eyre & Spottiswoode, 1947.

Wasson, R. Gordon, *Soma, Divine Mushroom of Immortality*, New York, 1972.

Wheeler, Alwyne, *The Fishes of the British Isles and North-west Europe*, Macmillan, 1969.

White, Florence, *Flowers as Food*, London, 1934.

White, Gilbert, *Natural History of Selbourne*, 1832; Penguin Books, 1977.

Wilson, Colin, *The Outsider*, Gollancz, 1956.

Wilson, John, *Scotland's Malt Whiskies*, Famedram Press, Gartocharn, 1974.

Wise, Dorothy, comp., *Home Made Country Wines*, Hamlyn, 1970.

Wood, Eric S., *Field Guide to Archaeology*, 4th edn., Collins, 1975.

Woodforde, John, *A Strange Story of False Teeth*, Routledge, 1968.

Wren, R. C., ed., *Potter's Cyclopaedia of Botanical Drugs and Preparations*, 6th edn., 1950.

Books Recommended for Identification

BIRDS *The Birds of Britain and Europe* by Roger Peterson, Guy Mountfort and P. A. D. Hollom, Collins, 1977.

FISH *The Oxford Book of Vertebrates* by Marion Nixon, OUP, 1972.

The Freshwater Fishes of Britain and Europe by Bent J. Muus and Preben Dahlstrom, Collins.

The Sea Fishes of Britain and North-western Europe by Bent J. Muus and Preben Dahlstrom, Collins, 1977.

FUNGI *Mushrooms and Toadstools* by Morten Lange and F. Bayard Hora, Collins, 1977.

Edible and Poisonous Fungi (Ministry of Agriculture Bulletin No. 43) HMSO, 1947.

INSECTS *The Oxford Book of Insects* by John Burton and others, OUP, 1968.

Field Guide to the Insects of Britain and Europe by Michael Chinery, Collins, 1974.

LICHEN *The Oxford Book of Flowerless Plants* by F. H. Brightman, OUP, 1966.

MAMMALS *The Oxford Book of Vertebrates* by Marion Nixon, OUP, 1972.

The Mammals of Britain and Europe by F. H. van den Brink, Collins.

MOLLUSCS *The Oxford Book of Invertebrates* by David Nichols and John Cooke, OUP, 1971.

The Sea Shore by John Barrett and C. M. Yonge, Collins, 1977.

PLANTS *The Concise British Flora in Colour* by W. Keble Martin, 2nd edn., Ebury Press and Michael Joseph, 1969.

Excursion Flora of the British Isles by A. R. Clapham, T. G. Tutin and E. F. Warburg, 2nd end., CUP, 1968.

British Poisonous Plants (Ministry of Agriculture Bulletin No. 161), HMSO, 1954.

REPTILES *The Oxford Book of Vertebrates* by Marion Nixon, OUP, 1972.

SEAWEED *The Sea Shore* by John Barrett and C. M. Yonge, Collins, London, 1977.

The Oxford Book of Flowerless Plants by F. H. Brightman, OUP, 1966.

TREES *Field Guide to the Trees of Britain and Northern Europe* by Alan Mitchell, Collins, 1974.

Notes

1. Thoreau, H. D., *Walden*, Boston, 1884.
2. Lekai, Louis J., *The White Monks: A History of the Cistercian Order*, Wisconsin, 1953.
3. Wilson, Colin, *The Outsider*, Gollancz, 1956.
4. Sandford, Jeremy, *Gypsies: Interviews with British Gypsies*, Secker & Warburg, 1973.
5. Huxley, Aldous, *Selected Essays*, ed. Harold Raymond, Chatto & Windus, 1967.
6. Digby, Sir Kenelm, *The Closet of the Eminently Learned Sir Kenelm Digby Knight Opened*, 1669 (reprinted Philip Lee Warner, 1910).
7. Beeton, Mrs Isabella, *Book of Household Management*, 1st Edition, S.O. Beeton, 1861.
8. Simmonds, P. L., *Animal Food Resources of Different Nations*, London, 1885.
9. Simon, André L., *Guide to Good Food and Wines – A Concise Encyclopaedia of Gastronomy Complete and Unabridged*, Collins, 1956.
10. Hobson, Dr Richard, *Charles Waterton, 1782–1865*, London, 1866.
11. Venners, *Via Recta and Vitam Longam*, London, 1628.
12. White, Rev. Gilbert, *Natural History of Selbourne*, London, 1832 (Penguin Books, 1977).
13. Elyot, Sir T., *Castel of Health*, London, 1539.
14. *Country Life*, 29 June 1940, p. 644.
15. Pulman, George P. R., *The Book of the Axe*, 1875 (reprinted Kingsmead Reprints, 1969).
16. *Country Life*, 20 February 1953, p. 503.
17. *Country Life*, 20 April 1953, p. 1003.
18. Boswell, James, *Journal of a Tour to the Hebrides with Samuel Johnson*, 1887.
19. Galton, Francis, *The Art of Travel*, Murray, 1860.
20. Curtis, A. T., and Speakman, F. J., *A Poacher's Tale*, G. Bell, 1960.
21. Tolstoy, Leo, *Anna Karenina*, tr. C. Garnett, Heinemann, 1901.
22. Trevelyan, G. M., *English Social History, A Survey of Six Centuries, Chaucer to Queen Victoria*, Penguin Books, 1964.

23. Arber, Agnes, *The Graminaea, A study of cereals, bamboo and grass*, CUP, 1934.
24. Ewart Evans, G., *Ask the Fellows Who Cut the Hay*, Faber, 1956.
25. Danaher, Kevin, *In Ireland Long Ago*, Cork, Mercier Press, 1962.
26. Gerard, John, *The Herbal or Generall Historie of Plantes*, London, 1597 (reprinted Minerva Press, 1971).
27. Hartley, Dorothy, *Food in England*, Macdonald, 1954.
28. *Country Life*, 21 June 1941, p. 551.
29. Smith, J. E., *English Botany*, illustrated by J. Sowerby, 3rd edn., ed. J. T. Boswell Syme, London, 1890–92.
30. Clare, John, 'Remembrance' in *Selected Poems*, Dent, 1965.
31. Joyce, P. W., *A Social History of Ireland*, Longmans, 1906.
32. Woolf, Virginia, *Moments of Being – A Sketch of the Past*, Hogarth Press, 1977.
33. White, Florence, *Good Things in England*, Jonathan Cape, 1932.
34. Acton, Eliza, *Modern Cookery in all its Branches*, Longmans, 1854.
35. O'Gorman, *The Practice of Angling*, Vol. 2, 1845.
36. Falkus, Hugh, and Buller, Fred, *Freshwater Fishing*, Macdonald & Janes, 1975.
37. Barker, Thomas, *The Art of Angling*, London, 1651.
38. Trench, C. Chenevix, *The Poacher and the Squire*, Longmans, 1967.
39. *Country Life*, February 1941.
40. Jekyll, Gertrude, and Jones, Sydney R., *Old English Household Life*, Batsford, 1944–5.
41. Kephart, Horace, *Camping and Woodcraft*, Collier-Macmillan, 1947.
42. Swan, John, *Speculum Mundi*, London, 1643.
43. Turner, W., *Herbal*, Cologne, 1568.
44. David, Elizabeth, *Spices, Salt and Aromatics in the English Kitchen*, Penguin Books, 1971.
45. Holt, Vincent M., *Why Not Eat Insects?*, E. W. Classey, 33 Hanworth Road, Hampton, Middlesex.
46. *Country Life* 23 September 1939, p. 312.
47. Irwin, Florence, *Irish Cookery Recipes*, Belfast, 1937.
48. Lord, W. B., and Baines, T., *Camplife, Travel and Exploration*, London, 1876.
49. Greenbank, A., *A Book of Survival*, Wolfe Publications, 1967.
50. Vesey Fitzgerald, Brian, *It's My Delight*, Eyre & Spottiswoode, 1947.
51. McDowall, M., *Nature and Men.*
52. London, J. R., *The Art and Mystery of Curing, Preserving and Pottering All Kinds of Meats, Game and Fish*, Chapman & Hall, 1864.
53. Mott, John, *Cook to the Duke of Bolton, The Receipt Book*, 1723.
54. Craig, Elizabeth, *Cookery and Household Management*, Odhams, 1936.

55. Ketton-Cremer, R. W., *Horace Walpole*, Methuen, 1940.
56. David, Elizabeth, *French Provincial Cooking*, Michael Joseph, 1960; Penguin Books, 1964.
57. Grieve, M. R., *A Modern Herbal*, Cape, 1931; Penguin Books, 1976.
58. Dickinson, C., *British Seaweeds*, Eyre & Spottiswoode, 1963.
59. Clare, John, 'Journey Out of Essex'.
60. *Country Life*, 1941, April, p. 350.
61. Martineau, G., *Common Commodities of Commerce, Sugar, Cane and Beet*, Pitman, 1910.
62. Kennedy-Herbert, Col., *Culinary Jottings from Madras*, Madras, Higginbotham & Co., 1885.
63. Smith, J. T., *Nollekens and His Times*, Turnstile Press, 1949.
64. Ray, Cyril, in *Daily Telegraph Magazine*, 21 October 1971.
65. Underhill, T., *Heaths and Heathers*, David & Charles, Newton Abbot, 1971.
66. *Country Life*, 7 September 1945, p. 429.
67. Blackmore, Richard, *Lorna Doone*, London, 1888.
68. Grey, Eric Lloyd, *William Morris*, Cassell, 1949.
69. Clifton-Taylor, Alec, *The Pattern of English Building*, revised edn., Faber, 1972.
70. Hoskins, W. G., *Midland England, A Survey of the Country between the Chilterns and the Trent*, Batsford, 1949.
71. Hartley, Dorothy, *Water in England*, Macdonald, 1964.
72. Hughes, Therle, *Old English Furniture*, Lutterworth Press, 1949.
73. Wade Labarge, M., *A Baronial Household of the Thirteenth Century*, 1965.
74. Defoe, Daniel, *Robinson Crusoe*, London, 1855.
75. Shakespeare, William, *Cymbeline*, I, vii, 124–5.
76. Shakespeare, William, *Henry VI*, II, v, 8–9.
77. Leach, Bernard, *Hamada Potter*, Thames & Hudson, 1976.
78. Leach, Bernard, *A Potter's Book*, Faber, 1940.
79. Cooper, C., *The English Table in History and Literature*, 1929.
80. *Country Life*, 'Patricia Szpiganowicz, The Peg-Maker', 1963.
81. *Country Life*, 1 September 1960, p. 441.
82. *Country Life*, correspondence column, 7 December 1940.
83. Boulger, G. S., *Wood: A Manual of the Natural History and Industrial Application of the Timbers of Commerce*, Edward Arnold, 1902.
84. Powell, H. J., *Glassmaking in England*, 1923.
85. Grigson, G., *A Herbal of All Sorts*, Phoenix House, 1959.
86. Evelyn, John, *Sylva*, London, 1664.
87. Carson, Rachel, *The Sea Around Us*, Staples Press, 1953.
88. Mairet, Ethel M., *Vegetable Dyes*, Faber, 1940.

89. Oakley, Kenneth P., *Man the Tool-Maker*, British Museum (Natural History), 1972.
90. Deering, C., *Catalogus Stirpinum*, London, 1738.
91. Chaucer, Geoffrey, 'The Nonne Preestes Tale'.
92. Fitzherbert, Anthony, *Book of Husbandrie*, London, 1523.
93. Septimus Piesse, G. V., *Art of Perfumes*, 1770.
94. Poucher, W. A., *Perfumes, Cosmetics and Soaps*, Vol. 1 and 2, Chapman & Hall, 1925–6.
95. Vicary, T., *The Englishmans Treasure*, 1577.
96. Carron, A., *A Lady's Toilet*, W. H. Wyatt, London, 1808.
97. *Country Life*, 'Gypsy Recipes and Remedies' by R. Croft Cooke, 31 October 1947, p. 877.